Introduction
to
AI
Robotics

Intelligent Robots and Autonomous Agents
Ronald C. Arkin, editor

Behavior-Based Robotics, Ronald C. Arkin, 1998

Robot Shaping: An Experiment in Behavior Engineering, Marco Dorigo and Marco Colombetti, 1998

Layered Learning in Multiagent Systems: A Winning Approach to Robotic Soccer, Peter Stone, 2000

Evolutionary Robotics: The Biology, Intelligence, and Technology of Self-Organizing Machines, Stefano Nolfi and Dario Floreano, 2000

Reasoning about Rational Agents, Michael Wooldridge, 2000

Introduction to AI Robotics, Robin R. Murphy, 2000

Introduction
to
AI
Robotics

Robin R. Murphy

A Bradford Book
The MIT Press
Cambridge, Massachusetts
London, England

Typeset in 10/13 Lucida Bright by the author using LATEX 2$_\varepsilon$.
Printed and bound in the United States of America.

Library of Congress Cataloging-in-Publication Data

Murphy, Robin, 1957–
   Introduction to AI robotics / Robin R. Murphy.
      p.   cm.—(Intelligent robotics and autonomous agents. A Bradford Book.)
   Includes bibliographical references and index.
   ISBN 0-262-13383-0 (hc. : alk. paper)
   1. Robotics. 2. Artificial intelligence. I. Title. II. Series
TJ211.M865   2000
629.8'6263—dc21   00-033251

10 9 8 7 6 5 4

To Kevin

...and Carlyle Ramsey, Monroe Swilley, Chris Trowell

Brief Contents

Contents

Preface

This book is intended to serve as a textbook for advanced juniors and seniors and first-year graduate students in computer science and engineering. The reader is not expected to have taken a course in artificial intelligence (AI), although the book includes pointers to additional readings and advanced exercises for more advanced students. The reader should have had at least one course in object-oriented programming in order to follow the discussions on how to implement and program robots using the structures described in this book. These programming structures lend themselves well to laboratory exercises on commercially available robots, such as the Khepera, Nomad 200 series, and Pioneers. Lego Mindstorms and Rug Warrior robots can be used for the first six chapters, but their current programming interface and sensor limitations interfere with using those robots for the more advanced material. A background in digital circuitry is not required, although many instructors may want to introduce laboratory exercises for building reactive robots from kits such as the Rug Warrior or the Handy Board.

Introduction to AI Robotics attempts to cover all the topics needed to program an artificially intelligent robot for applications involving sensing, navigation, path planning, and navigating with uncertainty. Although machine perception is a separate field of endeavor, the book covers enough computer vision and sensing to enable students to embark on a serious robot project or competition. The book is divided into two parts. Part I defines what are intelligent robots and introduces why artificial intelligence is needed. It covers the "theory" of AI robotics, taking the reader through a historical journey from the Hierarchical to the Hybrid Deliberative/Reactive Paradigm for organizing intelligence. The bulk of the seven chapters is concerned with the Reactive Paradigm and behaviors. A chapter on sensing and programming techniques for reactive behaviors is included in order to permit a class to get a head start on a programming project. Also, Part I covers the coordination and control of teams of multi-agents. Since the fundamental mission of a mobile robot involves moving about in the world, Part II devotes three chapters to qualitative and metric navigation and path planning techniques, plus work in uncertainty management. The book concludes with an overview of how advances in computer vision are now being integrated into robots, and how successes in robots are driving the web-bot and know-bot craze.

Since *Introduction to AI Robotics* is an introductory text, it is impossible to cover all the fine work that has been in the field. The guiding principle has been to include only material that clearly illuminates a specific topic. References to other approaches and systems are usually included as an advanced reading question at the end of the chapter or as an end note. *Behavior-based Robotics*[10] provides a thorough survey of the field and should be an instructor's companion.

Acknowledgments

It would be impossible to thank all of the people involved in making this book possible, but I would like to try to list the ones who made the most obvious contributions. I'd like to thank my parents (I think this is the equivalent of scoring a goal and saying "Hi Mom!" on national TV) and my family (Kevin, Kate, and Allan). I had the honor of being in the first AI robotics course taught by my PhD advisor Ron Arkin at Georgia Tech (where I was also his first PhD student), and much of the material and organization of this book can be traced back to his course. I have tried to maintain the intellectual rigor of his course and excellent book while trying to distill the material for a novice audience. Any errors in this book are strictly mine. David Kortenkamp suggested that I write this book after using my course notes for a class he taught, which served as a very real catalyst. Certainly the students at both the Colorado School of Mines (CSM), where I first developed my robotics courses, and at the University of South Florida (USF) merit special thanks for being guinea pigs. I would like to specifically thank Leslie Baski, John Blitch, Glenn Blauvelt, Ann Brigante, Greg Chavez, Aaron Gage, Dale Hawkins, Floyd Henning, Jim Hoffman, Dave Hershberger, Kevin Gifford, Matt Long, Charlie Ozinga, Tonya Reed Frazier, Michael Rosenblatt, Jake Sprouse, Brent Taylor, and Paul Wiebe from my CSM days and Jenn Casper, Aaron Gage, Jeff Hyams, Liam Irish, Mark Micire, Brian Minten, and Mark Powell from USF.

Special thanks go to the numerous reviewers, especially Karen Sutherland and Ken Hughes. Karen Sutherland and her robotics class at the University of Wisconsin-LaCrosse (Kristoff Hans Ausderau, Teddy Bauer, Scott David Becker, Corrie L. Brague, Shane Brownell, Edwin J. Colby III, Mark Erickson, Chris Falch, Jim Fick, Jennifer Fleischman, Scott Galbari, Mike Halda, Brian Kehoe, Jay D. Paska, Stephen Pauls, Scott Sandau, Amy Stanislowski, Jaromy Ward, Steve Westcott, Peter White, Louis Woyak, and Julie A. Zander) painstakingly reviewed an early draft of the book and made extensive suggestions and added review questions. Ken Hughes also deserves special thanks; he also provided a chapter by chapter critique as well as witty emails. Ken always comes to my rescue.

Likewise, the book would not be possible without my ongoing involvement in robotics research; my efforts have been supported by NSF, DARPA, and ONR. Most of the case studies came from work or through equipment sponsored by NSF. Howard Moraff, Rita Rodriguez, and Harry Hedges were always very encouraging, beyond the call of duty of even the most dedicated NSF program director. Michael Mason also provided encouragement, in many forms, to hang in there and focus on education.

My editor, Bob Prior, and the others at the MIT Press (Katherine Innis, Judy Feldmann, Margie Hardwick, and Maureen Kuper) also have my deepest appreciation for providing unfailingly good-humored guidance, technical assistance, and general savvy. Katherine and especially Judy were very patient and nice— despite knowing that I was calling with Yet Another Crisis. Mike Hamilton at AAAI was very helpful in making available the various "action shots" used throughout the book. Chris Manning provided the LaTeX 2_ε style files, with adaptations by Paul Anagnostopoulos. Liam Irish and Ken Hughes contributed helpful scripts.

Besides the usual suspects, there are some very special people who indirectly helped me. Without the encouragement of three liberal arts professors, Carlyle Ramsey, Monroe Swilley, and Chris Trowell, at South Georgia College in my small hometown of Douglas, Georgia, I probably wouldn't have seriously considered graduate school in engineering and computer science. They taught me that learning isn't a place like a big university but rather a personal discipline. The efforts of my husband, Kevin Murphy, were, as always, essential. He worked hard to make sure I could spend the time on this book without missing time with the kids or going crazy. He also did a serious amount of editing, typing, scanning, and proofreading. I dedicate the book to these four men who have influenced my professional career as much as any academic mentor.

PART I

Robotic Paradigms

Contents:

Overview

The eight chapters in this part are devoted to describing what is *AI robotics* and the three major paradigms for achieving it. These paradigms character- ize the ways in which intelligence is organized in robots. This part of the book also covers architectures that provide exemplars of how to transfer the principles of the paradigm into a coherent, reusable implementation on a single robot or teams of robots.

What Are Robots?

One of the first questions most people have about robotics is "what is a ro- bot?" followed immediately by "what can they do?"

In popular culture, the term "robot" generally connotes some anthropo- morphic (human-like) appearance; consider robot "arms" for welding. The tendency to think about robots as having a human-like appearance may stem from the origins of the term "robot." The word "robot" came into the popu- lar consciousness on January 25, 1921, in Prague with the first performance of Karel Capek's play, R.U.R. (Rossum's Universal Robots).[37] In R.U.R., an unseen inventor, Rossum, has created a race of workers made from a vat of biological parts, smart enough to replace a human in any job (hence "univer- sal"). Capek described the workers as robots, a term derived from the Czech word "robota" which is loosely translated as menial laborer. Robot workers implied that the artificial creatures were strictly meant to be servants to free "real" people from any type of labor, but were too lowly to merit respect. This attitude towards robots has disastrous consequences, and the moral of the rather socialist story is that work defines a person.

The shift from robots as human-like servants constructed from biological parts to human-like servants made up of mechanical parts was probably due to science fiction. Three classic films, *Metropolis* (1926), *The Day the Earth Stood Still* (1951), and *Forbidden Planet* (1956), cemented the connotation that robots were mechanical in origin, ignoring the biological origins in Capek's play. Meanwhile, computers were becoming commonplace in industry and accounting, gaining a perception of being literal minded. Industrial automation confirmed this suspicion as robot arms were installed which would go through the motions of assembling parts, even if there were no parts. Eventually, the term robot took on nuances of factory automation: mindlessness and good only for well-defined repetitious types of work. The notion of anthropomorphic, mechanical, and literal-minded robots complemented the viewpoint taken in many of the short stories in Isaac Asimov's perennial favorite collection, *I, Robot*.[15] Many (but not all) of these stories involve either a "robopsychologist," Dr. Susan Calvin, or two erstwhile trouble shooters, Powell and Donovan, diagnosing robots who behaved logically but did the wrong thing.

The shift from human-like mechanical creatures to whatever shape gets the job done is due to reality. While robots are mechanical, they don't have to be anthropomorphic or even animal-like. Consider robot vacuum cleaners; they look like vacuum cleaners, not janitors. And the HelpMate Robotics, Inc., robot which delivers hospital meals to patients to permit nurses more time with patients, looks like a cart, not a nurse.

It should be clear from Fig. I.1 that appearance does not form a useful definition of a robot. Therefore, the definition that will be used in this book is *an intelligent robot is a mechanical creature which can function autonomously.* "Intelligent" implies that the robot does not do things in a mindless, repetitive way; it is the opposite of the connotation from factory automation. The "mechanical creature" portion of the definition is an acknowledgment of the fact that our scientific technology uses mechanical building blocks, not biological components (although with recent advances in cloning, this may change). It also emphasizes that a robot is not the same as a computer. A robot may use a computer as a building block, equivalent to a nervous system or brain, but the robot is able to interact with its world: move around, change

INTELLIGENT ROBOT

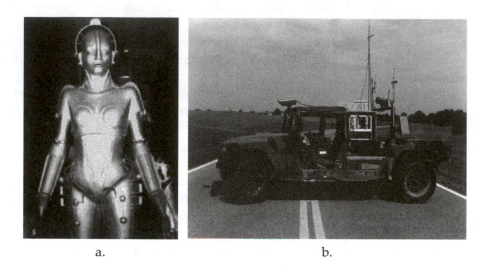

a.   b.

Figure I.1 Two views of robots: a) the humanoid robot from the 1926 movie Metropolis (image courtesty Fr. Doug Quinn and the Metropolis Home Page), and b) a HMMWV military vehicle capable of driving on roads and open terrains. (Photograph courtesy of the National Institute for Standards and Technology.)

it, etc. A computer doesn't move around under its own power. "Function autonomously" indicates that the robot can operate, self-contained, under all reasonable conditions without requiring recourse to a human operator. Autonomy means that a robot can adapt to changes in its environment (the lights get turned off) or itself (a part breaks) and continue to reach its goal.

Perhaps the best example of an intelligent mechanical creature which can function autonomously is the Terminator from the 1984 movie of the same name. Even after losing one camera (eye) and having all external coverings (skin, flesh) burned off, it continued to pursue its target (Sarah Connor). Extreme adaptability and autonomy in an extremely scary robot! A more practical (and real) example is *Marvin*, the mail cart robot, for the Baltimore FBI office, described in a Nov. 9, 1996, article in the Denver Post. Marvin is able to accomplish its goal of stopping and delivering mail while adapting to people getting in its way at unpredictable times and locations.

What are Robotic Paradigms?

PARADIGM   A *paradigm is a philosophy or set of assumptions and/or techniques which charac-
terize an approach to a class of problems.* It is both a way of looking at the world
and an implied set of tools for solving problems. No one paradigm is right;
rather, some problems seem better suited for different approaches. For example, consider calculus problems. There are problems that could be solved
by differentiating in cartesian (X, Y, Z) coordinates, but are much easier to
solve if polar coordinates (r, θ) are used. In the domain of calculus problems,
Cartesian and polar coordinates represent two different paradigms for viewing and manipulating a problem. Both produce the correct answer, but one
takes less work for certain problems.

Applying the right paradigm makes problem solving easier. Therefore,
knowing the paradigms of AI robotics is one key to being able to successfully
program a robot for a particular application. It is also interesting from a historical perspective to work through the different paradigms, and to examine
the issues that spawned the shift from one paradigm to another.

ROBOTIC PARADIGMS   There are currently three paradigms for organizing intelligence in robots:
hierarchical, reactive, and hybrid deliberative/reactive. The paradigms are
described in two ways.

1. **By the relationship between the three commonly accepted primitives
of robotics: SENSE, PLAN, ACT.** The functions of a robot can be divided
ROBOT PARADIGM   into three very general categories. If a function is taking in information
PRIMITIVES   from the robot's sensors and producing an output useful by other functions, then that function falls in the SENSE category. If the function is
taking in information (either from sensors or its own knowledge about
how the world works) and producing one or more tasks for the robot to
perform (go down the hall, turn left, proceed 3 meters and stop), that function is in the PLAN category. Functions which produce output commands
to motor actuators fall into ACT (turn 98°, clockwise, with a turning velocity of 0.2mps). Fig. I.2 attempts to define these three primitives in terms
of inputs and outputs; this figure will appear throughout the chapters in
Part I.

2. **By the way sensory data is processed and distributed through the system.** How much a person or robot or animal is influenced by what it
senses. So it is often difficult to adequately describe a paradigm with just
a box labeled SENSE. In some paradigms, sensor information is restricted
to being used in a specific, or dedicated, way for each function of a robot;

ROBOT PRIMITIVES	INPUT	OUTPUT
SENSE	Sensor data	Sensed information
PLAN	Information (sensed and/or cognitive)	Directives
ACT	Sensed information or directives	Actuator commands

Figure I.2 Robot primitives defined in terms of inputs and outputs.

SENSING
ORGANIZATION IN
ROBOT PARADIGMS

in that case processing is *local* to each function. Other paradigms expect all sensor information to be first processed into one *global* world model and then subsets of the model distributed to other functions as needed.

Overview of the Three Paradigms

In order to set the stage for learning details, it may be helpful to begin with a general overview of the robot paradigms. Fig. I.3 shows the differences between the three paradigms in terms of the SENSE, PLAN, ACT primitives.

HIERARCHICAL
PARADIGM

The *Hierarchical Paradigm* is the oldest paradigm, and was prevalent from 1967–1990. Under it, the robot operates in a top-down fashion, heavy on planning (see Fig. I.3). This was based on an introspective view of how people think. "I see a door, I decide to head toward it, and I plot a course around the chairs." (Unfortunately, as many cognitive psychologists now know, introspection is not always a good way of getting an accurate assessment of a thought process. We now suspect no one actually plans how they get out of a room; they have default schemas or behaviors.) Under the Hierarchical Paradigm, the robot senses the world, plans the next action, and then acts (SENSE, PLAN, ACT). Then it senses the world, plans, acts. At each step, the robot explicitly plans the next move. The other distinguishing feature of the Hierarchical paradigm is that all the sensing data tends to be gathered into one global world model, a single representation that the planner can use and can be routed to the actions. Constructing generic global world models

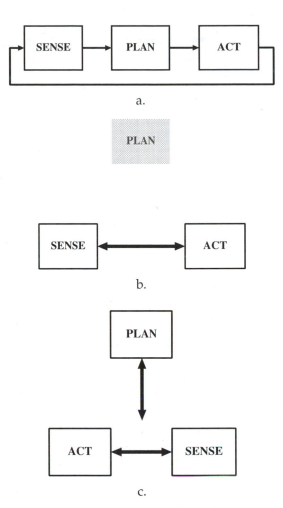

Figure I.3 Three paradigms: a.) Hierarchical, b.) Reactive, and c.) Hybrid deliberative/reactive.

turns out to be very hard and brittle due to the *frame problem* and the need for a *closed world assumption*.

Fig. I.4 shows how the Hierarchical Paradigm can be thought of as a transitive, or Z-like, flow of events through the primitives given in Fig. I.4. Unfortunately, the flow of events ignored biological evidence that sensed information can be directly coupled to an action, which is why the sensed information input is blacked out.

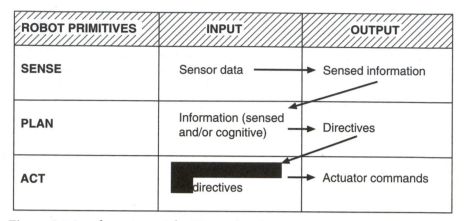

Figure I.4 Another view of the Hierarchical Paradigm.

The *Reactive Paradigm* was a reaction to the Hierarchical Paradigm, and led to exciting advances in robotics. It was heavily used in robotics starting in 1988 and continuing through 1992. It is still used, but since 1992 there has been a tendency toward hybrid architectures. The Reactive Paradigm was made possible by two trends. One was a popular movement among AI researchers to investigate biology and cognitive psychology in order to examine living exemplars of intelligence. Another was the rapidly decreasing cost of computer hardware coupled with the increase in computing power. As a result, researchers could emulate frog and insect behavior with robots costing less than $500 versus the $100,000s Shakey, the first mobile robot, cost.

The Reactive Paradigm threw out planning all together (see Figs. I.3b and I.5). It is a SENSE-ACT (S-A) type of organization. Whereas the Hierarchical Paradigm assumes that the input to a ACT will always be the result of a PLAN, the Reactive Paradigm assumes that the input to an ACT will always be the direct output of a sensor, SENSE.

If the sensor is directly connected to the action, why isn't a robot running under the Reactive Paradigm limited to doing just one thing? The robot has multiple instances of SENSE-ACT couplings, discussed in Ch. 4. These couplings are concurrent processes, called behaviors, which take local sensing data and compute the best action to take independently of what the other processes are doing. One behavior can direct the robot to "move forward 5 meters" (ACT on drive motors) to reach a goal (SENSE the goal), while another behavior can say "turn 90°" (ACT on steer motors) to avoid a collision

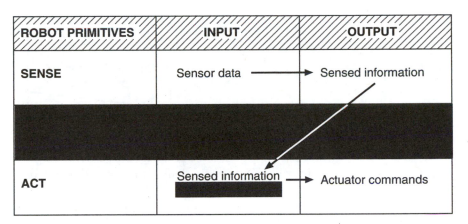

ROBOT PRIMITIVES	INPUT	OUTPUT
SENSE	Sensor data ⟶	Sensed information
ACT	Sensed information ⟶	Actuator commands

Figure I.5 The reactive paradigm.

with an object dead ahead (**SENSE** obstacles). The robot will do a combination of both behaviors, swerving off course temporarily at a 45° angle to avoid the collision. Note that neither behavior directed the robot to **ACT** with a 45° turn; the final **ACT** emerged from the combination of the two behaviors.

While the Reactive Paradigm produced exciting results and clever robot insect demonstrations, it quickly became clear that throwing away planning was too extreme for general purpose robots. In some regards, the Reactive Paradigm reflected the work of Harvard psychologist B. F. Skinner in stimulus-response training with animals. It explained how some animals accomplished tasks, but was a dead end in explaining the entire range of human intelligence.

But the Reactive Paradigm has many desirable properties, especially the fast execution time that came from eliminating any planning. As a result, the Reactive Paradigm serves as the basis for the *Hybrid Deliberative/Reactive Paradigm*, shown in Fig.I.3c. The Hybrid Paradigm emerged in the 1990's and continues to be the current area of research. Under the Hybrid Paradigm, the robot first plans (deliberates) how to best decompose a task into subtasks (also called "mission planning") and then what are the suitable behaviors to accomplish each subtask, etc. Then the behaviors start executing as per the Reactive Paradigm. This type of organization is **PLAN, SENSE-ACT (P, S-A)**, where the comma indicates that planning is done at one step, then sensing and acting are done together. Sensing organization in the Hybrid Paradigm is also a mixture of Hierarchical and Reactive styles. Sensor data gets routed to each behavior that needs that sensor, but is also available to the planner

HYBRID DELIBERA-
TIVE/REACTIVE
PARADIGM

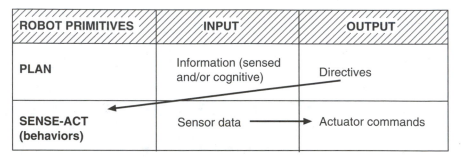

ROBOT PRIMITIVES	INPUT	OUTPUT
PLAN	Information (sensed and/or cognitive)	Directives
SENSE-ACT (behaviors)	Sensor data	Actuator commands

Figure I.6 The hybrid deliberative/reactive paradigm.

for construction of a task-oriented global world model. The planner may also "eavesdrop" on the sensing done by each behavior (i.e., the behavior identifies obstacles that could then be put into a map of the world by the planner). Each function performs computations at its own rate; deliberative planning, which is generally computationally expensive may update every 5 seconds, while the reactive behaviors often execute at 1/60 second. Many robots run at 80 centimeters per second.

Architectures

Determining that a particular paradigm is well suited for an application is certainly the first step in constructing the AI component of a robot. But that step is quickly followed with the need to use the tools associated with that paradigm. In order to visualize how to apply these paradigms to real-world applications, it is helpful to examine representative architectures. These architectures provide templates for an implementation, as well as examples of what each paradigm really means.

What is an architecture? Arkin offers several definitions in his book, *Behavior-Based Robots*.[10] Two of the definitions he cites from other researchers capture how the term will be used in this book. Following Mataric,[89] an architecture provides a principled way of organizing a control system. However, in addition to providing structure, it imposes constraints on the way the control problem can be solved. Following Dean and Wellman,[43] an architec- ARCHITECTURE ture describes a set of architectural components and how they interact. This book is interested in the components common in robot architectures; these are the basic building blocks for programming a robot. It also is interested in the principles and rules of thumb for connecting these components together.

To see the importance of an architecture, consider building a house or a car. There is no "right" design for a house, although most houses share the same components (kitchens, bathrooms, walls, floors, doors, etc.). Likewise with designing robots, there can be multiple ways of organizing the components, even if all the designs follow the same paradigm. This is similar to cars designed by different manufacturers. All internal combustion engine types of cars have the same basic components, but the cars look different (BMWs and Jaguars look quite different than Hondas and Fords). The internal combustion (IC) engine car is a paradigm (as contrasted to the paradigm of an electric car). Within the IC engine car community, the car manufacturers each have their own architecture. The car manufacturers may make slight modifications to the architecture for sedans, convertibles, sport-utility vehicles, etc., to throw out unnecessary options, but each style of car is a particular instance of the architecture. The point is: by studying representative robot architectures and the instances where they were used for a robot application, we can learn the different ways that the components and tools associated with a paradigm can be used to build an artificially intelligent robot.

Since a major objective in robotics is to learn how to build them, an important skill to develop is evaluating whether or not a previously developed architecture (or large chunks of it) will suit the current application. This skill will save both time spent on re-inventing the wheel and avoid subtle problems that other people have encountered and solved. Evaluation requires a set of criteria. The set that will be used in this book is adapted from *Behavior-Based Robotics*:[10]

MODULARITY
1. **Support for modularity:** does it show good software engineering principles?

NICHE TARGETABILITY
2. **Niche targetability:** how well does it work for the intended application?

PORTABILITY
3. **Ease of portability to other domains:** how well would it work for other applications or other robots?

ROBUSTNESS
4. **Robustness:** where is the system vulnerable, and how does it try to reduce that vulnerability?

Note that niche targetability and ease of portability are often at odds with each other. Most of the architectures described in this book were intended to be generic, therefore emphasizing portability. The generic structures, however, often introduce undesirable computational and storage overhead, so in practice the designer must make trade-offs.

Layout of the Section

This section is divided into eight chapters, one to define robotics and the other seven to intertwine both the theory and practice associated with each paradigm. Ch. 2 describes the Hierarchical Paradigm and two representative architectures. Ch. 3 sets the stage for understanding the Reactive Paradigm by reviewing the key concepts from biology and ethology that served to motivate the shift from Hierarchical to Reactive systems. Ch. 4 describes the Reactive Paradigm and the architectures that originally popularized this approach. It also offers definitions of primitive robot behaviors. Ch. 5 provides guidelines and case studies on designing robot behaviors. It also introduces issues in coordinating and controlling multiple behaviors and the common techniques for resolving these issues. At this point, the reader should be almost able to design and implement a reactive robot system, either in simulation or on a real robot. However, the success of a reactive system depends on the sensing. Ch. 6 discusses simple sonar and computer vision processing techniques that are commonly used in inexpensive robots. Ch. 7 describes the Hybrid Deliberative-Reactive Paradigm, concentrating on architectural trends. Up until this point, the emphasis is towards programming a single robot. Ch. 8 concludes the section by discussing how the principles of the three paradigms have been transferred to teams of robots.

End Note

Robot paradigm primitives.
While the SENSE, PLAN, ACT primitives are generally accepted, some researchers are suggesting that a fourth primitive be added, LEARN. There are no formal architectures at this time which include this, so a true paradigm shift has not yet occurred.

1 *From Teleoperation To Autonomy*

Chapter Objectives:

- Define *intelligent robot*.

- Be able to describe at least two differences between AI and Engineering approaches to robotics.

- Be able to describe the difference between *telepresence* and *semi-autonomous control*.

- Have some feel for the history and societal impact of robotics.

1.1 Overview

This book concentrates on the role of artificial intelligence for robots. At first, that may appear redundant; aren't robots intelligent? The short answer is "no," most robots currently in industry are not intelligent by any definition. This chapter attempts to distinguish an intelligent robot from a non-intelligent robot.

The chapter begins with an overview of artificial intelligence and the social implications of robotics. This is followed with a brief historical perspective on the evolution of robots towards intelligence, as shown in Fig. 1.1. One way of viewing robots is that early on in the 1960's there was a fork in the evolutionary path. Robots for manufacturing took a fork that has focused on engineering robot arms for manufacturing applications. The key to success in industry was precision and repeatability on the assembly line for mass production, in effect, industrial engineers wanted to automate the workplace. Once a robot arm was programmed, it should be able to operate for weeks and months with only minor maintenance. As a result, the emphasis was

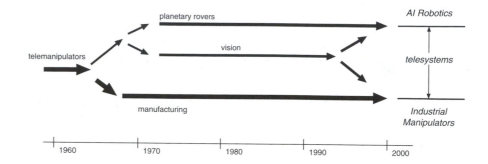

Figure 1.1   A timeline showing forks in development of robots.

placed on the mechanical aspects of the robot to ensure precision and repeatability and methods to make sure the robot could move precisely and
repeatable, quickly enough to make a profit. Because assembly lines were
engineered to mass produce a certain product, the robot didn't have to be
able to notice any problems. The standards for mass production would make
it more economical to devise mechanisms that would ensure parts would be
in the correct place. A robot for automation could essentially be blind and
senseless.

Robotics for the space program took a different fork, concentrating instead
on highly specialized, one-of-a-kind planetary rovers. Unlike a highly automated manufacturing plant, a planetary rover operating on the dark side of
the moon (no radio communication) might run into unexpected situations.
Consider that on Apollo 17, astronaut and geologist Harrison Schmitt found
an orange rock on the moon; an orange rock was totally unexpected. Ideally,
a robot would be able to notice something unusual, stop what it was doing
(as long as it didn't endanger itself) and investigate. Since it couldn't be pre-
programmed to handle all possible contingencies, it had to be able to notice
its environment and handle any problems that might occur. At a minimum,
a planetary rover had to have some source of sensory inputs, some way of
interpreting those inputs, and a way of modifying its actions to respond to
a changing world. And the need to sense and adapt to a partially unknown
environment is the need for intelligence.

The fork toward AI robots has not reached a termination point of truly autonomous, intelligent robots. In fact, as will be seen in Ch. 2 and 4, it wasn't
until the late 1980's that any visible progress toward that end was made. So
what happened when someone had an application for a robot which needed

real-time adaptability before 1990? In general, the lack of machine intelligence was compensated by the development of mechanisms which allow a human to control all, or parts, of the robot remotely. These mechanisms are generally referred to under the umbrella term: teleoperation. Teleoperation can be viewed as the "stuff" in the middle of the two forks. In practice, intelligent robots such as the Mars Sojourner are controlled with some form of teleoperation. This chapter will cover the flavors of teleoperation, given their importance as a stepping stone towards truly intelligent robots.

The chapter concludes by visiting the issues in AI, and argues that AI is imperative for many robotic applications. Teleoperation is simply not sufficient or desirable as a long term solution. However, it has served as a reasonable patch.

It is interesting to note that the two forks, manufacturing and AI, currently appear to be merging. Manufacturing is now shifting to a "mass customization" phase, where companies which can economically make short runs of special order goods are thriving. The pressure is on for industrial robots, more correctly referred to as industrial manipulators, to be rapidly reprogrammed and more forgiving if a part isn't placed exactly as expected in its workspace. As a result, AI techniques are migrating to industrial manipulators.

1.2   How Can a Machine Be Intelligent?

ARTIFICIAL
INTELLIGENCE

The science of making machines act intelligently is usually referred to as *artificial intelligence*, or AI for short. Artificial Intelligence has no commonly accepted definitions. One of the first textbooks on AI defined it as "the study of ideas that enable computers to be intelligent,"[143] which seemed to beg the question. A later textbook was more specific, "AI is the attempt to get the computer to do things that, for the moment, people are better at."[120] This definition is interesting because it implies that once a task is performed successfully by a computer, then the technique that made it possible is no longer AI, but something mundane. That definition is fairly important to a person researching AI methods for robots, because it explains why certain topics suddenly seem to disappear from the AI literature: it was perceived as being solved! Perhaps the most amusing of all AI definitions was the slogan for the now defunct computer company, Thinking Machines, Inc., "... making machines that will be proud of us."

The term AI is controversial, and has sparked ongoing philosophical debates on whether a machine can ever be intelligent. As Roger Penrose notes in his book, The Emperor's New Mind: "Nevertheless, it would be fair to say that, although many clever things have indeed been done, the simulation of anything that could pass for genuine intelligence is yet a long way off."[115] Engineers often dismiss AI as wild speculation. As a result of such vehement criticisms, many researchers often label their work as "intelligent systems" or "knowledge-based systems" in an attempt to avoid the controversy surrounding the term "AI."

A single, precise definition of AI is not necessary to study AI robotics. AI robotics is the application of AI techniques to robots. More specifically, AI robotics is the consideration of issues traditional covered by AI for application to robotics: learning, planning, reasoning, problem solving, knowledge representation, and computer vision. An article in the May 5, 1997 issue of Newsweek, "Actually, Chess is Easy," discusses why robot applications are more demanding for AI than playing chess. Indeed, the concepts of the reactive paradigm, covered in Chapter 4, influenced major advances in traditional, non-robotic areas of AI, especially planning. So by studying AI robotics, a reader interested in AI is getting exposure to the general issues in AI.

1.3   What Can Robots Be Used For?

Now that a working definition of a robot and artificial intelligence has been established, an attempt can be made to answer the question: what can intelligent robots be used for? The short answer is that robots can be used for just about any application that can be thought of. The long answer is that robots are well suited for applications where 1) a human is at significant risk (nuclear, space, military), 2) the economics or menial nature of the application result in inefficient use of human workers (service industry, agriculture), and 3) for humanitarian uses where there is great risk (demining an area of land mines, urban search and rescue). Or as the well-worn joke among roboticists

THE 3 D'S   goes, robots are good for *the 3 D's*: jobs that are dirty, dull, or dangerous.

Historically, the military and industry invested in robotics in order to build nuclear weapons and power plants; now, the emphasis is on using robots for environmental remediation and restoration of irradiated and polluted sites. Many of the same technologies developed for the nuclear industry for processing radioactive ore is now being adapted for the pharmaceutical industry; processing immune suppressant drugs may expose workers to highly toxic chemicals.

Another example of a task that poses significant risk to a human is space exploration. People can be protected in space from the hard vacuum, solar radiation, etc., but only at great economic expense. Furthermore, space suits are so bulky that they severely limit an astronaut's ability to perform simple tasks, such as unscrewing and removing an electronics panel on a satellite. Worse yet, having people in space necessitates more people in space. Solar radiation embrittlement of metals suggests that astronauts building a large space station would have to spend as much time repairing previously built portions as adding new components. Even more people would have to be sent into space, requiring a larger structure. the problem escalates. A study by Dr. Jon Erickson's research group at NASA Johnson Space Center argued that a manned mission to Mars was not feasible without robot drones capable of constantly working outside of the vehicle to repair problems introduced by deadly solar radiation.[51] (Interestingly enough, a team of three robots which did just this were featured in the 1971 film, *Silent Running*, as well as by a young R2D2 in *The Phantom Menace*.)

Nuclear physics and space exploration are activities which are often far removed from everyday life, and applications where robots figure more prominently in the future than in current times.

The most obvious use of robots is manufacturing, where repetitious activities in unpleasant surroundings make human workers inefficient or expensive to retain. For example, robot "arms" have been used for welding cars on assembly lines. One reason that welding is now largely robotic is that it is an unpleasant job for a human (hot, sweaty, tedious work) with a low tolerance for inaccuracy. Other applications for robots share similar motivation: to automate menial, unpleasant tasks—usually in the service industry. One such activity is janitorial work, especially maintaining public rest rooms, which has a high turnover in personnel regardless of payscale. The janitorial problem is so severe in some areas of the US, that the Postal Service offered contracts to companies to research and develop robots capable of autonomously cleaning a bathroom (the bathroom could be designed to accommodate a robot).

Agriculture is another area where robots have been explored as an economical alternative to hard to get menial labor. Utah State University has been working with automated harvesters, using GPS (global positioning satellite system) to traverse the field while adapting the speed of harvesting to the rate of food being picked, much like a well-adapted insect. The Department of Mechanical and Material Engineering at the University of Western Australia developed a robot called *Shear Majic* capable of shearing a live sheep. People available for sheep shearing has declined, along with profit margins, increasing the pressure on the sheep industry to develop economic alternatives. Possibly the most creative use of robots for agriculture is a mobile automatic milker developed in the Netherlands and in Italy.[68;32] Rather than have a person attach the milker to a dairy cow, the roboticized milker arm identifies the teats as the cow walks into her stall, targets them, moves about to position itself, and finally reaches up and attaches itself.

Finally, one of the most compelling uses of robots is for humanitarian purposes. Recently, robots have been proposed to help with detecting unexploded ordinance (land mines) and with urban search and rescue (finding survivors after a terrorist bombing of a building or an earthquake). Humanitarian land demining is a challenging task. It is relatively easy to demine an area with bulldozer, but that destroys the fields and improvements made by the civilians and hurts the economy. Various types of robots are being tested in the field, including aerial and ground vehicles.[73]

1.3.1   Social implications of robotics

While many applications for artificially intelligent robots will actively reduce risk to a human life, many applications appear to compete with a human's livelihood. Don't robots put people out of work? One of the pervasive themes in society has been the impact of science and technology on the dignity of people. Charlie Chaplin's silent movie, *Modern Times*, presented the world with visual images of how manufacturing-oriented styles of management reduces humans to machines, just "cogs in the wheel."

Robots appear to amplify the tension between productivity and the role of the individual. Indeed, the scientist in *Metropolis* points out to the corporate ruler of the city that now that they have robots, they don't need workers anymore. People who object to robots, or technology in general, are often called *Luddites*, after Ned Ludd, who is often credited with leading a short-lived revolution of workers against mills in Britain. Prior to the industrial revolution in Britain, wool was woven by individuals in their homes or collectives as a cottage industry. Mechanization of the weaving process changed the jobs associated with weaving, the status of being a weaver (it was a skill), and required people to work in a centralized location (like having your telecommuting job terminated). Weavers attempted to organize and destroyed looms and mill owners' properties in reaction. After escalating vi-

LUDDITES

olence in 1812, legislation was passed to end worker violence and protect the mills. The rebelling workers were persecuted. While the Luddite movement may have been motivated by a quality-of-life debate, the term is often applied to anyone who objects to technology, or "progress," for any reason. The connotation is that Luddites have an irrational fear of technological progress.

The impact of robots is unclear, both what is the real story and how people interact with robots. The HelpMate Robotics, Inc. robots and janitorial robots appear to be competing with humans, but are filling a niche where it is hard to get human workers at any price. Cleaning office buildings is menial and boring, plus the hours are bad. One janitorial company has now invested in mobile robots through a Denver-based company, Continental Divide Robotics, citing a 90% yearly turnover in staff, even with profit sharing after two years. The Robotics Industries Association, a trade group, produces annual reports outlining the need for robotics, yet possibly the biggest robot money makers are in the entertainment and toy industries.

The cultural implications of robotics cannot be ignored. While the sheep shearing robots in Australia were successful and were ready to be commercialized for significant economic gains, the sheep industry reportedly rejected the robots. One story goes that the sheep ranchers would not accept a robot shearer unless it had a 0% fatality rate (it's apparently fairly easy to nick an artery on a squirming sheep). But human shearers accidently kill several sheep, while the robots had a demonstrably better rate. The use of machines raises an ethical question: is it acceptable for an animal to die at the hands of a machine rather than a person? What if a robot was performing a piece of intricate surgery on a human?

1.4   A Brief History of Robotics

Robotics has its roots in a variety of sources, including the way machines are controlled and the need to perform tasks that put human workers at risk.

In 1942, the United States embarked on a top secret project, called the Manhattan Project, to build a nuclear bomb. The theory for the nuclear bomb had existed for a number of years in academic circles. Many military leaders of both sides of World War II believed the winner would be the side who could build the first nuclear device: the Allied Powers led by USA or the Axis, led by Nazi Germany.

One of the first problems that the scientists and engineers encountered was handling and processing radioactive materials, including uranium and

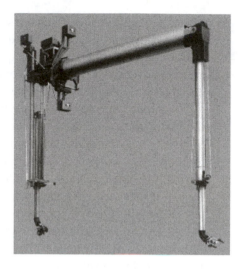

Figure 1.2   A Model 8 Telemanipulator. The upper portion of the device is placed in the ceiling, and the portion on the right extends into the hot cell. (Photograph courtesy Central Research Laboratories.)

plutonium, in large quantities. Although the immensity of the dangers of working with nuclear materials was not well understood at the time, all the personnel involved knew there were health risks. One of the first solutions was the *glove box*. Nuclear material was placed in a glass box. A person stood (or sat) behind a leaded glass shield and stuck their hands into thick rubberized gloves. This allowed the worker to see what they were doing and to perform almost any task that they could do without gloves.

But this was not an acceptable solution for highly radioactive materials, and mechanisms to physically remove and completely isolate the nuclear materials from humans had to be developed. One such mechanism was TELEMANIPULATOR   a force reflecting *telemanipulator*, a sophisticated mechanical linkage which translated motions on one end of the mechanism to motions at the other end. A popular telemanipulator is shown in Fig. 1.2.

A nuclear worker would insert their hands into (or around) the telemanipulator, and move it around while watching a display of what the other end of the arm was doing in a containment cell. Telemanipulators are similar in principle to the power gloves now used in computer games, but much harder to use. The mechanical technology of the time did not allow a perfect mapping of hand and arm movements to the robot arm. Often the operator had to make non-intuitive and awkward motions with their arms to get the robot arm to perform a critical manipulation—very much like working in front of a mirror. Likewise, the telemanipulators had challenges in providing force feedback so the operator could feel how hard the gripper was holding an object. The lack of naturalness in controlling the arm (now referred to as a poor Human-Machine Interface) meant that even simple tasks for an unencumbered human could take much longer. Operators might take years of practice to reach the point where they could do a task with a telemanipulator as quickly as they could do it directly.

After World War II, many other countries became interested in producing a nuclear weapon and in exploiting nuclear energy as a replacement for fossil fuels in power plants. The USA and Soviet Union also entered into a nuclear arms race. The need to mass-produce nuclear weapons and to support peaceful uses of nuclear energy kept pressure on engineers to design robot arms which would be easier to control than telemanipulators. Machines that looked more like and acted like robots began to emerge, largely due to advances in control theory. After WWII, pioneering work by Norbert Wiener allowed engineers to accurately control mechanical and electrical devices using cybernetics.

1.4.1   Industrial manipulators

Successes with at least partially automating the nuclear industry also meant the technology was available for other applications, especially general manufacturing. Robot arms began being introduced to industries in 1956 by Unimation (although it wouldn't be until 1972 before the company made a profit).[37] The two most common types of robot technology that have evolved for industrial use are robot arms, called industrial manipulators, and mobile carts, called automated guided vehicles (AGVs).

INDUSTRIAL
MANIPULATOR

An *industrial manipulator*, to paraphrase the Robot Institute of America's definition, is a reprogrammable and multi-functional mechanism that is designed to move materials, parts, tools, or specialized devices. The emphasis in industrial manipulator design is being able to program them to be able to perform a task repeatedly with a high degree of accuracy and speed. In order to be multi-functional, many manipulators have multiple degrees of freedom, as shown in Fig. 1.4. The MOVEMASTER arm has five degrees of freedom, because it has five joints, each of which is capable of a single rotational degree of freedom. A human arm has three joints (shoulder, el-

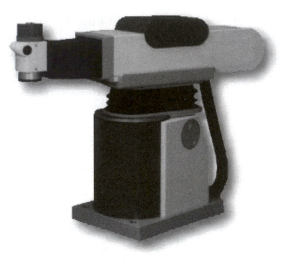

Figure 1.3 An RT3300 industrial manipulator. (Photograph courtesy of Seiko Instruments.)

bow, and wrist), two of which are complex (shoulder and wrist), yielding six degrees of freedom.

Control theory is extremely important in industrial manipulators. Rapidly moving around a large tool like a welding gun introduces interesting problems, like when to start decelerating so the gun will stop in the correct location without overshooting and colliding with the part to be welded. Also, oscillatory motion, in general, is undesirable. Another interesting problem is the joint configuration. If a robot arm has a wrist, elbow and shoulder joints like a human, there are redundant degrees of freedom. Redundant degrees of freedom means there are multiple ways of moving the joints that will accomplish the same motion. Which one is better, more efficient, less stressful on the mechanisms?

It is interesting to note that most manipulator control was assumed to be *ballistic control*, or *open loop control*. In ballistic control, the position trajectory and velocity profile is computed once, then the arm carries it out. There are no "in-flight" corrections, just like a ballistic missile doesn't make any course corrections. In order to accomplish a precise task with ballistic control, everything about the device and how it works has to be modeled and figured into the computation. The opposite of ballistic control is *closed-loop control*, where the error between the goal and current position is noted by a sensor(s),

BALLISTIC CONTROL
OPEN LOOP CONTROL

CLOSED-LOOP
CONTROL

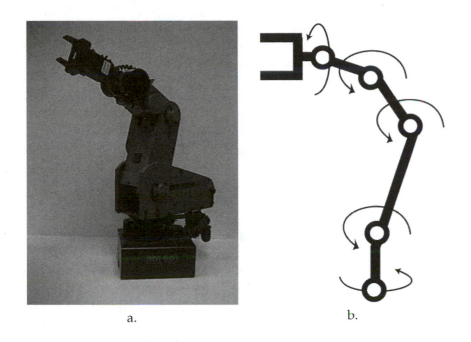

a.   b.

Figure 1.4   A MOVEMASTER robot: a.) the robot arm and b.) the associated joints.

and a new trajectory and profile is computed and executed, then modified on
the next update, and so on. Closed-loop control requires external sensors to
provide the error signal, or *feedback*.

In general, if the structural properties of the robot and its cargo are known,
these questions can be answered and a program can be developed. In practice, the control theory is complex. The dynamics (how the mechanism moves
and deforms) and kinematics (how the components of the mechanism are
connected) of the system have to be computed for each joint of the robot, then
those motions can be propagated to the next joint iteratively. This requires a
computationally consuming change of coordinate systems from one joint to
the next. To move the gripper in Fig 1.4 requires four changes of coordinates
to go from the base of the arm to the gripper. The coordinate transformations
often have singularities, causing the equations to perform divide by zeros. It
can take a programmer weeks to reprogram a manipulator.

One simplifying solution is to make the robot rigid at the desired velocities,
reducing the dynamics. This eliminates having to compute the terms for
overshooting and oscillating. However, a robot is made rigid by making it

heavier. The end result is that it is not uncommon for a 2 ton robot to be able to handle only a 200 pound payload. Another simplifying solution is to avoid the computations in the dynamics and kinematics and instead have the programmer use a teach pendant. Using a *teach pendant* (which often looks like a joystick or computer game console), the programmer guides the robot through the desired set of motions. The robot remembers these motions and creates a program from them. Teach pendants do not mitigate the danger of working around a 2 ton piece of equipment. Many programmers have to direct the robot to perform delicate tasks, and have to get physically close to the robot in order to see what the robot should do next. This puts the programmer at risk of being hit by the robot should it hit a singularity point in its joint configuration or if the programmer makes a mistake in directing a motion. You don't want to have your head next to a 2 ton robot arm if it suddenly spins around!

Automatic guided vehicles, or AGVs, are intended to be the most flexible conveyor system possible: a conveyor which doesn't need a continuous belt or roller table. Ideally an AGV would be able to pick up a bin of parts or manufactured items and deliver them as needed. For example, an AGV might receive a bin containing an assembled engine. It could then deliver it automatically across the shop floor to the car assembly area which needed an engine. As it returned, it might be diverted by the central computer and instructed to pick up a defective part and take it to another area of the shop for reworking.

However, navigation (as will be seen in Part II) is complex. The AGV has to know where it is, plan a path from its current location to its goal destination, and to avoid colliding with people, other AGVs, and maintenance workers and tools cluttering the factory floor. This proved too difficult to do, especially for factories with uneven lighting (which interferes with vision) and lots of metal (which interferes with radio controllers and on-board radar and sonar). Various solutions converged on creating a trail for the AGV to follow. One method is to bury a magnetic wire in the floor for the AGV to sense. Unfortunately, changing the path of an AGV required ripping up the concrete floor. This didn't help with the flexibility needs of modern manufacturing. Another method is to put down a strip of photochemical tape for the vehicle to follow. The strip is unfortunately vulnerable, both to wear and to vandalism by unhappy workers. Regardless of the guidance method, in the end the simplest way to thwart an AGV was to something on its path. If the AGV did not have range sensors, then it would be unable to detect an expensive piece of equipment or a person put deliberately in its path. A

TEACH PENDANT

AUTOMATIC GUIDED
VEHICLES

few costly collisions would usually led to the AGV's removal. If the AGV did have range sensors, it would stop for anything. A well placed lunch box could hold the AGV for hours until a manager happened to notice what was going on. Even better from a disgruntled worker's perspective, many AGVs would make a loud noise to indicate the path was blocked. Imagine having to constantly remove lunch boxes from the path of a dumb machine making unpleasant siren noises.

From the first, robots in the workplace triggered a backlash. Many of the human workers felt threatened by a potential loss of jobs, even though the jobs being mechanized were often menial or dangerous. This was particularly true of manufacturing facilities which were unionized. One engineer reported that on the first day it was used in a hospital, a HelpMate Robotics cart was discovered pushed down the stairs. Future models were modified to have some mechanisms to prevent malicious acts.

BLACK FACTORY   Despite the emerging Luddite effect, industrial engineers in each of the economic powers began working for a *black factory* in the 1980's. A black factory is a factory that has no lights turned on because there are no workers. Computers and robots were expected to allow complete automation of manufacturing processes, and courses in "Computer-Integrated Manufacturing Systems" became popular in engineering schools.

But two unanticipated trends undermined industrial robots in a way that the Luddite movement could not. First, industrial engineers did not have experience designing manufacturing plants with robots. Often industrial manipulators were applied to the wrong application. One of the most embarrassing examples was the IBM Lexington printer plant. The plant was built with a high degree of automation, and the designers wrote numerous articles on the exotic robot technology they had cleverly designed. Unfortunately, IBM had grossly over-estimated the market for printers and the plant sat mostly idle at a loss. While the plant's failure wasn't the fault of robotics, per se, it did cause many manufacturers to have a negative view of automation in general. The second trend was the changing world economy. Customers were demanding "mass customization." Manufacturers who could make short runs of a product tailored to each customer on a large scale were the ones making the money. (Mass customization is also referred to as "agile manufacturing.") However, the lack of adaptability and difficulties in programming industrial robot arms and changing the paths of AGVs interfered with rapid retooling. The lack of adaptability, combined with concerns over worker safety and the Luddite effect, served to discourage companies from investing in robots through most of the 1990's.

a.   b.

Figure 1.5   Motivation for intelligent planetary rovers: a.) Astronaut John Young awkwardly collecting lunar samples on Apollo 16, and b.) Astronaut Jim Irwin stopping the lunar rover as it slides down a hill on Apollo 15. (Photographs courtesy of the National Aeronautics and Space Administration.)

1.4.2   Space robotics and the AI approach

While the rise of industrial manipulators and the engineering approach to robotics can in some measure be traced to the nuclear arms race, the rise of the AI approach can be said to start with the space race. On May 25, 1961, spurred by the success of the Soviet Union's Sputnik space programs, President John F. Kennedy announced that United States would put a man on the moon by 1970. Walking on the moon was just one aspect of space exploration. There were concerns about the Soviets setting up military bases on the Moon and Mars and economic exploitation of planetary resources.

Clearly there was going to be a time lag of almost a decade before humans from the USA would go to the Moon. And even then, it would most likely be with experimental spacecraft, posing a risk to the human astronauts. Even without the risk to humans, the bulk of spacesuits would make even trivial tasks difficult for astronauts to perform. Fig. 1.5a shows astronaut John Young on Apollo 16 collecting samples with a lunar rake. The photo shows the awkward way the astronaut had to bend his body and arms to complete the task.

Planetary rovers were a possible solution, either to replace an astronaut or assist him or her. Unfortunately, rover technology in the 1960's was limited. Because of the time delays, a human would be unable to safely control a rover over the notoriously poor radio links of the time, even if the rover went very slow. Therefore, it would be desirable to have a robot that was autonomous. One option would be to have mobile robots land on a planetary conduct preliminary explorations, conduct tests, etc., and radio back the results. These automated planetary rovers would ideally have a high degree of autonomy, much like a trained dog. The robot would receive commands from Earth to explore a particular region. It would navigate around boulders and not fall into canyons, and traverse steep slopes without rolling over. The robot might even be smart enough to regulate its own energy supply, for example, by making sure it was sheltered during the planetary nights and to stop what it was doing and position itself for recharging its solar batteries. A human might even be able to speak to it in a normal way to give it commands.

Getting a mobile robot to the level of a trained dog immediately presented new issues. Just by moving around, a mobile robot could change the world-for instance, by causing a rock slide. Fig. 1.5b shows astronaut Jim Irwin rescuing the lunar rover during an extra-vehicular activity (EVA) on Apollo 15 as it begins to slide downhill. Consider that if an astronaut has difficulty finding a safe parking spot on the moon, how much more challenging it would be for an autonomous rover. Furthermore, an autonomous rover would have no one to rescue it, should it make a mistake.

Consider the impact of uncertain or incomplete information on a rover that didn't have intelligence. If the robot was moving based on a map taken from a telescope or an overhead command module, the map could still contain errors or at the wrong resolution to see certain dangers. In order to navigate successfully, the robot has to compute its path with the new data or risk colliding with a rock or falling into a hole. What if the robot did something broke totally unexpected or all the assumptions about the planet were wrong? In theory, the robot should be able to diagnose the problem and attempt to continue to make progress on its task. What seemed at first like an interim solution to putting humans in space quickly became more complicated.

Clearly, developing a planetary rover and other robots for space was going to require a concentrated, long-term effort. Agencies in the USA such as NASA *Jet Propulsion Laboratory (JPL)* in Pasadena, California, were given the task of developing the robotic technology that would be needed to prepare the way for astronauts in space. They were in a position to take advantage of the outcome of the *Dartmouth Conference*. The Dartmouth Conference was a gathering hosted by the Defense Advanced Research Projects Agency (DARPA) in 1955 of prominent scientists working with computers or on the theory for computers. DARPA was interested in hearing what the potential uses for computers were. One outcome of the conference was the term "artificial intelligence"; the attending scientists believed that computers might become powerful enough to understand human speech and duplicate human reasoning. This in turn suggested that computers might mimic the capabilities of animals and humans sufficiently for a planetary rover to survive for long periods with only simple instructions from Earth.

As an indirect result of the need for robotics converging with the possibility of artificial intelligence, the space program became one of the earliest proponents of developing AI for robotics. NASA also introduced the notion that AI robots would of course be mobile, rather than strapped to a factory floor, and would have to integrate all forms of AI (understanding speech, planning, reasoning, representing the world, learning) into one program—a daunting task which has not yet been reached.

1.5   Teleoperation

TELEOPERATION
Teleoperation is when a human operator controls a robot from a distance (*tele* means "remote"). The connotation of teleoperation is that the distance is too great for the operator to see what the robot is doing, so radio controlled toy cars are not considered teleoperation systems. The operator and robot have some type of master-slave relationship. In most cases, the human operator sits at a workstation and directs a robot through some sort of interface, as seen in Fig. 1.6.

LOCAL
REMOTE
The control interface could be a joystick, virtual reality gear, or any number of innovative interfaces. The human operator, or teleoperator, is often referred to as the *local* (due to being at the local workstation) and the robot as the *remote* (since it is operating at a remote location from the teleoperator). The local must have some type of display and control mechanisms, while the remote must have sensors, effectors, power, and in the case of mobile robots, mobility.[141] The teleoperator cannot look at what the remote is doing directly, either because the robot is physically remote (e.g., on Mars) or the local has to be shielded (e.g., in a nuclear or pharmaceutical processing plant hot cell).

SENSORS
DISPLAY
COMMUNICATION LINK
Therefore, the *sensors* which acquire information about the remote location, the *display* technology for allowing the operator to see the sensor data, and the *communication link* between the local and remote are critical components of a telesystem.[141]

Teleoperation is a popular solution for controlling remotes because AI technology is nowhere near human levels of competence, especially in terms of

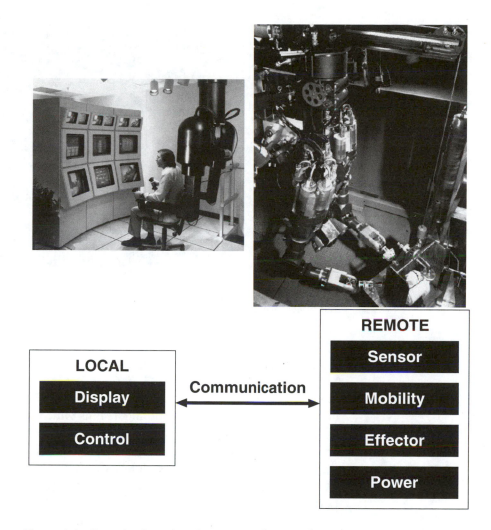

Figure 1.6 Organization of a telesystem. (Photographs courtesy of Oak Ridge National Laboratory.)

perception and decision making. One example of teleoperation is the exploration of underwater sites such as the Titanic. Having a human control a robot is advantageous because a human can isolate an object of interest, even partially obscured by mud in murky water as described by W. R. Uttal.[141] Humans can also perform dextrous manipulation (e.g., screwing a nut on a bolt), which is very difficult to program a manipulator to do.

Figure 1.7   Sojourner Mars rover. (Photograph courtesy of the National Aeronautics and Space Administration.)

Another example is the Sojourner robot (shown in Fig. 1.7) which explored Mars from July 5 to September 27, 1997, until it ceased to reply to radio commands. Since there was little data before Sojourner on what Mars is like, it is hard to develop sensors and algorithms which can detect important attributes or even control algorithms to move the robot. It is important that any unusual rocks or rock formations (like the orange rock Dr. Schmitt found on the Moon during Apollo 17) be detected. Humans are particularly adept at perception, especially seeing patterns and anomalies in pictures. Current AI perceptual abilities fall far short of human abilities. Humans are also adept at problem solving. When the Mars Pathfinder craft landed on Mars, the air bags that had cushioned the landing did not deflate properly. When the petals of the lander opened, an airbag was in the way of Sojourner. The solution? The ground controllers sent commands to retract the petals and open them again. That type of problem solving is extremely difficult for the current capabilities of AI.

But teleoperation is not an ideal solution for all situations. Many tasks are repetitive and boring. For example, consider using a joystick to drive a radio-controlled car; after a few hours, it tends to get harder and harder to pay attention. Now imagine trying to control the car while only looking through a small camera mounted in front. The task becomes much harder because of the limited field of view; essentially there is no peripheral vision. Also, the camera may not be transmitting new images very fast because the communication link has a limited bandwidth, so the view is jerky. Most people quickly experience *cognitive fatigue*; their attention wanders and they may even experience headaches and other physical symptoms of stress. Even if the visual display is excellent, the teleoperator may get *simulator sickness* due to the discordance between the visual system saying the operator is moving and the inner ear saying the operator is stationary. [141]

COGNITIVE FATIGUE

SIMULATOR SICKNESS

Another disadvantage of teleoperation is that it can be inefficient to use for applications that have a *large time delay*. [128] A large time delay can result in the teleoperator giving a remote a command, unaware that it will place the remote in jeopardy. Or, an unanticipated event such as a rock fall might occur and destroy the robot before the teleoperator can see the event and command the robot to flee. A rule of thumb, or *heuristic*, is that the time it takes to do a task with traditional teleoperation grows linearly with the transmission delay. A teleoperation task which took 1 minute for a teleoperator to guide a remote to do on the Earth might take 2.5 minutes to do on the Moon, and 140 minutes on Mars. [142] Fortunately, researchers have made some progress with *predictive displays*, which immediately display what the simulation result of the command would be.

TELEOPERATION
HEURISTIC

PREDICTIVE DISPLAYS

The impact of time delays is not limited to planetary rovers. A recent example of an application of teleoperation are unmanned aerial vehicles (UAV) used by the United States to verify treaties by flying overhead and taking videos of the ground below. Advanced prototypes of these vehicles can fly autonomously, but take-offs and landings are difficult for on-board computer control. In this case of the Darkstar UAV (shown in Fig. 1.8), human operators were available to assume teleoperation control of the vehicle should it encounter problems during take-off. Unfortunately, the contingency plan did not factor in the 7 second delay introduced by using a satellite as the communications link. Darkstar no. 1 did indeed experience problems on take-off, but the teleoperator could not get commands to it fast enough before it crashed. As a result, it earned the unofficial nickname "Darkspot."

Another practical drawback to teleoperation is that there is at least one person per robot, possibly more. The Predator unmanned aerial vehicle has been used by the United States for verification of the Dayton Accords in Bosnia. One Predator requires at least one teleoperator to fly the vehicle and another teleoperator to command the sensor payload to look at particular areas. Other UAVs have teams composed of up to four teleoperators plus a fifth team member who specializes in takeoffs and landings. These teleop-

Figure 1.8 Dark Star unmanned aerial vehicle. (Photograph courtesy of DefenseLink, Office of the Assistant Secretary of Defense-Public Affairs.)

erators may have over a year of training before they can fly the vehicle. In the case of UAVs, teleoperation permits a dangerous, important task to be completed, but with a high cost in manpower.

TASK
CHARACTERISTICS

According to Wampler,[142] teleoperation is best suited for applications where:

1. The tasks are unstructured and not repetitive.

2. The task workspace cannot be engineered to permit the use of industrial manipulators.

3. Key portions of the task intermittently require dextrous manipulation, especially hand-eye coordination.

4. Key portions of the task require object recognition, situational awareness, or other advanced perception.

5. The needs of the display technology do not exceed the limitations of the communication link (bandwidth, time delays).

6. The availability of trained personnel is not an issue.

1.5.1 Telepresence

An early attempt at reducing cognitive fatigue was to add more cameras with faster update rates to widen the field of view and make it more consistent with how a human prefers to look at the world. This may not be practical for many applications because of limited bandwidth. Video telephones, picture phones, or video-conferencing over the Internet with their jerky, asynchronous updates are usually examples of annoying limited bandwidth. In these instances, the physical restrictions on how much and how fast information can be transmitted result in image updates much slower than the rates human brains expect. The result of limited bandwidth is jerky motion and increased cognitive fatigue. So adding more cameras only exacerbates the problem by adding more information that must be transmitted over limited bandwidth.

TELEPRESENCE

VIRTUAL REALITY

One area of current research in teleoperation is the use of *telepresence* to reduce cognitive fatigue and simulator sickness by making the human-robot interface more natural. Telepresence aims for what is popularly called *virtual reality*, where the operator has complete sensor feedback and feels as if she were the robot. If the operator turns to look in a certain direction, the view from the robot is there. If the operator pushes on a joystick for the robot to move forward and the wheels are slipping, the operator would hear and feel the motors straining while seeing that there was no visual change. This provides a more natural interface to the human, but it is very expensive in terms of equipment and requires very high bandwidth rates. It also still requires one person per robot. This is better than traditional teleoperation, but a long way from having one teleoperator control multiple robots.

1.5.2   Semi-autonomous control

SEMI-AUTONOMOUS
CONTROL
SUPERVISORY CONTROL

Another line of research in teleoperation is *semi-autonomous control*, often called *supervisory control*, where the remote is given an instruction or portion of a task that it can safely do on its own. There are two flavors of semi-autonomous control: continuous assistance, or *shared control*, and *control trading*.

SHARED CONTROL

In continuous assistance systems, the teleoperator and remote share control. The teleoperator can either delegate a task for the robot to do or can do it via direct control. If the teleoperator delegates the task to the robot, the human must still monitor to make sure that nothing goes wrong. This is particularly useful for teleoperating robot arms in space. The operator can relax (relatively) while the robot arm moves into the specified position near a panel, staying on alert in case something goes wrong. Then the operator can take over and perform the actions which require hand-eye coordination. Shared control helps the operator avoid cognitive fatigue by delegating boring, repetitive control actions to the robot. It also exploits the ability of a human to perform delicate operations. However, it still requires a high communication bandwidth.

CONTROL TRADING   An alternative approach is *control trading*, where the human initiates an action for the robot to complete autonomously. The human only interacts with the robot to give it a new command or to interrupt it and change its orders. The overall scheme is very much like a parent giving a 10-year old child a task to do. The parent knows what the child is able to do autonomously (e.g., clean their room). They have a common definition (clean room means go to the bedroom, make the bed, and empty the wastebaskets). The parent doesn't care about the details of how the child cleans the room (e.g., whether the wastebasket is emptied before the bed is made or vice versa). Control trading assumes that the robot is capable of autonomously accomplishing certain tasks without sharing control. The advantage is that, in theory, the local operator can give a robot a task to do, then turn attention to another robot and delegate a task to it, etc. A single operator could control multiple robots because they would not require even casual monitoring while they were performing a task. Supervisory control also reduces the demand on bandwidth and problems with communication delays. Data such as video images need to be transferred only when the local is configuring the remote for a new task, not all the time. Likewise, since the operator is not involved in directly controlling the robot, a 2.5 minute delay in communication is irrelevant; the robot either wrecked itself or it didn't. Unfortunately, control trading assumes that robots have actions that they can perform robustly even in unexpected situations; this may or may not be true. Which brings us back to the need for artificial intelligence.

Sojourner exhibited both flavors of supervisory control. It was primarily programmed for traded control, where the geologists could click on a rock and Sojourner would autonomously navigate close to it, avoiding rocks, etc. However, some JPL employees noted that the geologists tended to prefer to use shared control, watching every movement. A difficulty with most forms of shared control is that it is assumed that the human is smarter than the robot. This may be true, but the remote may have better sensor viewpoints and reaction times.

1.6   The Seven Areas of AI

Now that some possible uses and shortcomings of robots have been covered, it is motivating to consider what are the areas of artificial intelligence and how they could be used to overcome these problems. The Handbook of Artificial Intelligence[64] divides up the field into seven main areas: *knowledge representation, understanding natural language, learning, planning and problem solving, inference, search,* and *vision.*

1. **Knowledge representation**. An important, but often overlooked, issue is how does the robot represent its world, its task, and itself. Suppose a robot is scanning a pile of rubble for a human. What kind of data structure and algorithms would it take to represent what a human looks like? One way is to construct a structural model: a person is composed of an oval head, a cylindrical torso, smaller cylindrical arms with bilateral symmetry, etc. Of course, what happens if only a portion of the human is visible?

2. **Understanding natural language**. Natural language is deceptively challenging, apart from the issue of recognizing words which is now being done by commercial products such as Via Voice and Naturally Speaking. It is not just a matter of looking up words, which is the subject of the following apocryphal story about AI. The story goes that after Sputnik went up, the US government needed to catch up with the Soviet scientists. However, translating Russian scientific articles was time consuming and not many US citizens could read technical reports in Russian. Therefore, the US decided to use these newfangled computers to create translation programs. The day came when the new program was ready for its first test. It was given the proverb: the spirit is willing, but the flesh is weak. The reported output: the vodka is strong, but the meat is rotten.

3. **Learning.** Imagine a robot that could be programmed by just watching a human, or by just trying the task repeatedly itself.

4. **Planning and problem solving.** Intelligence is associated with the ability to plan actions needed to accomplish a goal and solve problems with those plans or when they don't work. One of the earliest childhood fables, the Three Pigs and the Big, Bad Wolf, involves two unintelligent pigs who don't plan ahead and an intelligent pig who is able to solve the problem of why his brothers' houses have failed, as well as plan an unpleasant demise for the wolf.

5. **Inference.** Inference is generating an answer when there isn't complete information. Consider a planetary rover looking at a dark region on the ground. Its range finder is broken and all it has left is its camera and a fine AI system. Assume that depth information can't be extracted from

the camera. Is the dark region a canyon? Is it a shadow? The rover will need to use inference to either actively or passively disambiguate what the dark region is (e.g., kick a rock at the dark area versus reason that there is nothing nearby that could create that shadow).

SEARCH

6. **Search**. Search doesn't necessarily mean searching a large physical space for an object. In AI terms, search means efficiently examining a knowledge representation of a problem (called a "search space") to find the answer. Deep Blue, the computer that beat the World Chess master Gary Kasparov, won by searching through almost all possible combinations of moves to find the best move to make. The legal moves in chess given the current state of the board formed the search space.

VISION

7. **Vision**. Vision is possibly the most valuable sense humans have. Studies by Harvard psychologist Steven Kosslyn suggest that much of problem solving abilities stem from the ability to visually simulate the effects of actions in our head. As such, AI researchers have pursued creating vision systems both to improve robotic actions and to supplement other work in general machine intelligence.

Finally, there is a temptation to assume that the history of AI Robotics is the story of how advances in AI have improved robotics. But that is not the case. In many regards, robotics has played a pivotal role in advancing AI. Breakthroughs in methods for planning (operations research types of problems) came after the paradigm shift to reactivity in robotics in the late 1980's showed how unpredictable changes in the environment could actually be exploited to simplify programming. Many of the search engines on the world wide web use techniques developed for robotics. These programs are called

SOFTWARE AGENTS
WEB-BOT

software agents: autonomous programs which can interact with and adapt to their world just like an animal or a smart robot. The term *web-bot* directly reflects on the robotic heritage of these AI systems. Even animation is being changed by advances in AI robotics. According to a keynote address given by Danny Hillis at the 1997 Autonomous Agents conference, animators for Disney's *Hunchback of Notre Dame* programmed each cartoon character in the crowd scenes as if it were a simulation of a robot, and used methods that will be discussed in Ch. 4.

1.7 Summary

AI robotics is a distinct field, both historically and in scope, from industrial robotics. Industrial robots has concentrated on control theory issues, particularly solving the dynamics and kinematics of a robot. This is concerned with having the stationary robot perform precise motions, repetitively in a structured factory environment. AI robotics has concentrated on how a mobile robot should handle unpredictable events in an unstructured world. The design of an AI robot should consider how the robot will represent knowledge about the world, whether it needs to understand natural language, can it learn tasks, what kind of planning and problem solving will it have to do, how much inference is expected, how can it rapidly search its database and knowledge for answers, and what mechanisms will it use for perceiving the world.

Teleoperation arose as an intermediate solution to tasks that required automation but for which robots could not be adequately programmed to handle. Teleoperation methods typically are cognitive fatiguing, require high communication bandwidths and short communication delays, and require one or more teleoperators per remote. Telepresence techniques attempt to create a more natural interface for the human to control the robot and interpret what it is doing and seeing, but at a high communication cost. Supervisory control attempts to delegate portions of the task to the remote, either to do autonomously (traded control) or with reduced, but continuous, human interaction (shared control).

1.8 Exercises

Exercise 1.1

List the four attributes for evaluating an architecture. Based on what you know from your own experience, evaluate MS Windows 95/98/2000 as an architecture for teleoperating a robot.

Exercise 1.2

Name the three primitives for expressing the components of a robotics paradigm.

Exercise 1.3

Name the three robotic paradigms, and draw the relationship between the primitives.

Exercise 1.4

What is an intelligent robot?

Exercise 1.5

What is a Luddite?

Exercise 1.6

Describe at least two differences between AI and Engineering approaches to robotics.

Exercise 1.7

List three problems with teleoperation.

Exercise 1.8

Describe the components and the responsibilities of the local and the remote members of a telesystem.

Exercise 1.9

Describe the difference between telepresence and semi-autonomous control.

Exercise 1.10

List the six characteristics of applications that are well suited for teleoperation. Give at least two examples of potentially good applications for teleoperation not covered in the chapter.

Exercise 1.11   [*World Wide Web*]

Search the world wide web for sites that permit clients to use a robot remotely (one example is Xavier at Carnegie Mellon University). Decide whether each site is using human supervisory or shared control, and justify your answer.

Exercise 1.12   [*World Wide Web*]

Search the world wide web for applications and manufacturers of intelligent robots.

Exercise 1.13   [*World Wide Web*]

Dr. Harrison "Jack" Schmitt is a vocal proponent for space mining of Near Earth Objects (NEOs) such as mineral-rich asteroids. Because of the economics of manned mission, the small size of NEOs, human safety concerns, and the challenges of working in micro-gravity, space mining is expected to require intelligent robots. Search the web for more information on space mining, and give examples of why robots are needed.

Exercise 1.14   [*Programming*]

(This requires a robot with an on-board video camera and a teleoperation interface.) Teleoperate the robot through a slalom course of obstacles while keeping the robot in view as if controlling a RC car. Now looking only at the output of the video camera, repeat the obstacle course. Repeat the comparison several times, and keep track of the time to complete the course and number of collisions with obstacles. Which viewpoint led to faster completion of the course? Fewer collisions? Why?

Exercise 1.15   [*Advanced Reading*]

Read "Silicon Babies," Scientific American, December 1991, pp 125-134, on the challenges of AI robotics. List the 7 topics of AI and give examples of robots or researchers addressing each topic.

Exercise 1.16   [*Science Fiction*]

Read "Stranger in Paradise," Isaac Asimov, The Complete Robot, Doubleday, 1982, and enumerate the problems with telepresence illustrated by this story.

Exercise 1.17   [*Science Fiction*]

Watch the movie *Star Gate*. The military uses a teleoperated vehicle (in reality, NASA Jet Propulsion Laboratory's Hazbot) to first go through the star gate and test the environmental conditions on the other side. Discuss other ways in which the team could have continued to use the robot to their advantage.

Exercise 1.18   [*Science Fiction*]

Watch the 1971 movie, *The Andromeda Strain*, by Michael Crichton. The movie has several nerve wracking scenes as the scientists try to telemanipulate an unknown, deadly organism as fast as possible without dropping it. What do you think can be done with today's robots?

1.9   End Notes

Finding robots in the popular press
There is no one-stop-shopping publication or web site for robot applications. *Robotics World* is a business oriented publication which often has interesting blurbs. *Popular Mechanics* and *Popular Science* often contain short pieces on new robots and applications, although those short bits are often enthusiastically optimistic. A new magazine, *Robot Science and Technology*, appears to be bridging the gap between hobby 'bots and research 'bots. In addition to surfing the web, annual proceedings from the IEEE International Conference on Robotics and Automation (ICRA) and IEEE/RSJ International Conference on Intelligent Robots and Systems (IROS) contain scientific articles on the newest robots emerging from university and government laboratories. *Intelligent Robotic Systems*, ed. by S.G. Tzafestas, Marcel Dekker Inc, NY, 1991. This is a collection of chapters by various researchers and laboratory managers. The work is a bit dated now, but gives some feel for the variety of applications.

About Joe Engleberger
Joe Engleberger is often referred to as the "Father of Industrial Robots." His impressive resume includes having formed Unimation. His most recent robotics company made the HelpMate robot for hospitals. Engleberger participates in many robotics

forums, where his sartorial style (he always wears a bow tie) and verbal style (stridently pro-robotics, and that his company should get more money) make him easily recognizable.

Science fiction and robotics
For science fiction enthusiasts, take a look at Clute, John, and Nicholls, Peter, "Grolier Science Fiction: The Multimedia Encyclopedia of Science Fiction," Grolier Electronic Publishing, Danbury, CT, 1995. This entertaining CD provides a very detailed, cross-referenced look at robots as a theme in science fiction and a lengthy list (and review) of movies and books with robots in them. One of the most technically accurate movies about robots is *Silent Running*. It was directed by Douglas Trumbull who gained fame for his work in special effects, including *2001: A Space Odyssey*, *Close Encounters of the Third Kind*, and *Blade Runner*. The bulk of the movie concerns the day to day life of Bruce Dern and three waist-high robots. The robots and how they interact with Dern and their environment are very realistic and consistent with AI robotics. The only downside is a laughably ecologically correct plot (written in part by Steven Bochco and Michael Cimino) complete with songs by Joan Baez. Well worth watching for the 'bots, especially if the audience is curious about the hippie movement.

Robot name trivia
Marvin, the mail robot, may be named after the cantankerous robot Marvin in *The Hitchhiker's Guide to the Galaxy*. That Marvin is widely assumed to be named after the cantankerous AI researcher, Dr. Marvin Minksy, at MIT.

Have Spacesuit, Will Travel.
John Blitch brought to my attention the difficulty the Apollo astronauts had in accomplishing simple tasks due to the bulky space suits.

2 *The Hierarchical Paradigm*

Chapter Objectives:

- Describe the Hierarchical Paradigm in terms of the three robot paradigms and its organization of sensing.

- Name and evaluate one representative Hierarchical architecture in terms of: support for modularity, niche targetability, ease of portability to other domains, robustness.

- Solve a simple navigation problem using Strips, given a world model, operators, difference table, and difference evaluator. The state of the world model should be shown after each step.

- Understand the meaning of the following terms as applied to robotics: precondition, closed world assumption, open world, frame problem.

- Describe the mission planner, navigator, pilot organization of the Nested Hierarchical Controller.

- List two advantages and disadvantages of the Hierarchical Paradigm.

2.1 Overview

The Hierarchical Paradigm is historically the oldest method of organizing intelligence in mainstream robotics. It dominated robot implementations from 1967, with the inception of the first AI robot, Shakey (Fig. 2.1) at SRI, up until the late 1980's when the Reactive Paradigm burst onto the scene.

This chapter begins with a description of the Hierarchical Paradigm in terms of the **SENSE, PLAN, ACT** primitives and by its sensing representation. The chapter then covers the use of Strips in Shakey to reason and plan

Figure 2.1   Shakey, the first AI robot. It was built by SRI for DARPA 1967–70. (Photograph courtesy of SRI.)

a path. Strips will serve to motivate the reader as to the computer challenges inherent in even as simple a task as walking across a room. However, Strips is not an architecture, per se, just an interesting technique which emerged from trying to build an architecture. Two representative architectures are presented, NHC and RCS, that serve as examples of robot architectures popular at the time. The chapter concludes with programming considerations.

2.2   Attributes of the Hierarchical Paradigm

As noted in Part I, a robotic paradigm is defined by the relationship between the three primitives (SENSE, PLAN, ACT) and by the way sensory data is processed and distributed through the system.

The Hierarchical Paradigm is sequential and orderly, as shown in Figs. 2.2 and 2.3. First the robot senses the world and constructs a global world map. Then "eyes" closed, the robot plans all the directives needed to reach the

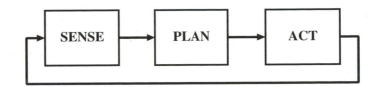

Figure 2.2   S,P,A organization of Hierarchical Paradigm.

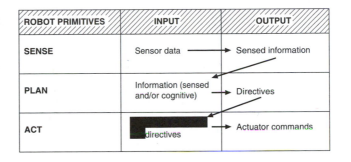

Figure 2.3   Alternative description of how the 3 primitives interact in the Hierarchical Paradigm.

goal. Finally, the robot acts to carry out the first directive. After the robot has carried out the **SENSE-PLAN-ACT** sequence, it begins the cycle again: eyes open, the robot senses the consequence of its action, replans the directives (even though the directives may not have changed), and acts.

As shown in Fig. 2.3, sensing in the Hierarchical Paradigm is monolithic: all the sensor observations are fused into one global data structure, which the WORLD MODEL   planner accesses. The global data structure is generally referred to as a *world model*. The term world model is very broad; "world" means both the outside world, and whatever meaning the robot ascribes to it. In the Hierarchical Paradigm, the world model typically contains

A PRIORI   1. an *a priori* (previously acquired) representation of the environment the robot is operating in (e.g., a map of the building),

2. sensing information (e.g., "I am in a hallway, based on where I've traveled, I must be in the northwest hallway"), plus

3. any additional cognitive knowledge that might be needed to accomplish a task (e.g., all packages received in the mail need to be delivered to Room 118).

Creating a single representation which can store all of this information can be very challenging. Part of the reason for the "sub-turtle" velocity was the lack of computing power during the 1960's. However, as roboticists in the 1980's began to study biological intelligence, a consensus arose that even with increased computing power, the hierarchical, logic-based approach was unsatisfactory for navigational tasks which require a rapid response time to an open world.

2.2.1   Strips

ALGORITHM

Shakey, the first AI mobile robot, needed a generalized algorithm for planning how to accomplish goals. (An *algorithm* is a procedure which is correct and terminates.) For example, it would be useful to have the same program allow a human to type in that the robot is in Office 311 and should go to Office 313 or that the robot is in 313 and should the red box.

GENERAL PROBLEM
SOLVER (GPS)
STRIPS
MEANS-ENDS ANALYSIS

The method finally selected was a variant of the *General Problem Solver* method, called *Strips*. Strips uses an approach called *means-ends analysis*, where if the robot can't accomplish the task or reach the goal in one "movement", it picks a action which will reduce the difference between what state it was in now (e.g., where it was) versus the goal state (e.g., where it wanted to be). This is inspired by cognitive behavior in humans; if you can't see how to solve a problem, you try to solve a portion of the problem to see if it gets you closer to the complete solution.

GOAL STATE
INITIAL STATE

OPERATOR
DIFFERENCE

DIFFERENCE
EVALUATOR

Consider trying to program a robot to figure out how to get to the Stanford AI Lab (SAIL). Unless the robot is at SAIL (represented in Strips as a variable `goal state`), some sort of transportation will have to arranged. Suppose the robot is in Tampa, Florida (`initial state`). The robot may represent the decision process of how to get to a location as function called an `operator` which would consider the Euclidean distance (a variable named `difference`) between the `goal state` and `initial state`. The difference between locations could be computed for comparison purposes, or evaluation, by the square of the hypotenuse (`difference evaluator`). For example using an arbitrary frame of reference that put Tampa at the center of the world with made-up distances to Stanford:

`initial state:`	Tampa, Florida (0,0)
`goal state:`	Stanford, California (1000,2828)
`difference:`	3,000

DIFFERENCE TABLE

This could lead to a data structure called a `difference table` of how to make decisions:

difference	operator
d≥200	fly
100<d < 200	ride_train
d ≤ 100	drive
d< 1	walk

Different modes of transportation are appropriate for different distances. A mode of transportation, `fly`, `ride_train`, `drive`, `walk`, in the table is really a function in the robot's program. It is also called an `operator`, because it reduces the value stored in `difference` as to the distance from being in the `initial state` of Tampa and wanting to be at the `goal state`. A robot following this difference table would begin by flying as close as it could to SAIL.

But suppose the robot flew into the San Francisco airport. It'd be within 100 miles of SAIL, so the robot appears to have made an intelligent decision. But now the robot has a new difference to reduce. It examines the difference table with a new value of `difference`. The table says the robot should `drive`. Drive what? A car? Ooops: if the robot did have a personal car, it would be back in Tampa. The robot needs to be able to distinguish between driving its car and driving a rental car. This is done by listing

PRECONDITIONS

the `preconditions` that have to be true in order to execute that particular operator. The preconditions are a column in the difference table, where a single operator can have multiple preconditions. In practice, the list of preconditions is quite lengthy, but for the purposes of this example, only `drive_rental`, `drive_personal` will be shown with preconditions.

difference	operator	preconditions
d≤200	fly	
100<d<200	ride_train	
d≤100	drive_rental	at airport
	drive_personal	at home
d<1	walk	

The difference table is now able to handle the issue of deciding to drive a rental car. But this introduces a new issue: how does the robot know where it is at? This is done by monitoring the state of the robot and its world. If it took an airplane from Tampa to the San Francisco airport, its state has changed. Its `initial state` is now at the San Francisco airport, and no

ADD-LIST
DELETE-LIST

longer Tampa. Therefore, whenever the robot executes an operator, there is almost always something that has to be added to the robot's knowledge of the world state (which is entered into a `add-list`) and something that has to be deleted (`delete-list`). This two lists are stored in the difference table so that when the robot picks an operator based on the difference and operator, it can easily apply the appropriate modifications to the world. The difference table below is expanded to show the add and delete lists.

difference	operator	pre-conditions	add-list	delete-list
d≤200	fly		at Y at airport	at X
100<d<200	train		at Y at station	at X
d≤100	drive_rental	at airport		
	drive_personal	at home		
d<1	walk			

Of course, the above difference table is fairly incomplete. Driving a rental car should have a precondition that there is a rental car available. (And that the robot have a waiver from the state highway patrol to drive as an experimental vehicle and a satisfactory method of payment.) The number of facts and preconditions that have to be explicitly represented seem to be growing explosively. Which is Very Bad from a programming standpoint.

The main point is that the difference table appears to be a good data structure for representing what a robot needs in planning a trip. It should be apparent that a recursive function can be written which literally examines each entry in the table for the first operator that reduces the difference. The resulting list of operators is actually the plan: a list of the steps (operators) that the robot has to perform in order to reach a goal. The robot actually constructs the plan before handing it off to another program to execute.

At this point in time, it isn't likely that a robot will get on a plane and then drive. So perhaps the criticisms of Strips is because the example used too complicated a task to be realistic. Let's see if Strips is more streamlined with a simple task of getting from one room to another.

2.2.2 More realistic Strips example

CONSTRUCTING A
WORLD MODEL

The first step in creating a Strips planner is to construct a Strips-based representation of the world, or `world model`. Everything in the world that is

AXIOMS
PREDICATES
relevant to the problem is represented by facts, or *axioms*, in predicate logic. *Predicates* are functions that evaluate to TRUE or FALSE. By years of AI programming convention, predicates are usually written in uppercase.

Consider the problem of a robot named IT in a room, R1, who needs to go to another room, R2, in the house shown in Fig. 2.4. In order to solve this problem using Strips, the robot has to be given a way of representing the world, which will in turn influence the difference table, a difference evaluator, and how the add and delete lists are written. The world model in the previous example was never formally defined.

A world model is generally built up from static facts (represented as predicates) from a set of candidates, and things in the world, like the robot. The robot's name is in all capitals because it exists (and therefore is TRUE). Lowercase identifiers indicate that the thing is a variable, that a real thing hasn't been assigned to that placeholder yet.

Suppose the robot was limited to knowing only whether a movable object was in a room, next to a door or another movable object, and whether a door was open or closed and what rooms it connected. In a programming sense, there would be only three types of things in the world: movable_object (such as the robot, boxes it should pick up), room, and door. The robot's knowledge could be represented by the following predicates:

INROOM(x, r)	where x is an object of type movable_object,
	r is type room
NEXTTO(x, t)	where x is a movable_object,
	t is type door or movable_object
STATUS(d, s)	where d is type door,
	s is an enumerated type: OPEN or CLOSED
CONNECTS(d, rx, ry)	where d is type door,
	rx, ry are the room

With the above predicates, the world model for the initial state of the world in Fig. 2.4 would be represented by:

```
initial state:
INROOM(IT, R1)
INROOM(B1,R2)
CONNECTS(D1, R1, R2)
CONNECTS(D1, R2, R1)
STATUS(D1,OPEN)
```

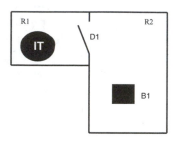

Figure 2.4   An example for Strips of two rooms joined by an open door.

This world model captures that a specific `movable_object` named `IT` is in a room named `R1`, and `B1` is in another room labeled `R2`. A door `D1` connects a room named `R1` to `R2` and it connects `R2` to `R1`. (Two different `CONNECTS` predicates are used to represent that a robot can go through the door from either door.) A door called `D1` has the enumerated value of being `OPEN`. The `NEXTTO` predicate wasn't used, because it wasn't true and there would be nothing to bind the variables to.

Under this style of representation, the world model for the `goal state` would be:

```
goal state:
INROOM(IT,R2)
INROOM(B1,R2)
CONNECTS(D1, R1, R2)
CONNECTS(D1, R2, R1)
STATUS(D1,OPEN)
```

CONSTRUCTING THE   Once the world model is established, it is possible to construct the differ-
DIFFERENCE TABLE   ence table. The partial difference table is:

operator	preconditions	add-list	delete-list
OP1: GOTODOOR(IT,dx)	INROOM(IT,rk) CONNECT(dx,rk,rm)	NEXTTO(IT,dx)	
OP2: GOTHRUDOOR(IT,dx)	CONNECT(dx,rk,rm) NEXTTO(IT,dx) STATUS(dx, OPEN) INROOM(IT,rk)	INROOM(IT,rm)	INROOM(IT,rk)

This difference table says the robot is programmed for only two operations: go to a door, and go through a door. The GOTODOOR operator can be applied only if the following two preconditions are true:

- INROOM(IT, rk) The robot is in a room, which will be assigned to the identifier rk.

- CONNECT(dx, rk, rm) There is a door, which will be assigned to the identifier dx, which connects rk to some other room called rm.

The label IT is used to constrain the predicates. Notice that only the variables dx and rk get bound when GOTODOOR is called. rm can be anything. If GOTODOOR is executed, the robot is now next to the door called dx. Nothing gets deleted from the world state because the robot is still in room rk, the door dx still connects the two rooms rk and rm. The only thing that has changed is that the robot is now in a noteworthy position in the room: next to the door.

The difference table specifies that the GOTHRUDOOR operator will only work if the robot is in the room next to the door, the door is open, and the door connects the room the robot is in to another room. In this case, predicates must be added and deleted from the world model when the operator executes. When the robot is in room rk and goes through the door, it is now in room rm (which must be added to the world model) and is no longer in room rk (which must be deleted).

So far, the world model and difference table should seem reasonable, although tedious to construct. But constructing a difference table is pointless without an evaluation function for differences. (Notice that there wasn't a column for the difference in the above table.) The difference evaluator in the travel example was Euclidean distance. In this example, the evaluator is predicate calculus, where the initial state is logically subtracted from the goal state. The logical difference between the initial state goal state is simply:

¬INROOM(IT, R2) or INROOM(IT, R2)=FALSE

REDUCING
DIFFERENCES

Reducing differences is a bit like a jigsaw puzzle where Strips tries different substitutions to see if a particular operator will reduce the difference. In order to reduce the difference, Strips looks in the difference table, starting at the top, under the add-list column for a match. It looks in the add-list rather than a separate differences column because the add-list expresses what the result of the operator is. If Strips finds an operator that produces the goal state, then that operator eliminates the existing difference between the initial and goal states.

The add-list in OP2: GOTHRUDOOR has a match on form. If rm=R2, then the result of OP2 would be INROOM(IT, R2). This would eliminate the difference, so OP2 is a candidate operator.

Before the OP2 can be applied, Strips must check the preconditions. To do this, rm must be replaced with R2 in every predicate in the preconditions. OP2 has two preconditions, only CONNECTS(dx, rk, rm) is affected. It becomes CONNECTS(dx, rk, R2). Until dx and rk are bound, the predicate doesn't have a true or false value. Essentially dx, rk are wildcards, CONNECTS(*, *, R2). To fill in values for these variables, Strips looks at the current state of the world model to find a match. The predicate in the current state of the world CONNECTS(D1, R1, R2) matches CONNECTS(*, *, R2). D1 is now bound to dx and R1 is bound to rk.

Now Strips propagates the bindings to the next precondition on the list: NEXTTO(IT, dx). NEXTTO(IT, D1) is FALSE because the predicate is

FAILED
PRECONDITIONS

not in the current world state. NEXTTO(IT, D1) is referred to as a *failed precondition*. An informal interpretation is that GOTHRUDOOR(IT, D1) will get the robot to the goal state, but before it can do that, IT has to be next to D1.

RECURSION TO
RESOLVE DIFFERENCES

Rather than give up, STRIPS *recurses* (uses the programming technique of recursion) to repeat the entire procedure. It marks the original goal state as G0, pushes it on a stack, then it creates a new sub-goal state, G1.

The difference between NEXTTO(IT, D1) and the current world state is:

```
¬NEXTTO(IT, D1)
```

Strips once again searches through the add-list in the difference table to find an operator that would negate this. Indeed, OP1: GOTODOOR(IT, dx) has a match in the add-list of NEXTTO(IT, dx). Strips has to start over with reassigning values to the identifiers because the program has entered a new programming scope, so dx=D1.

Again, Strips examines the preconditions. This time `rk=R1` and `rm=R2` can be matched with `CONNECTS(dx, rk, rm)`, and all preconditions are satisfied (that is, they evaluate to true). Strips puts the operator `OP1` on the plan stack and applies the operator to the world model, changing the state. (Note that this is the equivalent of a "mental operation"; the robot doesn't actually physically go to the door, it just changes the state to imagine what would happen if it did.)

To recall, the initial state of the world model was:

```
initial state:
INROOM(IT, R1)
INROOM(B1,R2)
CONNECTS(D1, R1, R2)
CONNECTS(D1, R2, R1)
STATUS(D1,OPEN)
```

Applying the operator `OP1` means making the changes on the add-list and delete-list. There is only a predicate on the add-list and none on the delete-list. After adding `NEXTTO(IT, D1)`, the state of the world is:

```
state after OP1:
INROOM(IT, R1)
INROOM(B1,R2)
CONNECTS(D1, R1, R2)
CONNECTS(D1, R2, R1)
STATUS(D1,OPEN)
NEXTTO(IT, D1)
```

Strips then returns control back to the previous call. It resumes where it left off in evaluating the preconditions for `OP2` with `dx=D1`, `rm=R2` and `rk=R1`, only now the world model has changed. Both `STATUS(D1, OPEN)` and INROOM(IT, R1) are true, so all the preconditions for `OP2` are satisfied. Strips puts `OP2` on its plan stack and changes the world model by applying the add-list and delete-list predicates. This results in what the state of the world will be when the plan executes:

```
state after OP2:
INROOM(IT, R2)
INROOM(B1,R2)
```

```
CONNECTS(D1, R1, R2)
CONNECTS(D1, R2, R1)
STATUS(D1,OPEN)
NEXTTO(IT, D1)
```

Strips exits and the plan for the robot to physically execute (in reverse order on the stack) is: GOTODOOR(IT, D1), GOTHRUDOOR(IT, D1).

2.2.3   Strips summary

Strips works recursively; if it can't reach a goal directly, it identifies the problem (a failed precondition), then makes the failed precondition a subgoal. Once the subgoal is reached, Strips puts the operator for reaching the subgoal on a list, then backs up (pops the stack) and resumes trying to reach the previous goal. Strips plans rather than execute: it creates a list of operators to apply; it does not apply the operator as it goes. Strips implementations requires the designer to set up a:

- world model representation

- difference table with operators, preconditions, add, and delete lists

- difference evaluator

The steps in executing Strips are:

1. Compute the difference between the goal state and the initial state using the difference evaluation function. If there is no difference, terminate.

2. If there is a difference, reduce the difference by selecting the first operator from the difference table whose add-list has a predicate which negates the difference.

3. Next, examine the preconditions to see if a set of bindings for the variables can be obtained which are all true. If not, take the first false precondition, make it the new goal and store the original goal by pushing it on a stack. Recursively reduce that difference by repeating step 2 and 3.

4. When all preconditions for an operator match, push the operator onto the plan stack and update a copy of the world model. Then return to the operator with the failed precondition so it can apply its operator or recurse on another failed precondition.

2.3   Closed World Assumption and the Frame Problem

CLOSED WORLD
ASSUMPTION
FRAME PROBLEM

Strips sensitized the robotics community to two pervasive issues: the *closed world assumption* and the *frame problem*. As defined earlier, the closed world assumption says that the world model contains everything the robot needs to know: there can be no surprises. If the closed world assumption is violated, the robot may not be able to function correctly. But, on the other hand, it is very easy to forget to put all the necessary details into the world model. As a result, the success of the robot depends on how well the human programmer can think of everything.

But even assuming that the programmer did come up with all the cases, the resulting world model is likely to be huge. Consider how big and cumbersome the world model was just for moving between 2 rooms. And there were no obstacles! People began to realize that the number of facts (or axioms) that the program would have to sort through for each pass through the difference table was going to become intractable for any realistic application. The problem of representing a real-world situation in a way that was computationally tractable became known as the frame problem. The opposite of the closed world assumption is known as the *open world assumption*. When roboticists say that "a robot must function in the open world," they are saying the closed world assumption cannot be applied to that particular domain.

OPEN WORLD
ASSUMPTION

The above example, although trivial, shows how tedious Strips is (though computers are good at tedious algorithms). In particular, the need to formally represent the world and then maintain every change about it is non-intuitive. It also illustrates the advantage of a closed-world assumption: imagine how difficult it would be to modify the planning algorithm if the world model could suddenly change. The algorithm could get lost between recursions. The example should also bring home the meaning of the frame problem: imagine what happens to the size of the world model if a third room is added with boxes for the robot to move to and pick up! And this is only for a world of rooms and boxes. Clearly the axioms which frame the world will become too numerous for any realistic domain.

One early solution was ABStrips which tried to divide the problem into multiple layers of abstraction, i.e., solve the problem on a coarse level first. That had its drawbacks, and soon many people who had started out in robotics found themselves working on an area of AI called planning. The two fields became distinct, and by the 1980's, the planning and robotics researchers had separate conferences and publications. Many roboticists during the 1970's and 1980's worked on either computer vision related issues, trying to get the robots to be able to better sense the world, or on path planning, computing the most efficient route around obstacles, etc. to a goal location.

2.4   Representative Architectures

As mentioned in Part I an architecture is a method of implementing a paradigm, of embodying the principles in some concrete way. Ideally, an architecture is generic; like a good object-oriented program design, it should have many reusable pieces for other robot platforms and tasks.

Possibly the two best known architectures of the Hierarchical period are the Nested Hierarchical Controller (NHC) developed by Meystel[93] and the NIST Realtime Control System (RCS) originally developed by Albus,[1] with its teleoperation version for JPL called NASREM.

2.4.1   Nested Hierarchical Controller

As shown in Fig. 2.5, the Nested Hierarchical Controller architecture has components that are easily identified as either SENSE, PLAN, or ACT. The robot begins by gathering observations from its sensors and combining those observations to form the World Model data structure through the SENSE activity. The World Model may also contain *a priori* knowledge about the world, for example, maps of a building, rules saying to stay away from the foyer during the start and finish of business hours, etc. After the World Model has been created or updated, then the robot can PLAN what actions it should take. Planning for navigation has a local procedure consisting of three steps executed by the Mission Planner, Navigator, and Pilot. Each of these modules has access to the World Model in order to compute their portion of planning. The last step in planning is for the Pilot module to generate specific actions for the robot to do (e.g., Turn left, turn right, move straight at a velocity of 0.6 meters per second). These actions are translated into actuator control signals (e.g., Velocity profile for a smooth turn) by the Low-Level Controller. Together, the Low-Level Controller and actuators form the ACT portion of the architecture.

The major contribution of NHC was its clever decomposition of planning into 3 different functions or subsystems aimed at supporting navigation: the *Mission Planner*, the *Navigator*, and the *Pilot*. As shown in Fig. 2.6, the Mission Planner either receives a mission from a human or generates a mission

MISSION PLANNER
NAVIGATOR
PILOT

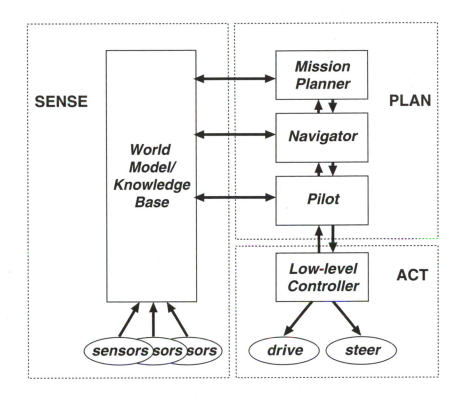

Figure 2.5 Nested Hierarchical Controller.

for itself, for example: pick up the box in the next room. The Mission Planner is responsible for operationalizing, or translating, this mission into terms that other functions can understand: box=B1; rm=ROOM311. The Mission Planner then accesses a map of the building and locates where the robot is and where the goal is. The Navigator takes this information and generates a path from the current location to the goal. It generates a set of waypoints, or straight lines for the robot to follow. The path is passed to the Pilot. The Pilot takes the first straight line or path segment and determines what actions the robot has to do to follow the path segment. For instance, the robot may need to turn around to face the way point before it can start driving forward.

What happens if the Pilot gives directions for a long path segment (say 50 meters) or if a person suddenly walks in front of the robot? Unlike Shakey, under NHC, the robot is not necessarily walking around with its eyes closed. After the Pilot gives the Low-Level Controller commands and the controller

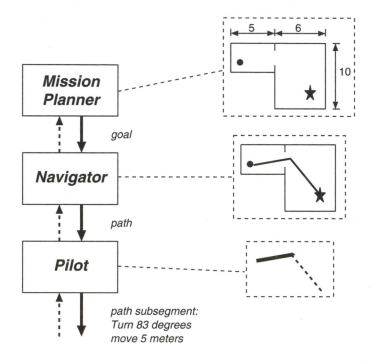

Figure 2.6   Examination of planning components in the NHC architecture.

sends actuator signals, the robot polls its sensors again. The World Model is updated. However, the entire planning cycle does not repeat. Since the robot has a plan, it doesn't need to rerun the Mission Planner or the Navigator. Instead, the Pilot checks the World Model to see if the robot has drifted off the path subsegment (in which case it generates a new control signal), has reached the waypoint, or if an obstacle has appeared. If the robot has reached its waypoint, the Pilot informs the Navigator. If the waypoint isn't the goal, then there is another path subsegment for the robot to follow, and so the Navigator passes the new subsegment to the Pilot. If the waypoint is the goal, then the Navigator informs the Mission Planner that the robot has reached the goal. The Mission Planner may then issue a new goal, e.g., Return to the starting place. If the robot has encountered an obstacle to its path, the Pilot passes control back to the Navigator. The Navigator must compute a new path, and subsegments, based on the updated World Model. Then it gives the updated path subsegment to the Pilot to carry out.

NHC has several advantages. It differs from Strips in that it interleaves planning and acting. The robot comes up with a plan, starts executing it, then changes it if the world is different than it expected. Notice that the decomposition is inherently hierarchical in intelligence and scope. The Mission Planner is "smarter" than the Navigator, who is smarter than the Pilot. The Mission Planner is responsible for a higher level of abstraction then the Navigator, etc. We will see that other architectures, both in the Hierarchical and Hybrid paradigms, will make use of the NHC organization.

One disadvantage of the NHC decomposition of the planning function is that it is appropriate only for navigation tasks. The division of responsibilities seems less helpful, or clear, for tasks such as picking up a box, rather than just moving over to it. The role of a Pilot in controlling end-effectors is not clear. At the time of its initial development, NHC was never implemented and tested on a real mobile robot; hardware costs during the Hierarchical period forced most roboticists to work in simulation.

2.4.2   NIST RCS

Jim Albus at the National Bureau of Standards (later renamed the National Institute of Standards and Technology or NIST) anticipated the need for intelligent industrial manipulators, even as engineering and AI researchers were splitting into two groups. He saw that one of the major obstacles in applying AI to manufacturing robots was that there were no common terms, no common set of design standards. This made industry and equipment manufacturers leery of AI, for fear of buying an expensive robot that would not be compatible with robots purchased in the future. He developed a very detailed architecture called the Real-time Control System (RCS) Architecture to serve as a guide for manufacturers who wanted to add more intelligence to their robots. RCS used NHC in its design, as shown in Fig. 2.7.

SENSE activities are grouped into a set of modules under the heading of sensory perception. The output of the sensors is passed off to the world modeling module which constructs a global map using information in its associated knowledge database about the sensors and any domain knowledge (e.g., the robot is operating underwater). This organization is similar to NHC. The main difference is that the sensory perception module introduces a useful preprocessing step between the sensor and the fusion into a world model. As will be seen in Ch. 6, sensor preprocessing is often referred to as *feature extraction*.

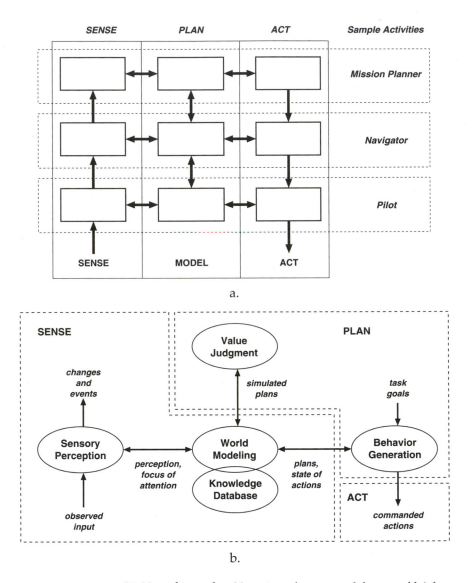

Figure 2.7 Layout of RCS: a.) hierarchical layering of sense-model-act, and b.) functional decomposition.

The Value Judgment module provides most of the functionality associated with the **PLAN** activity: it plans, then simulates the plans to ensure they will work. Then, as with Shakey, the Planner hands off the plan to another module, Behavior Generation, which converts the plans into actions that the robot can actually perform (**ACT**). Notice that the Behavior Generation module is similar to the Pilot in NHC, but there appears to be less focus on navigation tasks. The term "behavior" will be used by Reactive and Hybrid Deliberative/Reactive architectures. (This use of "behavior" in RCS is a bit of retrofit, as Albus and his colleagues at NIST have attempted to incorporate new advances. The integration of all sensing into a global world model for planning and acting keeps RCS a Hierarchical architecture.) There is another module, operator interface, which is not shown which allows a human to "observe" and debug what a program constructed with the architecture is doing.

The standard was adapted by many government agencies, such as NASA and the US Bureau of Mines, who were contracting with universities and companies to build robot prototypes. RCS serves as a blueprint for saying: "here's the types of sensors I want, and they'll be fused by this module into a global map, etc." The architecture was considered too detailed and restrictive when it was initially developed by most AI researchers, who continued development of new architectures and paradigms on their own. Fig. 2.8 shows three of the diverse mobile robots that have used RCS.

A close inspection of the NHC and RCS architectures suggests that they are well suited for semi-autonomous control. The human operator could provide the world model (via eyes and brain), decide the mission, decompose it into a plan, and then into actions. The lower level controller (robot) would carry out the actions. As robotics advanced, the robot could replace more functions and "move up" the autonomy hierarchy. For example, taking over the pilot's responsibilities; the human could instruct the robot to stay on the road until the first left turn. As AI advanced, the human would only have to serve as the Mission Planner: "go to the White House." And so on. Albus noted this and worked with JPL to develop a version of RCS for

NASREM teleoperating a robot arm in space. This is called the *NASREM* architecture and is still in use today.

2.4.3 Evaluation of hierarchical architectures

Recall from Part I that there are four criteria for evaluating an architecture: support for modularity, niche targetability, ease of portability to other domains, and robustness. NHC and RCS both provide some guidelines in how

a.   b.

c.

Figure 2.8   Three of the diverse mobile robots that have used RCS: a.) a commercial floor cleaning robot, b.) a mining robot, and c.) a submersible or underwater robot. (Photographs courtesy of the National Institute of Standards and Technology.)

to decompose a robot program into intuitive modules. The NHC decomposition of mission planner, navigator, and pilot was focused strictly on navigation, while RCS appears broader. Both have been used recently for successful vehicle guidance, with RCS being used to control mining equipment, submarines, and cars. So both have reasonable niche targetability. The ease of portability to other domains is unclear. The architectures are expressed at a very broad level, akin to "a house should have bedrooms, bathrooms, and a kitchen." Architectures which are more specific, "there should be one bathroom for every two bedrooms," and which have associated techniques simplify portability. It is hard to see how the code written for a mining machine could be reused for a submarine, especially since RCS is not object-oriented. In terms of robustness, RCS does attempt to provide some explicit mechanisms. In particular, it assumes the Value Judgment module simulates a plan to confirm that it should be successful when deployed. The use of simulation is common for operating equipment in a well-known environment where every piece of equipment is known. The most notable example is a nuclear processing cell. With such detailed information, it is fairly straightforward (although computationally expensive) to simulate whether a particular course for a robot would collide with equipment and cause a spill. This is a very limited form of robustness. The disadvantage is the time delay caused by the robot mentally rehearsing its actions prior to executing them. Simulation may not be appropriate for all actions; if a piece of the ceiling is falling on the robot, it needs to get out of the way immediately or risk coming up with the best place to move too late to avoid being crushed.

2.5 Advantages and Disadvantages

Robots built in the time period before 1990 typically had a Hierarchical style of software organization. They were generally developed for a specific application rather than to serve as a generic architecture for future applications. The robots are interesting because they illustrate the diversity and scope of applications being considered for mobile robots as far back as 15 or 20 years ago.

The primary advantage of the Hierarchical Paradigm was that it provides an ordering of the relationship between sensing, planning, and acting. The primary disadvantage was planning. Every update cycle, the robot had to update a global world model and then do some type of planning. The sensing and planning algorithms of the day were extremely slow (and many still are), so this introduced a significant bottleneck. Notice also that sensing and acting are always disconnected. This effectively eliminated any stimulus-response types of actions ("a rock is crashing down on me, I should move *anywhere*") that are seen in nature.

The dependence on a global world model is related to the frame problem. In Strips, in order to do something as simple as opening a door, the robot had to reason over all sorts of details that were irrelevant (like other rooms, other doors). NHC and RCS represent attempts to divide up the world model into pieces best suited for the type of actions; for example, consider the roles of the Mission Planner, Navigator, and Pilot. Unfortunately, these decompositions appear to be dependent on a particular application. As a result, robotics gained a reputation as being more of an art than a science.

Another issue that was never really handled by architectures in the Hierarchical Paradigm was uncertainty. Uncertainty comes in many forms, such as semantic (how close does NEXTTO mean anyway?), sensor noise, and actuator errors. Another important aspect of uncertainty is action completion: did the robot actually accomplish the action? One robotics researcher said that their manipulator was only able to pick up a cup 60% of the attempts; therefore they had to write a program to check to see if it was holding a cup and then restart the action if it wasn't. Because Shakey essentially closed its eyes during planning and acting, it was vulnerable to uncertainty in action completion.

2.6   Programming Considerations

It is interesting to note that the use of predicate logic and recursion by Strips favors languages like Lisp and PROLOG. These languages were developed by AI researchers specifically for expressing logical operations. These languages do not necessarily have good real-time control properties like C or C++. However, during the 1960's the dominant scientific and engineering language was FORTRAN IV which did not support recursion. Therefore, researchers in AI robotics often chose the lesser of two evils and programmed in Lisp. The use of special AI languages for robotics may have aided the split between the engineering and AI approaches to robotics, as well as slowed down the infusion of ideas from the the two communities. It certainly discouraged non-AI researchers from becoming involved in AI robotics.

The Hierarchical Paradigm tends to encourage monolithic programming, rather than object-oriented styles. Although the NHC decomposes the planning portion of intelligence, the decomposition is strictly functional. In particular, NHC and RCS don't provide much guidance on how to build modular, reusable components.

2.7   Summary

The Hierarchical Paradigm uses a **SENSE** then **PLAN** then **ACT** (S,P,A). It organizes sensing into a global data structure usually called a world model that may have an associated knowledge base to contain *a priori* maps or knowledge relevant to a task. Global data structures often flag that an architecture will suffer from the frame problem. The Hierarchical Paradigm was introduced in the first mobile robot, Shakey. Strips is an important planning technique that came out of the Shakey project at SRI, which focused on the **PLAN** primitive in robotics. Concepts and terms which emerged that continue to play an important role in defining robotics are: preconditions, the closed and open world assumptions, and the frame problem. Hierarchical systems have largely fallen out of favor except for the NIST Realtime Control Architecture. The decline in popularity is due in part to its focus on strong niche targetability at the expense of true modularity and portability. However, as will be seen in the following chapters, insights from biology and cognitive science have led to paradigms with more intuitive appeal. One often overlooked property of most hierarchical architectures is that they tend to support the evolution of intelligence from semi-autonomous control to fully autonomous control.

2.8 Exercises

Exercise 2.1

Describe the Hierarchical Paradigm in terms of a) the **SENSE, PLAN, ACT** primitives and b) sensing organization.

Exercise 2.2

Define the following terms in one or two sentences. Give an example of how each arises in a robotic system:

a. precondition

b. closed world assumption

c. open world

d. frame problem

Exercise 2.3

Consider the frame problem. Suppose the World Model for a Strips-based robot consisted of 100 facts. Each fact requires 1KB of memory storage. Every time a new object is added to the world model, it increases the model by 100 (a linear increase). One object, 100 facts, 100KB of storage; two objects, 200 facts, 200KB. How many objects would fill 64KB of memory?

Exercise 2.4

Redo the above exercise where the number of facts in the world model doubles every time a new object is added (exponential). One object, 100 facts, 1KB, two objects, 200 facts, 200KB, three objects, 400 facts, 400KB. Which is a more reasonable rate to assume the world model would increase at, linear or exponential?

Exercise 2.5

Describe the mission planner, navigator, pilot organization of the Nested Hierarchical Controller. Write down how it would handle the problem in Sec. 2.2.2.

Exercise 2.6

List 2 advantages and disadvantages of the Hierarchical Paradigm.

Exercise 2.7

Solve the following navigation problem using Strips. Return to the world in Sec 2.2.2. The robot will move to the box `B1` and pick it up.

a. Add a new operator `pickup` to the difference table.

b. Use the world model, difference table, difference evaluator to construct a plan. Failed preconditions and new subgoals should be shown after each step.

c. Show the changes in the world model after *each* operator is applied.

Exercise 2.8

Name and evaluate one representative Hierarchical architecture in terms of: support for modularity, niche targetability, ease of portability to other domains, robustness.

Exercise 2.9   [*World Wide Web*]

Search the web for interactive versions of Strips and experiment with them.

2.9   End Notes

A robot that did take a cross-country trip.
Robot vehicles do in fact need special authorization to drive on public roads. In 1996, the Carnegie Mellon University Navlab vehicle project led by Dean Pomerleau steered itself (the driver handled the gas pedal and brakes) over 90% of the way across the USA from Washington, DC, to Los Angeles in the "No Hands Across America" trip. The Navlab (a modified Saturn station wagon) was reportedly pulled over by the Kansas State Highway Patrol for driving an experimental vehicle without permission. The entire trip was placed in jeopardy, but eventually the Navlab was allowed to continue, and the team and vehicle appeared on the David Letterman show in Los Angeles. As impressive as the Carnegie Mellon feat was, a group of German researchers under the direction of Ernst Dickmanns and Volker Graefe have been fielding even more advanced autonomous highway driving vehicles since 1988.

Shakey.
It can be debated whether Shakey is really the first mobile robot. There was a tortoise built by Grey Walter, but this was never really on the main branch of AI research. See *Behavior-Based Robots*[10] for details.

Robot name trivia.

Regardless of how Shakey got its name, SRI continued the tradition with Shakey's successor being called *Flakey*, followed by Flakey's successor, *Erratic*.

Strips.

The description of Strips and the robot examples are adapted from *The Handbook of Artificial Intelligence*, A. Barr and E. Feigenbaum, editors, vol. 1, William Kaufmann, Inc., Los Altos, CA, 1981.

Jim Albus.

Jim Albus is one of the statesmen of robotics. Although his RCS architecture is a representative of the Hierarchical Paradigm, Albus was heavily by cognitive studies—so much so that he wrote *Brains, Behaviors and Robots* (1981). What's odd is that exploiting biological and cognitive studies is commonly associated with the Reactive Paradigm. The RCS architecture was never meant to be totally static, and in recent years, it has begun to resemble what will be referred to as a model-oriented style of the Hybrid Paradigm.

3 Biological Foundations of the Reactive Paradigm

Chapter Objectives:

- Describe the three levels in a *computational theory*.

- Explain in one or two sentences each of the following terms: *reflexes, taxes, fixed-action patterns, schema, affordance.*

- Be able to write pseudo-code of an animal's behaviors in terms of *innate releasing mechanisms*, identifying the releasers for the behavior.

- Given a description of an animal's sensing abilities, its task, and environment, identify an *affordance* for each behavior.

- Given a description of an animal's sensing abilities, its task, and environment, define a set of behaviors using schema theory to accomplish the task.

3.1 Overview

Progress in robotics in the 1970's was slow. The most influential robot was the Stanford Cart developed by Hans Moravec, which used stereo vision to see and avoid obstacles protruding from the ground. In the late 1970's and early 80's, Michael Arbib began to investigate models of animal intelligence from the biological and cognitive sciences in the hopes of gaining insight into what was missing in robotics. While many roboticists had been fascinated by animals, and many, including Moravec, had used some artifact of animal behavior for motivation, no one approached the field with the seriousness and dedication of Arbib.

At nearly the same time, a slender volume by Valentino Braitenberg, called *Vehicles: Experiments in Synthetic Psychology*,[25] appeared. It was a series of gedanken or entirely hypothetical thought experiments, speculating as to how machine intelligence could evolve. Braitenberg started with simple thermal sensor-motor actuator pair (Vehicle 1) that could move faster in warm areas and slower in cold areas. The next, more complex vehicle had two thermal sensor-motor pairs, one on each side of the vehicle. As a result of the differential drive effect, Vehicle 2 could turn around to go back to cold areas. Throughout the book, each vehicle added more complexity. This layering was intuitive and seemed to mimic the principles of evolution in primates. *Vehicles* became a cult tract among roboticists, especially in Europe.

Soon a new generation of AI researchers answered the siren's call of biological intelligence. They began exploring the biological sciences in search of new organizing principles and methods of obtaining intelligence. As will be seen in the next chapter, this would lead to the Reactive Paradigm. This chapter attempts to set the stage for the Reactive Paradigm by recapping influential studies and discoveries, and attempting to cast them in light of how they can contribute to robotic intelligence.

The chapter first covers animal behaviors as the fundamental primitive for sensing and acting. Next, it covers the work of Lorenz and Tinbergen in defining how concurrent simple animal behaviors interact to produce complex behaviors through Innate Releasing Mechanisms (IRMs). A key aspect of an animal behavior is that perception is needed to support the behavior. The previous chapter on the Hierarchical Paradigm showed how early roboticists attempted to fuse all sensing into a global world map, supplemented with a knowledge base. This chapter covers how the work of cognitive psychologists Ulrich Neisser[109] and J.J. Gibson[59] provides a foundation for thinking about robotic perception. Gibson refuted the necessity of global world models, a direct contradiction to the way perception was handled in the hierarchical paradigm. Gibson's use of *affordances*, also called *direct perception*, is an important key to the success of the Reactive Paradigm. Later work by Neisser attempts to define when global models are appropriate and when an affordance is more elegant.

ETHOLOGY
COGNITIVE
PSYCHOLOGY

Many readers find the coverage on *ethology* (study of animal behavior) and *cognitive psychology* (study of how humans think and represent knowledge) to be interesting, but too remote from robotics. In order to address this concern, the chapter discusses specific principles and how they can be applied to robotics. It also raises issues in transferring animal models of behavior to robots. Finally, the chapter covers *schema theory*, an attempt in cognitive psychology to formalize aspects of behavior. Schema theory has been used successfully by Arbib to represent both animal and robot behavior. It is implicitly object-oriented and so will serve as the foundation of discussions through out the remainder of this book.

3.1.1 Why explore the biological sciences?

Why should roboticists explore biology, ethology, cognitive psychology and other biological sciences? There is a tendency for people to argue against considering biological intelligence with the analogy that airplanes don't flap their wings. The counter-argument to that statement is that almost everything else about a plane's aerodynamics duplicates a bird's wing: almost all the movable surfaces on the wing of a plane perform the same functions as parts of a bird's wing. The advances in aeronautics came as the Wright Brothers and others extracted aerodynamic principles. Once the principles of flight were established, mechanical systems could be designed which adhered to these principles and performed the same functions but not necessarily in the same way as biological systems. The "planes don't flap their wings" argument turns out to be even less convincing for computer systems: animals make use of innate capabilities, robots rely on compiled programs.

Many AI roboticists often turn to the biological sciences for a variety of reasons. Animals and man provide existence proofs of different aspects of intelligence. It often helps a researcher to know that an animal can do a particular task, even if it isn't known how the animal does it, because the researcher at least knows it is possible. For example, the issue of how to combine information from multiple sensors (sensor fusion) has been an open question for years. At one point, papers were being published that robots shouldn't even try to do sensor fusion, on the grounds that sensor fusion was a phenomenon that sounded reasonable but had no basis in fact. Additional research showed that animals (including man) do perform sensor fusion, although with surprisingly different mechanisms than most researchers had considered.

OPEN WORLD
ASSUMPTION
CLOSED WORLD
ASSUMPTION

FRAME PROBLEM

The principles of animal intelligence are extremely important to roboticists. Animals live in an *open world*, and roboticists would like to overcome the *closed world assumption* that presented so many problems with Shakey. Many "simple" animals such as insects, fish, and frogs exhibit intelligent behavior yet have virtually no brain. Therefore, they must be doing something that avoids the frame problem.

3.1.2 Agency and computational theory

AGENT
Even though it seems reasonable to explore biological and cognitive sciences for insights in intelligence, how can we compare such different systems: carbon and silicon "life" forms? One powerful means of conceptualizing the different systems is to think of an abstract intelligent system. Consider something we'll call an *agent*. The agent is self-contained and independent. It has its own "brains" and can interact with the world to make changes or to sense what is happening. It has self-awareness. Under this definition, a person is an agent. Likewise, a dog or a cat or a frog is an agent. More importantly, an intelligent robot would be an agent, even certain kinds of web search engines which continue to look for new items of interest to appear, even after the user has logged off. Agency is a concept in artificial intelligence that allows researchers to discuss the properties of intelligence without discussing the details of how the intelligence got in the particular agent. In OOP terms, "agent" is the superclass and the classes of "person" and "robot" are derived from it.

COMPUTATIONAL
THEORY
Of course, just referring to animals, robots, and intelligent software packages as "agents" doesn't make the correspondences between intelligence any clearer. One helpful way of seeing correspondences is to decide the level at which these entities have something in common. The set of levels of commonality lead to what is often called a *computational theory*[88] after David Marr. Marr was a neurophysiologist who tried to recast biological vision processes into new techniques for computer vision. The levels in a computational theory can be greatly simplified as:

Level 1: Existence proof of what can/should be done. Suppose a roboticist is interested in building a robot to search for survivors trapped in a building after an earthquake. The roboticist might consider animals which seek out humans. As anyone who has been camping knows, mosquitoes are very good at finding people. Mosquitoes provide an existence proof that it is possible for a computationally simple agent to find a human being using heat. At Level 1, agents can share a commonality of purpose or functionality.

Level 2: Decomposition of "what" into inputs, outputs, and transformations. This level can be thought of as creating a flow chart of "black boxes." Each box represents a transformation of an input into an output. Returning to the example of a mosquito, the roboticist might realize from biology that the mosquito finds humans by homing on the heat of a human (or any warm blooded animal). If the mosquito senses a hot area, it flies toward it. The roboticist can model this process as: `input=thermal image`, `output=steering command`. The "black box" is how the mosquito transforms the input into the output. One good guess might be to take the centroid of the thermal image (the centroid weighted by the heat in each area of the image) and steer to that. If the hot patch moves, the thermal image will change with the next sensory update, and a new steering command will be generated. This might not be exactly how the mosquito actually steers, but it presents an idea of how a robot could duplicate the functionality. Also notice that by focusing on the process rather than the implementation, a roboticist doesn't have to worry about mosquitoes flying, while a search and rescue robot might have wheels. At Level 2, agents can exhibit common processes.

Level 3: How to implement the process. This level of the computational theory focuses on describing how each transformation, or black box, is implemented. For example, in a mosquito, the steering commands might be implemented with a special type of neural network, while in a robot, it might be implemented with an algorithm which computes the angle between the centroid of heat and where the robot is currently pointing. Likewise, a researcher interested in thermal sensing might examine the mosquito to see how it is able to detect temperature differences in such a small package; electro-mechanical thermal sensors weigh close to a pound! At Level 3, agents may have little or no commonality in their implementation.

It should be clear that Levels 1 and 2 are abstract enough to apply to any agent. It is only at Level 3 that the differences between a robotic agent and a biological agent really emerge. Some roboticists actively attempt to emulate biology, reproducing the physiology and neural mechanisms. (Most roboticists are familiar with biology and ethology, but don't try to make exact duplicates of nature.) Fig. 3.1 shows work at Case Western Reserve's Bio-Bot Laboratory under the direction of Roger Quinn, reproducing a cockroach on a neural level.

In general, it may not be possible, or even desirable, to duplicate how a biological agent does something. Most roboticists do not strive to precisely replicate animal intelligence, even though many build creatures which resemble animals, as seen by the insect-like Genghis in Fig. 3.2. But by focusing on Level 2 of a computational theory of intelligence, roboticists can gain insights into how to organize intelligence.

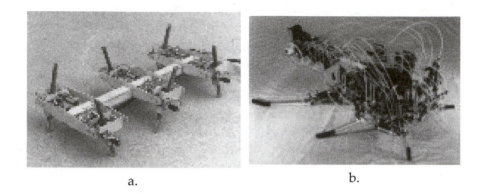

a.   b.

Figure 3.1   Robots built at the Bio-Bot Laboratory at Case Western Reserve University which imitate cockroaches at Level 3: a.) Robot I, an earlier version, and b.) Robot III. (Photographs courtesy of Roger Quinn.)

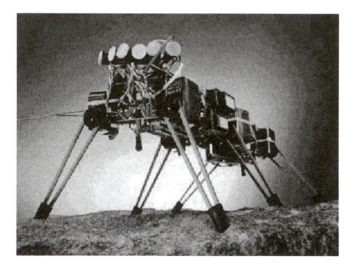

Figure 3.2   Genghis, a legged robot built by Colin Angle, IS Robotics, which imitates an insect at Levels 1 and 2. (Photograph courtesy of the National Aeronautics and Space Administration.)

Figure 3.3   Graphical definition of a behavior.

3.2   What Are Animal Behaviors?

BEHAVIOR

Scientists believe the fundamental building block of natural intelligence is a behavior. A *behavior* is a mapping of sensory inputs to a pattern of motor actions which then are used to achieve a task. For example, if a horse sees a predator, it flattens its ears, lowers its head, and paws the ground. In this case, the sensory input of a predator triggers a recognizable pattern of a defense behavior. The defensive motions make up a pattern because the actions and sequence is always the same, regardless of details which vary each episode (e.g., how many times the horse paws the ground). See Fig. 3.3.

Scientists who study animal behaviors are called *ethologists*. They often spend years in the field studying a species to identify its behaviors. Often the pattern of motor actions is easy to ascertain; the challenging part is to discover the sensory inputs for the behavior and why the behavior furthers the species survival.

REFLEXIVE BEHAVIOR
STIMULUS-RESPONSE

REACTIVE BEHAVIOR

CONSCIOUS BEHAVIOR

Behaviors can be divided into three broad categories.[10] *Reflexive behaviors* are *stimulus-response (S-R)*, such as when your knee is tapped, it jerks upward. Essentially, reflexive behaviors are "hardwired"; neural circuits ensure that the stimulus is directly connected to the response in order to produce the fastest response time. *Reactive behaviors* are learned, and then consolidated to where they can be executed without conscious thought. Any behavior that involves what is referred to in sports as "muscle memory" is usually a reactive behavior (e.g., riding a bike, skiing). Reactive behaviors can also be changed by conscious thought; a bicyclist riding over a very narrow bridge might "pay attention" to all the movements. *Conscious behaviors* are deliberative (assembling a robot kit, stringing together previously developed behaviors, etc.).

The categorization is worthy of note for several reasons. First, the Reactive Paradigm will make extensive use of reflexive behaviors, to the point that some architectures only call a robot behavior a behavior if it is S-R. Second, the categorization can help a designer determine what type of behavior to use, leading to insights about the appropriate implementation. Third, the use of the word "reactive" in ethology is at odds with the way the word is used in robotics. In ethology, reactive behavior means learned behaviors or a skill; in robotics, it connotes a reflexive behavior. If the reader is unaware of these differences, it may be hard to read either the ethological or AI literature without being confused.

3.2.1 Reflexive behaviors

Reflexive types of behaviors are particularly interesting, since they imply no need for any type of cognition: if you sense it, you do it. For a robot, this would be a hardwired response, eliminating computation and guaranteed to be fast. Indeed, many kit or hobby robots work off of reflexes, represented by circuits.

Reflexive behaviors can be further divided into three categories:[10]

REFLEXES

1. *reflexes*: where the response lasts only as long as the stimulus, and the response is proportional to the intensity of the stimulus.

TAXES

2. *taxes*: where the response is to move to a particular orientation. Baby turtles exhibit *tropotaxis*; they are hatched at night and move to the brightest light. Until recently the brightest light would be the ocean reflecting the moon, but the intrusion of man has changed that. Owners of beach front property in Florida now have to turn off their outdoor lights during hatching season to avoid the lights being a source for tropotaxis. Baby turtles hatch at night, hidden from shore birds who normally eat them. It had been a mystery as to how baby turtles knew which way was the ocean when they hatched. The story goes that a volunteer left a flashlight on the sand while setting up an experiment intended to show that the baby turtles used magnetic fields to orient themselves. The magnetic field theory was abandoned after the volunteers noticed the baby turtles heading for the flashlight! Ants exhibit a particular taxis known as *chemotaxis*; they follow trails of pheromones.

FIXED-ACTION
PATTERNS

3. *fixed-action patterns*: where the response continues for a longer duration than the stimulus. This is helpful for fleeing predators. It is important to keep in mind that a taxis can be any orientation relative to a stimulus, not just moving towards.

The above categories are not mutually exclusive. For example, an animal going over rocks or through a forest with trees to block its view might persist (fixed-action patterns) in orienting itself to the last sensed location of a food source (taxis) when it loses sight of it.

The tight coupling of action and perception can often be quantified by mathematical expressions. An example of this is orienting in angelfish. In order to swim upright, an angelfish uses an internal (*idiothetic*) sense of gravity combined with its vision sense (*allothetic*) to see the external percept of the horizon line of the water to swim upright. If the fish is put in a tank with prisms that make the horizon line appear at an angle, the angelfish will swim cockeyed. On closer inspection, the angle that the angelfish swims at is the vector sum of the vector parallel to gravity with the vector perpendicular to the perceived horizon line! The ability to quantify animal behavior suggests that computer programs can be written which do likewise.

IDIOTHETIC
ALLOTHETIC

3.3 Coordination and Control of Behaviors

KONRAD LORENZ
NIKO TINBERGEN

Konrad Lorenz and Niko Tinbergen were the founding fathers of ethology. Each man independently became fascinated not only with individual behaviors of animals, but how animals acquired behaviors and selected or coordinated sets of behaviors. Their work provides some insight into four different ways an animal might acquire and organize behaviors. Lorenz and Tinbergen's work also helps with a computational theory Level 2 understanding of how to make a process out of behaviors.

The four ways to acquire a behavior are:

INNATE

1. to be born with a behavior (*innate*). An example is the feeding behavior in baby arctic terns. Arctic terns, as the name implies, live in the Arctic where the terrain is largely shades of black and white. However, the Arctic tern has a bright reddish beak. When babies are hatched and are hungry, they peck at the beak of their parents. The pecking triggers a regurgitation reflex in the parent, who literally coughs up food for the babies to eat. It turns out that the babies do not recognize their parents, per se. Instead, they are born with a behavior that says: if hungry, peck at the largest red blob you see. Notice that the only red blobs in the field of vision should be the beaks of adult Arctic terns. The largest blob should be the nearest parent (the closer objects are, the bigger they appear). This is a simple, effective, and computationally inexpensive strategy.

SEQUENCE OF INNATE
BEHAVIORS

2. to be born with a *sequence of innate behaviors*. The animal is born with a sequence of behaviors. An example is the mating cycle in digger wasps.

A female digger wasp mates with a male, then builds a nest. Once it sees the nest, the female lays eggs. The sequence is logical, but the important point is the role of stimulus in triggering the next step. The nest isn't built until the female mates; that is a change in internal state. The eggs aren't laid until the nest is built; the nest is a visual stimulus releasing the next step. Notice that the wasp doesn't have to "know" or understand the sequence. Each step is triggered by the combination of internal state and the environment. This is very similar to Finite State Machines in computer science programming, and will be discussed later in Ch. 5.

INNATE WITH MEMORY 3. to be born with behaviors that need some initialization (*innate with memory*). An animal can be born with innate behaviors that need customizing based on the situation the animal is born in. An example of this is bees. Bees are born in hives. The location of a hive is something that isn't innate; a baby bee has to learn what its hive looks like and how to navigate to and from it. It is believed that the curious behavior exhibited by baby bees (which is innate) allows them to learn this critical information. A new bee will fly out of the hive for a short distance, then turn around and come back. This will get repeated, with the bee going a bit farther along the straight line each time. After a time, the bee will repeat the behavior but at an angle from the opening to the hive. Eventually, the bee will have circumnavigated the hive. Why? Well, the conjecture is that the bee is learning what the hive looks like from all possible approach angles. Furthermore, the bee can associate a view of the hive with a motor command ("fly left and down") to get the bee to the opening. The behavior of zooming around the hive is innate; what is learned about the appearance of the hive and where the opening is requires memory.

LEARN 4. to *learn* a set of behaviors. Behaviors are not necessarily innate. In mammals and especially primates, babies must spend a great deal of time learning. An example of learned behaviors is hunting in lions. Lion cubs are not born with any hunting behaviors. If they are not taught by their mothers over a period of years, they show no ability to fend for themselves. At first it might seem strange that something as fundamental as hunting for food would be learned, not innate. However, consider the complexity of hunting for food. Hunting is composed of many sub-behaviors, such as searching for food, stalking, chasing, and so on. Hunting may also require teamwork with other members of the pride. It requires great sensitivity to the type of the animal being hunted and the terrain. Imagine trying to write a program to cover all the possibilities!

While the learned behaviors are very complex, they can still be represented by innate releasing mechanisms. It is just that the releasers and actions are learned; the animal creates the program itself.

Note that the number of categories suggests that a roboticist will have a spectrum of choices as to how a robot can acquire one or more behaviors: from being pre-programmed with behaviors (innate) to somehow learning them (learned). It also suggests that behaviors can be innate but require memory. The lesson here is that while S-R types of behaviors are simple to preprogram or hardwire, robot designers certainly shouldn't exclude the use of memory. But as will be seen in Chapter 4, this is a common constraint placed on many robot systems. This is especially true in a popular style of hobby robot building called BEAM robotics (biology, electronics, aesthetics, and mechanics), espoused by Mark Tilden. Numerous BEAM robot web sites guide adherents through construction of circuits which duplicate memoryless innate reflexes and taxes.

INTERNAL STATE
MOTIVATION

An important lesson that can be extracted from Lorenz and Tinbergen's work is that the internal state and/or motivation of an agent may play a role in releasing a behavior. Being hungry is a stimulus, equivalent to the pain introduced by a sharp object in the robot's environment. Another way of looking at it is that motivation serves as a stimulus for behavior. Motivations can stem from survival conditions (like being hungry) or more abstract goals (e.g., need to check the mail). One of the most exciting insights is that behaviors can be sequenced to create complex behaviors. Something as complicated as mating and building a nest can be decomposed into primitives or certainly more simple behaviors. This has an appeal to the software engineering side of robotics.

3.3.1   Innate releasing mechanisms

INNATE RELEASING
MECHANISMS

RELEASER

Lorenz and Tinbergen attempted to clarify their work in how behaviors are coordinated and controlled by giving it a special name *innate releasing mechanisms* (IRM). An IRM presupposes that there is a specific stimulus (either internal or external) which releases, or triggers, the stereotypical pattern of action. The IRM activates the behavior. A *releaser* is a latch or a Boolean variable that has to be set. One way to think of IRMs is as a process of behaviors. In a computational theory of intelligence using IRMs, the basic black boxes of the process would be behaviors. Recall that behaviors take sensory input and produce motor actions. But IRMs go further and specify when a behav-

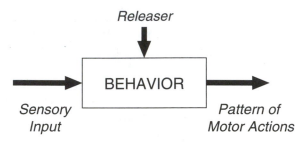

Figure 3.4   Innate Releasing Mechanism as a process with behaviors.

ior gets turned on and off. The releaser acts as a control signal to activate a behavior. If a behavior is not released, it does not respond to sensory inputs and does not produce motor outputs. For example, if a baby arctic tern isn't hungry, it doesn't peck at red, even if there is a red beak nearby.

Another way to think of IRMs is as a simple computer program. Imagine the agent running a C program with a continuous `while` loop. Each execution through the loop would cause the agent to move for one second, then the loop would repeat.

```
enum            Releaser={PRESENT, NOT_PRESENT};
Releaser        predator;
while (TRUE)
{
   predator = sensePredators();
   if (predator == PRESENT)
     flee();
}
```

In this example, the agent does only two things: sense the world and then flees if it senses a predator. Only one behavior is possible: `flee`. `flee` is released by the presence of a predator. A predator is of type `Releaser` and has only two possible values: it is either present or it is not. If the agent does not sense the releaser for the behavior, the agent does nothing. There is no "default" behavior.

This example also shows filtering of perception. In the above example, the agent only looks for predators with a dedicated detection function, `sense-Predators()`. The dedicated predator detection function could be a specialized sense (e.g., retina is sensitive to the frequency of motions associated with predator movement) or a group of neurons which do the equivalent of a computer algorithm.

COMPOUND RELEASERS

Another important point about IRMs is that the releaser can be a *compound of releasers*. Furthermore, the releaser can be a combination of either external (from the environment) or internal (motivation). If the releaser in the compound isn't satisfied, the behavior isn't triggered. The pseudo-code below shows a compound releaser.

```
enum            Releaser={PRESENT, NOT_PRESENT};
Releaser        food;
while (TRUE)
{
   food = senseFood();
   hungry = checkState();
      if (food == PRESENT && hungry==PRESENT)
      feed();
}
```

IMPLICIT CHAINING

The next example below shows what happens in a sequence of behaviors, where the agent eats, then nurses its young, then sleeps, and repeats the sequence. The behaviors are implicitly chained together by their releasers. Once the initial releaser is encountered, the first behavior occurs. It executes for one second (one "movement" interval), then control passes to the next statement. If the behavior isn't finished, the releasers remain unchanged and no other behavior is triggered. The program then loops to the top and the original behavior executes again. When the original behavior has completed, the internal state of the animal may have changed or the state of the environment may have been changed as a result of the action. When the motivation and environment match the stimulus for the releaser, the second behavior is triggered, and so on.

```
enum            Releaser={PRESENT, NOT_PRESENT};
Releaser        food, hungry, nursed;
while (TRUE) {
   food = sense();
   hungry = checkStateHunger();
   child = checkStateChild();
   if (hungry==PRESENT)
      searchForFood(); //sets food = PRESENT when done
   if (hungry==PRESENT && food==PRESENT)
      feed(); // sets hungry = NOT_PRESENT when done
```

```
if (hungry== NOT_PRESENT && parent==PRESENT)
   nurse(); // set nursed = PRESENT when done
if (nursed ==PRESENT)
   sleep();
}
```

The example also reinforces the nature of behaviors. If the agent sleeps and wakes up, but isn't hungry, what will it do? According to the releasers created above, the agent will just sit there until it gets hungry.

In the previous example, the agent's behaviors allowed it to feed and enable the survival of its young, but the set of behaviors did not include fleeing or fighting predators. Fleeing from predators could be added to the program as follows:

```
enum            Releaser={PRESENT, NOT_PRESENT};
Releaser        food, hungry, nursed, predator;
while (TRUE) {
   predator = sensePredator();
   if (predator==PRESENT)
      flee();
   food = senseFood();
   hungry = checkStateHunger();
   parent = checkStateParent();
   if (hungry==PRESENT)
      searchForFood();
   if (hungry==PRESENT && food==PRESENT)
      feed();
   if (hungry== NOT_PRESENT && parent==PRESENT)
      nurse();
   if (nursed ==PRESENT)
      sleep();
}
```

Notice that this arrangement allowed the agent to flee the predator regardless of where it was in the sequence of feeding, nursing, and sleeping because predator is checked for first. But fleeing is temporary, because it did not change the agent's internal state (except possibly to make it more hungry which will show up on the next iteration). The code may cause the agent to flee for one second, then feed for one second.

One way around this is to *inhibit*, or turn off, any other behavior until fleeing is completed. This could be done with an if-else statement:

```
while (TRUE) {
   predator = sensePredator();
   if (predator==PRESENT)
      flee();
   else {
      food = senseFood();
      hungry = checkStateHunger();
      ...
   }
}
```

The addition of the `if-else` prevents other, less important behaviors from executing. It doesn't solve the problem with the predator releaser disappearing as the agents runs away. If the agent turns and the predator is out of view (say, behind the agent), the value of `predator` will go to NOT_PRESENT in the next update. The agent will go back to foraging, feeding, nursing, or sleeping. Fleeing should be a fixed-pattern action behavior which persists for some period of time, T. The fixed-pattern action effect can be accomplished with:

```
#define T LONG_TIME
while (TRUE) {
   predator = sensePredator();
   if (predator==PRESENT)
      for(time = T; time > 0; time--)
         flee();
   else {
      food = senseFood();
      ...
   }
}
```

The C code examples were implemented as an implicit sequence, where the order of execution depended on the value of the releasers. An implementation of the same behaviors with an explicit sequence would be:

```
Releaser        food, hungry, nursed, predator;
while (TRUE) {

   predator = sensePredator();
   if (predator==PRESENT)
```

```
      flee();
   food = senseFood();
   hungry = checkStateHunger();
   parent = checkStateParent();
   if (hungry==PRESENT)
      searchForFood();
   feed();
   nurse();
   sleep();
}
```

The explicit sequence at first may be more appealing. It is less cluttered and the compound releasers are hidden. But this implementation is not equivalent. It assumes that instead of the loop executing every second and the behaviors acting incrementally, each behavior takes control and runs to completion. Note that the agent cannot react to a predator until it has finished the sequence of behaviors. Calls to the fleeing behavior could be inserted between each behavior or fleeing could be processed on an interrupt basis. But every "fix" makes the program less general purpose and harder to add and maintain.

The main point here is: *simple behaviors operating independently can lead to what an outside observer would view as a complex sequence of actions.*

3.3.2   Concurrent behaviors

An important point from the examples with the IRMs is that behaviors can, and often do, execute concurrently and independently. What appears to be a fixed sequence may be the result of a normal series of events. However, some behaviors may violate or ignore the implicit sequence when the environment presents conflicting stimuli. In the case of the parent agent, fleeing a predator was mutually exclusive of the feeding, nursing, and sleeping behaviors.

Interesting things can happen if two (or more) behaviors are released that usually are not executed at the same time. It appears that the strange interactions fall into the following categories:

EQUILIBRIUM
- *Equilibrium (the behaviors seem to balance each other out):* Consider feeding versus fleeing in a squirrel when the food is just close enough to a person on a park bench. A squirrel will often appear to be visibly undecided as to whether to go for the food or to stay away.

DOMINANCE
- *Dominance of one (winner take all):* you're hungry and sleepy. You do one or the other, not both simultaneously.

CANCELLATION
- *Cancellation (the behaviors cancel each other out):* Male sticklebacks (fish) when their territories overlap get caught between the need to defend their territory and to attack the other fish. So the males make another nest! Apparently the stimuli cancels out, leaving only the stimulus normally associated with nest building.

Unfortunately, it doesn't appear to be well understood when these different mechanisms for conflicting behaviors are employed. Clearly, there's no one method. But it does emphasize that a roboticist who works with behaviors should pay close attention to how the behaviors will interact. This will give rise to the differences in architectures in the Reactive and Hybrid Paradigms, discussed in later chapters.

3.4 Perception in Behaviors

While Lorenz and Tinbergen's work provides some insights into behaviors, it's clear that behaviors depend on perception. Ulrich Neisser, who literally created the term "cognitive psychology" in his book, *Cognition and Reality*, argued that perception cannot be separated from action.[109] As will be seen in this section, J.J. Gibson, a very controversial cognitive psychologist, spent his career advocating an ecological approach to perception. The ecological approach is the opposite of the top-down, model-based reasoning about the environment approach favored by psychologists, including Neisser. Interestingly enough, Neisser took a position at Cornell where J.J. Gibson was, and they became close colleagues. Since then, Neisser has spent significant time and thought trying to reconcile the two views based on studies; this has led to his identification of two perceptual systems.

3.4.1 Action-perception cycle

ACTION-PERCEPTION
CYCLE
The *action-perception cycle* illustrates that perception is fundamental to any intelligent agent. A simple interpretation of the cycle is: When an agent acts, it interacts with its environment because it is situated in that environment; it is an integral part of the environment. So as it acts, it changes things or how it perceives it (e.g., move to a new viewpoint, trigger a rock slide, etc.). Therefore the agent's perception of the world is modified. This new perception is

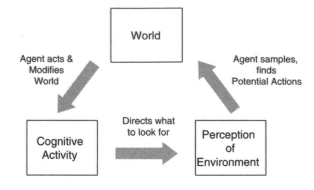

Figure 3.5   Action-Perception Cycle.[7]

then used for a variety of functions, including both cognitive activities like planning for what to do next as well as reacting. The term cognitive activity includes the concepts of feedback and feedforward control, where the agent senses an error in what it attempted to do and what actually happened. An equally basic cognitive activity is determining what to sense next. That activity can be something as straightforward as activating processes to look for releasers, or as complex as looking for a particular face in a crowd.

Regardless of whether there is an explicit conscious processing of the senses or the extraction of a stimulus or releaser, the agent is now directed in terms of what it is going to perceive on the next update(s). This is a type of selective attention or focus-of-attention. As it perceives, the agent perceptually samples the world. If the agent actually acts in a way to gather more perception before continuing with its primary action, then that is sometimes referred to as active perception. Part of the sampling process is to determine the potential for action. Lorenz and Tinbergen might think of this as the agent having a set of releasers for a task, and now is observing whether they are present in the world. If the perception supports an action, the agent acts. The action modifies the environment, but it also modifies the agent's assessment of the situation. In the simplest case, this could be an error signal to be used for control or a more abstract difference such as at the level of those used in STRIPS/MEA.

In some regards, the action-perception cycle appears to bear a superficial resemblance to the Hierarchical Paradigm of **SENSE, PLAN, ACT**. However, note that 1) there is no box which contains ACT, and 2) the cycle does not require the equivalent of planning to occur at each update. Action is implicit in an agent; the interesting aspect of the cycle is where perception and cognition come in. The agent may have to act to acquire more perception or to accomplish a task. Also, the agent may or may not need to "plan" an action on each update.

3.4.2   Two functions of perception

Perception in behavior serves two functions. First, as we saw with IRMs, it serves to *release* a behavior. However, releasing a behavior isn't necessarily the same as the second function: perceiving the information needed to accomplish the behavior. For example, consider an animal in a forest fire. The fire activates the fleeing. But the fleeing behavior needs to extract information about open spaces to run through obstacles in order to *guide* the behavior. A frightened deer might bolt right past a hunter without apparently noticing.

RELEASE

GUIDE

In both roles as a releaser and as a guide for behavior, perception filters the incoming stimulus for the task at hand. This is often referred to as action-oriented perception by roboticists, when they wish to distinguish their perceptual approach from the more hierarchical global models style of perception. Many animals have evolved specialized detectors which simplify perception for their behaviors. Some frogs which sit in water all day with just half their eyes poking up have a split retina: the lower half is good for seeing in water, the upper half in air.

3.4.3   Gibson: Ecological approach

The central tenet of Gibson's approach is that "... the world is its own best representation." Gibson's work is especially interesting because it complements the role of perception in IRM and is consistent with the action-perception cycle. Gibson postulated (and proved) the existence of affordances. *Affordances are perceivable potentialities of the environment for an action.* For example, to a baby arctic tern, the color red is perceivable and represents the potential for feeding. So an affordance can be a more formal way of defining the external stimulus in IRM. But like IRMs, an affordance is only a potential— it doesn't count until all the other conditions are satisfied (the baby tern is hungry). An affordance can also be the percept that guides the behavior. The presence of red to a hungry baby arctic tern releases the feeding behavior. But the feeding behavior consists of pecking at the red object. So in this case, red is also the percept being used to guide the action, as well as release it.

AFFORDANCES

Gibson referred to his work as an "ecological approach" because he believed that perception evolved to support actions, and that it is silly to try to discuss perception independently of an agent's environment, and its survival behaviors. For example, a certain species of bees prefers one special type of poppy. But for a long time, the scientists couldn't figure out how the bees recognized that type of poppy because as color goes, it was indistinguishable from another type of poppy that grows in the same area. Smell? Magnetism? Neither. They looked at the poppy under UV and IR light. In the non-visible bands that type of poppy stood out from other poppy species. And indeed, the scientists were able to locate retinal components sensitive to that bandwidth. The bee and poppy had co-evolved, where the poppy's color evolved to a unique bandwidth while at the same time the bee's retina was becoming specialized at detecting that color. With a retina "tuned" for the poppy, the bee didn't have to do any reasoning about whether there was a poppy in view, and, if so, was it the right species of poppy. If that color was present, the poppy was there.

Fishermen have exploited affordances since the beginning of time. A fishing lure attempts to emphasize those aspects of a fish's desired food, presenting the strongest stimulus possible: if the fish is hungry, the stimulus of the lure will trigger feeding. As seen in Fig. 3.6, fishing lures often look to a human almost nothing like the bait they imitate.

DIRECT PERCEPTION

What makes Gibson so interesting to roboticists is that an affordance is directly perceivable. Direct perception means that the sensing process doesn't require memory, inference, or interpretation. This means minimal computation, which usually translates to very rapid execution times (near instantaneous) on a computer or robot.

But can an agent actually perceive anything meaningful without some memory, inference, or interpretation? Well, certainly baby arctic terns don't need memory or inference to get food from a parent. And they're definitely not interpreting red in the sense of: "oh, there's a red blob. It's a small oval, which is the right shape for Mom, but that other one is a square, so it must be a graduate ethology student trying to trick me." For baby arctic terns, it's simply: `red = food, bigger red = better`.

Does this work for humans? Consider walking down the hall and somebody throws something at you. You will most likely duck. You also probably ducked without recognizing the object, although later you may determine it was only a foam ball. The response happens too fast for any reasoning: "Oh look, something is moving towards me. It must be a ball. Balls are usually hard. I should duck." Instead, you probably used a phenomena so basic that

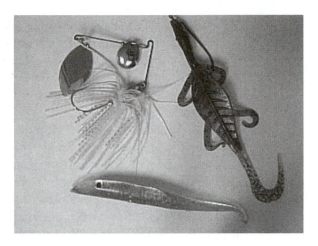

Figure 3.6 A collection of artificial bait, possibly the first example of humans exploiting affordances. Notice that the lures exaggerate one or more attributes of what a fish might eat.

OPTIC FLOW you haven't noticed it, called *optic flow.* Optic flow is a neural mechanism for determining motion. Animals can determine time to contact quite easily with it. You probably are somewhat familiar with optic flow from driving in a car. When driving or riding in a car, objects in front seem to be in clear focus but the side of the road is a little blurry from the speed. The point in space that the car is moving to is the focus of expansion. From that point outward, there is a blurring effect. The more blurring on the sides, the faster the car is going. (They use this all the time in science fiction movies to simulate faster-than-light travel.) That pattern of blurring is known as a flow field (because it can be represented by vectors, like a gravitational or magnetic field). It is TIME TO CONTACT straightforward, neurally, to extract the time to contact, represented in the cognitive literature by τ.

Gannets and pole vaulters both use optic flow to make last-minute, precise movements as reflexes. Gannets are large birds which dive from high altitudes after fish. Because the birds dive from hundreds of feet up in the air, they have to use their wings as control surfaces to direct their dive at the targeted fish. But they are plummeting so fast that if they hit the water with their wings open, the hollow bones will shatter. Gannets fold their wings just before hitting the water. Optic flow allows the time to contact, τ, to be a stimulus: when the time to contact dwindles below a threshold, fold those wings!

Pole vaulters also make minute adjustments in where they plant their pole as they approach the hurdle. This is quite challenging given that the vaulter is running at top speed. It appears that pole vaulters use optic flow rather than reason (slowly) about where the best place is for the pole. (Pole vaulting isn't the only instance where humans use optic flow, just one that has been well-documented.)

In most applications, a fast computer program can extract an affordance. However, this is not the case (so far) with optic flow. Neural mechanisms in the retina have evolved to make the computation very rapid. It turns out that computer vision researchers have been struggling for years to duplicate the generation of an optical flow field from a camera image. Only recently have we seen any algorithms which ran in real-time on regular computers.[48] The point is that affordances and specialized detectors can be quite challenging to duplicate in computers.

Affordances are not limited to vision. A common affordance is knowing when a container is almost filled to the top. Think about filling a jug with water or the fuel tank of a car. Without being able to see the cavity, a person knows when the tank is almost filled by the change in sound. That change in sound is directly perceivable; the person doesn't need to know anything about the size or shape of the volume being filled or even what the liquid is.

One particularly fascinating application of affordances to robotics, which also serves to illustrate what an affordance is, is the research of Louise Stark and Kevin Bowyer.[135] A seemingly unsurmountable problem in computer vision has been to have a computer recognize an object from a picture. Literally, the computer should say, "that's a chair" if the picture is of a chair.

STRUCTURAL MODELS   The traditional way of approaching the problem has been to use *structural models*. A structural model attempts to describe an object in terms of physical components: "A chair has four legs, a seat, and a back." But not all chairs fit the same structural model. A typing chair has only one leg, with supports at the bottom. Hanging baskets don't have legs at all. A bench seat doesn't have a back. So clearly the structural approach has problems: instead of one structural representation, the computer has to have access to many different models. Structural models also lack flexibility. If the robot is presented with a new kind of chair (say someone has designed a chair to look like your toilet or an upside down trash can), the robot would not be able to recognize it without someone explicitly constructing another structural model.

Stark and Bowyer explored an alternative to the structual approach called GRUFF. GRUFF identifies chairs by *function* rather than form. Under Gibsonian perception, a chair should be a chair because it affords sitting, or serves

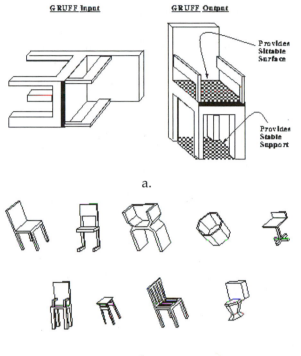

Figure 3.7   The GRUFF system: a.) input, and b.) different types of chairs recognized by GRUFF. (Figures courtesy of Louise Stark.)

the function of sittability. And that affordance of sittability should be something that can be extracted from an image:

- Without memory (the agent doesn't need to memorize all the chairs in the world).

- Without inference (the robot doesn't need to reason: "if it has 4 legs, and a seat and a back, then it's a chair; we're in an area which should have lots of chairs, so this makes it more likely it's a chair").

- Without an interpretation of the image (the robot doesn't need to reason: "there's an arm rest, and a cushion, ..."). A computer should just be able to look at a picture and say if something in that picture is sittable or not.

Stark and Bowyer represented sittability as a reasonably level and continuous surface which is at least the size of a person's butt and at about the height of their knees. (Everything else like seat backs just serve to specify the kind of chair.) Stark and Bowyer wrote a computer program which accepted CAD/CAM drawings from students who tried to come up with non-intuitive things that could serve as chairs (like toilets, hanging basket chairs, trash cans). The computer program was able to correctly identify sittable surfaces that even the students missed.

It should be noted that Stark and Bowyer are hesitant to make claims about what this says about Gibsonian perception. The computer vision algorithm can be accused of some inference and interpretation ("that's the seat, that's the right height"). But on the other hand, that level of inference and interpretation is significantly different than that involved in trying to determine the structure of the legs, etc. And the relationship between seat size and height could be represented in a special neural net that could be *released* whenever the robot or animal got tired and wanted to sit down. The robot would start noticing that it could sit on a ledge or a big rock if a chair or bench wasn't around.

3.4.4   Neisser: Two perceptual systems

At this point, the idea of affordances should seem reasonable. A chair is a chair because it affords sittability. But what happens when someone sits in *your* chair? It would appear that humans have some mechanism for recognizing specific instances of objects. Recognition definitely involves memory ("my car is a blue Ford Explorer and I parked it in slot 56 this morning"). Other tasks, like the kind of sleuthing Sherlock Holmes does, may require inference and interpretation. (Imagine trying to duplicate Sherlock Holmes in a computer. It's quite different than mimicking a hungry baby arctic tern.)

So while affordances certainly are a powerful way of describing perception in animals, it is clearly not the only way animals perceive. Neisser postulated that there are two perceptual systems in the brain (and cites neurophysiological data):[110]

DIRECT PERCEPTION   1. *direct perception*. This is the "Gibsonian," or ecological, track of the brain, and consists of structures low in the brain which evolved earlier on and accounts for affordances.

RECOGNITION   2. *recognition*. This is more recent perceptual track in the brain, which ties in with the problem solving and other cognitive activities. This part accounts for the use of internal models to distinguish "your coffee cup" from "my coffee cup." This is where top-down, model-based perception occurs.

On a more practical note, Neisser's dichotomy suggests that the first decision in designing a behavior is to determine whether a behavior can be accomplished with an affordance or requires recognition. If it can be accomplished with an affordance, then there may be a simple and straightforward way to program it in a robot; otherwise, we will most certainly have to employ a more sophisticated (and slower) perceptual algorithm.

3.5   Schema Theory

Schema theory provides a helpful way of casting some of the insights from above into an object-oriented programming format.[6] Psychologists have used schema theory since the early 1900's. It was first brought to the serious attention of AI roboticists by Michael Arbib while at the University of Massachusetts, and later used extensively by Arkin and Murphy for mobile robotics, Lyons and Iberall for manipulation,[75] and Draper et al. for vision.[46]

SCHEMA

Schemas were conceived of by psychologists as a way of expressing the basic unit of activity. A *schema* consists both of the knowledge of how to act and/or perceive (knowledge, data structures, models) as well as the computational process by which it is uses to accomplish the activity (the algorithm). The idea of a schema maps nicely onto a class in object-oriented programming (OOP). A *schema class* in C++ or Java would contain both data (knowledge, models, releasers) and methods (algorithms for perceiving and acting), as shown below.

SCHEMA CLASS

```
Schema:
```
Data
Methods

A schema is a generic template for doing some activity, like riding a bicycle. It is a template because a person can ride different bicycles without starting the learning process all over. Since a schema is parameterized like a class, parameters (type of bicycle, height of the bicycle seat, position of the handlebars) can be supplied to the object at the time of instantiation (when an object is created from the class). As with object-oriented programming, the creation of a specific schema is called a *schema instantiation (SI)*.

SCHEMA
INSTANTIATION (SI)

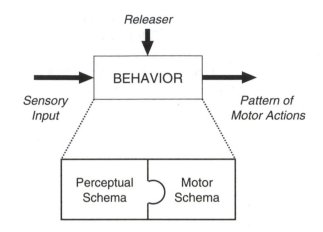

Figure 3.8   Behaviors decomposed into perceptual and motor schemas.

The schema instantiation is the object which is constructed with whatever parameters are needed to tailor it to the situation. For example, there could be a `move_to_food` schema where the agent always heads in a straight line to the food. Notice that the "always heads in a straight line" is a template of activity, and a reusable algorithm for motion control. However, it is just a method; until the `move_to_food` schema is instantiated, there is no specific goal to head for, e.g., the candy bar on the table. The same schema could be instantiated for moving to a sandwich.

3.5.1   Behaviors and schema theory

COMPOSITION OF A
BEHAVIOR
MOTOR SCHEMA
PERCEPTUAL SCHEMA

In the Arbibian application of schema theory towards a computational theory of intelligence, a *behavior* is a schema which is composed of a motor schema and a perceptual schema. The *motor schema* represents the template for the physical activity, the *perceptual schema* embodies the sensing. The motor schema and perceptual schema are like pieces of a puzzle; both pieces must be together in place before there is a behavior. This idea is shown below in Fig. 3.8.

Essentially, the perceptual and motor schema concept fits in with ethology and cognitive psychology as follows:

- A behavior takes sensory inputs and produces motor actions as an output.

- A behavior can be represented as a schema, which is essentially an object-oriented programming construct.

- A behavior is activated by releasers.

- The transformation of sensory inputs into motor action outputs can be divided into two sub-processes: a perceptual schema and a motor schema.

In OOP terms, the motor schema and perceptual schema classes are derived from the schema class. A primitive behavior just has one motor and one perceptual schema.

Behavior::Schema

Data	
Methods	perceptual_schema()
	motor_schema()

Recall from IRMs, more sophisticated behaviors may be constructed by sequencing behaviors. In the case of a sequence of behaviors, the overall behavior could be represented in one of two ways. One way is to consider the behavior to be composed of several primitive behaviors, with the releasing logic to serve as the knowledge as to when to activate each primitive behaviors. This is probably the easiest way to express a "meta" behavior.

A meta-behavior composed of three behaviors can be thought of as:

Behavior::Schema

Data	releaser1
	releaser2
	releaser3
	IRM_logic()
Methods	behavior1()
	behavior2()
	behavior3()

However, in more advanced applications, the agent may have a choice of either perceptual or motor schemas to tailor its behavior. For example, a person usually uses vision (the default perceptual schema) to navigate out of a room (motor schema). But if the power is off, the person can use touch (an alternate perceptual schema) to feel her way out of a dark room. In this case, the schema-specific knowledge is knowing which perceptual schema to use for different environmental conditions. Schema theory is expressive enough to represent basic concepts like IRMs, plus it supports building new behaviors out of primitive components. This will be discussed in more detail in later chapters.

This alternative way of creating a behavior by choosing between alternative perceptual and motor schemas can be thought of as:

Behavior::Schema

Data	environmental_state
Methods	choose_PS(environmental_state)
	perceptual_schema_1()
	perceptual_schema_2()
	motor_schema()

RANA COMPUTATRIX

Arbib and colleagues did work constructing computer models of visually guided behaviors in frogs and toads. They used schema theory to represent the toad's behavior in computational terms, and called their model *rana computatrix* (rana is the classification for toads and frogs). The model explained Ingle's observations as to what occasionally happens when a toad sees two flies at once.[33] Toads and frogs can be characterized as responding visually to either small, moving objects and large, moving objects. Small, moving objects release the feeding behavior, where the toad orients itself towards the object (taxis) and then snaps at it. (If the object turns out not to be a fly, the toad can spit it out.) Large moving objects release the fleeing behavior, causing the toad to hop away. The feeding behavior can be modeled as a behavioral schema, or template, shown in Fig. 3.9.

When the toad sees a fly, an instance of the behavior is instantiated; the toad turns toward that object and snaps at it. Arbib's group went one level further on the computational theory.[7] They implemented the taxis behavior as a vector field: rana computatrix would literally feel an attractive force along the direction of the fly. This direction and intensity (magnitude) was represented as a vector. The direction indicated where rana had to turn and the magnitude indicated the strength of snapping. This is shown in Fig. 3.10.

What is particularly interesting is that the rana computatrix program predicts what Ingle saw in real toads and frogs when they are presented with two flies simultaneously. In this case, each fly releases a separate instance of the feeding behavior. Each behavior produces the vector that the toad needs to turn to in order to snap at that fly, without knowing that the other be-

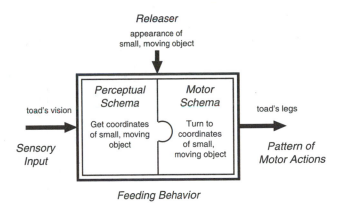

Figure 3.9   Toad's feeding behavior represented as a behavior with schema theory.

havior exists. According to the vector field implementation of the schema model, the toad now receives two vectors, instead of one. What to do? Well, *rana computatrix* summed the two vectors, resulting in a third vector in between the original two! The toad snaps at neither fly, but in the middle. The unexpected interaction of the two independent instances probably isn't that much of a disadvantage for a toad, because if there are two flies in such close proximity, eventually one of them will come back into range.

This example illustrates many important lessons for robotics. First, it validates the idea of a computational theory, where functionality in an animal and a computer can be equivalent. The concept of behaviors is Level 1 of the computational theory, schema theory (especially the perceptual and motor schemas) expresses Level 2, and Level 3 is the vector field implementation of the motor action. It shows the property of emergent behavior, where the agent appears to do something fairly complex, but is really just the result of interaction between simple modules. The example also shows how behaviors correspond to object-orienting programming principles.

Another desirable aspect of schema theory is that it supports reflex behaviors. Recall that in reflex behaviors, the strength of the response is proportional to the strength of the stimulus. In schema theory, the perceptual schema is permitted to pass both the percept and a gain to the motor schema. The motor schema can use the gain to compute a magnitude on the output action. This is an example of how a particular schema can be tailored for a behavior.

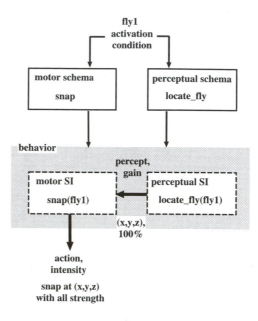

Figure 3.10   Schema theory of a frog snapping at a fly.

Schema theory does not specify how the output from concurrent behaviors is combined; that is a Level 3, or implementation, issue. Previous examples in this chapter have shown that in some circumstances the output is combined or summed, in others the behaviors would normally occur in a sequence and not overlap, and sometimes there would be a winner-take-all effect. The winner-take-all effect is a type of inhibition, where one behavior inhibits the instantiation of another behavior.

INHIBITION   Arbib and colleagues also modeled an instance of *inhibition* in frogs and toads.[7] Returning to the example of feeding and fleeing, one possible way to model this behavior is with two behaviors. The `feeding` behavior would consist of a motor schema for moving toward an object, with a perceptual schema for finding small, moving objects. The `fleeing` behavior would be similar only with a motor schema for moving away from the perception of large moving objects. Lesion studies with frogs showed something different. The `feeding` behavior actually consists of moving toward *any* moving object. So the perceptual schema is more general than anticipated. The frog would try to eat anything, including predators. The perceptual schema in the `fleeing` behavior detects large moving objects. It flees from them, but

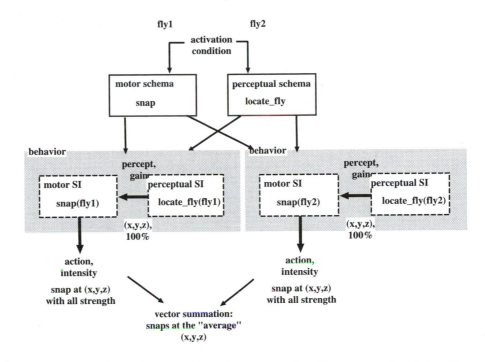

Figure 3.11   Schema theory of a frog snapping at a fly when presented with two flies equidistant.

it also inhibits the perceptual schema for feeding. As a result, the inhibition keeps the frog from trying to both flee from predators and eat them.

3.6   Principles and Issues in Transferring Insights to Robots

To summarize, some general principles of natural intelligence which may be useful in programming robots:

PRINCIPLES FOR
PROGRAMMING

- Programs should decompose complex actions into independent behaviors, which tightly couple sensing and acting. Behaviors are inherently parallel and distributed.

- In order to simplify control and coordination of behaviors, an agent should rely on straightforward, boolean activation mechanisms (e.g. IRM).

- In order to simplify sensing, perception should filter sensing and consider only what is relevant to the behavior (action-oriented perception).

- Direct perception (affordances) reduces the computational complexity of sensing, and permits actions to occur without memory, inference, or interpretation.

- Behaviors are independent, but the output from one 1) may be combined with another to produce a resultant output, or 2) may serve to inhibit another (competing-cooperating).

Unfortunately, studying natural intelligence does not give a complete picture of how intelligence works. In particular there are several unresolved UNRESOLVED ISSUES   issues:

- *How to resolve conflicts between concurrent behaviors?* Robots will be required to perform concurrent tasks; for example, a rescue robot sent in to evacuate a building will have to navigate hallways while looking for rooms to examine for people, as well as look for signs of a spreading fire. Should the designer specify dominant behaviors? Combine? Let conflicting behaviors cancel and have alternative behavior triggered? Indeed, one of the biggest divisions in robot architectures is how they handle concurrent behaviors.

- *When are explicit knowledge representations and memory necessary?* Direct perception is wonderful in theory, but can a designer be sure that an affordance has not been missed?

- *How to set up and/or learn new sequences of behaviors?* Learning appears to be a fundamental component of generating complex behaviors in advanced animals. However, the ethological and cognitive literature is unsure of the mechanisms for learning.

It is also important to remember that natural intelligence does not map perfectly onto the needs and realities of programming robots. One major advantage that animal intelligence has over robotic intelligence is evolution. Animals evolved in a way that leads to survival of the species. But robots are expensive and only a small number are built at any given time. Therefore, individual robots must "survive," not species. This puts tremendous pressure on robot designers to get a design right the first time. The lack of evolutionary pressures over long periods of time makes robots extremely vulnerable to design errors introduced by a poor understanding of the robot's ecology.

Ch. 5 will provide a case study of a robot which was programmed to follow white lines in a path-following competition by using the affordance of white. It was distracted off course by the white shoes of a judge. Fortunately that design flaw was compensated for when the robot got back on course by reacting to a row of white dandelions in seed.

Robots introduce other challenges not so critical in animals. One of the most problematic attributes of the Reactive Paradigm, Ch. 4, is that roboticists have no real mechanism for completely predicting emergent behaviors. Since a psychologist can't predict with perfect certainty what a human will do under a stressful situation, it seems reasonable that a roboticist using principles of human intelligence wouldn't be able to predict what a robot would do either. However, robotics end-users (military, NASA, nuclear industry) have been reluctant to accept robots without a guarantee of what it will do in critical situations.

3.7   Summary

A behavior is the fundamental element of biological intelligence, and will serve as the fundamental component of intelligence in most robot systems. BEHAVIOR A *behavior* is defined as a mapping of sensory inputs to a pattern of motor actions which then are used to achieve a task. Innate Releasing Mechanisms are one model of how intelligence is organized. IRMs model intelligence at Level 2 of a computational theory, describing the process but not the implementation. In IRM, releasers activate a behavior. A releaser may be either an internal state (motivation) and/or an environmental stimulus. Unfortunately, IRMs do not make the interactions between concurrent, or potentially concurrent, behaviors easy to identify or diagram.

Perception in behaviors serves two roles, either as a releaser for a behavior or as the percept which guides the behavior. The same percept can be used both as a releaser and a guide; for example, a fish can respond to a lure and follow it. In addition to the way in which perception is used, there appear to be two pathways for processing perception. The direct perception pathway uses affordances: perceivable potentialities for action inherent in the environment. Affordances are particularly attractive to roboticists because they can be extracted without inference, memory, or intermediate representations. The recognition pathway makes use of memory and global representations to identify and label specific things in the world.

Important principles which can be extracted from natural intelligence are:

- Agents programs should decompose complex actions into independent behaviors (or objects), which tightly couple sensing and acting. Behaviors are inherently parallel and distributed.

- In order to simplify control and coordination of behaviors, an agent should rely on straightforward, boolean activation mechanisms (e.g. IRM).

- In order to simplify sensing, perception should filter sensing and consider only what is relevant to the behavior (action-oriented perception).

- Direct perception (affordances) reduces the computational complexity of sensing, and permits actions to occur without memory, inference, or interpretation.

- Behaviors are independent, but the output from one 1) may be combined with another to produce a resultant output, or 2) may serve to inhibit another (competing-cooperating).

Schema theory is an object-oriented way of representing and thinking about behaviors. The important attributes of schema theory for behaviors are:

- Schema theory is used to represent behaviors in both animals and computers, and is sufficient to describe intelligence at the first two levels of a computational theory.

- A behavioral schema is composed of at least one motor schema and at least one perceptual schema, plus local, behavior-specific knowledge about how to coordinate multiple component schemas.

- More than one behavior schema can be instantiated at a time, but the schemas act independently.

- A behavior schema can have multiple instantiations which act independently, and are combined.

- Behaviors or schemas can be combined, sequenced, or inhibit one another.

3.8   Exercises

Exercise 3.1

Describe the three levels in a Computational Theory.

Exercise 3.2

Explain in one or two sentences each of the following terms: reflexes, taxes, fixed-action patterns, schema, affordance.

Exercise 3.3

Represent a schema, behavior, perceptual schema, and motor schema with an Object-Oriented Design class diagram.

Exercise 3.4

Many mammals exhibit a camouflage meta-behavior. The animal freezes when it sees motion (an affordance for a predator) in an attempt to become invisible. It persists until the predator is very close, then the animal flees. (This explains why squirrels freeze in front of cars, then suddenly dash away, apparently flinging themselves under the wheels of a car.) Write pseudo-code of the behaviors involved in the camouflage behavior in terms of innate releasing mechanisms, identifying the releasers for each behavior.

Exercise 3.5

Consider a mosquito hunting for a warm-blooded mammal and a good place to bite them. Identify the affordance for a warm-blooded mammal and the associated behavior. Represent this with schema theory (perceptual and motor schemas).

Exercise 3.6

One method for representing the IRM logic is to use finite state automata (FSA), which are commonly used in computer science. If you have seen FSAs, consider a FSA where the behaviors are states and releasers serve as the transitions between state. Express the sequence of behaviors in a female digger wasp as a FSA.

Exercise 3.7

Lego Mindstorms and Rug Warrior kits contain sensors and actuators which are coupled together in reflexive behaviors. Build robots which:

a. Reflexive avoid: turn left when they touch something (use touch sensor and two motors)

b. Phototaxis: follow a black line (use the IR sensor to detect the difference between light and dark)

c. Fixed-action pattern avoid: back up and turn right when robot encounters a "negative obstacle" (a cliff)

Exercise 3.8

What is the difference between direct perception and recognition?

Exercise 3.9

Consider a cockroach, which typically hides when the lights are turned on. Do you think the cockroach is using direct perception or recognition of a hiding place? Explain why. What are the percepts for the cockroach?

Exercise 3.10

Describe how cancellation could happen as a result of concurrency and incomplete FSA.

Exercise 3.11   [*Advanced Reading*]

Read the first four chapters in Braitenberg's *Vehicles*.[25] Write a 2-5 page paper:

a. List and describe the principles of behaviors for robotics in Ch. 3.

b. Discuss how *Vehicles* is consistent with the biological foundations of reactivity. Be specific, citing which vehicle illustrates what principle or attribute discussed in the book.

c. Discuss any flaws in the reasoning or inconsistency between *Vehicles* with the biological foundations of reactivity or computer science.

Exercise 3.12   [*Advanced Reading*]

Read "Sensorimotor transformations in the worlds of frogs and robots," by Arbib and Liaw.[7]

a. List and describe how the principles of schema theory and potential fields for robotics given in Ch. 3.

b. Summarize the main contributions of the paper.

3.9   End Notes

For the roboticist's bookshelf.
Valentino Braitenberg's *Vehicles: Experiments in Synthetic Psychology*[25] is the cult classic of AI roboticists everywhere. It doesn't require any hardware or programming experience, just a couple hours of time and an average imagination to experience this radical departure from the mainstream robotics of the 1970's.

About David Marr.
David Marr's idea of a computational theory was an offshoot of his work bridging the gap between vision from a neurophysiological perspective (his) and computer vision. As is discussed in his book, *Vision*,[88] Marr had come from England to work in the MIT AI lab on computer vision. The book represented his three years there, and he finished it while literally on his deathbed with leukemia. His preface to the book is heartbreaking.

A Brief History of Cognitive Science.
Howard Gardner's *The Mind's New Science*[56] gives a nice readable overview of cognitive psychology. He conveys a bit of the controversy Gibson's work caused.

J.J. and E.J. Gibson.

While J.J. Gibson is very well-known, his wife Jackie (E.J. Gibson) is also a prominent cognitive psychologist. They met when he began teaching at Smith College, where she was a student. She raised a family, finished a PhD, and publishes well-respected studies on learning. At least two of the Gibson's students followed their husband-wife teaming: Herb Pick was a student of J.J. Gibson, while his wife, Anne Pick, was a student of E.J. Gibson. The Picks are at the University of Minnesota, and Herb Pick has been active in the mobile robotics community.

Susan Calvin, robopsychologist.

Isaac Asimov's robot stories often feature Dr. Susan Calvin, the first robopsychologist. In the stories, Calvin is often the only person who can figure out the complex interactions of concurrent behaviors leading to a robot's emergent misbehavior. In some regards, Calvin is the embarrassing Cold War stereotype of a woman scientist: severe, unmarried, too focused on work to be able to make small talk.

4 *The Reactive Paradigm*

Chapter Objectives:

- Define what the reactive paradigm is in terms of i) the three primitives SENSE, PLAN, and ACT, and ii) sensing organization.

- List the characteristics of a reactive robotic system, and discuss the connotations surrounding the reactive paradigm.

- Describe the two dominant methods for combining behaviors in a reactive architecture: *subsumption* and *potential field summation*.

- Evaluate subsumption and potential fields architectures in terms of: *support for modularity, niche targetability, ease of portability to other domains, robustness.*

- Be able to program a behavior using a potential field methodology.

- Be able to construct a new potential field from primitive potential fields, and sum potential fields to generate an emergent behavior.

4.1 Overview

This chapter will concentrate on an overview of the reactive paradigm and two representative architectures. The Reactive Paradigm emerged in the late 1980's. The Reactive Paradigm is important to study for at least two reasons. First, robotic systems in limited task domains are still being constructed using reactive architectures. Second, the Reactive Paradigm will form the basis for the Hybrid Reactive-Deliberative Paradigm; everything covered here will be used (and expanded on) by the systems in Ch. 7.

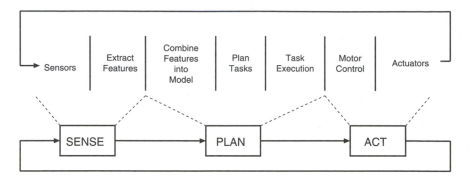

Figure 4.1 Horizontal decomposition of tasks into the S,P,A organization of the Hierarchical Paradigm.

The Reactive Paradigm grew out of dissatisfaction with the hierarchical paradigm and with an influx of ideas from ethology. Although various reactive systems may or may not strictly adhere to principles of biological intelligence, they generally mimic some aspect of biology. The dissatisfaction with the Hierarchical Paradigm was best summarized by Rodney Brooks,[27] who HORIZONTAL characterized those systems as having a *horizontal decomposition* as shown in DECOMPOSITION Fig. 4.1.

Instead, an examination of the ethological literature suggests that intelligence is layered in a *vertical decomposition*, shown in Fig. 4.2. Under a vertical decomposition, an agent starts with primitive survival behaviors and evolves new layers of behaviors which either reuse the lower, older behaviors, inhibit the older behaviors, or create parallel tracks of more advanced behaviors. The parallel tracks can be thought of layers, stacked vertically. Each layer has access to sensors and actuators independently of any other layers. If anything happens to an advanced behavior, the lower level behaviors would still operate. This return to a lower level mimics degradation of autonomous functions in the brain. Functions in the brain stem (such as breathing) continue independently of higher order functions (such as counting, face recognition, task planning), allowing a person who has brain damage from a car wreck to still breathe, etc.

Work by Arkin, Brooks, and Payton focused on defining behaviors and on mechanisms for correctly handling situations when multiple behaviors are active simultaneously. Brooks took an approach now known as subsumption and built insect-like robots with behaviors captured in hardware circuitry.

HORIZONTAL
DECOMPOSITION

VERTICAL
DECOMPOSITION

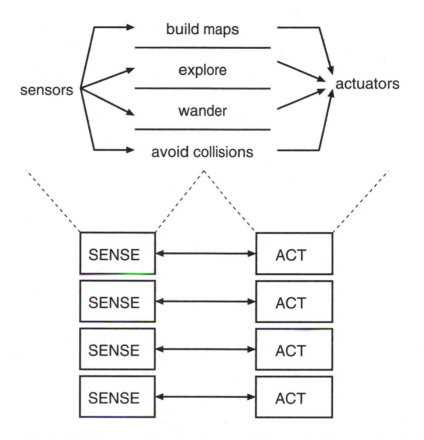

Figure 4.2 Vertical decomposition of tasks into an S-A organization, associated with the Reactive Paradigm.

Arkin and Payton used a potential fields methodology, favoring software implementations. Both approaches are equivalent. The Reactive Paradigm was initially met with stiff resistance from traditional customers of robotics, particularly the military and nuclear regulatory agencies. These users of robotic technologies were uncomfortable with the imprecise way in which discrete behaviors combine to form a rich emergent behavior. In particular, reactive behaviors are not amenable to mathematical proofs showing they are sufficient and correct for a task. In the end, the rapid execution times associated with the reflexive behaviors led to its acceptance among users, just as researchers shifted to the Hybrid paradigm in order to fully explore layering of intelligence.

The major theme of this chapter is that all reactive systems are composed of behaviors, though the meaning of a behavior may be slightly different in each reactive architecture. Behaviors can execute concurrently and/or sequentially. The two representative architectures, subsumption and potential fields, are compared and contrasted using the same task as an example. This chapter will concentrate on how architecture handles concurrent behaviors to produce an emergent behavior, deferring sequencing to the next chapter.

4.2   Attributes of Reactive Paradigm

BEHAVIORS

The fundamental attribute of the reactive paradigm is that all actions are accomplished through behaviors. As in ethological systems, *behaviors are a direct mapping of sensory inputs to a pattern of motor actions that are then used to achieve a task.* From a mathematical perspective, behaviors are simply a transfer function, transforming sensory inputs into actuator commands. For the purposes of this book, a behavior will be treated as a schema, and will consist of at least one motor schema and one perceptual schema. The motor schema contains the algorithm for generating the pattern of action in a physical actuator and the perceptual schema contains the algorithm for extracting the percept and its strength. Keep in mind that few reactive robot architectures describe their behaviors in terms of schemas. But in practice, most behavioral implementations have recognizable motor and perceptual routines, even though they are rarely referred to as schemas.

The Reactive Paradigm literally threw away the PLAN component of the SENSE, PLAN, ACT triad, as shown in Fig. 4.3. The SENSE and ACT components are tightly coupled into behaviors, and all robotic activities emerge as the result of these behaviors operating either in sequence or concurrently.

SENSE-ACT
ORGANIZATION

The S-A organization does not specify how the behaviors are coordinated and controlled; this is an important topic addressed by architectures.

BEHAVIOR-SPECIFIC
(LOCAL) SENSING

Sensing in the Reactive Paradigm is local to each behavior, or behavior-specific. Each behavior has its own dedicated sensing. In many cases, this is implemented as one sensor and perceptual schema per behavior. But in other cases, more than one behavior can take the same output from a sensor and process it differently (via the behavior's perceptual schema). One behavior literally does not know what another behavior is doing or perceiving. Fig. 4.4 graphically shows the sensing style of the Reactive Paradigm.

Note that this is fundamentally opposite of the global world model used in the hierarchical paradigm. Sensing is immediately available to the be-

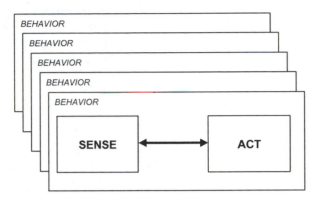

Figure 4.3 S-A organization of the Reactive Paradigm into multiple, concurrent behaviors.

havior's perceptual schema, which can do as little or as much processing as needed to extract the relevant percept. If a computationally inexpensive affordance is used, then the sensing portion of the behavior is nearly instantaneous and action is very rapid.

As can be seen from the previous chapter on the biological foundations of the reactive paradigm, behaviors favor the use of affordances. In fact, Brooks was fond of saying (loudly) at conferences, "we don't need no stinking representations." It should be noted that often the perceptual schema portion of the behavior has to use a behavior-specific representation or data structure to substitute for specialized detectors capable of extracting affordances. For example, extracting a red region in an image is non-trivial with a computer compared with an animal seeing red. The point is that while a computer program may have to have data structures in order to duplicate a simple neural function, the behavior does not rely on any central representation built up from all sensors.

In early implementations of the reactive paradigm, the idea of "one sensor, one behavior" worked well. For more advanced behaviors, it became useful to fuse the output of multiple sensors within one perceptual schema to have increased precision or a better measure of the strength of the stimulus. This type of sensor fusion is permitted within the reactive paradigm as long as the fusion is local to the behavior. Sensor fusion will be detailed in Ch. 6.

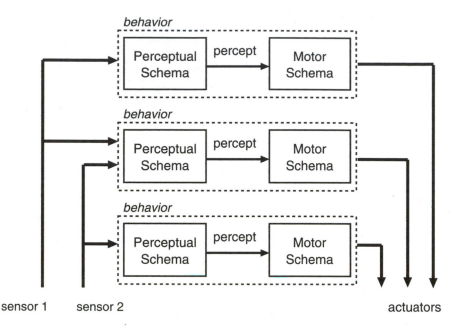

Figure 4.4   Behavior-specific sensing organization in the Reactive Paradigm: sensing is local, sensors can be shared, and sensors can be fused locally by a behavior.

4.2.1   Characteristics and connotations of reactive behaviors

As seen earlier, a reactive robotic system decomposes functionality into behaviors, which tightly couple perception to action without the use of intervening abstract (global) representations. This is a broad, vague definition. Over the years, the reactive paradigm has acquired several connotations and characteristics from the way practitioners have used the paradigm.

The primary connotation of a reactive robotic system is that it executes rapidly. The tight coupling of sensing and acting permits robots to operate in real-time, moving at speeds of 1-2 cm per second. Behaviors can be implemented directly in hardware as circuits, or with low computational complexity algorithms (O(n)). This means that behaviors execute quickly regardless of the processor. Behaviors execute not only fast in their own right, they are particularly fast when compared to the execution times of Shakey and the Stanford Cart. A secondary connotation is that reactive robotic systems have no memory, limiting reactive behaviors to what biologists would call pure stimulus-response reflexes. In practice, many behaviors exhibit a fixed-action pattern type of response, where the behavior persists for a short period of time without the direct presence of the stimulus. The main point is that behaviors are controlled by what is happening in the world, duplicating the spirit of innate releasing mechanisms, rather than by the program storing and remembering what the robot did last. The examples in the chapter emphasize this point.

The five characteristics of almost all architectures that follow the Reactive Paradigm are:

SITUATED AGENT

1. *Robots are situated agents operating in an ecological niche.* As seen earlier in Part I, *situated agent* means that the robot is an integral part of the world. A robot has its own goals and intentions. When a robot acts, it changes the world, and receives immediate feedback about the world through sensing. What the robot senses affects its goals and how it attempts to meet them, generating a new cycle of actions. Notice that situatedness is defined by Neisser's Action-Perception Cycle. Likewise, the goals of a robot, the world it operates in, and how it can perceive the world form the eco-logical niche of the robot. To emphasize this, many robotic researchers say they are working on *ecological robotics.*

ECOLOGICAL ROBOTICS

2. *Behaviors serve as the basic building blocks for robotic actions, and the overall behavior of the robot is emergent.* Behaviors are independent, computational entities and operate concurrently. The overall behavior is emergent: there is no explicit "controller" module which determines what will be done, or functions which call other functions. There may be a coordinated control program in the schema of a behavior, but there is no external controller of all behaviors for a task. As with animals, the "intelligence" of the robot is in the eye of the beholder, rather than in a specific section of code. Since the overall behavior of a reactive robot emerges from the way its individual behaviors interact, the major differences between reactive architectures is usually the specific mechanism for interaction. Recall from Chapter 3 that these mechanisms include combination, suppression, and cancellation.

EGO-CENTRIC

3. *Only local, behavior-specific sensing is permitted.* The use of explicit abstract representational knowledge in perceptual processing, even though it is behavior-specific, is avoided. Any sensing which does require represen-tation is expressed in *ego-centric* (robot-centric) coordinates. For example, consider obstacle avoidance. An ego-centric representation means that it does not matter that an obstacle is in the world at coordinates (x,y,z), only

where it is relative to the robot. Sensor data, with the exception of GPS, is inherently ego-centric (e.g., a range finder returns a distance to the nearest object from the transducer), so this eliminates unnecessary processing to create a world model, then extract the position of obstacles relative to the robot.

4. *These systems inherently follow good software design principles.* The modularity of these behaviors supports the decomposition of a task into component behaviors. The behaviors are tested independently, and behaviors may be assembled from primitive behaviors.

5. *Animal models of behavior are often cited as a basis for these systems or a particular behavior.* Unlike in the early days of AI robotics, where there was a conscious effort to not mimic biological intelligence, it is very acceptable under the reactive paradigm to use animals as a motivation for a collection of behaviors.

4.2.2 Advantages of programming by behavior

Constructing a robotic system under the Reactive Paradigm is often referred to as programming by behavior, since the fundamental component of any implementation is a behavior. Programming by behavior has a number of advantages, most of them consistent with good software engineering principles. Behaviors are inherently modular and easy to test in isolation from the system (i.e., they support unit testing). Behaviors also support incremental expansion of the capabilities of a robot. A robot becomes more intelligent by having more behaviors. The behavioral decomposition results in an implementation that works in real-time and is usually computationally inexpensive. Although we'll see that sometimes duplicating specialized detectors (like optic flow) is slow. If the behaviors are implemented poorly, then a reactive implementation can be slow. But generally, the reaction speeds of a reactive robot are equivalent to stimulus-response times in animals.

LOW COUPLING
HIGH COHESION

Behaviors support good software engineering principles through decomposition, modularity and incremental testing. If programmed with as high a degree of independence (also called *low coupling*) as possible, and *high cohesion*, the designer can build up libraries of easy to understand, maintain, and reuse modules that minimize side effects. Low coupling means that the modules can function independently of each other with minimal connections or interfaces, promoting easy reuse. Cohesion means that the data and operations contained by a module relate only to the purpose of that module.

Higher cohesion is associated with modules that do one thing well, like the SQRT function in C. The examples in Sec. 4.3 and 4.4 attempt to illustrate the choices a designer has in engineering the behavioral software of a robot.

4.2.3 Representative architectures

In order to implement a reactive system, the designer must identify the set of behaviors necessary for the task. The behaviors can either be new or use existing behaviors. The overall action of the robot emerges from multiple, concurrent behaviors. Therefore a reactive architecture must provide mechanisms for 1) triggering behaviors and 2) for determining what happens when multiple behaviors are active at the same time. Another distinguishing feature between reactive architectures is how they define a behavior and any special use of terminology. Keep in mind that the definitions presented in Sec. 4.2 are a generalization of the trends in reactive systems, and do not necessarily have counterparts in all architectures.

RULE ENCODING

There are many architectures which fit in the Reactive Paradigm. The two best known and most formalized are the subsumption and potential field methodologies. Subsumption refers to how behaviors are combined. Potential Field Methodologies require behaviors to be implemented as potential fields, and the behaviors are combined by summation of the fields. A third style of reactive architecture which is popular in Europe and Japan is *rule encoding*, where the motor schema component of behaviors and the combination mechanism are implemented as logical rules. The rules for combining behaviors are often ad hoc, and so will not be covered in this book. Other methods for combining behaviors exist, including fuzzy methods and winner-take-all voting, but these tend to be implementation details rather than an over-arching architecture.

4.3 Subsumption Architecture

Rodney Brooks' subsumption architecture is the most influential of the purely Reactive Paradigm systems. Part of the influence stems from the publicity surrounding the very naturalistic robots built with subsumption. As seen in Fig. 4.5, these robots actually looked like shoe-box sized insects, with six legs and antennae. In many implementations, the behaviors are embedded directly in the hardware or on small micro-processors, allowing the robots to have all on-board computing (this was unheard of in the processor-impoverished mid-1980's). Furthermore, the robots were the first to be able

Figure 4.5 "Veteran" robots of the MIT AI Laboratory using the subsumption architecture. (Photograph courtesy of the MIT Artificial Intelligence Laboratory.)

to walk, avoid collisions, and climb over obstacles without the "move-think-move-think" pauses of Shakey.

The term "behavior" in the subsumption architecture has a less precise meaning than in other architectures. A behavior is a network of sensing and acting modules which accomplish a task. The modules are augmented finite state machines AFSM, or finite state machines which have registers, timers, and other enhancements to permit them to be interfaced with other modules. An AFSM is equivalent to the interface between the schemas and the coordinated control strategy in a behavioral schema. In terms of schema theory, a subsumption behavior is actually a collection of one or more schemas into an abstract behavior.

Behaviors are released in a stimulus-response way, without an external program explicitly coordinating and controlling them. Four interesting aspects of subsumption in terms of releasing and control are:

LAYERS OF
COMPETENCE
1. Modules are grouped into *layers of competence*. The layers reflect a hierarchy of intelligence, or competence. Lower layers encapsulate basic survival functions such as avoiding collisions, while higher levels create

more goal-directed actions such as mapping. Each of the layers can be viewed as an abstract behavior for a particular task.

LAYERS CAN SUBSUME LOWER LAYERS

2. Modules in a higher layer can override, or subsume, the output from behaviors in the next lower layer. The behavioral layers operate concurrently and independently, so there needs to be a mechanism to handle potential conflicts. The solution in subsumption is a type of winner-take-all, where the winner is always the higher layer.

NO INTERNAL STATE

3. The use of internal state is avoided. Internal state in this case means any type of local, persistent representation which represents the state of the world, or a model. Because the robot is a situated agent, most of its information should come directly from the world. If the robot depends on an internal representation, what it believes may begin to dangerously diverge from reality. Some internal state is needed for releasing behaviors like being scared or hungry, but good behavioral designs minimize this.

4. A task is accomplished by activating the appropriate layer, which then activates the lower layers below it, and so on. However, in practice, subsumption style systems are not easily *taskable*, that is, they can't be ordered to do another task without being reprogrammed.

TASKABLE

4.3.1 Example

These aspects are best illustrated by an example, extensively modified from Brooks' original paper[27] in order to be consistent with schema theory terminology and to facilitate comparison with a potential fields methodology. A robot capable of moving forward while not colliding with anything could be represented with a single layer, Level 0. In this example, the robot has multiple sonars (or other range sensors), each pointing in a different direction, and two actuators, one for driving forward and one for turning.

LEVEL 0: AVOID

Following Fig. 4.6, the SONAR module reads the sonar ranges, does any filtering of noise, and produces a *polar plot*. A polar plot represents the range readings in polar coordinates, (r, θ), surrounding the robot. As shown in Fig. 4.7, the polar plot can be "unwound."

POLAR PLOT

If the range reading for the sonar facing dead ahead is below a certain threshold, the COLLIDE module declares a collision and sends the halt signal to the FORWARD drive actuator. If the robot was moving forward, it now stops. Meanwhile, the FEELFORCE module is receiving the same polar plot. It treats each sonar reading as a repulsive force, which can be represented

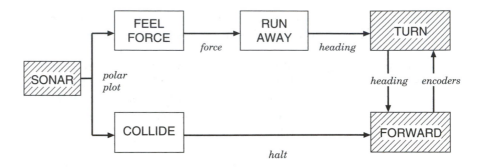

Figure 4.6   Level 0 in the subsumption architecture.

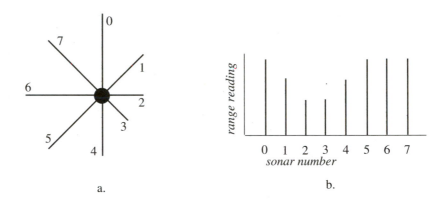

Figure 4.7   Polar plot of eight sonar range readings: a.) "robo-centric" view of range readings along acoustic axes, and b.) unrolled into a plot.

as a vector. Recall that a vector is a mathematical construct that consists of a magnitude and a direction. FEELFORCE can be thought of as summing the vectors from each of the sonar readings. This results in a new vector. The repulsive vector is then passed to the TURN module. The TURN module splits off the direction to turn and passes that to the steering actuators. TURN also passes the vector to the FORWARD module, which uses the magnitude of the vector to determine the magnitude of the next forward motion (how far or how fast). So the robot turns and moves a short distance away from the obstacle.

The observable behavior is that the robot will sit still if it is in an unoccupied space, until an obstacle comes near it. If the obstacle is on one side of

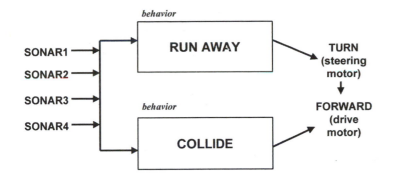

Figure 4.8 Level 0 recast as primitive behaviors.

the robot, the robot will turn 180° the other way and move forward; essentially, it runs away. This allows a person to herd the robot around. The robot can react to an obstacle if the obstacle (or robot) is motionless or moving; the response is computed at each sensor update.

However, if part of the obstacle, or another obstacle, is dead ahead (someone tries to herd the robot into a wall), the robot will stop, then apply the results of RUNAWAY. So it will stop, turn and begin to move forward again. Stopping prevents the robot from side-swiping the obstacle while it is turning and moving forward. Level 0 shows how a fairly complex set of actions can emerge from very simple modules.

It is helpful to recast the subsumption architecture in the terms used in this book, as shown in Fig. 4.8. Note how this looks like the vertical decomposition in Fig. 4.2: the sensor data flows through the concurrent behaviors to the actuators, and the independent behaviors cause the robot to do the right thing. The SONAR module would be considered a global interface to the sensors, while the TURN and FORWARD modules would be considered part of the actuators (an interface). For the purposes of this book, a behavior must consist of a perceptual schema and a motor schema. Perceptual schemas are connected to a sensor, while motor schemas are connected to actuators. For Level 0, the perceptual schemas would be contained in the FEELFORCE and COLLIDE modules. The motor schemas are RUNAWAY and COLLIDE modules. COLLIDE combines both perceptual processing (extracts the vector for the sonar facing directly ahead) and the pattern of action (halt if there is a

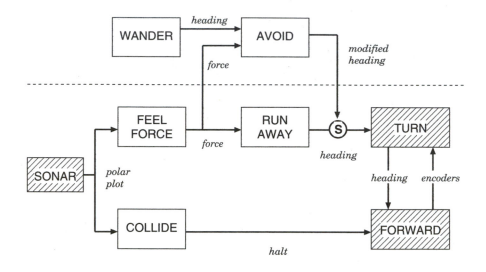

Figure 4.9 Level 1: wander.

reading). The primitive behaviors reflect the two paths through the layer. One might be called the runaway behavior and the other the collide behavior. Together, the two behaviors create a rich obstacle avoidance behavior, or a layer of competence.

It should also be noticed that the behaviors used direct perception, or affordances. The presence of a range reading indicated there was an obstacle; the robot did not have to know what the obstacle was.

LEVEL 1: WANDER

Consider building a robot which actually wandered around instead of sitting motionless, but was still able to avoid obstacles. Under subsumption, a second layer of competence (Level 1) would be added, shown in Fig. 4.9. In this case, Level 1 consists of a WANDER module which computes a random heading every n seconds. The random heading can be thought of as a vector. It needs to pass this heading to the TURN and FORWARD modules. But it can't be passed to the TURN module directly. That would sacrifice obstacle avoidance, because TURN only accepts one input. One solution is to add another module in Level 1, AVOID, which combines the FEELFORCE vector with the WANDER vector. Adding a new avoid module offers an opportunity to create a more sophisticated response to obstacles. AVOID combines the direction of the force of avoidance with the desired heading. This results in the actual heading being mostly in the right direction rather than having the robot turn

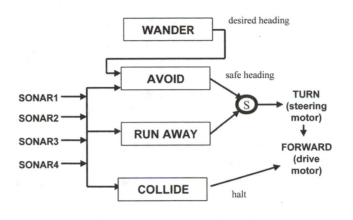

Figure 4.10   Level 1 recast as primitive behaviors.

around and lose forward progress. (Notice also that the AVOID module was able to "eavesdrop" on components of the next lower layer.) The heading output from AVOID has the same representation as the output of RUNAWAY, so TURN can accept from either source.

The issue now appears to be when to accept the heading vector from which layer. Subsumption makes it simple: the output from the higher level subsumes the output from the lower level. Subsumption is done in one of two ways:

INHIBITION
1. *inhibition.* In inhibition, the output of the subsuming module is connected to the output of another module. If the output of the subsuming module is "on" or has any value, the output of the subsumed module is blocked or turned "off." Inhibition acts like a faucet, turning an output stream on and off.

SUPPRESSION
2. *suppression.* In suppression, the output of of the subsuming module is connected to the input of another module. If the output of the subsuming module is on, it *replaces* the normal input to the subsumed module. Suppression acts like a switch, swapping one input stream for another.

In this case, the AVOID module suppresses (marked in the diagram with a S) the output from RUNAWAY. RUNAWAY is still executing, but its output doesn't go anywhere. Instead, the output from AVOID goes to TURN.

The use of layers and subsumption allows new layers to be built on top of less competent layers, without modifying the lower layers. This is good software engineering, facilitating modularity and simplifying testing. It also adds some robustness in that if something should disable the Level 1 behaviors, Level 0 might remain intact. The robot would at least be able to preserve its self-defense mechanism of fleeing from approaching obstacles.

Fig. 4.10 shows Level 1 recast as behaviors. Note that FEELFORCE was used by both RUNAWAY and AVOID. FEELFORCE is the perceptual component (or schema) of both behaviors, with the AVOID and RUNAWAY modules being the motor component (or schema). As is often the case, behaviors are usually named after the observable action. This means that the behavior (which consists of perception and action) and the action component have the same name. The figure does not show that the AVOID and RUNAWAY behaviors share the same FEELFORCE perceptual schema. As will be seen in the next chapter, the object-oriented properties of schema theory facilitate the reuse and sharing of perceptual and motor components.

LEVEL 2: FOLLOW CORRIDORS

Now consider adding a third layer to permit the robot to move down corridors, as shown in Fig. 4.11. (The third layer in Brooks' original paper is "explore," because he was considering a mapping task.) The LOOK module examines the sonar polar plot and identifies a corridor. (Note that this is another example of behaviors sharing the same sensor data but using it locally for different purposes.) Because identifying a corridor is more computationally expensive than just extracting range data, LOOK may take longer to run than behaviors at lower levels. LOOK passes the vector representing the direction to the middle of the corridor to the STAYINMIDDLE module. STAYINMIDDLE subsumes the WANDER module and delivers its output to the AVOID module which can then swerve around obstacles.

But how does the robot get back on course if the LOOK module has not computed a new direction? In this case, the INTEGRATE module has been observing the robots actual motions from shaft encoders in the actuators. This gives an estimate of how far off course the robot has traveled since the last update by LOOK. STAYINMIDDLE can use the dead reckoning data with the intended course to compute the new course vector. It serves to fill in the gaps in mismatches between updates rates of the different modules. Notice that LOOK and STAYINMIDDLE are quite sophisticated from a software perspective.

INTEGRATE is an example of a module which is supplying a dangerous internal state: it is actually substituting for feedback from the real world. If for some reason, the LOOK module never updates, then the robot could op-

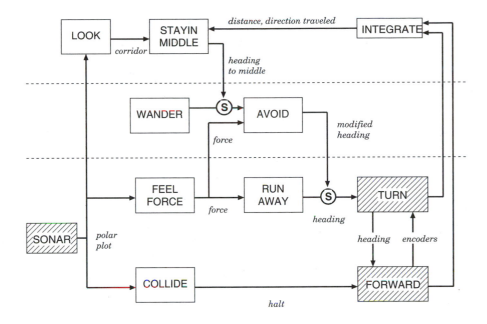

Figure 4.11   Level 2: follow corridors.

erate without any sensor data forever. Or at least until it crashed! Therefore, subsumption style systems include time constants on suppression and inhibition. If the suppression from STAYINMIDDLE ran for longer than n seconds with out a new update, the suppression would cease. The robot would then begin to wander, and hopefully whatever problem (like the corridor being totally blocked) that had led to the loss of signal would fix itself.

Of course, a new problem is how does the robot know that it hasn't started going down the hallway it just came up? Answer: it doesn't. The design assumes that that a corridor will always be present in the robot's ecological niche. If it's not, the robot does not behave as intended. This is an example of the connotation that reactive systems are "memory-less."

4.3.2   Subsumption summary

To summarize subsumption:

- Subsumption has a loose definition of behavior as a tight coupling of sensing and acting. Although it is not a schema-theoretic architecture, it can be described in those terms. It groups schema-like modules into layers of competence, or abstract behaviors.

- Higher layers may subsume and inhibit behaviors in lower layers, but behaviors in lower layers are never rewritten or replaced. From a programming standpoint, this may seem strange. However, it mimics biological evolution. Recall that the fleeing behavior in frogs (Ch. 3) was actually the result of two behaviors, one which always moved toward moving objects and the other which actually suppressed that behavior when the object was large.

- The design of layers and component behaviors for a subsumption implementation, as with all behavioral design, is hard; it is more of an art than a science. This is also true for all reactive architectures.

- There is nothing resembling a STRIPS-like plan in subsumption. Instead, behaviors are released by the presence of stimulus in the environment.

- Subsumption solves the frame problem by eliminating the need to model the world. It also doesn't have to worry about the open world being non-monotonic and having some sort of truth maintenance mechanism, because the behaviors do not remember the past. There may be some perceptual persistence leading to a fixed-action pattern type of behavior (e.g., corridor following), but there is no mechanism which monitors for changes in the environment. The behaviors simply respond to whatever stimulus is in the environment.

- Perception is largely direct, using affordances. The releaser for a behavior is almost always the percept for guiding the motor schema.

- Perception is ego-centric and distributed. In the wander (layer 2) example, the sonar polar plot was relative to the robot. A new polar plot was created with each update of the sensors. The polar plot was also available to any process which needed it (shared global memory), allowing user modules to be distributed. Output from perceptual schemas can be shared with other layers.

4.4   Potential Fields Methodologies

Another style of reactive architecture is based on potential fields. The specific architectures that use some type of potential fields are too numerous to describe here, so instead a generalization will be presented. Potential field styles of behaviors always use *vectors* to represent behaviors and *vector summation* to combine vectors from different behaviors to produce an emergent behavior.

4.4.1 Visualizing potential fields

The first tenet of a potential fields architecture is that the motor action of a behavior must be represented as a potential field. A potential field is an array, or field, of vectors. As described earlier, a vector is a mathematical construct which consists of a magnitude and a direction. Vectors are often used to represent a force of some sort. They are typically drawn as an arrow, where the length of the arrow is the magnitude of the force and the angle of the arrow is the direction. Vectors are usually represented with a boldface capital letter, for example, **V**. A vector can also be written as a tuple (m, d), where m stands for magnitude and d for direction. By convention the magnitude is a real number between 0.0 and 1, but the magnitude can be any real number.

The array represents a region of space. In most robotic applications, the space is in two dimensions, representing a bird's eye view of the world just like a map. The map can be divided into squares, creating a (x,y) grid. Each element of the array represents a square of space. Perceivable objects in the world exert a force field on the surrounding space. The force field is analogous to a magnetic or gravitation field. The robot can be thought of as a particle that has entered the field exuded by an object or environment. The vector in each element represents the force, both the direction to turn and the magnitude or velocity to head in that direction, a robot would feel if it were at that particular spot. Potential fields are continuous because it doesn't matter how small the element is; at each point in space, there is an associated vector.

Fig. 4.12 shows how an obstacle would exert a field on the robot and make it run away. If the robot is close to the obstacle, say within 5 meters, it is inside the potential field and will fell a force that makes it want to face directly away from the obstacle (if it isn't already) and move away. If the robot is not within range of the obstacle, it just sits there because there is no force on it. Notice that the field represents what the robot should do (the motor schema) based on if the robot perceives an obstacle (the perceptual schema). The field isn't concerned with how the robot came to be so close to the obstacle; the robot feels the same force if it were happening to move within range or if it was just sitting there and someone put their hand next to the robot.

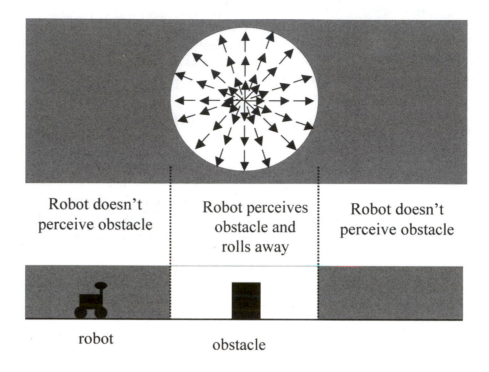

Figure 4.12   Example of an obstacle exerting a repulsive potential field over the radius of 1 meter.

One way of thinking about potential fields is to imagine a force field acting on the robot. Another way is to think of them as a potential energy surface in three dimensions (gravity is often represented this way) and the robot as a marble. In that case, the vector indicates the direction the robot would "roll" on the surface. Hills in the surface cause the robot to roll away or around (vectors would be pointing away from the "peak" of the hill), and valleys would cause the robot to roll downward (vectors pointing toward the bottom).

FIVE PRIMITIVE FIELDS

UNIFORM FIELD

There are five basic potential fields, or primitives, which can be combined to build more complex fields: *uniform, perpendicular, attractive, repulsive,* and *tangential*. Fig. 4.13 shows a uniform field. In a uniform field, the robot would feel the same force no matter where it was. No matter where it got set down and at what orientation, it would feel a need to turn to align itself to the direction the arrow points and to move in that direction at a velocity propor-

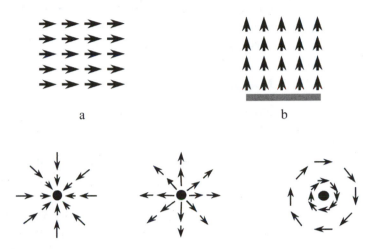

Figure 4.13 Five primitive potential fields: a.) uniform, b.) perpendicular, c.) attraction, d.) repulsion, and e.) tangential.

tional to the length of the arrow. A uniform field is often used to capture the behavior of "go in direction $n°$."

PERPENDICULAR FIELD

Fig. 4.13b shows a perpendicular field, where the robot is oriented perpendicular to some object or wall or border The field shown is directed away from the gray wall, but a perpendicular field can be pointed towards an object as well.

ATTRACTIVE FIELD

Fig. 4.13c illustrates an attractive field. The circle at the center of the field represents an object that is exerting an attraction on the robot. Wherever the robot is, the robot will "feel" a force relative to the object. Attractive fields are useful for representing a taxis or tropism, where the agent is literally attracted to light or food or a goal. The opposite of an attractive field is a repulsive field, shown in Fig. 4.13d. Repulsive fields are commonly associated with obstacles, or things the agent should avoid. The closer the robot is to the object, the stronger the repulsive force $180°$ away from it.

TANGENTIAL FIELD

The final primitive field is the tangential field in Fig. 4.13e. The field is a tangent around the object (think of a tangent vector as being perpendicular to radial lines extending outward from the object). Tangential fields can "spin" either clockwise or counterclockwise; Fig. 4.13 shows a clockwise spin. They are useful for directing a robot to go around an obstacle, or having a robot investigate something.

4.4.2   Magnitude profiles

Notice that in Fig. 4.13, the length of the arrows gets smaller closer to the object. The way the magnitude of vectors in the field change is called the MAGNITUDE PROFILE *magnitude profile*. (The term "magnitude profile" is used here because the term "velocity profile" is used by control engineers to describe how a robot's motors actually accelerate and decelerate to produce a particular movement without jerking.)

Consider the repulsive field in Fig. 4.12. Mathematically, the field can be represented with polar coordinates and the center of the field being the origin (0,0):

$$(4.1) \qquad \begin{aligned} V_{direction} &= -\phi \\ V_{magnitude} &= c \end{aligned}$$

In that case, the magnitude was a constant value, c: the length of the arrows was the same. This can be visualized with a plot of the magnitude shown in Fig. 4.14a.

This profile says that the robot will run away (the direction it will run is $-\phi$) at the same velocity, no matter how close it is to the object, as long as it is in the range of the obstacle. As soon as the robot gets out of range of the obstacle, the velocity drops to 0.0, stopping the robot. The field is essentially binary: the robot is either running away at a constant speed or stopped. In practice there is a problem with a constant magnitude. It leads to jerky motion on the perimeter of the range of the field. This is illustrated when a robot is heading in a particular direction, then encounters an obstacle. It runs away, leaving the field almost immediately, and turns back to its original path, encounters the field again, and so on.

Magnitude profiles solve the problem of a constant magnitude. They also REFLEXIVITY make it possible for a robot designer to represent reflexivity (that a response should be proportional to the strength of a stimulus) and to create interesting responses. Now consider the profile in Fig. 4.13c. It can be described as how

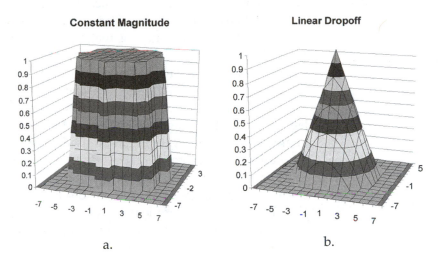

a.   b.

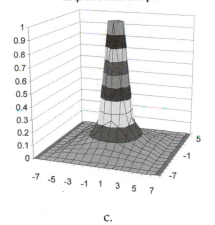

c.

Figure 4.14 Plots of magnitude profiles for a field of radius 5 units: a.) constant magnitude, b.) linear drop off with a slope of -1, and c.) exponential drop off.

an observer would see a robot behave in that field: if the robot is far away from the object, it will turn and move quickly towards it, then slow up to keep from overshooting and hitting the object. Mathematically, this is called

LINEAR DROP OFF
a *linear drop off*, since the rate at which the magnitude of the vectors drops off can be plotted as a straight line. The formula for a straight line is $y = mx + b$, where x is the distance and y is magnitude. b biases where the line starts, and m is the slope ($m = \frac{\Delta_y}{\Delta_x}$). Any value of m and b is acceptable. If it is not specified, $m = 1$ or -1 (a $45°$ slope up or down) and $b = 0$ in linear functions.

The linear profile in Fig. 4.14b matches the desired behavior of the designer: to have the robot react more, the closer it is. But it shares the problem of the constant magnitude profile in the sharp transition to 0.0 velocity. Therefore, another profile might be used to capture the need for a strong

EXPONENTIAL DROP OFF
reaction but with more of a taper. One such profile is a *exponential drop off* function, where the drop off is proportional to the square of the distance: for every unit of distance away from the object, the force on the robot drops in half. The exponential profile is shown in Fig. 4.14c.

As can be seen from the previous examples, almost any magnitude profile is acceptable. The motivation for using magnitude profiles is to fine-tune the behavior. It is important to note that the robot only computes the vectors acting on it at its current location. The figures display the entire field for all possible locations of the robot. The question then arises as to why do the figures show an entire field over space? First, it aids visualizing what the robot will do overall, not just at one particular time step. Second, since fields are continuous representations, it simplifies confirming that the field is correct and makes any abrupt transitions readily apparent.

4.4.3   Potential fields and perception

In the previous examples, the force of the potential field at any given point was a function of both the relative distance between the robot and an object and the magnitude profile. The strength of a potential field can be a function of the stimulus, regardless of distance. As an example recall from Ch. 3 the feeding behavior of baby arctic terns where the feeding behavior is guided by the stimulus "red." This can be modeled by an attractive field. The bigger and redder an object in the baby's field of view, the stronger the attraction, suggesting that a magnitude profile using an increasing exponential function. Another important point that has already been mentioned is that potential fields are ego-centric because robot perception is ego-centric.

4.4.4   Programming a single potential field

Potential fields are actually easy to program, especially since the fields are ego-centric to the robot. The visualization of the entire field may appear to indicate that the robot and the objects are in a fixed, absolute coordinate system, but they are not. The robot computes the effect of the potential field, usually as a straight line, at every update, with no memory of where it was previously or where the robot has moved. This should become clear through the following examples.

A primitive potential field is usually represented by a single function. The vector impacting the robot is computed each update. Consider the case of a robot with a single range sensor facing forward. The designer has decided that a repulsive field with a linear drop off is appropriate. The formula is:

$$(4.2) \qquad V_{direction} \;=\; -180°$$

$$V_{magnitude} \;=\; \begin{cases} \frac{(D-d)}{D} & \text{for } d <= D \\ 0 & \text{for } d > D \end{cases}$$

where D is the maximum range of the field's effect, or the maximum distance at which the robot can detect the obstacle. (D isn't always the detection range. It can be the range at which the robot should respond to a stimulus. For example, many sonars can detect obstacles 20 feet away, producing an almost infinitesimal response in emergent behavior but requiring the runtime overhead of a function call. In practice, a roboticist might set a D of 2 meters.) Notice that the formula produces a result where $0.0 \leq V_{magnitude} \leq 1.0$.

Below is a C code fragment that captures the repulsive field.

```
typedef struct {
   double    magnitude;
   double direction;
} vector;

vector repulsive(double d, double D)
{
   if (d <= D) {
     outputVector.direction = -180; //turn around!
     outputVector.magnitude = (D-d)/D; //linear dropoff
   }
   else {
```

```
        outputVector.direction=0.0
        outputVector.magnitude=0.0
    }
    return outputVector;
}
```

At this point, it is easy to illustrate how a potential field can be used by a behavior, runaway, for the robot with a single sensor. The runaway behavior will use the repulsive() function as the motor schema, and a function readSonar() as the perceptual schema. The output of the behavior is a vector. runaway is called by the robot on every update cycle.

```
vector runaway( ){
    double reading;
    reading=readSonar();//perceptual schema
    vector=repulsive (reading, MAX_DISTANCE); //motor schema
    return Voutput;
}
while (robot==ON)
{
    Vrunaway=runaway(reading); // motor schema
    turn(Vrunaway.direction);
    forward(Vrunaway.magnitude*MAX_VELOCITY);
}
```

4.4.5   Combination of fields and behaviors

As stated earlier in the chapter, the first attribute of a true potential fields methodology is that it requires all behaviors to be implemented as potential fields. The second attribute is that it combines behaviors not by one subsuming others, but by vector summation. A robot will generally have forces acting on it from multiple behaviors, all acting concurrently. This section provides two examples of how multiple behaviors arise and how they are implemented and combined.

The first example is simple navigation, where a robot is heading for a goal (specified as "10.3m in direction Θ") and encounters an obstacle. The motor

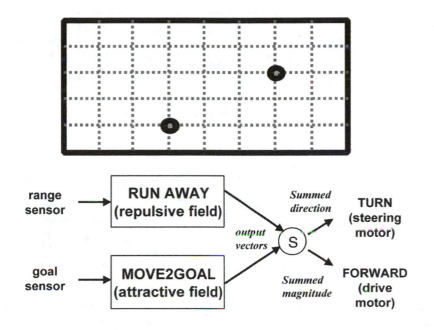

Figure 4.15   A bird's eye view of a world with a goal and obstacle, and the two active behaviors for the robot who will inhabit this world.

schema of the `move2goal` behavior is represented with an attractive potential field, which uses the shaft encoders on the robot to tell if it has reached the goal position. The `runaway` behavior is a repulsive field and uses a range sensor to detect if something is in front of it. Fig. 4.15 shows a bird's eye view of an area, and shows a visualization of the potential field. The `move2goal` behavior in Fig. 4.16b exerts an attractive field over the entire space; where ever the robot is, it will feel a force from the goal. The `runaway` behavior in Fig. 4.15 exerts a repulsive field in a radius around the obstacle (technically the repulsive field extends over all of the space as does the `move2goal`, but the magnitude of the repulsion is 0.0 beyond the radius). The combined field is shown in Fig. 4.16c.

Now consider the emergent behavior of the robot in the field if it starts in the lower right corner, shown in Fig. 4.17. At time t_0, the robot senses the world. It can only perceive the goal and cannot perceive the obstacle, so the only vector it feels is attraction (`runaway` returns a vector with magnitude

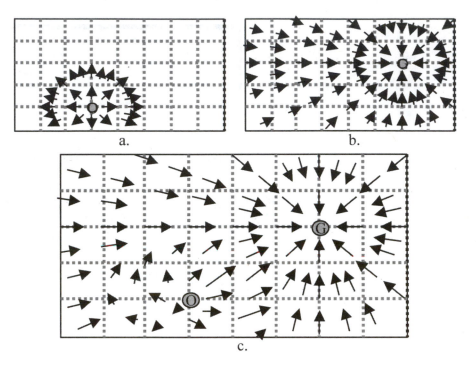

Figure 4.16   Potential fields from the world in Fig. 4.15: a.) repulsive from the obstacle, b.) attractive from the goal, and c.) combined.

of 0.0). It moves on a straight line for the goal. At t_2, it updates its sensors and now perceives both the goal and the obstacle. Both behaviors contribute a vector; the vectors are summed and the robot now moves off course. At t_3, the robot has almost moved beyond the obstacle and the goal is exerting the stronger force. At t_4, it resumes course and reaches the goal.

The example illustrates other points about potential fields methods: the impact of update rates, holonomicity, and local minima. Notice that the distance (length of the arrows) between updates is different. That is due to the changes in the magnitude of the output vector, which controls the robot velocity. If the robot has a "shorter" vector, it travels more slowly and, therefore, covers less distance in the same amount of time. It can also "overshoot" as seen between t_3 and t_4 where the robot actually goes farther without turning and has to turn back to go to the goal. As a result, the path is jagged with sharp lines. The resulting path will be smoother if the robot has a faster

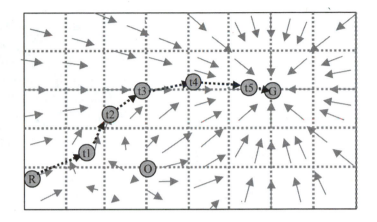

Figure 4.17   Path taken by the robot.

update interval. Another aspect of the update rate is that the robot can over-shoot the goal, especially if it is using shaft encoders (the goal is 10.3 meters from where the robot started). Sometimes designers use attractive fields with a magnitude that drops off as the robot approaches, slowing it down so the that the robot can tell with it has reached the goal. (Programmers usually put a tolerance around the goal location, for example instead of 10.3m, the goal is 10.3m+/- 0.5m.)

Potential fields treat the robot as if it were a particle that could change velocity and direction instantaneously. This isn't true for real robots. Research robots such as Kheperas (shown in Fig. 4.18) can turn in any direction in place, but they have to be stopped and there is a measurable amount of error due to the contact between the wheels and the surface. Many robots have Ackerman, or automobile, steering, and anyone who has tried to parallel park an automobile knows that a car can go only in certain directions.

A third problem is that the fields may sum to 0.0. Returning to Fig. 4.16, draw a line between the Goal and the Obstacle. Along that line behind the Obstacle, the vectors have only a head (direction of the arrow) and no body (length of the arrow). This means that the magnitude is 0.0 and that if the robot reaches that spot, it will stop and not move again. This is called the local minima problem, because the potential field has a minima, or valley, that traps the robot. Solutions to the local minima problem will be described at the end of the chapter.

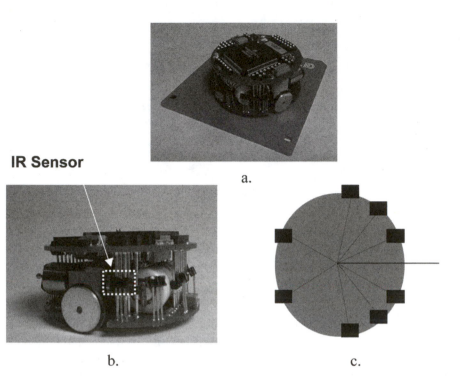

Figure 4.18   Khepera miniature robot: a.) a khepera on a floppy disk, b.) IR sensors (small black squares) along the "waistline," and c.) orientation of the IR sensors.

4.4.6   Example using one behavior per sensor

As another example of how powerful this idea of vector summation is, it is useful to consider how obstacle avoidance runaway is commonly implemented on real robots. Fig. 4.18 shows a layout of the IR range sensors on a Khepera robot. Since the sensors are permanently mounted on the platform, their angle α_i relative to the front is known. If a sensor receives a range reading, something is in front of that sensor. Under a repulsive field RUN-AWAY, the output vector will be $180°$ opposite α_i. The IR sensor isn't capable of telling that the obstacle may be a little off the sensor axis, so a reading is treated as if an obstacle was straight in front of that sensor and perpendicular to it.

If this sensor were the only sensor on the robot, the RUNAWAY behavior is very straightforward. But what if, as in the case of a Khepera, the robot has multiple range sensors? Bigger obstacles will be detected by multiple sensors at the same time. The common way is to have a RUNAWAY behavior for each sensor. This called multiple instantiations of the same behavior. Below is a code fragment showing multiple instantiations; all that had to be done is add a for loop to poll each sensor. This takes advantage of two properties of vector addition: it is associative (a+b+c+d can be performed as $((a + b) + c) + d$), and it is commutative (doesn't matter what order the vectors are summed).

```
while (robot==ON) {
    vector.mag=vector.dir=0.0; //initialize to 0
    for (i=0; i<=numberIR; i++) {
      vectorCurrent=Runaway(i); // accept a sensor number
      vectorOutput = VectorSum(tempVector,vectorCurrent);
    }
    turn(vector.direction);
    forward(vector.magnitude*MAX-VELOCITY);
}
```

BOX CANYON

As seen in Fig. 4.19, the robot is able to get out of the cave-like trap called a *box canyon* without building a model of the wall. Each instance contributes a vector, some of which have a X or Y component that cancels out.

From an ethological perspective, the above program is elegant because it is equivalent to behavioral instantiations in animals. Recall from Ch. 3 the model of *rana computrix* and its real-life toad counterpart where each eye sees and responds to a fly independently of the other eye. In this case, the program is treating the robot as if it had 8 independent eyes!

From a robotics standpoint, the example illustrates two important points. First, the direct coupling of sensing to action works. Second, behavioral programming is consistent with good software engineering practices. The

FUNCTIONAL
COHESION

RUNAWAY function exhibits *functional cohesion*, where the function does one thing well and every statement in the function has something directly to do with the function's purpose.[122] Functional cohesion is desirable, because it means the function is unlikely to introduce side effects into the main program

DATA COUPLING

or be dependent on another function. The overall organization shows *data coupling*, where each function call takes a simple argument.[122] Data coupling is good, because it means all the functions are independent; for example, the program can be easily changed to accommodate more IRs sensors.

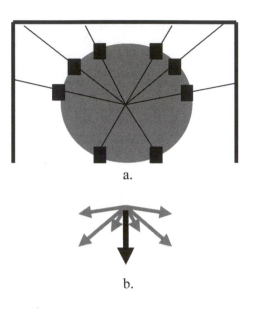

Figure 4.19 Khepera in a box canyon a.) range readings and b.) vectors from each instance of Runaway (gray) and the summed output vector.

The alternative to multiple instantiation is to have the perceptual schema for RUNAWAY process all 8 range readings. One approach is to sum all 8 vectors internally. (As an exercise show that the resulting vector is the same.) This is not as elegant from a software engineering perspective because the code is now specific to the robot (the function is said to have *procedural cohesion*),[122] and can be used only with a robot that has eight range sensors at those locations. Another approach, which produces a different emergent behavior, is to have the perceptual schema return the direction and distance of the single largest range reading. This makes the behavior more selective.

PROCEDURAL
COHESION

4.4.7 Pfields compared with subsumption

How can simple behaviors form a more complicated emergent behavior? The same way more complicated potential fields are constructed from primitive fields: combining multiple instantiations of primitive behaviors. This can be seen by revisiting the example behaviors used to describe the subsumption architecture. In the case of Level 0 in subsumption, if there are no obstacles within range, the robot feels no repulsive force and is motionless. If an obstacle comes within range and is detected by more than one sonar, each of the sonar readings create a vector, pointing the robot in the opposite direction. In the subsumption example, it could be imagined that these vectors were summed in the RUNAWAY module as shown in Fig. 4.20. In a potential fields system, each sonar reading would release an instance of the RUNAWAYpf behavior (the "pf" will be used to make it clear which runaway is being referred to). The RUNAWAYpf behavior uses a repulsive potential field. The output vectors would then be summed, and then the resultant vector would be used to guide the turn and forward motors.

```
while (robot==ON)
{
    vector.magnitude=vector.direction=0;
    for (i=0; i<=numberSonars; i++) {
        reading=readSonar();              //perceptual schema
        currentVector=runaway(reading); // motor schema
        vector = vectorSum(vector, currentVector);
    }
    turn(vector.direction);
    forward(vector.magnitude*MAX-VELOCITY);
}
```

The COLLIDE module in subsumption does not map over to a behavior in a potential fields methodology. Recall that the purpose of COLLIDE is to stop the robot if it touches an obstacle; in effect, if the RUNAWAY behavior has failed. This fits the definition of a behavior: it has a sensory input (range to obstacle = 0) and a recognizable pattern of motor activity (stop). But it doesn't produce a potential field, unless a uniform field of vectors with 0 magnitude is permissible. If it were treated as a behavior, the vector it contributes to would be summed with any other vectors contributed by other behaviors. But a vector with 0 magnitude is the identity function for vector addition, so a COLLISION vector would have no impact. Instead, collisions are often treated as "panic" situations, triggering an emergency response outside the potential field framework.

Some of the subtle differences between potential fields and subsumption appear when the case of Level 2 is considered. The same functionality can be accomplished by adding only a single instance of the WANDER behavior, as shown in Fig. 4.21. As before, the behavior generates a new direction

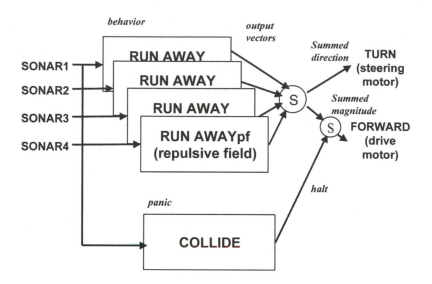

Figure 4.20   Level 0 redone as Potential Fields Methodology.

to move every n seconds. This would be represented by a uniform field where the robot felt the same attraction to go a certain direction, regardless of location, for n seconds. However, by combining the output of WANDER with the output vectors from RUNAWAYpf, the need for a new AVOID behavior is eliminated. The WANDER vector is summed with the repulsive vectors, and as a result, the robot moves both away from the obstacles and towards the desired direction. This is shown in Fig. 4.22. The primary differences in this example are that potential fields explicitly encapsulate sensing and acting into primitive behaviors, and it did not have to subsume any lower behaviors. As with subsumption, the robot became more intelligent when the WANDERpf behavior was added to the RUNAWAYpf behavior.

Now consider how Level 3, corridor following, would be implemented in a potential field system. This further illustrates the conceptual differences between the two approaches. The robot would have two concurrent behaviors: RUNAWAYpf and follow-corridor. RUNAWAYpf would remain the same as before, but WANDER would be discarded. In the parlance of potential fields, the task of following a corridor requires only two behaviors, while the task of wandering requires two different behaviors.

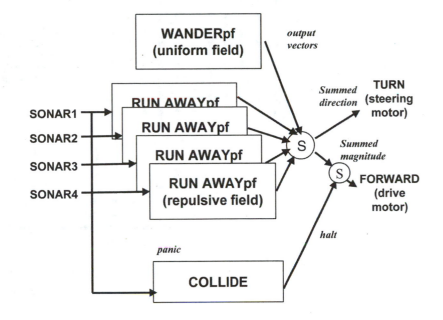

Figure 4.21   Level 1 redone with Potential Fields Methodology.

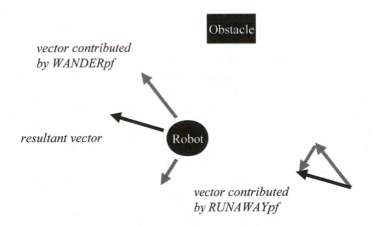

Figure 4.22   Example resultant vector of WANDERpf and RUNAWAYpf.

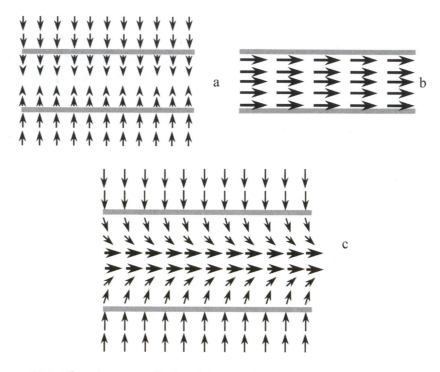

Figure 4.23 The a.) perpendical and b.) uniform fields combining into c.) a `follow-corridor` field.

The `follow-corridor` behavior is interesting, because it requires a more complex potential field. As shown in Fig. 4.23, it would be desirable for the robot to stay in the middle of the corridor. This can be accomplished using two potential fields: a uniform field perpendicular to the left boundary and pointing to the middle, and a uniform field perpendicular to the right boundary and pointing to the middle. Notice that both fields have a linear decrease in magnitude as the field nears the center of the corridor. In practice, this taper prevents the robot from see-sawing in the middle.

Also notice that the two uniform fields are not sufficient because they do not permit the robot to move forward; the robot would move to the middle of the corridor and just sit there. Therefore, a third uniform field is added which is parallel to the corridor. All three fields combined yield a smooth field which sharply pushes the robot back to the middle of the corridor as a function of its proximity to a wall. In the meantime, the robot is constantly making forward progress. The figure below shows the fields involved. Remember, in this example, the robot is not projecting past or future boundaries of the corridor; the visualization of the field makes it appear that way.

The `follow-corridor` behavior is using the same sonar data as `avoid`; therefore, walls will produce a repulsive field, which would generally push the robot onto the middle of the corridor. Why not just use a single uniform parallel field for `follow-corridor`? First, behaviors are independent. If there is a corridor following behavior, it must be able to follow halls without depending on side effects from other behaviors. Second, the polar symmetry of the repulsive fields may cause see-sawing, so there is a practical advantage to having a separate behavior.

The use of behavior-specific domain knowledge (supplied at instantiation time as an optional initialization parameter) can further improve the robot's overall behavior. If the robot knows the width of the hall *a priori*, `follow-corridor` can suppress instances of avoid which are using obstacles it decides form the boundary of the wall. Then it will only avoid obstacles that are in the hall. If there are no obstacles, `follow-corridor` will produce a smooth trajectory. If the obstacles are next to a wall, the `follow-corridor` will treat the profile of the obstacle as a wall and move closer to the center.

SEQUENCING AND PARAMETERIZING POTENTIAL FIELDS

The motor schemas for a behavior may be sequenced. One example of this is the `docking` behavior.[12] Docking is when a robot moves to a specific location and orientation relative to a docking station. This is useful for robots performing materials handling in industry. In order to accept a piece of material to carry, the robot has to be close enough to the correct side of the end of a conveyor and facing the right way. Because docking requires a specific position and orientation, it can't be done with an attraction motor schema. That field would have the robot make a bee-line for the dock, even if it was coming from behind; the robot would stop at the back in the wrong position and orientation. Instead, a *selective attraction* field is appropriate. Here the robot only "feels" the attractive force when it is within a certain angular range of the docking station, as shown in Fig. 4.24.

SELECTIVE ATTRACTION

Unfortunately selective attraction does not cover the case of when the robot approaches from behind or to the side. How does the robot move to an area where the selective attraction field can take effect? One way to do this is to have tangential field, which makes the robot orbit the dock until it gets into the selective attraction area. The combination of the two motor schema produces a very smooth field which funnels the robot into the correct position and orientation, as shown in Fig. 4.25.

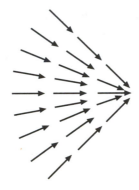

Figure 4.24   Selective attraction field, width of $\pm 45°$.

An interesting aspect of the docking behavior is that the robot is operating in close proximity to the dock. The dock will also release an instance of avoid, which would prevent the robot from getting near the desired position. In this case, the docking behavior would lower the magnitude (gain) of the output vector from an avoid instantiated in the dock area. Essentially, this partially inhibits the avoid behavior in selected regions. Also, the magnitude or gain can define the correct distance: the robot stops where the selective attraction of the dock balances with the repulsion.

The selective and tangential fields are not sufficient in practice, because of the limitations of perception. If the robot can't see the dock, it can't deploy the fields. But an industrial robot might know the relative direction of a dock, much as a bee recalls the direction to its hive. Therefore an attractive force attracts the robot to the vicinity of the dock, and then when the robot sees the dock, it begins the funnel effect into the correct position and orientation, even in the presence of obstacles, as seen in Fig. 4.26.

At least three perceptual schemas are needed for the docking behavior. One is needed to extract the relative direction of the dock for the regular attraction. Another is a perceptual schema capable of recognizing the dock in general, even from behind or the sides, in order to support the tangential field. The third perceptual schema is needed for the selective attention field; it has to be able to respond to the front of the dock and extract the robot's relative distance and orientation.

The docking behavior is now defined as having three perceptual schemas and three motor schemas (they could be grouped into 3 primitive behaviors). A schema-theoretic representation indicates that the behavior has some co-

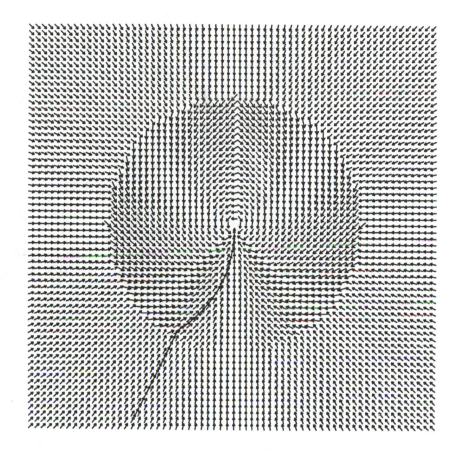

Figure 4.25   Docking potential field showing path of robot entering from slightly off course.

ordinated control program to coordinate and control these schemas. In the case of the docking behavior, a type of finite state machine is a reasonable choice for coordinating the sequence of perceptual and motor schemas. It provides a formal means of representing the sequence, and also reminds the designer to consider state transitions out of the ordinary. For instance, the robot could be moving toward the dock under the tangential plus selective attention fields when a person walks in front. This would occlude the view

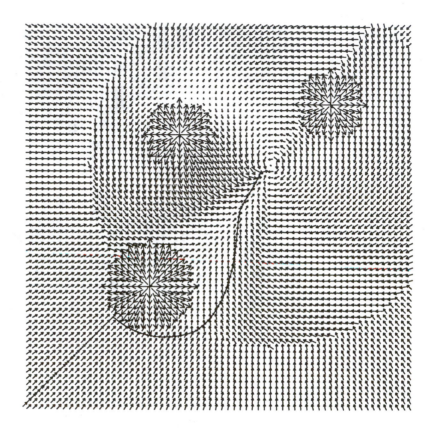

Figure 4.26   Visualization of the docking behavior with obstacles.

of the dock. The general attraction motor schema would then be reactivate, along with the associated perceptual schema to estimate the direction of the dock. This vector would allow the robot to avoid the human in a direction favorable as well as turn back towards the dock and try to re-acquire it.

The docking behavior also illustrates how the sensing capabilities of the robot impact the parameters of the motor schemas. Note that the angular size of the selective attention field would be determined by the angles at which the third perceptual schema could identify the dock. Likewise the radius of the tangential and selective attraction fields is determined by the distance at which the robot can perceive the dock.

4.4.8   Advantages and disadvantages

Potential field styles of architectures have many advantages. The potential field is a continuous representation that is easy to visualize over a large region of space. As a result, it is easier for the designer to visualize the robot's overall behavior. It is also easy to combine fields, and languages such as C++ support making behavioral libraries. The potential fields can be parameterized: their range of influence can be limited and any continuous function can express the change in magnitude over distance (linear, exponential, etc.). Furthermore, a two-dimensional field can usually be extended into a three-dimensional field, and so behaviors developed for 2D will work for 3D.

Building a reactive system with potential fields is not without disadvantages. The most commonly cited problem with potential fields is that multiple fields can sum to a vector with 0 magnitude; this is called the local minima problem. Return to Fig. 4.19, the box canyon. If the robot was being attracted to a point behind the box canyon, the attractive vector would cancel the repulsive vector and the robot would remain stationary because all forces would cancel out. The box canyon problem is an example of reaching a local minima. In practice, there are many elegant solutions to this problem. One of the earliest was to always have a motor schema producing vectors with a small magnitude from random noise. [12] The noise in the motor schema would serve to bump the robot off the local minima.

NAVIGATION
TEMPLATES
Another solution is that of *navigation templates* (NaTs), as implemented by Marc Slack for JPL. The motivation is that the local minima problem most often arises because of interactions between the avoid behavior's repulsive field and other behaviors, such as move-to-goal's attractive field. The minima problem would go away if the avoid potential field was somehow smarter. In NaTs, the avoid behavior receives as input the vector summed from the other behaviors. This vector represents the direction the robot would go if there were no obstacles nearby. For the purposes of this book, this will be referred to as the strategic vector the robot wants to go. If the robot has a strategic vector, that vector gives a clue as to whether an obstacle should be passed on the right or the left. For example, if the robot is crossing a bridge (see Fig. 4.27), it will want to pass to the left of obstacles on its right in order to stay in the middle. Note that the strategic vector defines what is left and what is right.

NaTs implement this simple heuristic in the potential field for RUNAWAY, promoting it to a true AVOID. The repulsion field is now supplemented with a tangential orbit field. The direction of the orbit (clockwise or counter-

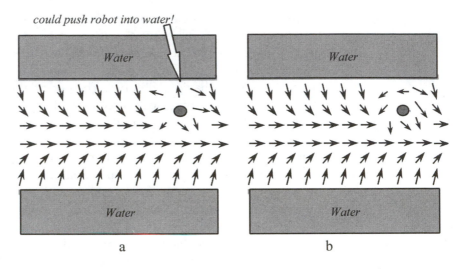

Figure 4.27   Problem with potential fields: a.) an example, and b.) the use of NaTs to eliminate the problem.

clockwise) is determined by whether the robot is to the right or left of the strategic vector. The output of the avoid behavior can be called a tactical vector, because it carries out the strategic goal of the robot in the face of immediate challenges, just as a military general might tell a captain to capture a fort but not specify each footstep.

A more recent solution to the local minima problem has been to express the fields as harmonic functions.[40] Potential fields implemented as harmonic functions are guaranteed not to have a local minima of 0. The disadvantage of this technique is that it is computationally expensive, and has to be implemented on a VLSI chip in order to run in real-time for large areas.

To summarize the major points about potential fields architectures:

- Behaviors are defined as consisting of one or more of both motor and perceptual schemas and/or behaviors. The motor schema(s) for a behavior must be a potential field.

- All behaviors operate concurrently and the output vectors are summed. Behaviors are treated equally and are not layered, although as will be seen in Ch. 5, there may be abstract behaviors which internally sequence behaviors. The coordinated control program is not specified; the designer can use logic, finite state machines, whatever is deemed appropriate. Sequencing is usually controlled by perceived cues or affordances in the environment, which are releasers.

- Although all behaviors are treated equally, behaviors may make varying contributions to the overall action of the robot. A behavior can change the gains on another behavior, thereby reducing or increasing the magnitude of its output. This means that behaviors can inhibit or excite other behaviors, although this is rarely used in practice.

- Perception is usually handled by direct perception or affordances.

- Perception can be shared by multiple behaviors. *A priori* knowledge can be supplied to the perceptual schemas, to emulate a specialized sensor being more receptive to events such as hall boundary spacing.

4.5 Evaluation of Reactive Architectures

As seen by the follow-corridor example, the two styles of architectures are very similar in philosophy and the types of results that they can achieve. Essentially, they are equivalent.

In terms of support for modularity, both decompose the actions and perceptions needed to perform a task into behaviors, although there is some disagreement over the level of abstraction of a behavior. Subsumption seems to favor a composition suited for a hardware implementation, while potential fields methods have nice properties for a software-oriented system.

The niche targetability is also high for both, assuming that the task can be performed by reflexive behaviors. Indeed, the use of direct perception emphasizes that reactive robots are truly constructed to fill a niche.

The issue of whether these architectures show an ease of portability to other domains is more open. Reactive systems are limited to applications which can be accomplished with reflexive behaviors. They cannot be transferred to domains where the robot needs to do planning, reasoning about resource allocation, etc. (this led to the Hybrid Paradigm to be described in Ch. 7). In practice, very few of the subsumption levels can be ported to new applications of navigating in an environment without some changes. The different applications create layers which need to subsume the lower layers differently. The potential fields methodology performs a bit better in that the designer can create a library of behaviors and schemas to choose from, with no implicit reliance on a lower layer.

Neither architecture presents systems which could be called genuinely robust. The layering of subsumption imparts some graceful degradation if an upper level is destroyed, but it has no mechanisms to notice that a degradation has occurred. The finite state mechanisms in the docking behavior show some resilience, but again, only for situations which can be anticipated and incorporated into the state diagram. As with animals, a reactive robot will also do something consistent with its perception of the world, but not always the right thing.

4.6   Summary

Under the Reactive Paradigm, systems are composed of behaviors, which tightly couple sensing and acting. The organization of the Reactive Paradigm is **SENSE-ACT** or S-A, with no **PLAN** component. Sensing in the Reactive Paradigm is local to each behavior, or behavior-specific. Each behavior has direct access to one or more sensors independently of the other behaviors. A behavior may create and use its own internal world representation, but there is no global world model as with the Hierarchical Paradigm. As a result, reactive systems are the fastest executing robotic systems possible.

There are four major characteristics of robots constructed under the Reactive Paradigm. Behaviors serve as the basic building blocks for robot actions, even though different designers may have different definitions of what a behavior entails. As a consequence of using behaviors, the overall behavior of the robot is emergent. Only local, behavior-specific sensing is permitted. The use of explicit representations in perceptual processing, even locally, is avoided in most reactive systems. Explicit representations of the world are often referred to as maintaining the state of the world internally, or internal state. Instead, reactive behaviors rely on the world to maintain state (as exemplified by the gripper controlling whether the robot was looking for soda cans or for the recycling bin). Animal models are often cited as a basis for a behavior or the architecture. Behaviors and groups of behaviors which were inspired by or simulate animal behavior are often considered desirable and more interesting than hacks. Finally, reactive systems exhibit good software engineering principles due to the "programming by behavior" approach. Reactive systems are inherently modular from a software design perspective. Behaviors can be tested independently, since the overall behavior is emergent. More complex behaviors may be constructed from primitive behaviors, or from mixing and matching perceptual and motor components. This supports good software engineering practices, especially low coupling and high cohesion.

The subsumption architecture is a popular reactive system. Behaviors are purely reflexive and may not use memory. Behaviors are arranged in layers of competence, where the lower levels encapsulate more general abilities. The coordination of layers is done by higher layers, which have more specific goal-directed behaviors, subsuming lower layers. Behaviors within a layer are coordinated by finite state automata, and can be readily implemented in hardware.

Potential fields methodologies are another popular reactive system. Behaviors in potential field systems must be implemented as potential fields. All active behaviors contribute a vector; the vectors are summed to produce a resultant direction and magnitude for travel. Pfields provide a continuous representation, which is easier to visualize than rule encoding, and are continuous. The fields can be readily implemented in software, and parameterized for flexibility and reuse. The vector summation effect formalizes how to combine behaviors, eliminating issues in how to design behaviors for subsumption. The fields are often extensible to three dimensions, adding to the re-usability and portability. In the example in this chapter, behaviors using potential fields were able to encapsulate several layers in subsumption into a set of concurrent peer behaviors with no layers. Ch. 5 will give examples of how to sequence, or assemble, behaviors into more abstract behaviors.

Despite the differences, subsumption and potential fields appear to be largely equivalent in practice. Both provide support for modularity and niche targetability. The ease of portability to other domains is relative to the complexity of the changes in the task and environment. Neither style of architecture explicitly addresses robustness, although in theory, if only a higher layer of a subsumption system failed, the lower layers should ensure robot survivability.

4.7 Exercises

Exercise 4.1

Define the reactive paradigm in terms of a.) the SENSE, PLAN, and ACT primitives, and b.) sensing organization.

Exercise 4.2

Describe the difference between robot control using a horizontal decomposition and a vertical decomposition.

Exercise 4.3

List the characteristics of a reactive robotic system.

Exercise 4.4

Describe the differences between two dominant methods for combining behaviors in a reactive architecture, subsumption and potential field summation.

Exercise 4.5

Evaluate the subsumption architecture in terms of: support for modularity, niche targetability, ease of portability to other domains, robustness.

Exercise 4.6

Evaluate potential field methodologies in terms of: support for modularity, niche targetability, ease of portability to other domains, robustness.

Exercise 4.7

What is the difference between the way the term "internal state" was used in ethology and the way "internal state" means in behavioral robotics?

Exercise 4.8

Diagram Level 2 in the subsumption example in terms of behaviors.

Exercise 4.9

When would an exponentially increasing repulsive field be preferable over a linear increasing repulsive field?

Exercise 4.10

Suppose you were to construct a library of potential fields of the five primitives. What parameters would you include as arguments to allow a user to customize the fields?

Exercise 4.11

Use a spreadsheet, such as Microsoft Excel, to compute various magnitude profiles.

Exercise 4.12

Return to Fig. 4.17. Plot the path of the robot if it started in the upper left corner.

Exercise 4.13

Consider the Khepera robot and its IR sensors with the RUNAWAY behavior instantiated for each sensor as in the example in Fig. 4.19. What happens if an IR breaks and always returns a range reading of N, meaning an obstacle is N cm away? What will be the emergent behavior? and so on. Can a reactive robot notice that it is malfunctioning? Why or why not?

Exercise 4.14

How does the Reactive Paradigm handle the frame problem and the open world assumption?

Exercise 4.15

An alternative RUNAWAY behavior is to turn 90° (either left or right, depending on whether its "left handed" or "right handed" robot) rather than 180°. Can this be represented by a potential field?

Exercise 4.16

Using rules, or if-then statements, is a method for representing and combining programming units which are often called behaviors; for example "if OBSTACLE-ON-LEFT and HEADING-RIGHT, then IGNORE." Can the layers in subsumption for hall-following be written as a series of rules? Can the potential fields? Are rules equivalent to these two methods? Do you think rules are more amenable to good software engineering practices?

Exercise 4.17

Some researchers consider random wandering as a primitive potential field. Recall that random wandering causes the robot to periodically swap to a new vector with a random direction and magnitude. How can a wander field be represented? Does the array of the field represent a physical area or time? Unlike regular potential fields, the vector is computed as a function of time, every n minutes, rather than on the robot's relationship to something perceivable in the world.

Exercise 4.18   [*Programming*]

Design and implement potential fields:

a. Construct a potential field to represent a "move through door" behavior from primitive potential fields. Why won't a simple attractive field work? ANS: if the robot is coming from a side, it will graze the door frame because the robot is not a point, it has width and limited turning radius.

b. What happens if a person is exiting the door as the robot enters? Design an appropriate "avoid" potential field, and show the emergent potential field when AVOID and MOVE-THRU-DOOR are activated at the same time.

c. Simulate this using the Khepera simulator for Unix systems found at: http://www.k-team.com.

d. Run this on a real khepera.

Exercise 4.19   [*Programming*]

Program two versions of a phototropic behavior using the Khepera simulator. Both versions should use the same motor schema, an attractive field, but different perceptual schemas. In one version, the perceptual schema processes light from a single sensor and the behavior is instantiated 8 times. In the second version, the perceptual schema processes light from all sensors and returns the brightest. Set up five interesting "worlds" in the simulator with different placements of lights. Compare the emergent behavior for each world.

Exercise 4.20   [*Digital Circuits*]

For readers with a background in digital circuits, build one or more of the simple creatures in Flynn and Jones' *Mobile Robots: Inspiration to Implementation*[76] using a Rug Warrior kit.

4.8   End Notes

For a roboticist's bookshelf.

The subsumption architecture favors a hardware implementation using inexpensive hardware. Part of the rapid acceptance of the reactive paradigm and the subsumption architecture was due to *Mobile Robots: Inspiration to Perspiration*[76] by students in the MIT AI Lab. The straightforward circuits allowed any hobbyist to produce intelligent robots. On a more theoretical note, Rodney Brooks has collected his seminal papers on subsumption into a volume entitled *Cambrian Intelligence*,[28] a nice play on the period in evolution and on Brooks' location in Cambridge, Massachusetts.

About Rodney Brooks.

Rodney Brooks is perhaps the best known roboticist, with his insect-like (Genghis, Attila, etc.) and anthropomorphic robots (Cog, Kismet) frequently appearing in the media. Brooks was one of four "obsessed" people profiled in a documentary by Errol Morris, *Fast, Cheap, and Out of Control*. The documentary is well worth watching, and there are some gorgeous shots of robots walking over broken glass giving the terrain a luminous quality. Brooks' reactive philosophy appears in an episode of *The X-Files* on robotic cockroaches called "War of the Corophages." The roboticist from the Massachusetts Institute of Robotics is a combination of Steven Hawking (the character is disabled), Joe Engleberger (the bow tie), Marvin Minsky (stern, professorial manner), and Rodney Brooks (the character says almost direct quotes from Brooks' interviews in science magazines).

About the "s" in subsumption.

Rodney Brooks' 1986 paper never officially named his architecture. Most papers refer to it as "Subsumption," sometimes without the capital "s" and sometimes with a capital.

Building a robot with petty cash.

Erann Gat and his then boss at NASA's Jet Propulsion Laboratory, David Miller, cite another advantage of behavioral robotics: you can build a mobile robot very cheaply. In the late 1980's, Miller's group wanted to build a small reactive robot to compare with the traditional Hierarchical vehicles currently used for research and to get experience with subsumption. Request after request was turned down. But they realized that the individual electronics were cheap. So they bought the parts for their small mobile robot in batches of $50 or less, which could be reimbursed out of petty cash. The resulting robot was about the size and capability of a Lego Mindstorms kit with a total cost around $500.

Robot name trivia.
The MIT robots used in the early days of subsumption were all named for conquerors: Attila, Genghis, etc. Ron Arkin did his initial work on potential fields methodology while pursuing his PhD at the University of Massachusetts. The robot he used was a Denning MRV called HARV (pronounced "Harvey"). HARV stood for Hardly Autonomous Robot Vehicle morphing into Harmful Autonomous Robot Vehicle, when military research sponsors were present. HARV was also considered a short version of "Harvey Wallbanger," both a description of the robot's emergent behavior and the name of a cocktail.

5 *Designing a Reactive Implementation*

Chapter objectives:

- Use schema theory to design and program behaviors using object-oriented programming principles.

- Design a complete behavioral system, including coordinating and controlling multiple concurrent behaviors.

- For a given behavioral system, draw a *behavioral table* specifying the releasers, perceptual schemas, and motor schemas for each behavior.

- Describe the two methods for assembling and coordinating primitive behaviors within an *abstract behavior: finite state automata* and *scripts*. Be able to represent a sequence of behaviors with a *state diagram* or with a pseudocode *script*.

5.1   Overview

By this point, the sheer simplicity and elegance of reactive behaviors tend to incite people to start designing and implementing their own robots. Kits such as Lego Mindstorms and the Rug Warrior permit the rapid coupling of sensors and actuators, enabling users to build reactive behaviors. However, the new issues are how to program more intelligence into the software and how to exploit better sensors than come with kits. Unfortunately, good intentions in robot programming are often frustrated by two deficits. First, designing behaviors tends to be an art, not a science. Novice roboticists often are uncertain as to how to even start the design process, much less how to know when they've got a reasonable system. The second deficit is more subtle. Once the designer has a few well-designed and tested behaviors, how are they integrated into a system? The Reactive movement and early work described in Ch. 4 was characterized by robots running a very small set of behaviors which were combined internally to produce an overall *emergent behavior*. The key components of a reactive architecture were shown to be the behaviors plus the mechanism for merging the output of the concurrent behaviors.

EMERGENT BEHAVIOR

SERIES OF BEHAVIORS

However, many applications are best thought of as a *series of behaviors*, each operating in a recognizable sequence. One of the first popular applications that many roboticists looked at was picking up and disposing of an empty soft drink can. This involved search for a can, move toward the can when it is found, pick up the can, search for the recycle bin, move toward the recycle bin, drop the can.[39;129;66] It's counterintuitive to think of these behaviors as being concurrent or merged. (There is certainly the possibility of concurrency, for example avoiding obstacles while moving to the soda can or recycle bin.) Therefore, new techniques had to be introduced for controlling sequences of behaviors. Most of these techniques are conceptually the equivalent of constructing a macro behavior, where the schema structure is used recursively to simplify programming the control program.

This chapter attempts to aid the novice designer in constructing a reactive robot system by addressing each of these two deficits. First, an object-oriented programming approach to designing behaviors is introduced. This approach is based on schema theory, which was introduced in Ch. 3. The "art" of design is presented in a flow chart following the waterfall method of software engineering, along with a case study of a winning entry in the 1994 International Association for Unmanned Systems' Unmanned Ground Robotics Competition. The case study emphasizes the importance of establishing the ecological niche of a reactive robot. Second, two techniques for managing sequences of behaviors are introduced: *finite-state automata* and *scripts*. As could be expected from the material presented in Ch. 3, both of these techniques will look very similar to the Innate Releasing Mechanisms from Tinbergen and Lorenz. Finally, the chapter shows how these techniques were applied to entries in the "Pick Up the Trash" events of the 1994 AAAI and 1995 IJCAI Mobile Robot Competitions. The focus of these examples is how the logic for coordinating a sequence of behaviors is developed, represented, and implemented. The use of schemas to "factor out" and program a small set of generic behaviors rather than designing a large set of specialized behaviors is emphasized throughout the chapter.

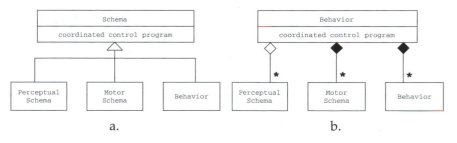

Figure 5.1 Classes: a.) schema and b.) behavior.

5.2   Behaviors as Objects in OOP

Although Object-Oriented Programming (OOP) had not become popular during the time that the Reactive Paradigm was developed, it is useful to cast behaviors in OOP terms. Schema theory is well suited for transferring theoretical concepts to OOP. Furthermore, schema theory will be used as a bridge between concepts in biological intelligence and robotics, enabling a practical implementation of reactivity exploiting innate releasing mechanisms and affordances.

Recall from software engineering that an object consists of data and methods, also called attributes and operations. As noted in Ch. 3, schemas contain specific knowledge and local data structures and other schemas. Fig. 5.1 shows how a schema might be defined. Following Arbib,[6] a schema as a programming object will be a class. The class will have an optional method called a *coordinated control program*. The coordinated control program is a function that coordinates any methods or schemas in the derived class.

COORDINATED
CONTROL PROGRAM

Three classes are derived from the Schema Class: Behavior, Motor Schema, and Perceptual Schema. Behaviors are composed of at least one Perceptual Schema and one Motor Schema; these schemas act as the methods for the Behavior class. A Perceptual Schema has at least one method; that method takes sensor input and transforms it into a data structure called a *percept*. A Motor Schema has at least one method which transforms the percept into a vector or other form of representing an action. Since schemas are independent, the Behavior object acts as a place holder or local storage area for the percept. The Perceptual Schema is linked to the sensor(s), while the Motor Schema is linked to the robot's actuators. The sensors and actuators can be represented by their own software classes if needed; this is useful when working with software drivers for the hardware.

PERCEPT

Using the Unified Modeling Language representation,[55] the Schema and Behavior classes look like Fig. 5.1. The OOP organization allows a behavior to be composed of multiple perceptual schema and motor schema and even behaviors. Another way of stating this is that the definition of a behavior is recursive. Why is it useful to have multiple perceptual schema and motor schema? In some cases, it might be helpful to have two perceptual schema, one for say daylight conditions using a TV camera and one for nighttime using infra-red. Sec. 5.2.2 provides a more detailed example of why multiple schemas in a behavior can be helpful.

PRIMITIVE BEHAVIOR   Recall that a *primitive behavior* is composed of only one perceptual schema and one motor schema; there is no need to have any coordinated control program. Primitive behaviors can be thought of being *monolithic*, where they do only one ("mono") thing. Because they are usually a simple mapping from stimulus to response, they are often programmed as a single method, not composed from multiple methods or objects. The concept of Perceptual and Motor Schema is there, but hidden for the sake of implementation.

ABSTRACT BEHAVIORS   Behaviors which are assembled from other behaviors or have multiple perceptual schema and motor schema will be referred to as *abstract behaviors*, because they are farther removed from the sensors and actuators than a primitive behavior. The use of the term "abstract behavior" should not be confused with an abstract class in OOP.

5.2.1 Example: A primitive move-to-goal behavior

This example shows how a primitive behavior can be designed using OOP principles. In 1994, the annual AAAI Mobile Robot Competitions had a "Pick Up the Trash" event, which was repeated in 1995 at the joint AAAI-IJCAI Mobile Robot Competition.[129;66] The basic idea was for a robot to be placed in an empty arena about the size of an office. The arena would have Coca-Cola cans and white Styrofoam cups placed at random locations. In two of the four corners, there would be a blue recycling bin; in the other two, a different colored trash bin. The robot who picked up the most trash and placed them in the correct bin in the allotted time was the winner. In most years, the strategy was to find and recycle the Coca-Cola cans first, because it was easier for the robot's vision processing algorithms to perceive red and blue.

One of the most basic behaviors needed for picking up a red soda can and moving to a blue bin is `move_to_goal`. When the robot sees a red can, it must move to it. When it has a can, it must find and then move to a blue bin.

It is better software engineering to write a general move to goal behavior, where only what is the goal—a red region or a blue region—varies. The goal for the current instance can be passed in at instantiation through the object constructor.

Writing a single generic behavior for `move_to_goal(color)` is more desirable than writing a `move_to_red` and a `move_to_blue` behaviors. From a software engineering perspective, writing two behaviors which do the same thing is an opportunity to introduce a programming bug in one of them and not notice because they are supposed to be the same. Generic behaviors also share the same philosophy as factoring in mathematics. Consider simplifying the equation $45x^2 + 90x + 45$. The first step is to factor out any common term to simplify the equation. In this case, 45 can be factored and the equation rewritten as $45(x + 1)^2$. The color of the goal, red or blue, was like the common coefficient of 45; it is important, but tends to hide that the key to the solution was the move-to-goal part, or x.

Modular, generic code can be handled nicely by schemas as shown in Fig. 5.2. The behavior `move_to_goal` would consist of a perceptual schema, which will be called `extract-goal`, and a motor schema, which uses an attractive field called `pfields.attraction`. `extract-goal` uses the affordance of color to extract where the goal is in the image, and then computes the angle to the center of the colored region and the size of the region. This

AFFORDANCE information forms the percept of the goal; the affordance of the Coke can is the color, while the information extracted from the perception is the angle and size. The attraction motor schema takes that percept and is responsible for using it to turn the robot to center on the region and move forward. It can do this easily by using an attractive field, where the larger the region, the stronger the attraction and the faster the robot moves.

The `move_to_goal` behavior can be implemented as a primitive behavior, where `goal_color` is a numerical means of representing different colors such as `red` and `blue`:

`move_to_goal(goal_color):`

Object	Behavioral Analog	Identifier
Data	percept	`goal_angle`
		`goal_strength`
Methods	`perceptual_schema`	`extract_goal(goal_color)`
	`motor_schema`	`pfields.attraction(goal_angle, goal_strength)`

The above table implies some very important points about programming with behaviors:

- The behavior is the "glue" between the perceptual and motor schemas. The schemas don't communicate in the sense that both are independent entities; the perceptual schema doesn't know that the motor schema exists. Instead, *the behavior puts the percept created by the perceptual schema in a local place where the motor schema can get it.*

- Behaviors can (and should) use libraries of schemas. The pfields suffix on the `pfields.attraction()` meant that attraction was a method within another object identified as pfields. The five primitive potential fields could be encapsulated into one class called `PFields`, which any motor schema could use. `PFields` would serve as a library. Once the potential fields in `PFields` were written and debugged, the designer doesn't ever have to code them again.

- Behaviors can be reused if written properly. In this example, the move to goal behavior was written to accept a structure (or object) defining a color and then moving to a region of that color. This means the behavior can be used with both red Coke cans and blue trash cans.

5.2.2   Example: An abstract follow-corridor behavior

The move to goal example used a single motor schema with a single perceptual schema. This example shows how a potential fields methodology can be implemented using schemas. In the corridor following example in Ch. 4, the `follow_corridor` potential field consisted of two primitive fields: two instances of `perpendicular` to the walls and one `uniform` parallel to the walls. The `follow_corridor` field could be implemented in schemas in at least two different ways as shown in Fig. 5.2. In one way, each of the primitive fields would be a separate motor schema. The follow corridor motor schema would consist of the three primitives and the coordinated control program. The coordinated control program would be the function that knows that one field is perpendicular from the left wall going towards the center of the corridor, which way is forward, etc. They were summed together by the coordinated control program in the behavioral schema to produce a single output vector. The perceptual schema for the follow corridor would examine the sonar polar plot and extract the relative location of the corridor walls. The perceptual schema would return the distance to the left wall and the right wall.

Another way to have achieved the same overall behavior is to have `fol-low_wall` composed of two instances of a follow wall behavior: `follow_-`

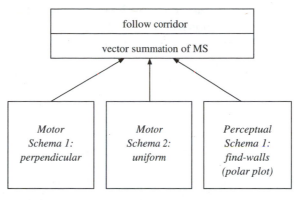

a.

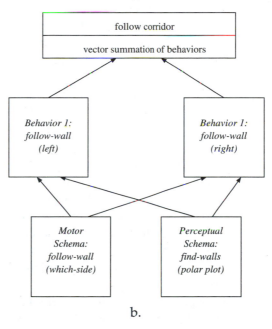

b.

Figure **5.2** Class diagrams for two different implementations of `follow_corridor`: a.) use of primitive fields, and b.) reuse of fields grouped into a `follow_wall` behavior.

wall (left) and follow_wall(right). Each instance of follow wall would receive the sonar polar plot and extract the relevant wall. The associated class diagram is shown on the right in Fig. 5.2.

In both implementations, the motor schema schemas ran continuously and the vectors were summed internally in order to produce a single output vector. Since there were multiple motor schemas, the coordinated control program for follow-corridor is not null as it was for move-to-goal. The vector summation and the concurrency form the conceptual coordinated control program in this case.

5.2.3   Where do releasers go in OOP?

TWO PURPOSES OF
PERCEPTION

The previous examples showed how behaviors can be implemented using OOP constructs, such as classes. Another important part of a behavior is how it is activated. As was discussed in Ch. 3, perception serves two purposes: *to release a behavior* and *to guide it*. Perceptual schemas are clearly used for guiding the behavior, either moving toward a distinctively colored goal or following a wall. But what object or construct contains the releaser and how is it "attached" to the behavior?

The answer to the first part of the question is that *the releaser is itself a perceptual schema*. It can execute independently of whatever else is happening with the robot; it is a perceptual schema not bound to a motor schema. For example, the robot is looking for red Coke cans with the extract_color perceptual schema. One way to implement this is when the schema sees red, it can signal the main program that there is red. The main program can determine that that is the releaser for the move to goal behavior has been satisfied, and instantiate move_to_goal with goal=red. move_to_goal can instantiate a new instance of extract_color or the main program can pass a pointer to the currently active extract_color. Regardless, move_to_goal has to instantiate pfield.attraction, since the attraction motor schema wouldn't be running. In this approach, the main program is responsible for calling the right objects at the right time; the releaser is attached to the behavior by the designer with little formal mechanisms to make sure it is correct. This is awkward to program.

Another, more common programming approach is to have the releaser be part of the behavior: the single perceptual schema does double duty. This programming style requires a coordinated control program. The behavior is always active, but if the releaser isn't satisfied, the coordinated control program short-circuits processing. The behavior returns an identity function, in the case of potential fields, a vector of (0.0,0.0), which is the same as if the behavior wasn't active at all. This style of programming can tie up some resources, but is generally a simple, effective way to program. Fig. 5.2 shows the two approaches.

Either way, once the robot saw red, the observable aspect of move to goal (e.g., moving directly toward the goal) would commence. The extract goal schema would update the percept data (relative angle of the goal and size of red region) every time it was called. This percept would then be available to the motor schema, which would in turn produce a vector.

As will be covered in Sec. 5.5, the releaser must be designed to support the correct sequence. Depending where the robot was in the sequence of activities, the robot uses move to goal to move to a red Coke can or a blue recycling bin. Otherwise, the robot could pursue a red Coke can and a blue recycling bin simultaneously. There is nothing in the OOP design to prevent that from happening—in fact, OOP makes it easy. In this situation, there would be two move to goal objects, one instantiated with goal of "red" and the other with goal of "blue." Notice that the move to goal behavior can use any perceptual schema that can produce a goal angle and goal strength. If the robot needed to move to a bright light (phototropism), only the perceptual schema would need to be changed. This is an example of software reusability.

5.3   Steps in Designing a Reactive Behavioral System

Fig. 5.3 shows the steps in designing a reactive behavioral system, which are taken from *Behavior-Based Robotics*[10] and a case study by Murphy.[98] This section will first give a broad discussion of the design process, then work through each step using the winning approach taken in the 1994 Unmanned Ground Vehicle Competition.

The methodology in Fig. 5.3 assumes that a designer is given a task for the robot to do, and a robot platform (or some constraints, if only budgetary). The goal is to design a robot as a situated agent. Therefore, the first three steps serve to remind the designer to specify the *ecological niche* of the robot.

The fourth step begins the iterative process of identifying and refining the set of behaviors for the task. It asks the question: *what does the robot do?* Defining the ecological niche defines constraints and opportunities but doesn't necessarily introduce major insights into the *situatedness* of the robot: *how it acts and reacts to the range of variability in its ecological niche.* This step is where a novice begins to recognize that designing behaviors is an art. Sometimes,

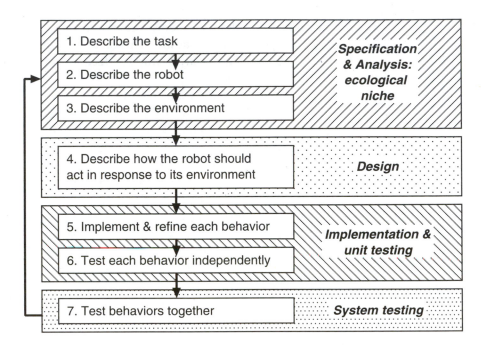

Figure 5.3   Steps in designing a reactive behavioral system, following basic software engineering phases.

a behavioral decomposition appears obvious to a roboticist after thinking about the ecological niche. For example, in the 1994 and 1995 Pick Up the Trash events, most of the teams used a partitioning along the lines of: random search until see red, move to red, pick up can, random search until see blue, move to blue, drop can.

Roboticists often attempt to find an analogy to a task accomplished by an animal or a human, then study the ethological or cognitive literature for more information on how the animal accomplishes that class of tasks. This, of course, sidesteps the question of how the roboticist knew what class of animal tasks the robot task is similar to, as well as implies a very linear thinking process by roboticists. In practice, roboticists who use biological and cognitive insights tend to read and try to stay current with the ethological literature so that they can notice a connection later on.

Steps 5-7 are less abstract. Once the candidate set of behaviors has been proposed, the designer works on designing each individual behavior, specifying its motor and perceptual schemas. This is where the designer has to write the algorithm for finding red blobs in a camera image for the random search until find red and move to red behaviors. The designer usually programs each schema independently, then integrates them into a behavior and tests the behavior thoroughly in isolation before integrating all behaviors. This style of testing is consistent with good software engineering principles, and emphasizes the practical advantages of the Reactive Paradigm.

The list of steps in implementing a reactive system can be misleading. Despite the feedback arrows, the overall process in Fig. 5.3 appears to be linear. In practice, it is iterative. For example, a supposed affordance may be impossible to detect reliably with the robot's sensors, or an affordance which was missed in the first analysis of the ecological niche suddenly surfaces. The single source of iteration may be testing all the behaviors together in the "real world." Software that worked perfectly in simulation often fails in the real world.

5.4 Case Study: Unmanned Ground Robotics Competition

This case study is based on the approach taken by the Colorado School of Mines team to the 1994 Unmanned Ground Robotics Competition.[98] The objective of the competition was to have a small unmanned vehicle (no larger than a golf cart) autonomously navigate around an outdoor course of white lines painted on grass. The CSM entry won first place and a $5,000 prize. Each design step is first presented in boldface and discussed. What was actually done by the CSM team follows in italics. This case study illustrates the effective use of only a few behaviors, incrementally developed, and the use of affordances combined with an understanding of the ecological niche. It also highlights how even a simple design may take many iterations to be workable.

Step 1: Describe the task. The purpose of this step is to specify what the robot has to do to be successful.

The task was for the robot vehicle to follow a path with hair pin turns, stationary obstacles in the path, and a sand pit. The robot which went the furthest without going completely out of bounds was the winner, unless two or more robots went the same distance or completed the course, then the winner was whoever went the fastest. The maximum speed was 5 mph. If the robot went partially out of bounds (one wheel or a portion of a tread remained inside), a distance penalty was subtracted. If the robot hit an obstacle enough to move it, another distance penalty was levied. Therefore, the competition favored an entry which could complete the course without accruing any penalties over a faster entry which might drift over a boundary line or bump an obstacle. Entrants were given three runs on one day and two days to prepare and test on a track near the course; the times of the heats were determined by lottery.

Step 2: Describe the robot. The purpose of this step is to determine the basic physical abilities of the robot and any limitations. In theory, it might be expected that the designer would have control over the robot itself, what it could do, what sensors it carries, etc. In practice, most roboticists work with either a commercially available research platform which may have limitations on what hardware and sensors can be added, or with relatively inexpensive kit type of platform where weight and power restrictions may impact what it can reasonably do. Therefore, the designer is usually handed some fixed constraints on the robot platform which will impact the design.

In this case, the competition stated that the robot vehicle had to have a footprint of at least 3ft by 3.5ft but no bigger than a golf cart. Furthermore, the robot had to carry its own power supply and do all computing on-board (no radio communication with an off-board processor was permitted), plus carry a 20 pound payload.

The CSM team was donated the materials for a robot platform by Omnitech Robotics, Inc. Fig. 5.4 shows Omnibot. The vehicle base was a Power Wheels battery powered children's jeep purchased from a toy store. The base met the minimum footprint exactly. It used Ackerman (car-like) steering, with a drive motor powering the wheels in the rear and a steering motor in the front. The vehicle had a 22° turning angle. The on-board computing was handled by a 33MHz 486 PC using Omnitech CANAMP motor controllers. The sensor suite consisted of three devices: shaft encoders on the drive and steer motors for dead reckoning, a video camcorder mounted on a mast near the center of the vehicle and a panning sonar mounted below the grille on the front. The output from the video camcorder was digitized by a black and white framegrabber. The sonar was a Polaroid lab grade ultrasonic transducer. The panning device could sweep 180°. All coding was done in C++.

Due to the motors and gearing, Omnibot could only go 1.5 mph. This limitation meant that it could only win if it went farther with less penalty points than any other entry. It also meant that the steering had to have at least a 150ms update rate or the robot could veer out of bounds without ever perceiving it was going off course. The black and white framegrabber eliminated the use of color. Worse yet, the update rate of the framegrabber was almost 150ms; any vision processing algorithm would have to be very fast or else the robot would be moving faster than it could react. The reflections from uneven grass reduced the standard range of the sonar from 25.5 ft to about 10 ft.

Figure 5.4   Omnibot, a mobile robot built from a Power Wheels battery-powered toy jeep by students and Omnitech Robotics, Inc.

Step 3: Describe the Environment. This step is critical for two reasons. First, it is a key factor in determining the situatedness of the robot. Second, it identifies perceptual opportunities for the behaviors, both in how a perceptual event will instantiate a new behavior, and in how the perceptual schema for a behavior will function. Recall from Chapter 4 that the Reactive Paradigm favors direct perception or affordance-based perception because it has a rapid execution time and involves no reasoning or memory.

The course was laid out on a grassy field with gentle slopes. The course consisted of a 10 foot wide lane marked in US Department of Transportation white paint, roughly in the shape of a kidney (see Fig. 5.5). The exact length of the course and layout of obstacles of the course were not known until the day of the competition, and teams were not permitted to measure the course or run trials on it. Obstacles were all stationary and consisted of bales of hay wrapped in either white or red plastic. The bales were approximately 2 ft by 4 ft and never extended more than 3 feet into the lane. The sonar was able to reliably detect the plastic covered bales at most angles of approach at 8 feet away. The vehicles were scheduled to run between 9am and 5pm on May 22, regardless of weather or cloud cover. In addition to the visual challenges of changing lighting due to clouds, the bales introduced shadows on the white lines between 9–11am and 3–5pm. The sand pit was only 4 feet long and placed on a straight segment of the course.

The analysis of the environment offered a simplification of the task. The placing of the obstacles left a 4 ft wide open area. Since Omnibot was only 3 ft wide, the course could be treated as having no obstacles if the robot could stay in the center of the lane

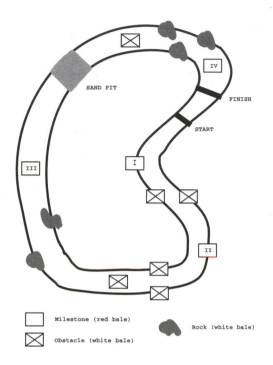

Figure 5.5   The course for the 1994 Ground Robotics Competition.

with a 0.5 ft tolerance. This eliminated the need for an avoid obstacle behavior.

The analysis of the environment also identified an affordance for controlling the robot. The only object of interest to the robot was the white line, which should have a high contrast to the green (dark gray) grass. But the exact lighting value of the white line changed with the weather. However, if the camera was pointed directly at one line, instead of trying to see both lines, the majority of the brightest points in the image would belong to the line (this is a reduction in the signal to noise ratio because more of the image has the line in it). Some of the bright points would be due to reflections, but these were assumed to be randomly distributed. Therefore, if the robot tried to keep the centroid of the white points in the center of the image, it would stay in the center of the lane.

Step 4: Describe how the robot should act in response to its environment. The purpose of this step is to identify the set of one or more candidate primitive behaviors; these candidates will be refined or eliminated later. As the designer describes how the robot should act, behaviors usually become apparent. It should be emphasized that the point of this step is to concentrate on what the robot should do, not how it will do it, although often the designer sees both the what and the how at the same time.

In the case of the CSM entry, only one behavior was initially proposed: follow-line. The perceptual schema would use the white line to compute the difference between where the centroid of the white line was versus where it should be, while the motor schema would convert that to a command to the steer motor.

BEHAVIOR TABLE

In terms of expressing the behaviors for a task, it is often advantageous to construct a *behavior table* as one way of at least getting all the behaviors on a single sheet of paper. The releaser for each behavior is helpful for confirming that the behaviors will operate correctly without conflict (remember, accidently programming the robotic equivalent of male sticklebacks from Ch. 3 is undesirable). It is often useful for the designer to classify the motor schema and the percept. For example, consider what happens if an implementation has a purely reflexive move-to-goal motor schema and an avoid-obstacle behavior. What happens if the avoid-obstacle behavior causes the robot to lose perception of the goal? Oops, the perceptual schema returns no goal and the move-to-goal behavior is terminated! Probably what the designer assumed was that the behavior would be a fixed-action pattern and thereby the robot would persist in moving toward the last known location of the goal.

Behavior Table

Releaser	Behavior	Motor Schema	Percept	Perceptual Schema
always on	follow-line()	stay-on-path(c_x)	c_x	compute-centroid(image,white)

As seen from the behavior table above, the CSM team initially proposed only one behavior, follow-line. The follow-line behavior consisted of a motor schema, stay-on-path(centroid), which was reflexive (stimulus-response) and taxis (it oriented the robot relative to the stimulus). The perceptual schema, compute-centroid(image,white), extracted an affordance of the centroid of white from the image as being the line. Only the x component, or horizontal location, of the centroid was used, c_x.

Step 5: Refine each behavior. By this point, the designer has an overall idea of the organization of the reactive system and what the activities are. This step concentrates on the design of each individual behavior. As the designer constructs the underlying algorithms for the motor and perceptual schemas, it is important to be sure to consider both the normal range of environmental conditions the robot is expected to operate in (e.g., the steady-state case) and when the behavior will fail.

The follow-line behavior was based on the analysis that the only white things in the environment were lines and plastic covered bales of hay. While this was a good assumption, it led to a humorous event during the second heat of the competition. As the robot was following the white line down the course, one of the judges stepped into view of the camera. Unfortunately, the judge was wearing white shoes, and Omnibot turned in a direction roughly in-between the shoes and the line. The CSM team captain, Floyd Henning, realized what was happening and shouted at the judge to move. Too late, the robot's front wheels had already crossed over the line; its camera was now facing outside the line and there was no chance of recovering. Suddenly, right before the leftmost rear wheel was about to leave the boundary, Omnibot straightened up and began going parallel to the line! The path turned to the right, Omnibot crossed back into the path and re-acquired the line. She eventually went out of bounds on a hair pin further down the course. The crowd went wild, while the CSM team exchanged confused looks.

What happened to make Omnibot drive back in bounds? The perceptual schema was using the 20% brightest pixels in the image for computing the centroid. When it wandered onto the grass, Omnibot went straight because the reflection on the grass was largely random and the positions cancelled out, leaving the centroid always in the center of the image. The groundskeepers had cut the grass only in the areas where the path was to be. Next to the path was a parallel swatch of uncut grass loaded with dandelion seed puffs. The row of white puffs acted just as a white line, and once in viewing range Omnibot obligingly corrected her course to be parallel to them. It was sheer luck that the path curved so that when the dandelions ran out, Omnibot continued straight and intersected with the path. While Omnibot wasn't programmed to react to shoes and dandelions, it did react correctly considering its ecological niche.

Step 6: Test each behavior independently. As in any software engineering project, modules or behaviors are tested individually. Ideally, testing occurs in simulation prior to testing on the robot in its environment. Many commercially available robots such as Khepera and Nomads come with impressive simulators. However, it is important to remember that simulators often only model the mechanics of the robot, not the perceptual abilities. This is useful for confirming that the motor schema code is correct, but often the only way to verify the perceptual schema is to try it in the real world.

Step 7: Test with other behaviors. The final step of designing and implementing a reactive system is to perform integration testing, where the behaviors are combined. This also includes testing the behaviors in the actual environment.

Although the follow-line behavior worked well when tested with white lines, it did not perform well when tested with white lines and obstacles. The obstacles, shiny plastic-wrapped bales of hay sitting near the line, were often brighter than the grass. Therefore the perceptual schema for follow-line included pixels belonging to the bale in computing the centroid. Invariably the robot became fixated on the bale, and followed its perimeter rather than the line. The bales were referred to as "visual distractions."

Fortunately, the bales were relatively small. If the robot could "close its eyes" for about two seconds and just drive in a straight line, it would stay mostly on course. This was called the move-ahead behavior. It used the direction of the robot (steering angle, dir) to essentially produce a uniform field. The issue became how to know when to ignore the vision input and deploy move-ahead.

The approach to the issue of when to ignore vision was to use the sonar as a releaser for move-ahead. The sonar was pointed at the line and whenever it returned a range reading, move-ahead took over for two seconds. Due to the difficulties in working with DOS, the CSM entry had to use a fixed schedule for all processes. It was easier and more reliable if every process ran every update cycle, even if the results were discarded. As a result the sonar releaser for move-ahead essentially inhibited follow-line, while the lack of a sonar releaser inhibited move-ahead. Both behaviors ran all the time, but only one had any influence on what the robot did. Fig. 5.6 shows this inhibition, while the new behavioral table is shown below.

New Behavior Table

Releaser	Inhibited by	Behavior	Motor Schema	Percept	Perceptual Schema
always on	near=read_sonar()	follow_line()	stay-on-path(c_x)	c_x	compute_centroid(image,white)
always on	far=read_sonar()	move_ahead(dir)	uniform(dir)	dir	dead_reckon(shaft-encoders)

The final version worked well enough for the CSM team to take first place. It went all the way around the track until about 10 yards from the finish line. The judges had placed a shallow sand pit to test the traction. The sand pit was of some concern since sand is a light color, and might be interpreted as part of the line. Since the sand was at ground level, the range reading could not be used as an inhibitor. In the end, the team decided that since the sand pit was only half the length of a bale, it wouldn't have enough effect on the robot to be worth changing the delicate schedule of existing processes.

The team was correct that the sand pit was too small to be a significant visual distraction. However, they forgot about the issue of traction. In order to get more traction, the team slipped real tires over the slick plastic wheels, but forgot to attach them. Once in the sand, the robot spun its wheels inside the tires. After the time limit was up, the team was permitted to nudge the robot along (done with a frustrated kick by the lead programmer) to see if it would have completed the entire course. Indeed it did. No other team made it as far as the sand pit.

It is clear that a reactive system was sufficient for this application. The use of primitive reactive behaviors was extremely computationally inexpensive,

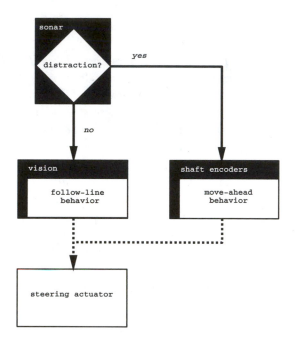

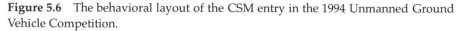

Figure 5.6   The behavioral layout of the CSM entry in the 1994 Unmanned Ground Vehicle Competition.

allowing the robot to update the actuators almost at the update rate of the vision framegrabber.

There are several important lessons that can be extracted from this case study:

- The CSM team evolved a robot which fit its ecological niche. However, it was a very narrow niche. The behaviors would not work for a similar domain, such as following sidewalks, or even a path of white lines with an intersection. Indeed, the robot reacted to unanticipated objects in the environment such as the judge's white shoes. The robot behaved "correctly" to features of the open world, but not in a desirable fashion.

- This example is a case where the releaser or inhibitor stimulus for a behavior was not the same perception as the percept needed to accomplish the task. The sonar was used to inhibit the behaviors. Follow-line used vision, while move-ahead integrated shaft encoder data to continue to move in the last good direction.

- This example also illustrates the tendency among purely reactive motor schema to assign one sensor per behavior.

5.5   Assemblages of Behaviors

The UGV competition case study illustrated the basic principles of the design of reactive behaviors. In that case, there were a trivial number of behaviors. What happens when there are several behaviors, some of which must run concurrently and some that run in a sequence? Clearly there are releasers somewhere in the system which determine the sequence. The issue is how to formally represent the releasers and their interactions into some sort of sequencing logic. If a set of behaviors form a prototypical pattern of action, they can be considered a "meta" or "macro" behavior, where a behavior is assembled from several other primitive behaviors into an *abstract behavior*. This raises the issue of how to encapsulate the set of behaviors and their sequencing logic into a separate module.

The latter issue of encapsulation is straightforward. The same OOP schema structure used to collect a perceptual schema and a motor schema into a behavior can be used to collect behaviors into an abstract behavior, as shown by a behavior being composed of behaviors in Fig. 5.1. The *coordinated control program* member of the abstract behavior expresses the releasers for the component behaviors.

SKILLS

This leaves the issue of how to formally represent the releasers in a way that both the robot can execute and the human designer can visualize and troubleshoot. There are three common ways of representing how a sequence of behaviors should unfold: *finite state automata, scripts* and *skills*. Finite state automata and scripts are logically equivalent, but result in slightly different ways about thinking about the implementation. Skills collect behavior-like primitives called Reaction-Action Packages (RAPs) into a "sketchy plan" which can be filled in as the robot executes. FSA-type of behavioral coordination and control were used successfully by the winning Georgia Tech team[19] in the 1994 AAAI Pick Up the Trash event, and the winning *LOLA* team in the 1995 IJCAI competition for the Pick Up the Trash event. Scripts were used by the Colorado School of Mines team in the 1995 competition; that entry performed behaviorally as well as the winning teams but did not place due to a penalty for not having a manipulator. Those three teams used at most eight behaviors, even though LOLA had a more sophisticated gripper than the Georgia Tech team. In contrast, *CHIP* the second place team in the IJCAI

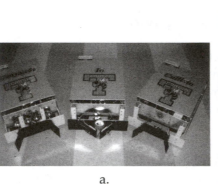

a.

b.

Figure 5.7   Two award-winning Pick Up the Trash competitors: a.) Georgia Tech's robots with the trash gripper (photograph courtesy of Tucker Balch and AAAI), and b.) University of North Carolina's LOLA (photograph courtesy of Rich LeGrand and AAAI).

competition required 34 skills and 80 RAPs to do the same task, in part because of the complexity of the arm.[53;54] Since in general skills lead to a more complex implementation than FSA and scripts, they will not be covered here. The most important point to remember in assembling behaviors is to try to make the world trigger, or *release*, the next step in the sequence, rather than rely on an internal model of what the robot has done recently.

5.5.1   Finite state automata

FINITE STATE
AUTOMATA

STATE DIAGRAM

Finite state automata (FSA) are a set of popular mechanisms for specifying what a program should be doing at a given time or circumstance. The FSA can be written as a table or drawn as a *state diagram*, giving the designer a visual representation. Most designers do both. There are many variants of

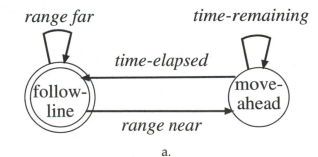

a.

$M : K =$ {follow-line, move-ahead}, $\Sigma =$ {range near, range far},
$s =$follow-line, $F =$ {follow-line, move-ahead}

q	σ	$\delta(q, \sigma)$
follow-line	range near	move-ahead
follow-line	range far	follow-line
move-ahead	time remaining	move-ahead
move-ahead	time elapsed	follow-line

b.

Figure 5.8   A FSA representation of the coordination and control of behaviors in the UGV competition: a.) a diagram and b.) the table.

FSA, but each works about the same way. This section follows the notation used in algorithm development.[86]

STATES

To begin with, the designer has to be able to specify a finite number of discrete *states* that the robot should be in. The set of states is represented by K, and each state, $q \in K$ is a listing of the behaviors that should be active at the same time. In the case of the UGR competition, there were only two states: following the line and moving forward. States are represented in a table under the heading q, and by circles in a graph. (See Fig. 5.8.) By convention, there is always a *Start state*, and the robot would always start there. The Start

START STATE

state is often written as s or q_o and drawn with a double circle. In the case of the UGR entry, the following-line state was the start state since the robot always starts with the follow-line behavior active and not suppressed.

The next part of the FSA is the inputs (also called the alphabet). Inputs are the behavioral releasers, and appear under the column heading σ. Unlike the IRM diagrams, the FSM table considers what happens to each state q for

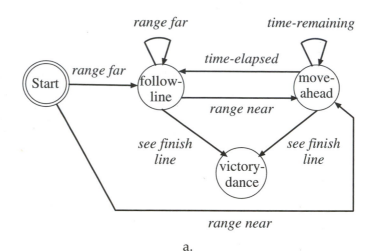

a.

$M: K = \{\text{follow-line, move-ahead}\}, \Sigma = \{\text{range near, range far}\},$
$s = \text{follow-line}, F = \{\text{follow-line, move-ahead}\}$

q	σ	$\delta(q, \sigma)$
follow-line	range near	move-ahead
follow-line	range far	follow-line
move-ahead	time remaining	move-ahead
move-ahead	time elapsed	follow-line

b.

Figure 5.9   An alternative FSA representation of the coordination and control of behaviors in the UGV competition: a.) a diagram and b.) the table.

all possible inputs. As shown in Fig. 5.8, there are only two releasers for the UGR example, so the table doesn't have many rows.

TRANSITION FUNCTION   The third part of the FSM is the *transition function*, called δ, which specifies what state the robot is in after it encounters an input stimulus, σ. The set of stimulus or affordances σ that can be recognized by the robot is represented by Σ (a capital σ). These stimuli are represented by arrows. Each arrow represents the *releaser* for a behavior. The new behavior triggered by the releaser depends on the state the robot is in. This is the same as with Innate Releasing Mechanisms, where the animal literally ignores releasers that aren't relevant to its current state.

Recall also in the serial program implementations of IRMs in Ch. 3 that the agent "noticed" releasers every second. At one iteration through the loop, it might be hungry and "enter" the state of feeding. In the next iteration, it might still be hungry and re-enter the state of feeding. This can be represented by having arrows starting at the feeding state and pointing back to the feeding state.

For the example in Fig. 5.8, the robot starts in the state of following a line. This means that the robot is not prepared to handle a visual distraction (range near) until it has started following a line. If it does, the program may fail because the FSA clearly shows it won't respond to the distraction for at least one update cycle. By that time, the robot may be heading in the wrong direction. Starting in the following-line state fine for the UGR competition, where it was known in advance that there were no bales of hay near the starting line. A more general case is shown in Fig. 5.9, where the robot can start either on a clear path or in the presence of a bale. The FSA doesn't make it clear that if the robot starts by a bale, it better be pointed straight down the path!

The fourth piece of information that a designer needs to know is when the robot has completed the task. Each state that the robot can reach that termi-

FINAL STATE   nates the task is a member of the set of *final state*, F. In the UGR example, the robot is never done and there is no final state—the robot runs until it is turned off manually or runs out of power. Thus, both states are final states. If the robot could recognize the finish line, then it could have a finish state. The finish state could just be stopped or it could be another behavior, such as a victory wag of the camera. Notice that this adds more rows to the FSA table, since there must be one row for each unique state.

In many regards, the FSA table is an extension of the behavioral table. The resulting table is known as a finite state machine and abbreviated M for machine. The notation:

$$M = \{K, \Sigma, \delta, s, F\}$$

is used as reminder that in order to use a FSA, the designer must know all the q states (K), the inputs σ the transitions between the states δ, the special starting state q_0, and the terminating state(s) (F). There must be one arrow in the state diagram for every row in the table. The table below summarizes the relationship of FSA to behaviors:

FSA	Behavioral analog
K	all the behaviors for a task
Σ	the releasers for each behavior in K
δ	the function that computes the new state
s	the behavior the robot starts in when turned on
F	the behavior(s) the robot must reach to terminate

In more complex domains, robots need to avoid obstacles (especially people). Avoidance should always be active, so it is often implicit in the FSA. move-to-goal often is shorthand for move-to-goal *and* avoid. This implicit grouping of "interesting task-related behaviors" and "those other behaviors which protect the robot" will be revisited in Ch. 7 as strategic and tactical behaviors.

Another important point about using FSA is that they describe the overall behavior of a system, but the implementation may vary. Fig. 5.8 is an accurate description of the state changes in the UGV entry. The control for the behaviors could have been implemented exactly as indicated by the FSA: if following-line is active and range returns range near, then move-ahead. However, due to timing considerations, the entry was programmed differently, though with the same result. The following examples will show how the FSA concept can be implemented with subsumption and schema-theoretic systems.

5.5.2   A Pick Up the Trash FSA

As another example of how to construct and apply an FSA, consider the Pick Up the Trash task. Assume that the robot is a small vehicle, such as the ones used by Georgia Tech shown in Fig. 5.7 or the Pioneer shown in Fig. 5.10, with a camera, and a bumper switch to tell when the robot has collided with something. In either case, the robot has a simple gripper. Assume that the robot can tell if the gripper is empty or full. One way to do this is to put an IR sensor across the jaw of the gripper. When the IR returns a short range, the gripper is full and it can immediately close, with a grasping reflex. One problem with grippers is that they are not as good as a human hand. As such, there is always the possibility that the can will slip or fall out of the gripper. Therefore the robot should respond appropriately when it is carrying a can or trash and loses it.

The Pick Up the Trash environment is visually simple, and there are obvious affordances. Coca-cola cans are the only red objects in the environment, and trash cans are the only blue objects. Therefore visually extracting red and blue blobs should be sufficient. All objects are on the floor, so the robot only has to worry about where the objects are in the x axis. A basic scenario is for the robot to start wandering around the arena looking for red blobs. It should head straight for the center of the largest red blob until it scoops the can in the forklift. Then it should try three times to grab the can, and if successful it should begin to wander around looking for a blue blob. There should only be one blue blob in the image at a time because the two trash cans are placed in diagonal corners of the arena. Once it sees a blue blob, the robot should move straight to the center of the blob until the blob gets a certain size in the image (looming). The robot should stop, let go of the can, turn around to a random direction and resume the cycle. The robot should avoid obstacles, so moving to a red or blue blob should be a fixed pattern action, rather than have the robot immediately forget where it was heading.

The behavior table is:

Releaser	Behavior	Motor Schema	Percept	Perceptual Schema
always on	avoid()	pfields.nat(goal_dir)	bumper_on	read_bumper()
EMPTY=gripper_status()	wander()	pfields.random()	time-remaining	countdown()
EMPTY=gripper_status() AND SEE_RED=extract_color(red)	move-to-goal(red)	pfields.attraction(c_x)	c_x	extract-color(red, c_x)
FULL=gripper_status()	grab-trash()	close_gripper()	status	gripper_status()
FULL=gripper_status() AND NO_BLUE=extract_color(blue)	wander()	pfields.random()	time_remaining	countdown()
FULL=gripper_status() AND SEE_BLUE=extract_color(blue)	move-to-goal(blue)	pfields.attraction(c_x)	c_x	extract-color(blue)
FULL=gripper_status() AND AT_BLUE=looming(blue, size=N)	drop_trash()	open_gripper() turn_new_dir(curr_dir)	curr_dir	read_encoders()

The function calls in the table only show the relevant arguments for brevity. The avoid behavior is interesting. The robot backs up either to the right or left (using a NaT) when it bumps something. It may bump an arena wall at several locations, but eventually a new wander direction will be set. If the robot bumps a can (as opposed to captures it in its gripper), backing up gives the robot a second chance. This table shows that the design relies on the gripper to maintain where the robot is in the nominal sequence. An empty gripper means the robot should be in the collecting the trash phase, either looking for a can or moving toward one. A full gripper means the robot is in the deposit phase. The looming releaser extracts the size of the blue region in pixels and compares it to the size N. If the region is greater than or equal

Figure 5.10 A Pioneer P2-AT with a forklift arm suitable for picking up soda cans. (Photograph courtesy of ActivMedia, Incorporated.)

to N, then the robot is "close enough" to the trash can and the robot can drop the can.

There are two problems with the behavior table. The first is that it doesn't show the sequence, or flow of control, clearly. The second is how did the designer come up with those behaviors? This is where a FSA is particularly helpful. It allows the designer to tinker with the sequence and represent the behavioral design graphically.

Fig. 5.11 shows a FSA that is equivalent to the behavior table. The FSA may be clearer because it expresses the sequence. It does so at the cost of not showing precisely how the sequence would be implemented and encouraging the designer to create internal states. A programmer might implement two wander behaviors, one which is instantiated by different releasers and terminates under different conditions, and two move-to-goal behaviors. Many designers draw and interpret FSA as carrying forward previous releasers. For example, the correct transition from Grab Trash to Wander For Trash can is FULL and NO_BLUE, but a designer may be tempted to label the arrow as only NO_BLUE, since to get that state, the gripper had to be FULL. This is a very dangerous mistake because it assumes that the implementation will be keeping up with what internal state the robot is in (by setting a vari-

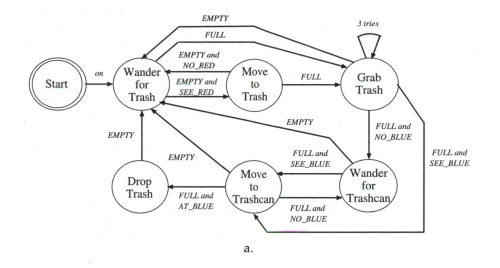

a.

K = {wander for trash, move to trash, grab trash, wander for trash can, move to trash can, drop trash }, Σ = {on, EMPTY, FULL, SEE_RED, NO_BLUE, SEE_BLUE, AT_BLUE}, $s = Start$, $F = K$

q	σ	$\delta(q, \sigma)$
start	on	wander for trash
wander for trash	EMPTY, SEE_RED	move to trash
wander for trash	FULL	grab trash
move to trash	FULL	grab trash
move to trash	EMPTY, NO_RED	wander for trash
grab trash	FULL, NO_BLUE	wander for trash can
grab trash	FULL, SEE_BLUE	move to trash can
grab trash	EMPTY	wander for trash
wander for trash can	EMPTY	wander for trash
wander for trash can	FULL, SEE_BLUE	move to trash can
move to trash can	EMPTY	wander for trash
move to trash can	FULL, AT_BLUE	drop trash
drop trash	EMPTY	wander for trash

b.

Figure 5.11   A FSA for picking up and recycling Coke cans: a.) state diagram, and b.) table showing state transitions.

able), instead of letting directly perceivable attributes of the world inform the robot as to what state it is in. Internal state is incompatible with reactivity.

The FSA also hid the role of the avoid behavior. The avoid behavior was always running, while the other behaviors were asynchronously being instantiated and de-instantiated. It is difficult to show behavioral concurrency with an FSA. Other techniques, most especially Petri Nets, are used in software engineering but have not been commonly used in robotics. The avoid behavior was not a problem in this case. It was always running and the output of the avoid potential field vector could be summed with the output of whatever other behavior was active.

5.5.3   Implementation examples

In a schema-theoretic implementation, the FSA logic would exist in one of two places. If the robot's sole task was to recycle soda cans, the controlling logic could be placed in the main program. If the robot had many tasks that it could do, the ability to recycle trash would be an *abstract behavior*, called by the main program whenever the robot needed to recycle trash. In that case, the FSA logic would be placed in the coordinated control program slot of the behavior schema.

Although the current discussion is on where the FSA goes, it might be useful to spend some time on the overall implementation. While the wander-to-goal and move-to-goal behaviors can be easily implemented with a potential fields methodology, drop-trash cannot. Drop-trash really isn't a navigation behavior. It fits the overall profile of a behavioral schema: it has an obvious motor schema (open the gripper, turn the wheels), a perceptual schema (read gripper encoders and wheel encoders), a coordinated control program (open THEN turn), and a releaser (at trash can). While schema-theoretic implementations use potential field methodologies and vector summation for effector control, not every behavior will generate a vector based on a potential field.

One advantage of FSA is that they are abstract, and can be implemented in a number of ways. The behavior table illustrated one way the FSA could be implemented with a schema-theoretic system. Fig. 5.12 shows one way it could be implemented in subsumption. This example shows the power of inhibition and suppression which is not well represented by FSA state diagrams.

In keeping with the idea of modularity and incrementally adding behaviors, the system starts with an explicit avoid behavior running on top of Level 0 (not shown). At the next level the robot wanders until it sees red. Then

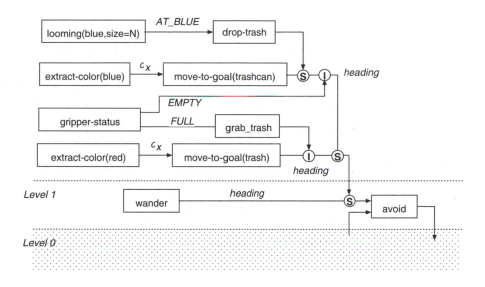

Figure 5.12 One possible Pick Up the Trash abstract behavior using subsumption.

move-to-trash suppresses wandering and replaces the heading with the direction to the trash. The move-to-trash behavior continues until the can is in the gripper. Once the gripper is full, the gripper closes and grabs the trash. Then the move-to-trash behavior is inhibited from executing. This prevents move-to-trash from sending any directions out, so the wandering direction is now again the output.

The next level of competency is to deposit trash in the trash can. When it sees the blue trash can, move-to-trash can begins to suppress wander and direct the robot to the trash can. If the gripper is empty, the output for move-to-trash can is inhibited. The robot is simultaneously looking for red and blue blobs, but as long as the gripper is empty, it only responds to red blobs.

Dropping trash also is constantly executing. If the robot happens to wander next to a blue trash can, it will signal to drop trash and turn around. The new heading suppresses any heading direction from move-to-trash can. But the robot will not open its gripper and turn around if the gripper is empty, because empty inhibits that whole line. The subsumption example produces a much less complex system than a direct FSA mapping.

5.5.4   Abstract behaviors

Finite state automata are a useful tool for expressing the coordinated control program of an abstract behavior. They fall short as a programming tool for abstract behaviors in a number of ways. First, in many cases, the assemblage of behaviors represents a prototypical sequence of events that should be slightly adapted to different situations, in essence, a *template* or *abstract behavior*.

TEMPLATE
ABSTRACT BEHAVIOR

In the Pick Up the Trash event, recycling Coke cans was only part of the task; the robots were also supposed to find white Styrofoam cups and deposit them in yellow trash cans. The behaviors represented by the FSA could be collected into an abstract behavior: `pick-up-the-trash(trash-color, trash can-color, size-trash can)`.

Second, templates need to handle different initialization conditions. Initialization wasn't a big problem for the Pick Up the Trash task, but it could be one for other applications. For example, the emergent behavior of the robot described in the Unmanned Ground Vehicle competition in Sec. 5.4 could be described as an abstract "follow-path" behavior. Recall that the robot's program assumed that it started facing the line. A more general purpose, reusable follow-path behavior would need to handle a broader range of starting conditions, such as starting facing a bale or not perfectly lined up with the line. Another common initialization behavior is *imprinting*, where

IMPRINTING

the robot is presented with an object and then records the perceived color (or other attribute) of the object for use with the nominal behavior. In the Pick Up the Trash competitions, several teams literally showed the robot the Coke can and let it determine the best values of "red" for the current lighting conditions. Likewise, some abstract behaviors would need special termination behavior. In the case of the UGR competition, the termination behaviors was NULL, but it could have been the victory dance.

Third, some times robots fail in their task; these events are often called

EXCEPTIONS

exceptions. An exception might be when the robot does not pick up a soda can in over 10 minutes. Another behavior can be substituted (do a raster scan rather than a random wander) or alternative set of parameters (use different values for red).

5.5.5   Scripts

SCRIPTS
SKILLS

Abstract behaviors often use *scripts*,[49;50;87;100] or a related construct called *skills*,[53;54] to create generic templates of assemblages of behaviors. Scripts provide a different way of generating the logic for an assemblage of behav-

Script	Collection of Behaviors	Example
Goal	Task	pick up and throw away a Coca-Cola can
Places	Applicability	an empty arena
Actors	Behaviors	WANDER_FOR_GOAL, MOVE_TO_GOAL, GRAB_TRASH, DROP_TRASH
Props, Cues	Percepts	red, blue
Causal Chain	Sequence of Behaviors	WANDER_FOR_GOAL(TRASH), MOVE_TO_GOAL(TRASH), GRAB_TRASH,WANDER_FOR_GOAL(TRASH CAN), MOVE_TO_GOAL(TRASH CAN), DROP_TRASH
Subscripts	Exception Handling	if have trash and drop, try GRAB_TRASH three times

Figure 5.13 Comparison of script structures to behaviors.

iors. They encourage the designer to think of the robot and the task literally in terms of a screenplay. Scripts were originally used in natural language processing (NLP) to help the audience (a computer) understand actors (people talking to the computer or writing summaries of what they did).[123] In the case of robots, scripts can be used more literally, where the actors are robots reading the script. The script has more room for improvization though, if the robot encounters an unexpected condition (an exception), the robot begins following a *sub-script*.

SUB-SCRIPT

Fig. 5.13 shows how elements of an actor's script compares to a robot script. The main sequence of events is called a *causal chain*. The causal chain is critical, because it embodies the coordination control program logic just as a FSA does. It can be implemented in the same way. In NLP, scripts allow the computer to keep up with a conversation that may be abbreviated. For example, consider a computer trying to read and translate a book where the main character has stopped in a restaurant. Good writers often eliminate all the details of an event to concentrate on the ones that matter. This missing, but implied, information is easy to extract. Suppose the book started with "John ordered lobster." This is a clue that serves as an index into the current or relevant event of the script (eating at a restaurant), skipping over past events (John arrived at the restaurant, John got a menu, etc.). They also focus the system's attention on the next likely event (look for a phrase that indicates John has placed an order), so the computer can instantiate the function which looks for this event. If the next sentence is "Armand brought out the lobster and refiled the white wine," the computer can infer that Armand is the waiter and that John had previously ordered and received white wine, without having been explicitly told.

CAUSAL CHAIN

In programming robots, people often like to abbreviate the routine portions of control and concentrate on representing and debugging the important sequence of events. Finite state automata force the designer to consider and enumerate every possible transition, while scripts simplify the specification. The concepts of *indexing* and *focus-of-attention* are extremely valuable for coordinating behaviors in robots in an efficient and intuitive manner. Effective implementations require asynchronous processing, so the implementation is beyond the scope of this book. For example, suppose a Pick Up the Trash robot boots up. The first action on the causal chain is to look for the Coke cans. The designer though realizes that this behavior could generate a random direction and move the robot, missing a can right in front of it. Therefore, the designer wants the code to permit the robot to skip searching the arena if it immediately sees a Coke can, and begin to pick up the can without even calling the wander-for-goal(red) behavior. The designer also knows that the next releaser after grab-trash exits to look for is blue, because the cue for moving to the trash can and dropping off trash is blue.

The resulting script for an abstract behavior to accomplish a task is usually the same as the programming logic derived from an FSA. In the case of Pick Up the Trash, the script might look like:

```
for each update...
\\ look for props and cues first: cans, trash cans, gripper
rStatus=extract_color(red, rcx, rSize); \\ ignore rSize
if (rStatus==TRUE)
  SEE_RED=TRUE;
else
  SEE_RED=FALSE;
bStatus=extract_color(blue, bcx, bSize);
if (bStatus==TRUE){
  SEE_BLUE=TRUE; NO_BLUE=FALSE;
} else {
  SEE_BLUE=FALSE; NO_BLUE=TRUE;
}
AT_BLUE=looming(size, bSize);
gStatus=gripper_status();
if (gStatus==TRUE) {
  FULL=TRUE; EMPTY=FALSE;
} else {
  FULL=FALSE; EMPTY=TRUE;
}
```

```
\\index into the correct step in the causal chain
if (EMPTY){
  if (SEE_RED){
    move_to_goal(red);
  else
    wander();
} else{
  grab_trash();
  if (NO_BLUE)
      wander();
  else if (AT_BLUE)
      drop_trash();
  else if (SEE_BLUE)
      move_to_goal(blue);
}
```

5.6 Summary

As defined in Ch. 4, a reactive implementation consists of one or more behaviors, and a mechanism for combining the output of concurrent behaviors. While an architectural style (subsumption, potential fields) may specify the structure of the implementation, the designer must invest significant effort into developing individual behaviors and into assembling them into a sequence or an abstract behavior.

Schema theory is highly compatible with Object Oriented Programming. A behavior is derived from the schema class; it is a schema that uses at least one perceptual and motor schema. If a behavior is composed of multiple schema, it must have a coordinated control program to coordinate them. Finite State Automata offer a formal representation of the coordination logic needed to control a sequence of behaviors. Scripts are an equivalent mechanism with a more natural story-like flow of control.

The steps in designing robot intelligence under the Reactive Paradigm are:

1. Describe the task,

2. Describe the robot,

3. Describe the environment,

4. Describe how the robot should act in response to its environment,

5. Refine each behavior,

6. Test each behavior independently,

7. Test with other behaviors,

and repeat the process as needed. A *behavior table* serves as a means of representing the component schemas and functions of the behavioral system. For each behavior, it shows the releasers, the motor schemas, the percept, and the perceptual schemas.

These steps emphasize the need to fully specify the ecological niche of the robot in order to design useful behaviors. Since the idea of behaviors in the Reactive Paradigm is derived from biology, it is not strange that the idea of a robot being evolved to fit its environment should also be part and parcel of the design process. Regardless of the implementation of the coordination program , the control should rely on the world to inform the robot as to what to do next, rather than rely on the program to remember and maintain state.

5.7   Exercises

Exercise 5.1

What is the difference between a *primitive* and an *abstract* behavior?

Exercise 5.2

Define:

a. behavior table

b. causal chain

c. coordinated control program†

Exercise 5.3

Can the perceptual schema and the motor schema for a behavior execute asynchronously, that is, have different update rates?

Exercise 5.4

Fig. 5.2 shows two methods of implementing a potential fields-based follow-corridor behavior. A third way is to have two instances of a move-away-from-wall (perpendicular) behavior with a move-parallel-to-wall behavior. What are the advantages and disadvantages of such an implementation?

Exercise 5.5

List and describe the steps in designing a reactive system.

Exercise 5.6

Consider the Pick Up the Trash example in Sec. 5.5.2. The example assumed the arena was empty except for walls, cans, and trash cans. What would happen if there were chairs and tables present? Could the gripper accidently scoop a chair or table leg? How would the system react? What changes, if any, would need to be made to the behavior table and FSA?

Exercise 5.7

Solve the 1994 International Association for Unmanned Systems Unmanned Ground Vehicle problem using STRIPS (Ch. 2). Be sure to include a world model and a difference table.†

Exercise 5.8

Solve the 1994 AAAI Pick Up the Trash problem using STRIPS (Ch. 2). Be sure to include a world model and a difference table.

Exercise 5.9

How is defining a robot's behaviors linked to the robot's ecological niche?†

Exercise 5.10

What is special about a primitive behavior in terms of perceptual and motor schema?†

Exercise 5.11

Construct a Behavioral Table of the behaviors needed for a robot to move from room to room.†

Exercise 5.12

What are the two main deficits encountered when designing and implementing reactive robotic systems?†

Exercise 5.13

Make up a task for a robot to complete. Describe what each of the 7 steps of the design methodology would require you to do to complete the task.†

Exercise 5.14

Describe the two methods for assembling primitive behaviors into abstract behaviors: finite state automata and scripts.†

Exercise 5.15

Assume that the CSM robot had been wider and needed to use an avoid-obstacle behavior. Make a Behavior Table to include this new behavior.†

Exercise 5.16

Assuming the state of the robot in question 1, describe how the coordinated control program should handle concurrent behaviors.†

Exercise 5.17

Recall how some mammals freeze when they see motion (an affordance for a predator) in an attempt to become invisible, and persist in this behavior until the predator is very close, then flee. Define this behavior using Behavior Tables.†

Exercise 5.18

Suppose the competition course described in Section 5.4 has been modified so that a hay bale can be placed directly on the white line. The robot must move around the bale and rejoin the line on the other side. Create a behavior table that not only follows the line but correctly responds to the bale so that it can continue following the line.†

Exercise 5.19   [*World Wide Web*]

Search the web for the International Association for Unmanned Systems competition home page and briefly describe three unmanned vehicle projects linked to the IAUS site.†

Exercise 5.20   [*World Wide Web*]

Identify at least 5 robot competitions, and for each describe the basic task. Can the task be accomplished with a reactive robot? Why or why not?

Exercise 5.21   [*Programming*]

Using Rug Warrior kits, Lego Mindstorms kits, or similar robotics tools, implement your own schools version of an IAUS Unmanned Ground Robotics Competition. Your class should decide on the course, the course objectives, rules, and prizes (if any). Groups should not begin construction of their robot without first describing the steps involved in designing a reactive behavioral system for the task at hand.†

Exercise 5.22   [*Programming*]

Write a script in pseudo-code for following a hallway. Consider that the robot may start in a hallway intersection facing away from the hallway it is supposed to take. Also the robot might start in the middle of a hall facing a wall, rather than having forward point to the long axis of the hall.

Exercise 5.23   [*Programming*]

The Pick Up the Trash competitions were a bit different than actually presented in this book. For example, the robots were actually permitted to cache up to three cans before going to the trash can, and the robots could go after white Styrofoam cups as trash. How would you integrate this into:

a. the FSA and

b. the script described in the book?

Exercise 5.24   [*Programming*]

Could the exception handling sub-scripts for picking up trash be implemented with the exception handling functionality provided by Ada or C++?

Exercise 5.25 *[Advanced Reading]*

Read Rodney Brooks' one paragraph introduction to Chapter 1 in *Cambrian Intelligence*[28] on the lack of mathematics in behavioral robotics. Now consider the behavior of the CSM robot around white shoes and dandelions. Certainly it would be useful to have theories which can prove when a behavioral system will fail. Is it possible?

Questions marked with a † were suggested by students from the University of Wisconsin Lacrosse.

5.8 End Notes

For the roboticist's bookshelf.
Artificial Intelligence and Mobile Robots[14] is a collection of case studies from top mobile robotics researchers, detailing successful entries in various robot competitions. The book provides many insights into putting theory into practice.

The IAUS Ground Robotics Competition.
The International Association for Unmanned Systems (formerly known as the Association for Unmanned Vehicle Systems) sponsors three annual robot competitions for student teams: Ground Robotics, Aerial Vehicle, and Underwater. The Ground Robotics competition is the oldest, having started in 1992. As noted in a Robotics Competition Corner column,[101] the competitions tend to reward teams for building platforms rather than programming them.

Reusability principle of software engineering and beer cans.
While researchers worried about picking up and disposing of soda cans, a popular magazine began discussing what it would take to have a robot go to the refrigerator and bring the user a beer. In an apparent acknowledgment of the lifestyle of someone who would have such a robot, the robot was expected to be able to recognize and avoid dirty underwear lying at random locations on the floor.

The 1995 IJCAI Mobile Robot Competition.
The competition was held in Montreal, Canada, and many competitors experienced delays shipping their robots due to delays at Customs. The University of New Mexico team spent the preparatory days of the competition frantically trying to locate where their robot was. Almost at midnight the evening before the preliminary rounds were to begin, a forklift drove up with the crate for their robot. All the teams looked up from their frantic testing and cheered in support of the New Mexicans. Until the fork lift came close enough and everyone could clearly see that the "This Side Up" arrow was pointing down... The New Mexicans didn't even bother to un-crate the robot to catalog the damage; they instead sought solace in Montreal's wonderful night life.

The teams with robots properly aligned with gravity went back to programming and fine tuning their entries.

Cheering at robot competitions.
The chant "Core Dump. Core Dump. Segmentation Fault!" has a nice cadence and is especially appropriate to yell at competitors using Unix systems.

Subsumption and Soda Cans.
Jon Connell addressed this task in 1989 in his thesis work at MIT,[39] applying subsumption to a robot arm, not a set of flappers. He used a special type of FSM called an Augmented Finite State Machines (AFSMs), and over 40 behaviors to accomplish the task.

Being in a Pick Up the Trash competition without a manipulator.
As often happens, robot competitions often pose problems that are a step beyond the capability of current hardware and software technology. In 1995, arms on mobile robots were rare; indeed Nomad introduced a forklift arm just in time for the competition. Participants, such as the Colorado School of Mines with an older robot and no arm, could have a "virtual manipulator" with a point deduction. The robot would move to within an agreed tolerance of the object, then either play a sound file or make a noise. The virtual manipulator—a human team member, either Tyler Devore, Dale Hawkins, or Jake Sprouse—would then physically either pick up the trash and place it on the robot or remove the trash. It made for an odd reversal of roles: the robot appeared to be the master, and the student, the servant!

About grippers maintaining the state of world.
The Pick Up the Trash event mutated in 1996 to picking up tennis balls in an empty arena, and in 1997 into a variation on sampling Mars. For the 1997 Find Life on Mars event, the sponsors brought in real rocks, painted black to contrast with the gray concrete floor and blue, green, red, and yellow "martians" or toy blocks. Because of weight considerations in shipping the rocks, the rocks were about the size of a couple of textbooks and not that much bigger than the martians. One team's purely reactive robot had trouble distinguishing colors during preliminary rounds. It would misidentify a rock as a martian during a random search, navigate to it, grip it, and then attempt to lift it. Since the rock was heavy, the gripper could not reach the full extension and trigger the next behavior. It would stay there, clutching the rock. Sometimes, the robot would grip a rock and the gripper would slip. The robot would then try to grip the rock two more times. Each time it would slip. The robot would give up, then resume a random search. Unfortunately, the search seemed to invariably direct the robot back to the same rock, where the cycle would repeat itself. Eventually the judges would go over and move the robot to another location.

Documentaries.

Scientific American Frontiers did an excellent special on robot competitions called "Robots Alive!" The special covered the AUVS Aerial Vehicle Competition (take away lesson: try your robot outdoors before you show up at an outdoor robot competition) and the 1996 AAAI Mobile Robot Competition where the robots picked up orange tennis balls instead of coca-cola cans.

6 *Common Sensing Techniques for Reactive Robots*

Chapter Objectives:

- Describe the difference between *active* and *passive* sensors, and give examples of each.

- Define each of the following terms in one or two sentences: *proprioception, exterception, exproprioception, proximity sensor, logical sensor, false positive, false negative, hue, saturation, image, pixel, image function, computer vision.*

- List the metrics for rating individual sensors and a sensor suite, and apply these metrics to a particular application.

- Describe the problems of *specular reflection, cross-talk,* and *foreshortening* with an ultrasonic transducer, and if given a 2D line drawing of surfaces, illustrate where each of these problems would likely occur.

- Describe the types of *behavioral sensor fusion* and be able to apply to a real-world problem.

- Write perceptual schemas from any logically equivalent range sensor to produce a polar plot percept for obstacle avoidance behavior.

- If given a small interleaved RGB image and a range of color values for a region, be able to 1) threshold the image on color and 2) construct a color histogram.

- Write computer vision code to enable a robot to imprint on and track a color.

6.1 Overview

To review Ch. 3, perception in a reactive robot system has two roles: *to release a behavior*, and *to support or guide the actions of the behavior*. All sensing is behavior-specific, where behaviors may tap into the same sensors, but use the data independently of each other. Also, the connotation of reactive robots is that behaviors are most often stimulus-response, relying on direct perception rather than require memory. Recognition is not compatible with reactivity. In order for a reactive robot to be successful in theory, it must have reliable perception since perception and action are tightly coupled. For it to be successful in practice, a robot has to have perceptual hardware and software which updates quickly. This chapter covers the most common sensing techniques for reactive robots. The sensors and sensing techniques described in this chapter also apply to robot architectures in the Hybrid paradigm, since Hybrid architectures use reactive behaviors.

SENSOR
TRANSDUCER

Regardless of sensor hardware or application, sensing and sensors can be thought of interacting with the world and robots as shown in Fig. 6.1. The *sensor* is a device that measures some attribute of the world. The term *transducer* is often used interchangeably with *sensor*. A transducer is the mechanism, or element, of the sensor that transforms the energy associated with what is being measured into another form of energy.[2] A sensor receives energy and transmits a signal to a display or a computer. Sensors use transducers to change the input signal (sound, light, pressure, temperature, etc.) into an analog or digital form capable of being used by a robot. In a reactive robot, the sensor observation is intercepted by a perceptual schema which extracts the relevant percept of the environment for the behavior. This percept is then used by the motor schema, which leads to an action.

PASSIVE SENSOR
ACTIVE SENSOR

A sensor is often classified as being either *passive sensor* or *active sensor*. Passive sensors rely on the environment to provide the medium for observation, e.g., a camera requires a certain amount of ambient light to produce a usable picture. Active sensors put out energy in the environment to either change the energy or enhance it. A sonar sends out sound, receives the echo, and measures the time of flight. An X-ray machine emits X-rays and measures the amount blocked by various types of tissue. Although a camera is a passive device, a camera with a flash is active. The term *active sensor* is not

ACTIVE SENSING

the same as *active sensing*. Active sensing connotes the system for using an effector to dynamically position a sensor for a "better look." A camera with a flash is an active sensor; a camera on a pan/tilt head with algorithms to direct the camera to turn to get a better view is using active sensing.

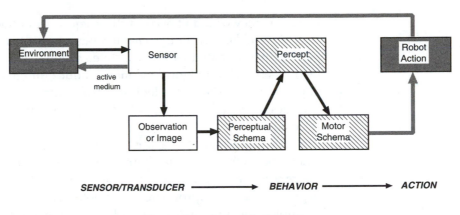

Figure 6.1   A model of sensing.

Different sensors measure different forms of energy. This in turns leads to different types of processing. Sensors which measure the same form of en-
MODALITY   ergy and process it in similar ways form a sensor *modality*. A sensor modality refers to what the raw input to the sensor is: sound, pressure, temperature, light, and so on. In some regards, modalities are similar to the five senses in humans. A modality can be further subdivided, for instance, vision can be decomposed into visible light, infrared light, X-rays, and other modalities.

6.1.1   Logical sensors

LOGICAL SENSORS   A powerful abstraction of sensors is *logical sensors*, first introduced by Henderson and Shilcrat.[65] A logical sensor is a unit of sensing or module that supplies a particular percept. It consists of the signal processing from the physical sensor and the software processing needed to extract the percept; it is the functional building block for perception. A logical sensor can be easily implemented as a perceptual schema.

An overlooked aspect of a logical sensor is that it contains all available alternative methods of obtaining that percept. For example, a percept commonly used for obstacle avoidance is a polar plot of range data. The logical sensor for the percept might be named `range_360` and return a data structure or object specifying the polar plot. The logical sensor would go further and list all the possible ways the robot had for constructing a polar plot of that form. The robot might be able to use sonar, a laser, stereo vision, or tex-
LOGICAL EQUIVALENCE   ture. Each of those modules would be *logically equivalent*; that is, they would return the same percept data structure so they can be used interchangeably.

However, they wouldn't necessarily be equivalent in performance or update rate. As will be seen in this chapter, the sonar is liable to produce a noisy percept in a second or two, while stereo vision may take minutes. Even different stereo vision algorithms may produce different results on the same data stream. Therefore, the logical sensor contains a selector function which specifies the conditions under which each alternative is useful and should be selected.

Notice that a logical sensor can be implemented as a perceptual schema, where the methods are the alternative means of generating the percept and the coordinated control strategy contains the knowledge as to when a particular method is appropriate. Also note that each individual method can be implemented as a perceptual schema, leading to the recursive, building-block effect.

In reactive systems, the term logical sensor has degenerated somewhat from its original usage and is essentially equivalent to a perceptual schema. "Logical sensor" is often used to connote information hiding, where the particular sensor and processing algorithm is hidden in the "package." This is useful because a robot might use the same physical sensor in two different ways. An avoid behavior might use a polar plot of sonar range data, while a panic-stop behavior might use the minimum of all the incoming sonar data. Since the perceptual schema use the raw sonar data differently, it is as if they were different sensors.

6.2 Behavioral Sensor Fusion

SENSOR FUSION

Sensor fusion is a broad term used for any process that combines information from multiple sensors into a single percept. The motivation for sensor fusion stems from three basic combinations of sensors: *redundant* (or competing), *complementary*, and *coordinated*. Although many researchers treat sensor fusion as a means of constructing a global world model in a hierarchical or deliberative system, sensor fusion can be incorporated into behaviors through *sensor fission*, *action-oriented sensor fusion*, and *sensor fashion*.

REDUNDANT
COMPLEMENTARY
COORDINATED

In some cases multiple sensors are used when a particular sensor is too imprecise or noisy to give reliable data. Adding a second sensor can give another "vote" for the percept. When a sensor leads the robot to believe that a percept is present, but it is not, the error is called a *false positive*. The robot has made a positive identification of percept, but it was false. Likewise, an error where the robot misses a percept is known as a *false negative*. Sensors

FALSE POSITIVE

FALSE NEGATIVE

Figure 6.2 Example of redundant top and bottom sonar rings.

will often produce different false positive and false negative rates. Whether a robot can tolerate a higher false positive or false negative rate depends on the task.

REDUNDANT PHYSICAL REDUNDANCY

LOGICALLY REDUNDANT

COMPETING SENSORS

When the sensors are both returning the same percept, the sensors are considered *redundant*. An example of *physical redundancy* is shown in Fig. 6.2, where a Nomad 200 has two sonar rings. The sonar software returns the minimum reading (shortest range) from the two, providing a more reliable reading for low objects which would ordinarily specularly reflect the beam from the upper sonar. Sensors can also be *logically redundant*, where they return identical percepts but use different modalities or processing algorithms. An example is extracting a range image from stereo cameras and from a laser range finder. Sometimes redundant sensors are called *competing sensors*, because the sensors can be viewed as competing to post the "winning" percept.

Complementary sensors provide disjoint types of information about a percept. In behavioral sensor fusion for urban search and rescue, a robot may search for survivors by fusing observations from a thermal sensor for body heat with a camera detecting motion. Both logical sensors return some aspect of a "survivor," but neither provides a complete view. Coordinated sensors use a sequence of sensors, often for cue-ing or providing focus-of-attention. A predator might see motion, causing it to stop and examine the scene more closely for signs of prey.

Most of the work on sensor fusion treats it as if it were a deliberative process: one that requires a global world model. Early work in reactive systems used robots with only a few simple sensors, a sonar or sonar ring for range and a camera for color, texture, or motion affordances. As a result, there was a philosophy of one sensor per behavior. Behaviors could share a sensor stream, but without knowing it. This philosophy led to the approach taken by Brooks that sensor fusion at the behavioral level was a mirage. Instead sensor fusion was really multiple instances of the same behavior with different sensor inputs being combined together. To an outside observer, it would look like some complicated process was being enacted inside the robot, but in fact it would be a simple competition with an emergent behavior.

SENSOR FISSION Brooks dubbed this *sensor fission* in part as a take off on the connotations of the word "fusion" in nuclear physics. In nuclear fusion, energy is created by forcing atoms and particles together, while in fission, energy is creating by separating atoms and particles. Fig. 6.3a shows a diagram of sensor fission.

Murphy reported on studies from cognitive psychology and neurophysiology showing that behavioral sensor fusion does occur in animals, and therefore should be part of a robot's behavioral repertoire.[99] The gist of the studies was that sensor fusion does occur in behaviors. The sensor pathways throughout the brain remain separate and can be routed to multiple behaviors in the superior colliculus. Only when the sensor signals routed to the portion of the brain associated with a particular behavior arrive at that location does there appear to be any transformation. The transformation appears to be a new common representation. Any or all of these sensor streams can be active and influence the resulting behavior. For example, consider the predation behavior in cats. If a cat hears a noise and sees a movement, it will react more strongly than if it has only a single stimulus. This type of sensor

ACTION-ORIENTED
SENSOR FUSION fusion is called *action-oriented sensor fusion* to emphasize that the sensor data is being transformed into a behavior-specific representation in order to support a particular action, not for constructing a world model. Fig. 6.3b shows a diagram of action-oriented sensor fusion.

Sensor fission and action-oriented sensor fusion cover competing and complementary sensing. Sensor fission is by definition a competitive method, though complementary sensors may be used to support a particular instance of a behavior. Action-oriented sensor fusion is not restricted to either competing or complementary sensors, since the behavior makes a local transformation anyway. This leaves the category of coordinated sensors untouched.

SENSOR FASHION Arkin filled in the apparent gap by calling coordination *sensor fashion*, an alliterative name intended to imply the robot was changing sensors with changing circumstances just as people change styles of clothes with the seasons. A

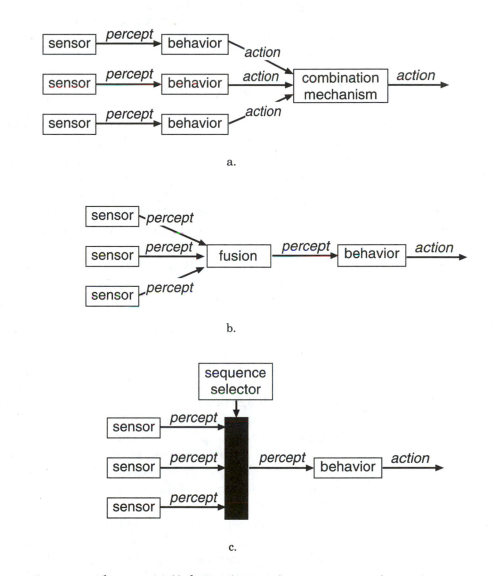

Figure 6.3   Three types of behavioral sensor fusion: a.) sensor fission, b.) action-oriented sensor fusion, and c.) sensor fashion.

diagram of sensor fashion is shown in Fig. 6.3c.

Murphy incorporated pathways for all three types of behavioral sensor fusion as well as other deliberative forms into the Sensor Fusion Effects (SFX) architecture. SFX will be covered in Ch. 7.

6.3 Designing a Sensor Suite

Historically, reactive robots used either inexpensive infrared (IR) or ultrasonic transducers to detect range. The earliest behaviors focused on basic navigational skills such as obstacle avoidance and wall following. The percept for these behaviors all involve knowing the distance to an occupied area of space. Now with the advent of inexpensive miniature cameras and laser range finders for consumer applications, computer vision is becoming increasingly common. In agricultural and transportation applications of reactive robots, GPS technology has become popular as well. This chapter attempts to cover the basics of these sensing modalities, and how they are used in mobile robots. Because the sensor market is rapidly changing, the chapter will focus on how to design a suite of sensors for use by a robot, rather the device details.

An artificially intelligent robot has to have some sensing in order to be considered a true AI robot. If it cannot observe the world and the effects of its actions, it cannot react. As noted in the chapter on "Action-Oriented Perception" in *Artificial Intelligence and Mobile Robots: Case Studies of Successful Robot Systems*, the design of a set of sensors for a robot begins with an assessment of the type of information that needs to be extracted.[14] This information can

PROPRIOCEPTION
EXTEROCEPTION
EXPROPRIOCEPTION

be either from *proprioception* (measurements of movements relative to an internal frame of reference), *exteroception* (measurements of the layout of the environment and objects relative to the robot's frame of reference) or *exproprioception* (measurement of the position of the robot body or parts relative to the layout of the environment).

The Colorado School of Mines fielded an entry to the 1995 UGV competition entry discussed in Ch. 5. This provides an example of different types of sensing for a path following robot. In 1995, the `follow-path` behavior was expanded to track both lines of the path using a wide angle lens on the camera. `follow-path` could be considered exteroceptive because it acquired information on the environment. However, the camera for the robot was mounted on a panning mast, which was intended to turn to keep the line in view, no matter what direction the path turned in. Therefore, the robot had to know where the camera was turned relative to the robot's internal frame of reference in order to correctly transform the location of a white line in image coordinates to a steering direction. This meant the information needed for `follow-path` had both proprioceptive and exteroceptive components, making the perception somewhat exproprioceptive. (If the robot was extracting the pose of its camera from exteroception, it would be clearly exproprioceptive.)

Due to a programming error, the follow-path behavior incorrectly assumed that the exteroceptive camera data had been transformed by the proprioceptive shaft encoder data from the panning mast into exproprioceptive data. The robot needed the exproprioception to determine where it should move next: turn to follow the path in camera coordinates, plus the compensation for the current camera pan angle. The programming error resulted in the robot acting as if the camera was aligned with the center of the robot at all times. But the camera might be turned slightly to maintain the view of both lines of the path through the `pan-camera` behavior. The resulting navigational command might be to turn, but too little to make a difference, or even to turn the wrong way. This subtle error surfaced as the robot went around hair pin turns, causing the robot to go consistently out of bounds.

6.3.1 Attributes of a sensor

As can be seen by the above example, robots may have dead reckoning capabilities, but will always have some type of exteroceptive sensor. Otherwise, the robot cannot be considered reactive: there would be no stimulus from the world to generate a reaction. The set of sensors for a particular robot is called a *sensor suite*. Following *Sensors for Mobile Robots*,[52] in order to construct a sensor suite, the following attributes should be considered for each sensor:

SENSOR SUITE

1. Field of view and range. Every exteroceptive sensor has a region of space that it is intended to cover. The width of that region are specified by the sensor's *field of view*, often abbreviated as FOV. The field of view is usually expressed in degrees; the number of degrees covered vertically may be different from the number of degrees covered horizontally. Field of view is frequently used in photography, where different lenses capture different size and shape areas. A wide angle lens will often cover up to 70°, while a "regular" lens may only have a field of view around 27°. The distance that the field extends is called the range.

FIELD OF VIEW (FOV)

The *field of view (FOV)* can be thought of in terms of egocentric spherical coordinates, where one angle is the *horizontal FOV* and the other is the *vertical FOV*. The other aspect is the *range,* or how far the sensor can make reliable measurements. In spherical coordinates, this would be the values of r that defined the depth of the operating range.

Field of view and range are obviously critical in matching a sensor to an application. If the robot needs to be able to detect an obstacle when it's 8 feet away in order to safely avoid it, then a sensor with a range of 5 feet will not be acceptable.

2. Accuracy, repeatability, and resolution. Accuracy refers to how correct the reading from the sensor is. But if a reading for the same conditions is accurate only 20% of the time, then the sensor has little repeatability. If the sensor is consistently inaccurate in the same way (always 2 or 3 cm low), then the software can apply a bias (add 2 centimeters) to compensate. If the inaccuracy is random, then it will be difficult to model and the applications where such a sensor can be used will be limited. If the reading is measured
RESOLUTION in increments of 1 meter, that reading has less *resolution* than a sensor reading which is measured in increments of 1 cm.

3. Responsiveness in the target domain. Most sensors have particular environments in which they function poorly. Another way of viewing this is that the environment must allow the signal of interest to be extracted from noise and interference (e.g., have a favorable signal-to-noise ratio). As will be seen below, sonar is often unusable for navigating in an office foyer with large amounts of glass because the glass reflects the sound energy in ways almost impossible to predict. It is important to have characterized the ecological niche of the robot in terms of what will provide, absorb, or deflect energy.

4. Power consumption. Power consumption is always a concern for robots. Since most robots operate off of batteries, the less power they consume, the longer they run. For example, the battery life on a Nomad 200, which carries five batteries, was improved from four hours to six by shutting off all sensors. Power is so restricted on most mobile robots that many robot manufacturers will swap microprocessor chips just to reduce the power drain (which was part of the motivation for the Transmeta Crusoe chip). Sensors which require a large amount of power are less desirable than those which do not. In general, passive sensors have less power demands than active sensors because they are not emitting energy into the environment.

The amount of power on a mobile robot required to support a sensor package (and any other electronics such as a microprocessor and communications
HOTEL LOAD links) is sometimes called the *hotel load*. The sensor suite is the "guest" of the

LOCOMOTION LOAD platform. The power needed to move the robot is called the *locomotion load*. Unfortunately, many robot manufacturers focus on only the locomotion load, balancing power needs with the desire to reduce the overall weight and size. This leads to a very small hotel load, and often prevents many sensors from being added to platform.

5. Hardware reliability. Sensors often have physical limitations on how well they work. For example, Polaroid sonars will produce incorrect range reading when the voltage drops below 12V. Other sensors have temperature and moisture constraints which must be considered.

6. Size. The size and weight of a sensor does affect the overall design. A microrover on the order of a shoebox will not have the power to transport a large camera or camcorder, but it may be able to use a miniature "Quick-Cam" type of camera.

The above list concentrated on considerations for the physical aspects of the sensor. However, the sensors only provide observations; without the software perceptual schemas, the behaviors cannot use the sensors. Therefore, the software that will process the information from a sensor must be considered as part of the sensor seletion process. **7. Computational complexity.** Computational complexity is the estimate of how many operations an algorithm or program performs. It is often written as a function O, called the "order," where $O(x)$ means the number of operations is proportional to x. x is often a function itself. Lower orders are better. An algorithm that executes with $O(n)$ equally consuming operations is faster than one with $O(n^2)$ operations. (If you doubt this, see if you can find a positive, whole number value of n such that $n > n^2$.) Computational complexity has become less critical for larger robots, with the rapid advances in processors and miniaturization of components. However, it remains a serious problem for smaller vehicles.

8. Interpretation reliability. The designer should consider how reliable the sensor will be for the ecological conditions and for interpretation. The robot will often have no way of determining when a sensor is providing incorrect information. As a result the robot may "hallucinate" (think it is seeing things that are not there) and do the wrong thing. Many sensors produce output which are hard for human to interpret without years of training; medical X-rays are one example, and synthetic aperature radar (SAR) which produces polar plots is another. If a sensor algorithm was not working properly in these modalities, the designer might not be skilled enough to notice it. Therefore, the algorithms themselves must be reliable.

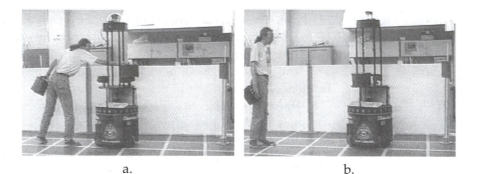

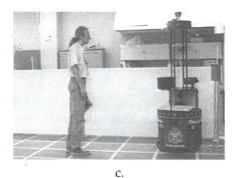

Figure 6.4   Sequence showing a Denning mobile robot with redundant cameras, responding to sensing failures introduced by Dave Hershberger.

6.3.2   Attributes of a sensor suite

Everett[52] recommends that the following attributes should be considered for the *entire sensing suite*:

   1. Simplicity. As with any design, simple sensors which have straightforward hardware and operating principles are more desirable than sensors which are complex and require constant maintenance.

   2. Modularity. In order to reconfigure a sensor suite (add new sensors, remove ones that aren't appropriate for the task), the designer must be able to remove one sensor and/or its perceptual schema without impacting any other sensing capability.

   3. Redundancy. In most military and industrial applications, it is imperative that the robot function correctly, since it would put people at risk to try to retrieve the robot and fix it. Sensors are especially important because a faulty sensor can cause the robot to "hallucinate." As a result, sensor suites may offer some sort of redundancy.

PHYSICAL REDUNDANCY

There are two types of redundancy. *Physical redundancy* means that there are several instances of physically identical sensors on the robot. Fig. 6.4 shows a robot with redundant cameras. In this case, the cameras are mounted 180° apart, and when one sensor fails, the robot has to "drive backwards" in order to accomplish its task.

LOGICAL REDUNDANCY

Logical redundancy means that another sensor using a different sensing modality can produce the same percept or releaser. For example, the Mars Sojourner mobile robot had a laser striping system for determining the range to obstacles, which emitted a line of light. If the surface was flat, a camera would see a flat line, whereas if the surface was rough the line would appear jagged. The robot also carried a second camera which could do obstacle detection via stereo triangulation. The laser striping sensor and the stereo cameras are logically redundant. They are not physically redundant, but they produce the same overall information: the location of obstacles relative to the robot. However, logically redundant sensors are not necessarily equivalent in processing speed or accuracy and resolution. A stereo range sensor and algorithm computes the range much slower than a laser striping system.

Physical redundancy introduces new issues which are the area of active research investigation. Possibly the most intriguing is how a robot can determine that a sensor (or algorithm) has failed and needs to be swapped out.

FAULT TOLERANCE

Surviving a failure is referred to as *fault tolerance*. Robots can be programmed in most cases to tolerate faults as long as they can identify when they occur.

6.4   Proprioceptive Sensors

Proprioception is dead reckoning, where the robot measures a signal originating within itself. In biology, this is usually some measure of how far an arm or leg has been extended or retracted. In robotics, actuators are generally

SHAFT ENCODER

motors. Many motors come with a *shaft encoder* which measures the number of turns the motor has made. If the gearing and wheel size is known, then the number of turns of the motor can be used to compute the number of turns of the robot's wheels, and that number can be used to estimate how far the robot has traveled.

Proprioception is often only an estimate. This is due to the impact of the environment on the actual movement of the robot. Arkin in his PhD thesis[8] showed that the same wheeled robot, HARV, traveled different distances for the same encoder count on a sidewalk, grass, and wet grass. The texture of the different surfaces caused the wheels of HARV mobile to slip to varying degrees. A robot on a tiled floor might slip twice as much as on dry grass.

6.4.1 Inertial navigation system (INS)

INERTIAL NAVIGATION
SYSTEMS (INS)

Aircraft, submarines, and missiles use *inertial navigation systems (INS)*. INS measure movements electronically through miniature accelerometers. As long as the movements are smooth, with no sudden jarring, and the samples are taken frequently, an INS can provide accurate dead reckoning to 0.1 percent of the distance traveled.[52] However, this technology is unsuitable for mobile robots for several reasons. The cost of an INS is prohibitive; units run from $50,000 to $200,000 USD. The cost is due in part to having to stabilize the accelerometers with gyroscopes, as well as the nature of precision electronics. Mobile robots often violate the constraint that motion must be smooth. A hard bump or sudden turn can exceed the accelerometers' measurement range, introducing errors. INS sytems are typically big; smaller devices have less accuracy. Sojourner, the Mars rover, carried an INS system. In one trek, it would have stopped 30 cm from a rock it was to sample if it had just used proprioception. Instead, by using exteroception, it got within 4 cm.

6.4.2 GPS

PRECISION
AGRICULTURE

GPS, or Global Positioning System, is becoming more common on robots, especially those used to automate farm equipment (an effort called *precision agriculture*). GPS systems work by receiving signals from satellites orbiting the Earth. The receiver triangulates itself relative to four GPS satellites, computing its position in terms of latitude, longitude, altitude, and change in time. GPS isn't a proprioceptive sensor per se since the robot must receive signals from the satellites, external to the robot. However, they are not exteroceptive sensors either, since the robot isn't computing its position relative to its environment. Since they tend to be used in place of dead reckoning on outdoor robots, only GPS will be covered here.

Currently the only sets of GPS satellites that a receiver can triangulate itself against are the Navstar "constellation" maintained by the United States Air Force Space Command or the Russian counterpart, GLONOSS, maintained by the Russian Federation Ministry of Defense. There are two types of channels on Navstar, one public, called the Standard Positioning System, and an encrypted signal, the Precise Positioning System. Until early in the year 2000, the U.S. military actually introduced an error in the satellite message as to where the satellite actually is, which could result in triangulation errors of up to 100 meters. The error was called *selective availability*, because it made accurate positioning available only to those users selected by the U.S. military. This was intended to prevent a hostile country from putting a GPS receiver on a guided missile and precisely targeting where the President is giving a talk. Selective availability was turned off in part because of the rise of civilian uses of GPS, and because it led to interoperability with groups working with the U.S. military who were using commercial, not military, GPS.

SELECTIVE AVAILABILITY

Many inexpensive hand-held receivers sold to hunters and hikers attempt to improve on localization by averaging or filtering the readings. This can reduce the error down to 10-15 meters. Surveyors and GPS specialty companies such as Trimble and Rockwell have found a way to subtract the error in the public channel and get performance near the Y-code's rumored accuracy of centimeters. The method is called *differential GPS (DGPS)*, where two GPS receivers are used. One remains stationary, while the other is put on the robot. If the two receivers are observing the same satellites, then any sudden change in position on the stationary "base" receiver is due to the induced error and can be subtracted from the readings at the robot GPS. The ultimate fix to the induced error will probably come in a few years due to the commercial sector. A consortium of private companies is planning to launch a new constellation of GPS satellites, Teledesic, which will emit accurate data at all times in a format that can be decoded only by chips licensed by the consortium. Teledesic is scheduled to go on-line in 2004.

DIFFERENTIAL GPS (DGPS)

GPS and DGPS are not complete solutions to the dead reckoning problem in mobile robots for at least two reasons. First, GPS does not work indoors in most buildings, especially offices or factories with large amounts of steel-reinforced concrete. As with cellular phones, these structures interrupt the reception of radio signals. Likewise, GPS may not work outdoors in major cities where skyscrapers act as *urban canyons* and interfere with reception. Second, commercial DGPS systems cost on the order of $30,000 USD, which is prohibitively high. Several web sites now offer free "do-it-yourself" DGPS code to create a DGPS from two inexpensive receivers.

URBAN CANYONS

6.5   Proximity Sensors

Proximity sensors measure the relative distance (range) between the sensor and objects in the environment. Since the sensor is mounted on the robot, it is a straightforward computation to translate a range relative to the sensor to a range relative to the robot at large. Most proximity sensors are active. Sonar, also called ultrasonics, is the most popular proximity sensor, with infrared, bump, and feeler sensors not far behind.

6.5.1   Sonar or ultrasonics

Sonar refers to any system for using sound to measure range. Sonars for different applications operate at different frequencies; for example, a sonar for underwater vehicles would use a frequency appropriate for traveling through water, while a ground vehicle would use a frequency more suited for air. Ground vehicles commonly use sonars with an ultrasonic frequency, just at the edge of human hearing. As a result the terms "sonar" and "ultrasonics" are used interchangeably when discussing extracting range from acoustic energy.

TIME OF FLIGHT

Ultrasonics is possibly the most common sensor on commercial robots operating indoors and on research robots. They are active sensors which emit a sound and measure the time it takes for the sound to bounce back. The *time of flight* (time from emission to bounce back) along with the speed of sound in that environment (remember, even air changes density with altitude) is sufficient to compute the range of the object.

Ultrasonics is common for several reasons. Its evolution paralleled the rise of the Reactive Paradigm. In the mid-1980's, Hans Moravec did impressive robot navigation with a ring of sonars. The ring configuration gave a 360° coverage as a polar plot. This ring was developed by one of the first mobile robot manufacturers, Denning Robotics, and since then sonar rings are often referred to as "Denning rings," regardless of manufacturer. Besides providing direct range measurements, the transducers were cheap, fast, and had terrific coverage. In the early 1980's, the Polaroid Land Corporation had developed small, inexpensive sonars for use as camera range finders. A bigger version, the Polaroid Lab Grade ultrasonic transducer, costs on the order of $30 USD and can measure ranges from 1 to 25 feet with inch resolution over a field of view of 30°. Furthermore, the measurement time was on the order of seconds versus hours for computer vision. Ultrasonics became the sensor of choice for behavior-based robots.

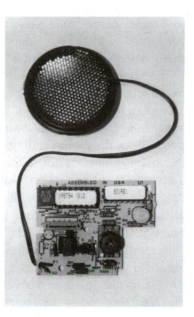

Figure 6.5 Polaroid ultrasonic transducer. The membrane is the disk.

A robotic sonar transducer is shown in Fig. 6.5. The transducer is about the size and thickness of a dollar coin, and consists of a thin metallic membrane. A very strong electrical pulse generates a waveform, causing the membrane on the transducer to produce a sound. The sound is audible as a faint clicking noise, like a crab opening and closing its pinchers. Meanwhile a timer ECHO is set, and the membrane becomes stationary. The reflected sound, or *echo*, vibrates the membrane which is amplified and then thresholded on return signal strength; if too little sound was received, then the sensor assumes the sound is noise and so ignores it. If the signal is strong enough to be valid, the timer is tripped, yielding the time of flight.

The key to how useful the data is requires understanding how the sound wave is generated by the transducer. In reality, the sound beam produces multiple secondary sound waves which interact over different regions of space around the transducer before dissipating. Secondary sound waves are SIDE LOBES called *side lobes*. Most robot systems assume that only sound from the main, or centermost, lobe is responsible for a range measurement. The width of the main lobe is often modeled as being 30° wide at about 5 meters away. However, in practice, reactive robots need to respond to obstacles in the 0.3

to 3 meter range. As a result many algorithms only treat the lobe as being between 8° and 15° wide depending on how reliable the range readings are in a particular environment. Ch. 11 will go over this in more detail.

The strength of the main lobe in the environment determines the maximum range that the sonar can extract reliability. In ideal indoor venues, a sonar might return ranges of up to 25 feet, while in the outdoors, the same sonar might go no further than 8 feet with any repeatability. So while the upper limit of the range reading depends on the sensor and the environment, the lower limit does not. Ultrasonic transducers have a "dead time" immediately following emission while the membrane vibration decays. The decay time translates into an inability to sense objects within 11 inches because measurements made during this period are unreliable because the membrane may not have stopped ringing.

Regardless of the maximum allowed range return (i.e., does the program ignore any reading over 3 meters?) and the width of the lobe, most computer programs divide the area covered by a sonar into the three regions shown in Fig. 6.6. Region I is the region associated with the range reading. It is an arc, because the object that returned the sound could be anywhere in the beam. The arc has a width, because there are some resolution and measurement errors; the width of Region I is the tolerance. Region II is the area that is empty. If that area was not empty, the range reading would have been shorter. Region III is the area that is theoretically covered by the sonar beam, but is unknown whether it is occupied or empty because it is in the shadow of whatever was in Region I. Region IV is outside of the beam and not of interest.

Although they are inexpensive, fast, and have a large operating range, ultrasonic sensors have many shortcomings and limitations which a designer should be aware of. Ultrasonic sensors rely on reflection, and so are suscep-

SPECULAR REFLECTION

tible to *specular reflection*. Specular reflection is when the wave form hits a surface at an acute angle and the wave bounces away from the transducer. Ideally all objects would have a flat surface perpendicular to the transducer, but of course, this rarely happens. To make matters worse, the reflected signal may bounce off of a second object, and so on, until by coincidence return some energy back to the transducer. In that case, the time of flight will not correspond to the true relative range.

Even with severely acute angles, the surface is usually rough enough to send some amount of sound energy back. An exception to this is glass, which is very common in hospitals and offices where mail robots operate, but induces serious specular reflection. Fortunately this energy is often sufficiently

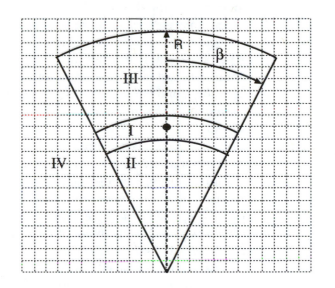

Figure 6.6   The regions of space observed by an ultrasonic sensor.

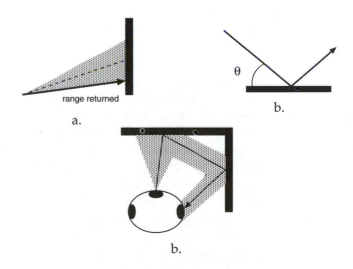

Figure 6.7   Three problems with sonar range readings: a.) foreshortening, b.) specular reflection, and c.) cross-talk.

strong to pass the thresholding in the transducer circuit. However, a new problem, *foreshortening*, may occur. Recall that a sonar has a 30° field of view. This means that sound is being broadcast in a 30° wide cone. If the surface is not perpendicular to the transducer, one side of the cone will reach the object first and return a range first. Most software assumes the reading is along the axis of the sound wave. If it uses the reading (which is really the reading for 15°), the robot will respond to erroneous data. There is no solution to this problem.

SPECULAR REFLECTION

Specular reflection is not only by itself a significant source of erroneous readings; it can introduce a new type of error in rings of sonars. Consider a ring of multiple sonars. Suppose the sonars fire (emit a sound) at about the same time. Even though they are each covering a different region around the robot, some specularly reflected sound from a sonar might wind up getting received by a completely different sonar. The receiving sonar is unable to tell the difference between sound generated by itself or by its peers. This source

CROSS-TALK

of wrong reading is called *cross-talk*, because the sound waves are getting crossed. Most robot systems stagger the firing of the sonars in a fixed pattern of four sonars, one from each quadrant of the ring) at a time. This helps some with cross-talk, but is not a complete or reliable solution. If the sonar sound frequency and firing rate can be changed (which is generally not the case), then sophisticated aliasing techniques can be applied. These techniques are outside the scope of this book.

One researcher, Monet Soldo, told a story of when she developed a reactive mobile robot for IBM's T.J.Watson Laboratories during the late 1980's. The robot used sonar as its primary sensors, and she had written behaviors to guide the robot through doors, rooms, and hall successfully at reasonable speeds. The day came for the big demonstration, which was to be held not in the hallways of the laboratory but in the front reception area. The robot navigated successfully out of the lab, down the halls, and then went berserk when it got to the atrium. She rebooted, and tried again, but with the same result. After days of trying to debug the code, she realized it wasn't a code problem, it was an environment problem: most of the atrium reception area consisted of glass partitions. The specular reflection and cross-talk caused the robot to hallucinate, although in different ways each time.

I had a similar problem when my robot started navigating in an office environment. In that environment, the robot was expected to navigate among office cubes, or work areas delimited by partitions. The partitions were covered with cloth to dampen the sound from the workers. Unfortunately, the cloth also absorbed the sound from the sonars! These stories emphasize the

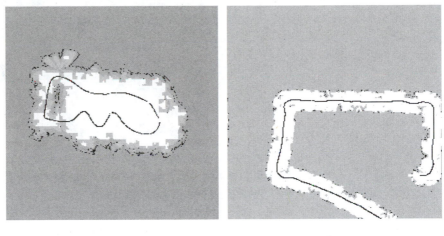

a.   b.

Figure 6.8 Maps produced by a mobile robot using sonars in: a.) a lab and b.) a hallway. (The black line is the path of the robot.)

need to consider the operating environment for the sensor and its impact on the signal.

The impact of the problems of specular reflection and cross talk become easier to see with plots of sonar returns overlaid with the perimeter of the area they were taken in; see Fig. 6.8. Some walls are invisible, others are too close. Clearly sonar readings have to be taken with a grain of salt.

The 30° cone also creates resolution problems. While sonars often have excellent resolution in depth, they can only achieve that at large distances if the object is big enough to send back a significant portion of the sound wave. The further away from the robot, the larger the object has to be. Most desk chairs and table tops present almost no surface area to the sensor and so the robot will often not perceive their presence and run right into them.

In practice, another problem leads to spurious sonar readings: power. The generation of a sound wave requires a significant pulse of energy. If the robot is operating at low power levels, the correct waveform will not be generated and the return signal worthless. This problem is often difficult to debug

Figure 6.9   The ring of IR sensors on a Khepera robot. Each black square mounted on three posts is an emitter and receiver.

by looking at the sonar returns, which often suggest specular reflection or crosstalk. One team in a robot competition attached a voltmeter next to the emergency stop button on their robot to ensure that this problem would not go undetected.

One method of eliminating spurious readings, regardless of cause, is to take the average of three readings (current plus the last two) from each sensor. This method is fairly common on purely reactive robots, but is ad hoc. As will be seen in later chapters, other approaches treat the reading as being uncertain and apply formal evidential reasoning techniques to refine the reading. These uncertainty techniques are employed by architectures operating under the Hybrid Paradigm, and will be covered in Ch. 11.

6.5.2   Infrared (IR)

Infrared sensors are another type of active proximity sensor. They emit near-infrared energy and measure whether any significant amount of the IR light is returned. If so, there is an obstacle present, giving a binary signal. IR sensors have a range of inches to several feet, depending on what frequency of light is used and the sensitivity of the receiver. The simplest IR proximity sensors can be constructed from LEDs, which emit light into the environment and have a range of 3-5 inches. Fig. 6.9 shows the IR emitters and receivers placed side by side in a single rectangular package on a Khepera robot. These often fail in practice because the light emitted is often "washed out" by bright ambient lighting or is absorbed by dark materials (i.e., the environment has too much noise).

In more sophisticated IR sensors, different IR bands can be selected or modulated to change the signal-to-noise ratio. This typically ensures that an object in range doesn't absorb the light, causing the sensor to miss the presence of the object. Nomad robots have an IR sensor option.

6.5.3 Bump and feeler sensors

TACTILE   Another popular class of robotic sensing is *tactile,* or touch, done with bump and feeler sensors. Feelers or whiskers can be constructed from sturdy wires. Bump sensors are usually a protruding ring around the robot consisting of two layers. Contact with an object causes the two layers to touch, creating an electrical signal. In theory, the sensitivity of a bump sensor can be adjusted for different contact pressures; some robots may want a "light" touch to create a signal rather than a "heavier" touch. In practice, bump sensors are annoyingly difficult to adjust. In the "Hors d'Oeuvres, Anyone?" event of the 1997 AAAI Mobile Robot Competition, humans were served finger food by robot "waiters." The robot waiters were various research robots with serving trays attached. Humans were supposed to communicate to the Colorado School of Mines' Nomad 200 robot waiter (seen in Fig. 6.10) that they were done eating by kicking the bump sensor. The sensitivity of the bump sensor was so low that it often required many kicks, producing a very comical scene with Bruce Lee overtones.

Placement of bump sensors is a very important issue. The bump sensors on a Nomad 200 base clearly protect the robot only from low obstacles not perceivable by sonar. The Denning mobile robot platforms built in the 1980's used a bump sensor that looked much like a thick piece of gray tape. Denning mobile robots look like a fat version of the Nomad 200's, and the bump sensor is wrapped around the cowling of the robot at the waist level. Unfortunately, in certain turning configurations, the wheels extend beyond the cowling. In those situations, the bump sensor is totally useless in preventing the expensive synchro-drive mechanism from being damaged in a collison.

Feeler sensors are whiskers or antennae, only not as sensitive as those on animals. Contact of a whisker and an object will trip a binary switch, whereas there is reason to believe that an insect or animal can extract much more information. Bump and feeler sensors are actually tactile sensors since they require the robot to be touching something in order to generate a reading.

a.

b.

Figure 6.10   CRISbot, the Colorado School of Mines' entry in the 1997 AAAI Mobile Robot Competition Hors d'Oeuvres, Anyone? event. a.) Interacting with the audience. b.) Audience members "communicated" by kicking the two protruding bumpers near the bottom of the robot. (Photographs courtesy of AAAI.)

However, they are often interchangeable with IR sensors because IR sensors often operate over the short range (inches) with less reliability.

6.6   Computer Vision

COMPUTER VISION

IMAGE

Computer vision refers to processing data from any modality which uses the electromagnetic spectrum which produces an image. An *image* is essentially a way of representing data in a picture-like format where there is a direct physical correspondence to the scene being imaged. Unlike sonar, which returns a single range reading which could correspond to an object anywhere within a 30° cone, an image implies multiple readings placed in a two-dimensional array or grid. Every element in the array maps onto a small region of space. The elements in image arrays are called *pixels*, a contraction

PIXELS

of the words "picture element." The modality of the device determines what the image measures. If a visible light camera is used, then the value stored at each pixel is the value of the light (e.g., color). If a thermal camera is used, then the value is the heat at that region. The function that converts a signal IMAGE FUNCTION into a pixel value is called an *image function*.

Computer vision includes cameras, which produce images over the same electromagnetic spectrum that humans see, to more exotic technologies: thermal sensors, X-rays, laser range finders, and synthetic aperature radar. Simple forms of computer vision are becoming more popular due to the drop in prices and miniaturization of cameras and because reactive robots need to exploit affordances such as color or texture.

As noted in the Introduction, computer vision is a separate field of study from robotics, and has produced many useful algorithms for filtering out noise, compensating for illumination problems, enhancing images, finding lines, matching lines to models, extracting shapes and building 3D representations. Reactive robots tend not to use those algorithms. Most of the algorithms, especially those that remove noise, require many computations on each pixel in the image; until recently, the algorithms were too computationally expensive to run in real-time. Also, there was a resistance to algorithms which required any type of memory or modeling. Therefore a robot designed to follow paths which used vision to extract the path boundary lines in the current image based on knowledge of the width, then predicted where the path boundary lines should be in the next image would be on the borderline of reactivity.

6.6.1 CCD cameras

Computer vision on reactive robots is most often from a video camera, which uses CCD (charged couple device) technology to detect visible light. A video camera, such as a camcorder, is arranged so that light falls on an array of closely spaced metal-oxide semiconductor (MOS) capacitors. Interestingly, the MOS capacitors are rectangular, not square, so there is some distortion in creating the image. The capacitors form a shift register, and output is either a line at a time ("line transfer") or the whole array at one time ("frame transfer").

The output of most consumer video signals is analog, and must be digitized for use by a computer. Consumer digital cameras post an analog signal, but the update rate is too slow at this time for real-time reactive robot control. The A/D conversion process takes longer than the CCD array can sense light, so the camera device can either have many frame buffers, which create a pipeline of images (but is expensive), or have a low frame rate.

FRAMEGRABBER   A *framegrabber* is a card which fits inside a computer, accepts analog camera signals and outputs the digitized results. The card has a software driver which allows the robot software to communicate with the board. Framegrabbers can produce a grayscale or a color digital image. In the early part of the 1990's, color-capable framegrabbers were prohibitively expensive, costing around $3,000 USD. Now color framegrabbers can be purchased from $300 to $500 USD, and TV tuners which can capture a single frame are available for $50 USD.

6.6.2   Grayscale and color representation

The framegrabber usually expresses the grayscale value of a pixel as an 8 bit number (1 byte of computer memory). This leads to 256 discrete values of gray, with 0 representing black and 255 representing white. (Remember, 256 values means 0...255.)

Color is represented differently. First, there are many different methods of expressing color. Home PC printers use a subtractive method, where cyan plus yellow make green. Most commercial devices in the U.S. use a NTSC (television) standard. Color is expressed as the sum of three measurements: red, green, and blue. This is simply abbreviated as *RGB*.

RGB   RGB is usually represented as three *color planes*, or axes of a 3D cube as COLOR PLANES   shown in Fig. 6.11. The cubic represents all possible colors. A specific color is represented by a tuple of three values to be summed: (R, G, B). Black is (0,0,0) or 0+0+0, or no measurements on any of the three color planes. White is (255, 255, 255). The pure colors of red, green, and blue are represented by (255,0,0), (0,255,0), and (0,0,255) respectively. This is the same as in color graphics.

Notice that the cube dimensions in the figure are 256 by 256 by 256, where 256 is the range of integers that can be expressed with 8 bits. Since there are three color dimensions, a manufacturer may refer to this as 24-bit color (3 x 8), to distinguish their framegrabber from ones which map color onto a linear grayscale. The 8-bit color model is what is used to colorize old black and white movies. There are only 256 values of color, which is quite limited, and the gray values are often ambiguous. The pixel values of a person's red lips might be 185, while their dark blue dress is also 185. A person may have to indicate which regions in each frame of the film where 185=red and 185=dark blue. 8-bit color is not often used for robots, unless the robot will

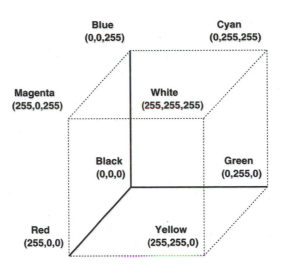

Figure 6.11   RGB color cube.

be operating in an environment where the only visible colors will not have an ambiguity.

24-bit color is usually sufficient for robotics. For other applications of computer vision such as medical imaging, weather forecasting, or military reconaissance, an 8 bit resolution is often insufficient. Those applications may use 10 bits for each color plane. Since 10 bits do not fall on a byte boundary, it can be awkward to program algorithms for representing and manipulating this kind of image. Companies such as Pixar make special computers for these applications.

In programming terms, 24-bit color image is often declared in computer programs in two ways:

1. *Interleaved.* Interleaved means the colors are stored together, RGB RGB RGB ..., and it is the more common representation. The order is almost always red, green, then blue, although there may be framegrabbers which do not follow that convention. Below is a code fragment where the color is displayed for a pixel at location row, col.

```
#define    RED    0
#define    GREEN  1
#define    BLUE   2
```

```
int            image[ROW][COLUMN][COLOR_PLANE];
    . . .
red = image[row][col][RED];
green = image[row][col][GREEN];
blue = image[row][col][BLUE];
display_color(red, green, blue);
```

2. *Separate.* Some framegrabbers store an image as three separate two-dimensional arrays, as shown below. Some framegrabbers have functions which return each color plane separately or interleaved. The equivalent code fragment is:

```
int            image_red[ROW][COLUMN];
int            image_green[ROW][COLUMN];
int            image_blue[ROW][COLUMN];
    . . .
red = image_red[row][col];
red = image_green[row][col];
red = image_blue[row][col];
display_color(red, green, blue);
```

The RGB representation has disadvantages for robotics. Color in RGB is a function of the wavelength of the light source, how the surface of the object modifies it (surface reflectance), and the sensitivity of the sensor. The first problem is that color is not absolute. RGB is based on the sensitivity of the three color sensing elements to reflected light. An object may appear to be at different values at different distances due to the intensity of the reflected light. Fig. 6.12 shows the same program and parameters to segment an orange landmark that is serving as a "flag" for tracking a small robot just outside of the image. The RGB segmentation in Fig. 6.12a is more correct than in Fig. 6.12b. The only difference is that the flagged robot has moved, thereby changing the incidence of the light. This degradation in segmentation qual-

VISUAL EROSION   ity is called *visual erosion*, because the object appears to erode with changes in lighting. Moreover, CCD devices are notoriously insensitive to red. This means that one of the three color planes is not as helpful in distinguishing colors.

Clearly a device which was sensitive to the absolute wavelength of the reflected light (the hue) would be more advantageous than having to work

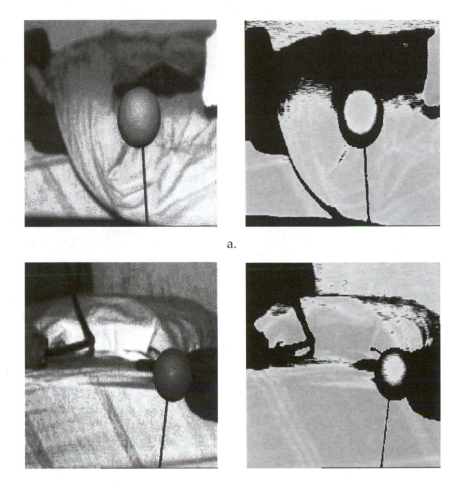

a.

b.

Figure 6.12   Images showing visual erosion of an orange landmark sticking up from a small robot (not visible): a.) Original image and RGB segmentation and b.) original image and degradation in RGB segmentation as robot moves farther from camera.

HSI
HUE

SATURATION
VALUE
INTENSITY

around the limitations of RGB. Such a device would work on the *HSI* (hue, saturation, intensity) representation of color. The *hue* is the dominant wavelength and does not change with the robot's relative position or the object's shape. *Saturation* is the lack of whiteness in the color; red is saturated, pink is less saturated. The *value* or *intensity* measure is the quantity of light received by the sensor. So HSV is a very different color scheme than RGB.

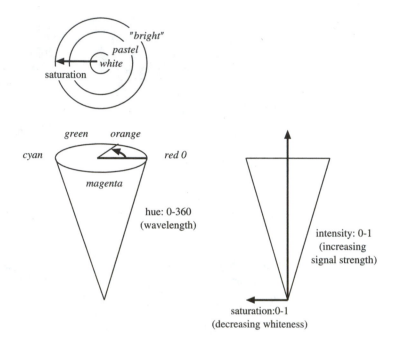

Figure 6.13   HSV space representation.

HSV is a three-dimensional space in that it has three variables, but it is definitely not a cube representation, more of a cone as seen in Fig. 6.13. The hue, or color, is measured in degrees from 0 to 360. Saturation and intensity are real numbers between 0 and 1. These are generally scaled to 8-bit numbers. Accordingly, red is both 0 and 255, orange is 17, green is at 85, blue is 170, with magenta at 200.

HSV space is challenging for roboticists for many reasons. First, it requires special cameras and framegrabbers to directly measure color in HSV space. This equipment is prohibitively expensive. Second, there is a software conversion from the RGB space measured by consumer electronics, but it is computationally expensive and has singularities (values of RGB where the conversion fails). These singularities occur at places where the three colors for a pixel are the same; the flatness of the red color plane in CCD cameras increases the likelihood that a singularity will occur.

An alternative color space that is currently being explored for robotics is the Spherical Coordinate Transform (SCT).[140] That color space was designed

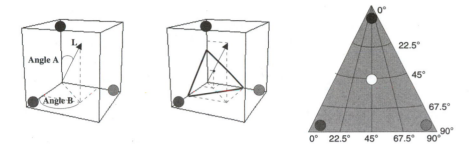

Figure 6.14   Spherical coordinate transform.

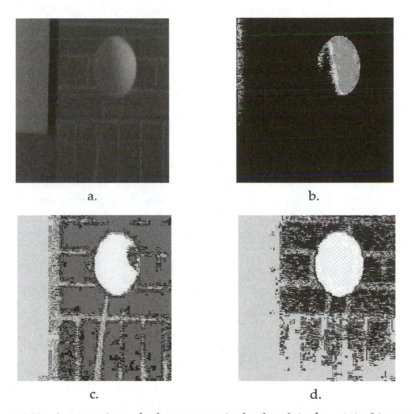

Figure 6.15   A comparison of color spaces: a.) a landmark in the original image, b.) RGB segementation, c.) HSI segmentation, and d.) SCT segmentation.

to transform RGB data to a color space that more closely duplicates the response of the human eye. It is used in biomedical imaging, but has not been widely considered for robotics. The shape of the color space is triangular, as shown in Fig. 6.14. Initial results indicate it is much more insensitive to changes in lighting.[74] Fig. 6.15 shows an image and the results of segmenting a color in RGB, HSI, and SCT spaces.

6.6.3 Region segmentation

REGION SEGMENTATION

The most ubiquitous use of computer vision in reactive robotics is to identify a region in the image with a particular color, a process called *region segmentation*. Region segmentation and color affordances are a staple perceptual algorithm for successful entries to many different international robot competitions, including the AAAI Mobile Robot Competition, RoboCup, and MIROSOT. There are many color region segmentation algorithms available and Newton Labs sells a *Cognachrome* board dedicated to the rapid extraction of colored regions. The basic concept is to identify all the pixels in an image which are part of the region and then navigate to the region's center (centroid). The first step is to threshold all pixels which share the same color (thresholding), then group those together and throw out any pixels which don't seem to be in the same area as the majority of the pixels (region growing).

BINARY IMAGE

THRESHOLDING

Ch. 5 described a robot which used red to signify a red Coca-Cola can for recycling. Ideally, the robot during the searching for the can behavior would see the world as a *binary image* (having only 2 values) consisting of red, not-red. This partitioning of the world can be achieved by *thresholding* the image and creating a binary image. A C/C++ code example is shown below:

```
for (i= = 0; i < numberRows; i++)
  for (j= = 0; j < numberColumns; j++) {
    if ((ImageIn[i][j][RED] == redValue)
        && (ImageIn[i][j][GREEN] == greenValue)
        && (ImageIn[i][I][BLUE] == blueValue)) {
            ImageOut[i][j] = 255;
    }
    else {
      ImageOut[i][j] = 0;
    }
}
```

Note that the output of a thresholded color image is a two-dimensional array, since there is no need to have more than one value attached at each pixel. Also, in theory a binary image would permit only values of 0 and 1. However, on many compilers there is no particular benefit to doing a bit level representation, and it can complicate code reuse. Also, most display software is used to displaying at least 256 values. The difference between 1 and 0 is not detectable by the human eye. Therefore, it is more common to replace the 1 with a 255 and use a full byte per pixel.

Thresholding works better in theory than in practice due to the lack of color constancy. The shape of an object will mean that even though a human sees the object as a solid color, the computer will see it as a set of similar colors. The common solution is to specify a range of high and low values on each color plane. The C/C++ code would now become:

```
for (i= = 0; i< numberRows; i++)
  for (j= = 0; j<numberColumns; j++) {
    if (((ImageIn[i][j][RED] >= redValueLow)
 && (ImageIn[i][j][RED] <= redValueHigh))
      &&((ImageIn[i][j][GREEN]>=greenValueLow)
        &&(ImageIn[i][j][GREEN] <= greenValueHigh))
      &&((ImageIn[i][j][BLUDE]>=blueValueLow)
 &&(ImageIn[i][j][BLUE] <= blueValueHigh))) {
            ImageOut[i][j] = 255;
    }
    else {
      ImageOut[i][j] = 0;
    }
}
```

The change in viewpoints and lighting means that the range which defines the object from the robot's current position is likely to change. The color range for the object has to be made even wider to include the set of color values the object will take. If the object color is unique for that environment, this increase in the color range is acceptable. Otherwise, if there are objects which have a color close enough to the object of interest, those objects may be mistaken for the target. In some circles, the object of interest is called the *foreground*, while everything else in the image is called the *background*. Thresholding an image requires a significant contrast between the background and foreground to be successful.

FOREGROUND
BACKGROUND

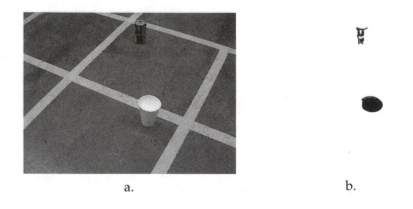

a.   b.

Figure 6.16   Segmentation of a red Coca Cola can: a.) original image and b.) resulting red regions. Note that some non-object pixels showed a reddish color.

Fig. 6.16 is the output of a threshold on color alone. If a robot was to move to the "red" in the image, how would it know which pixel to follow? The perceptual schema could be instantiated for each red pixel; this is simple, but it would waste a lot of execution cycles. The perceptual schema could take the weighted centroid of all the red pixels. In this case, it would be somewhat about where most people would say the center of the can was. Or, the perceptual schema could attempt to find the largest region where red pixels were adjacent to each other, then take the centroid of that region. (The region is often referred to as a "blob," and the extraction process is known as blob analysis.)

Color regions can also be helpful in cluttered environments. Fig. 6.17 shows a Denning mobile robot simulating a search of a collapsed building. The international orange vest of the workman provides an important cue. The robot can signal a teleoperator when it sees bright colors.

6.6.4   Color histogramming

COLOR
HISTOGRAMMING

Thresholding works well for objects which consist of one color or one dominant color. A different technique popularized by Mike Swain, called *color histogramming*, can be used to identify a region with several colors.[137] Essentially, color histogramming is a way to match the proportion of colors in a region.

a.   b.

c.

Figure 6.17   An urban search and rescue scene. a.) a Denning mobile robot searching, b.) image from the camera, and c.) segmentation for orange.

A color histogram is a type of histogram. A histogram is a bar chart of data. The user specifies the range of values for each bar, called buckets. The size of the bar is the number of data points whose value falls into the range for that bucket. For example, a histogram for a grayscale image might have 8 buckets (0-31, 32-63, 64-95, 96-127, 128-159, 160-191, 192-223, 224-251) and each bucket contains the number of pixels in the image that fell into that range. Constructing a color histogram is straightforward for a region in hue space, as shown in Fig. 6.18.

A color histogram in RGB or any other distributed color space is a bit harder to visualize. The grayscale and hue image histograms had only one axis for buckets, because these images have only one plane that matters. But a color image has 3 planes in the RGB coordinate system. As a result, it has buckets for each color plane or axis. Assuming that each plane is divided

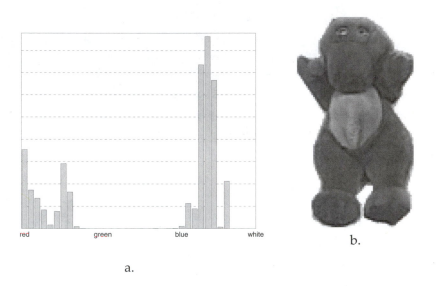

b.

a.

Figure 6.18   a.) A histogram for b.) the image of the children's toy, Barney.

into 8 buckets, the first bucket would be the number of pixels which fell into the range of (R, G, B) of (0-31, 0-31, 0-31).

The real advantage of a color histogram for reactive robots is that color histograms can be subtracted from each other to determine if the current image (or some portion), I, matches a previously constructed histogram, E. The histograms are subtracted bucket by bucket (j buckets total), and the difference indicates the number of pixels that didn't match. The number of mismatched pixels divided by the number of pixels in the image gives a percentage match. This is called the histogram intersection:

$$(6.1) \quad intersection \;\; = \;\; \frac{\sum_{j=1}^{n} min(I_j - E_j)}{\sum_{j=1}^{n} E_j}$$

For example, a robot can "wake up" and imprint the object in front of it by constructing the color histogram. Then a perceptual schema for a releaser or behavior can compute the color histogram intersection of the current image with the imprint. The robot can use the color histogram to determine if a particular object is of interest or not.

Because the color histogram of a current image can be matched with another image, the technique appears to be model-based, or recognition. But reactive systems do not permit recognition types of perception. Is this a contradiction? No; a color histogram is an example of a local, behavior-specific representation which can be directly extracted from the environment. For example, a robot could be shown a Barney doll with its distinct purple color with green belly as the percept for the goal for a move-to-goal behavior. However, the robot will follow a purple triangle with a green region, because the ratio of colors is the same. There is no memory and no inference, just a more complex stimulus.

Note that the intersection can be considered to be a measure of the strength of the stimulus, which is helpful in reactive robotics. In one set of experiments, a robot was presented a poster of Sylvester and Tweety. It learned the histogram, then after learning the object (e.g., fixating on it), it would begin to move towards it, playing a game of tag as a person moved the poster around. The robot used a simple attractive potential fields-based move-to-goal behavior, where the perceptual schema provided the location of the poster and the percent intersection. The motor schema used the location to compute the direction to the poster, but the intersection influenced the magnitude of the output vector. If the person moved the poster into a dark area or turned it at an angle, the intersection would be low and the robot would move slower. If the match was strong, the robot would speed up. Overall, it produced a very dog-like behavior where the robot appeared to play tag quickly (and happily) until the human made it too difficult. Then if the human moved the poster back to a more favorable position, the robot would resume playing with no hard feelings.

6.7 Range from Vision

STEREOPSIS
OPTIC FLOW

An important topic in computer vision is how to extract range information. Humans extract depth from vision. In most cases, though not always, depth perception is due to having two eyes and being able to triangulate as shown in Fig. 6.20, also known as *stereopsis*. Other times, perception of depth is related to *optic flow* and simple cues such as shadows, texture, and expected size of objects. This section covers three types of vision sensors which are commonly used to create an image representing a depth map: *stereo camera pairs*, *light stripers*, and *laser ranger finders*.

Figure 6.19   A Denning mobile robot using a color histogram to play tag with a poster of Sylvester and Tweety.

6.7.1   Stereo camera pairs

Using two cameras to extract range data is often referred to as *range from stereo, stereo disparity, binocular vision,* or just plain "stereo." One way to extract depth is to try to superimpose a camera over each eye as in Fig. 6.20a. Each camera finds the same point in each image, turns itself to center that point in the image, then measures the relative angle. The cameras are known as the *stereo pair*.

STEREO PAIR

This method has two challenges. The first is that it is hard to design and build a mechanism which can precisely move to verge on the points. (It is even harder to design and build an inexpensive vergence mechanism.) The second challenge is even more fundamental: *how does the robot know that it is looking at the same point in both images?* This problem is referred to as the *correspondence* problem, since the task is to find a point in one image that corresponds to a point in the other image. A common approach is to identify "interesting" or potentially uniquely valued pixels in the image, such as very bright or dark spots or edges. The algorithm that selects interesting pixels is called an *interest operator*. Since even minute changes in lighting make a difference in the image, there is no guarantee that the two images, even though acquired at precisely the same time from two cameras, will "see" the same values for corresponding pixels. Therefore, interest operator algorithms usually return a list of interesting pixels, not just one, and a matching algorithm tries to find the best correspondence between all of them. After the interest

CORRESPONDENCE

INTEREST OPERATOR

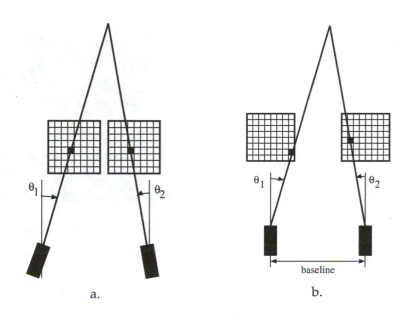

a.   b.

Figure 6.20 Ways of extracting depth from a pair of cameras: a.) vergence of the cameras to determine the depth of a point, and b.) a set of rectified stereo images.

points are established, the rest of the pixels have to be labeled with a depth relative to those points.

Fortunately, it is not necessary to have a mechanical vergence system. Instead, cameras can be mounted in place with the optic axes parallel to each other and perpendicular to the mount, producing *rectified images*.[41] This type of traditional stereo "head" is shown in Fig. 6.21. The space between the axes of two cameras is called the baseline. The distance in the location of the point of interest between the images is called the *disparity*; the distance of the point from the cameras is inversely proportional to disparity.[69] Fig. 6.20b shows the geometry behind a stereo pair.

While rectified images eliminate the need for expensive mechanical vergence systems, they don't solve the correspondence problem. If the cameras are aligned precisely, then one row in the left image will correspond to a row in the right image. These rows are said to be *epipolar lines* or projections of a *epipolar plane*. Whenever the robot finds an interesting point in one image, it only has to consider the pixels along the epipolar line in the other image. This is a tremendous computational savings. However, it only works if the

RECTIFIED IMAGES

DISPARITY

EPIPOLAR LINES
EPIPOLAR PLANE

Figure 6.21   A stereo camera pair mounted on a pan/tilt head.

cameras are perfectly matched optically and remain in alignment. In practice, robots move, bump, and suffer alignment drifts, plus the cameras may
have some flaws in their optics. The alignment can be periodically compen-
CAMERA CALIBRATION   sated for in software through a *camera calibration* process, where the robot
is presented with a standard and then creates a calibration look up table or
function. Fig. 6.22 shows the CMU Uranus robot calibrating its camera system. As a result, many researchers are turning to units which package a
stereo pair in one fixed case, where the alignment cannot be altered. Fig. 6.25
shows the results using a stereo range system using three cameras in a fixed
configuration.

The first robot to use stereo vision successfully was Hans Moravec's Stanford Cart shown in Fig. 6.23a Moravec worked on the Cart while at graduate
school at Stanford between 1973 and 1980. Fig. 6.23b shows the Marsokhod
rover developed in the late 1990's which used a stereo pair for real-time navigation. Longer baselines tend to be more accurate because a slight measurement error has a smaller impact, but smaller baselines have a smaller
"footprint," in effect, take up less room. The same point in both images still
has to be identified.

Fig. 6.24 shows the simplified flow of operations in extracting range from
a pair of images. The process begins with two images, the left-right pair, and
RANGE IMAGE   results in a third image called the *range image* or the *depth map*. The left-right
DEPTH MAP   pair can be grayscale or color, but the depth map is a grayscale map, where
intensity is proportional to the distance the pixel is away from the cameras.
Fig. 6.25 shows two stereo images and the resulting depth map.

Figure 6.22 Uranus undergoing calibration. (Photograph courtesy of Hans Moravec.)

The major drawback with extracting range information from vision is that the algorithms tend to be computationally complex. Stereo matching algorithms are typically on the order of $O(n^2 m^2)$. This means that to process an image of size 640 by 480 takes on the order of 9×10^{10} instructions, while to simply segment a color is on the order of $O(nm)$ or 3×10^5 instructions. Even with advances in microprocessors, a stereo range map can take minutes to compute.

6.7.2 Light stripers

Light striping, light stripers or *structured light detectors* work by projecting a colored line (or stripe), grid, or pattern of dots on the environment. Then a regular vision camera observes how the pattern is distorted in the image. For example, in Fig. 6.26a, the striper projects four lines. The lines should occur at specific, evenly spaced rows in the camera image if the surface is flat. If the surface is not flat, as shown in Fig. 6.26b, the lines will have breaks or

b.

a.

Figure 6.23 Robots and stereo: a.) The Stanford Cart developed in the late 1970's. (Photograph courtesy of Hans Moravec.) b.)The Marsokhod rover developed in the late 1990's jointly by scientists from McDonnell Douglas, Russia, and NASA Ames Research Center. (Image courtesy of the National Aeronautics and Space Administration.)

discontinuities. A vision algorithm can quickly scan each of the designated rows to see if the projected line is continuous or not. The location of the breaks in the line give information about the size of the obstacle. The vision algorithm can also look for where the dislocated line segments appears, since the distance in image coordinates is proportional to the depth of the object. The relative placement of the lines indicates whether the object is above the NEGATIVE OBSTACLE ground plane (an obstacle) or below (a hole or *negative obstacle*). The more lines or finer-grained grid, the more depth information.

Light stripers are less expensive for many reasons. First, since they are producing a line or pattern to be measured, expensive time-of-flight detectors are unnecessary. The detection is done by the camera. Second, producing a thick line that can be detected by a camera does not require a laser. Instead it can be done with structured light, an optical method which allows "regular" light to mimic desirable properties of laser light. Finally, light stripers pro-

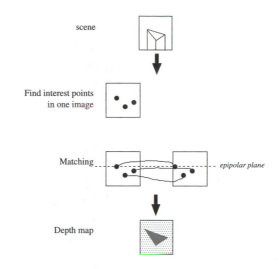

Figure 6.24   A simplified flow of operations in extracting range from a stereo pair.

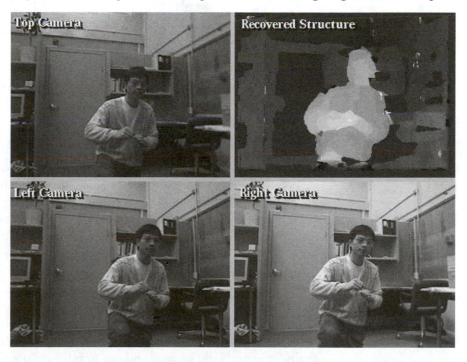

Figure 6.25   A set of stereo images from a Triclops stereo camera and resulting depth map. (Images courtesy of Chandra Kambhamettu.)

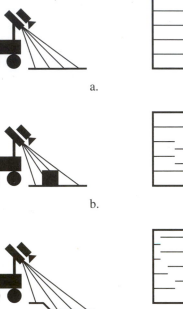

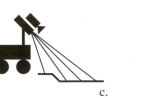

a.

b.

c.

Figure 6.26 Situations and resulting images of a.) flat surface, b.) an obstacle, and c.) a negative obstacle.

duce a fairly coarse pattern; they don't project a line or grid onto every pixel in the image. This means the device is overall less demanding, and therefore less expensive to build.

Light stripers were popular in the late 1980's and early 1990's, and laboratories such as the University of Pennsylvania's GRASP Lab under the direction of Ruzena Bajcsy produced excellent results in extracting 3D information. However, these efforts focused on using the depth map to recognize an object under laboratory conditions. The results did not transfer particularly well to mobile robots. Reactive robots are not concerned with recognition, so many of the algorithms were not particularly useful or provided a quick, reflexive response. Also, in the open world, objects were often the same color as the projected light or near enough to it to confuse the vision system. The amount and direction of lighting could also confuse the striper, with brightly lit rooms making it difficult to see the bright laser or structured light.

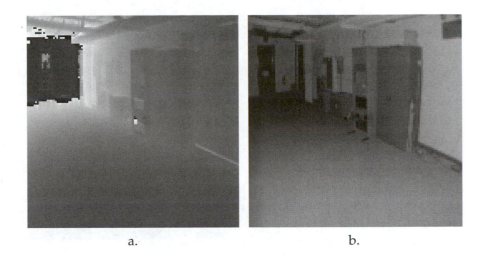

a.   b.

Figure 6.27   Lidar images from an Odetics LADAR camera: a.) range and b.) intensity.   (Images courtesy of University of South Florida and Oak Ridge National Laboratory.)

The Sojourner Mars rover used a light striping system for obstacle avoidance. The system projected five lines ahead of the vehicle.[134] This worked well because Mars has little color or light diversity. Interestingly enough, the light striper used one member of a stereo pair, but unlike the Marsokhod, Sojourner did not use stereo for navigation. Instead, the robot would periodically take a stereo pair for reconstruction and map-making on Earth.

6.7.3   Laser ranging

Ultrasonics introduces acoustic energy into the environment and measures the time of flight of the signal to return. The same principle can be used with lasers; a laser beam can emitted and then the reflectance measured. Unlike a sonar beam which has a very wide field of view (almost 30°), a laser produces an almost infinitesimal field of view. If the laser is directed in a scan, just like a raster scan on a CRT, the device can cover a reasonable area and produce an image, where the image function produces depth values. Devices which use lasers to produce a depth map or image are often called *laser radar*, *ladar*, or *lidar*. They can generate up to one million range pixels per second,[52] with a range of 30 meters and an accuracy of a few millimeters. The mechanical

LASER RADAR
LADAR
LIDAR

Figure 6.28   Sick laser, covering a 180° area.

scanning component makes lidars very expensive, on the order of $30,000 to $100,000 USD. A less expensive solution for navigation is to create a planar laser range finder.

A lidar produces two images: intensity and range. Fig. 6.27 shows the images produced by a Odetics laser range (LADAR) camera. The intensity map is essentially a black and white photograph and measures the intensity of the light reflected or absorbed by objects in the scene. This corresponds to how humans perceive the scene The image function for the range image is depth from the camera. Pixels that are black, or have a value of 0, are closer than white pixels. A flat floor usually appears as a radiating set of semi-circles going from near to far; trigonometry is then used to compute that the

RANGE SEGMENTATION circles represent a flat surface. This process is called *range segmentation* and can be quite difficult.

Lidars have some problems in practice. For example, Fig. 6.27 shows an area on the range image that is pure black or very near. But as can be seen from the intensity image the area is actually far away. Likewise, the black moulding between the wall and floor appear to be very far away on the range image. The errors were due to out of range conditions, absorption of the light (not enough light returned), or to the optical equivalent of specular reflection (light hitting corners gets reflected away from the receiver).

A planar laser range finder, such as the Sick shown in Fig. 6.28, provides a narrow horizontal range map. The map is essentially a high resolution polar plot. Robots such as Nomads and Pioneers originally came with Sick lasers mounted in parallel to the floor. This was useful for obstacle avoidance (as long as the obstacle was tall enough to break the laser plane), but not particularly helpful for extracting 3D information. Also, as with sonars, robots ran the risk of being decapitated by obstacles such as tables which did not appear in the field of view of the range sensor but could hit a sensor pod or antenna. To combat this problem, researchers have recently begun mounting planar laser range finders at a slight angle upward. As the robot moves forward, it gets a different view of upcoming obstacles. In some cases, researchers have mounted two laser rangers, one tilted slightly up and the other slightly down, to provide coverage of overhanging obstacles and negative obstacles.

6.7.4   Texture

The variety of sensors and algorithms available to roboticists can actually distract a designer from the task of designing an elegant sensor suite. In most cases, reactive robots use range for navigation; robots need a sensor to keep it from hitting things. Ian Horswill designed the software and camera system of Polly, shown in Fig. 6.29, specifically to explore vision and the relationship to the environment using subsumption.[70] Horswill's approach

LIGHTWEIGHT VISION   is called *lightweight vision*, to distinguish its ecological flavor from traditional model-based methods.

Polly served as an autonomous tour-guide at the MIT AI Laboratory and Brown University during the early 1990's. At that time vision processing was slow and expensive, which was totally at odds with the high update rates needed for navigation by a reactive mobile robot. The percept for the obstacle avoidance behavior was based on a clever affordance: texture. The halls of the AI Lab were covered throughout with the same carpet. The "color" of the carpet in the image tended to change due to lighting, but the overall texture or "grain" did not. In this case, texture was measured as edges per unit area, as seen with the fine positioning discussed in Ch. 3.

RADIAL DEPTH MAP   The robot divided the field of view into angles or sectors, creating a *radial depth map*, or the equivalent of a polar plot. Every sector with the texture of the carpet was marked empty. If a person was standing on the carpet, that patch would have a different texture and the robot would mark the area as occupied. Although this methodology had some problems—for example, strong shadows on the floor created "occupied" areas—it was fast and elegant.

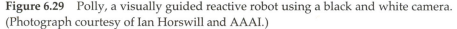

Figure 6.29   Polly, a visually guided reactive robot using a black and white camera. (Photograph courtesy of Ian Horswill and AAAI.)

6.8   Case Study: Hors d'Oeuvres, Anyone?

The University of South Florida's (USF) entry in the 1999 AAAI Mobile Robot Competition Hors d'Oeuvres, Anyone? event provides a case study of selecting sensors, constructing reactive behaviors, and using behavioral sensor fusion. The entry used two cooperative robots. The goal was to push the envelope in robotic sensing by using six different sensing modalities with 40 different physical devices on one robot and four modalities with 23 devices on the other. Although the robots executed under a hybrid deliberative/reactive style of architecture (covered later in Ch. 7), the basic design process followed the steps in Ch. 5, and produced a largely behavioral system. The entry won a Technical Achievement award of Best Conceptual and Artistic Design after a series of hardware and software timing failures prevented it from working at the competition.

a.   b.

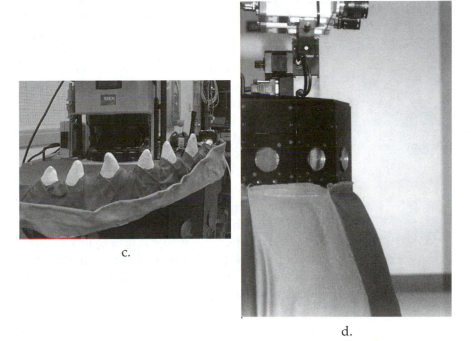

c.

d.

Figure 6.30 USF robots in the "Hors d'Oeuvres, Anyone?" event. a.) Family portrait, where Borg Shark is on the left, Puffer Fish on the right, with b.) the thermal sensor located as the Borg Shark's "third eye," c.) the SICK laser located behind the Borg Shark's teeth (head piece is removed for better view), and d.) a profile of Puffer Fish's skirt showing spatial relationship to sonar.

Step 1: Describe the task. The "Hors d'Oeuvres, Anyone?" event required fully autonomous robots to circulate in the reception area at the AAAI conference with a tray of finger food, find and approach people, interact with them, and refill the serving tray. Each robot was scored on covering the area, noticing when the tray needed refilling, interacting with people naturally, having a distinct personality, and recognizing VIPs. The USF entry used two robots, shown in Fig. 6.30, costumed by the USF Art Department in order to attract attention. The Borg Shark was the server robot, and navigated through audience following a pre-planned route. It would stop and serve at regular intervals or whenever a treat was removed from the tray. It used a DEC-talk synthesizer to broadcast audio files inviting audience members to remove a treat from its mouth, but it had no way of hearing and understanding natural language human commands. In order to interact more naturally with people, the Borg Shark attempted to maintain eye contact with people. If it saw a person, it estimated the location in image coordinates of where a VIP's colored badge might be, given the location of the face.

When the Borg Shark was almost out of food, she would call over radio ethernet her assistant robot, Puffer Fish. Puffer Fish would be stationary in sleep mode, inhaling and exhaling through her inflatable skirt and turning her cameras as if avoiding people crowding her. When Puffer Fish awoke, she would head with a full tray of food (placed on her stand by a human) to the coordinates given to her by Borg Shark. She would also look for Borg Shark's distinctive blue costume, using both dead reckoning and visual search to move to goal. Once within 2 meters of Borg Shark, Puffer Fish would stop. A human would physically swap trays, then kick the bumpers to signal that the transfer was over. Borg Shark would resume its serving cycle, while Puffer Fish would return to its home refill station.

Both robots were expected to avoid all obstacles: tables, chairs, people. Since there was a tendency for people to surround the robotos, preventing coverage of the area or refilling, the robots had different responses. Borg Shark, who was programmed to be smarmy, would announce that it was coming through and begin moving. Puffer Fish, with a grumpy, sullen personality, would vocally complain, then loudly inflate her skirt and make a rapid jerk forward, usually causing spectators to back up and give her room.

Step 2: Describe the robots. The robots used for the entry were Nomad 200 bases, each with a unique sensor suite.

The original sensors on Borg Shark included a pair of color cameras mounted on a pan-tilt head, redundant sonar rings, and a SICK planar laser:

Type	Modality	Devices
exteroceptive	vision	2 cameras
exteroceptive	laser	1 planar ranger
exteroceptive	sonar	15 ultrasonics (upper)
		15 ultrasonics (lower)
exteroceptive	tactile	1 bumper switch
proprioceptive	motor encoders	3 drive, steer, turret control
		2 pan, tilt control

The sensors on Puffer Fish were:

Type	Modality	Devices
exteroceptive	vision	2 cameras
exteroceptive	sonar	15 ultrasonics
exteroceptive	tactile	1 bumper switch
proprioceptive	motor encoders	3 drive, steer, turret control
		2 pan, tilt control

Step 3: Describe the environment. The environment was a convention center arena, with variable lighting and many people causally dressed. The major perceptual challenge was to maintain eye contact with people and to determine if a person is a VIP. The VIPs' badges were marked with distinctively colored ribbons, so if the robot was sure it was looking in the right area, the color would afford a VIP. However, the colors of the ribbon were fairly common. If the robot scanned at about chest height for ribbons, it would likely find a shirt of that color in the crowd who would be wear wearing bright tourist wear. This would cause it to mis-identify a VIP, losing points. Another approach was to use sonars to find a person: read a range, point the camera in that direction and tilt to the angle where the eyes would be for a person of average height. This focus-of-attention mechanism could be used to look in the likely location of a badge. However, it was known from experience that people rarely stood along the acoustic axis of a sonar. If a single person was picked up by two sonars, the robot would look for 10 seconds to the left of the person and then 10 seconds to the right. If multiple people were present, the robot would seem even more dysfunctional, and the focus-of-attention mechanism would not work correctly.

A better solution would be to detect a person using vision. Notice that detection is not the same thing as recognition. Detection means that the robot is able to identify a face, which is reactive. Recognition would label the face and be able to recognize it at a later time, which is a deliberative function, not reactive. Is there a simple visual affordance of a face? Actually, to a vision system human skin is remarkably similar in color, regardless of ethnicity. Once the robot had found a colored region about the size and shape of a head, it could then more reliably find the VIP badges.

The other opportunity for an affordance was Puffer Fish's navigation to Borg Shark. Although Puffer Fish would receive Borg Shark's coordinates, it was unlikely that Puffer Fish could reliably navigate to Borg Shark using only dead reckoning. The coordinates were likely to be incorrect from Borg Shark's own drift over time. Then Puffer Fish would accumulate dead reckoning error, more so if it had to stop and start and avoid people. Therefore, it was decided that Puffer Fish should look for Borg Shark. Borg Shark's head piece was deliberately made large and a distinctive blue color to afford visibility over the crowd and reduce the likelihood of fixating on someone's shirt.

Step 4-7: Design, test, and refine behaviors. The choice of sensors for other behaviors, such as treat removal, was influenced by the physical location of the sensors. For example, the SICK laser for Borg Shark came mounted on the research platform as shown in Fig. 6.30b. The research platform, nominally the top of the robot, was at hand height, making it a logical place to attach a tray for holding food. It was obvious that the laser could be used to monitor the food tray area. Other teams tried various approaches such as having a colored tray and counting the amount of that color visible (more color means fewer treats on the tray, covering the color). Another approach was to build a scale and monitor the change in weight.

An interesting aspect of the robots that impacted the sensor suite indirectly were the costumes. As part of giving the robots personality, each robot had a costume. The Puffer Fish had an inflatable skirt that puffed out when the robot was crowded or annoyed. The team had to empirically test and modify the skirt to make sure it would not interfere with the sonar readings. Fig. 6.30c shows the profile of the skirt.

As seen in the behavior table below, the only behavior using any form of sensor fusion was `move-to-goal` in Puffer Fish, which had two competing instances of the goal making it sensor fission.

The initial behaviors for Borg Shark are given in the behavior table below:

Releaser	Behavior	Motor Schema	Percept	Perceptual Schema
always on	avoid()	vfh()	most-open-direction	polar-plot(sonar)
FOOD-REMOVED= treat-removal(laser)	track-face	center-face(face-centroid) track-face() check-VIP()	face-centroid ribbon-color	find-face(vision) look-for-ribbon(VIP-color)
SERVING-TIME-OUT, TRAY-FULL=bumper()	move-to-goal	pfields.attraction(waypoint)	waypoint	list of waypoints
FOOD-DEPLETED= treat-removal(laser)	track-face	center-face(face-centroid)	face-centroid	find-face(vision)

The initial behavior table for Puffer Fish was:

Releaser	Behavior	Motor Schema	Percept	Perceptual Schema
always on	avoid()	vfh()	most-open-direction	polar-plot(sonar)
AT-HOME= dead-reckoning(encoders)	sleep()	turn-camera-head() cycle-skirt()	obstacle	polar-plot(sonar)
AWAKE=radio-signal()	move-to-goal()	pfields.attraction(location)	relative-location	read-encoders()
AWAKE=radio-signal()	move-to-goal()	pfields.attraction(shark)	shark	find-shark-blue(camera)
TRAY-FULL=bumper()	move-to-goal()	pfields.attraction(home)	relative-location	read-encoders()

The `vfh` behavior is an obstacle avoidance behavior using polar plots derived from models described in Ch. 11. As the team tested the behaviors individually, the `find-face` and `treat-removal` behaviors proved to be unreliable. While color was a reasonable affordance for a face, the algorithm often returned false negatives, missing faces unless in bright light. Meanwhile the laser appeared to occasionally get a reflection from the teeth, also generating false positives, and more than 75% of the time it would miss a person's hand if the motion was quick. The rates were:

logical sensor	False Positives	False Negatives
Face-Find	1.7%	27.5%
Food-Count	6.7%	76.7%

The solution to the `find-face` performance was to exploit another affordance of a human, one used by mosquitoes: heat. The problem was partial segmentation; candidate regions were getting rejected on being too small. Heat would make a good the decision criteria. If a candidate region was co-located with a hot region, then it was declared a face. Fortunately, the team was able to transfer an E^2T digital thermometer used on another robot to Borg Shark. The thermal sensor shown in Fig. 6.30 was intended for deter-

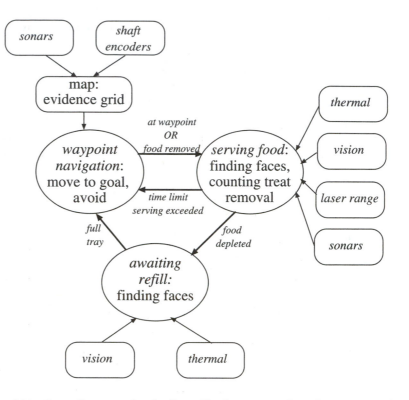

Figure 6.31 State diagrams for the Borg Shark, annotated to show sensors being used.

mining the temperature of a person on contact, but it was able to detect an increase in temperature above the ambient from a person up to two meters away.

Why wasn't the vision system simply replaced with the thermal sensor? This gets back to the attributes of sensors and how they fit with the environment. The thermal sensor has a 2° field of view, making it too slow to scan. Instead, the vision system covered a much wider field of view and could generate a small list of candidate regions. Then as the camera turned to center on the largest region, the thermal probe could decide whether this was really a person or not.

The problem with the food-count was greatly reduced by a simple AND function with the sonars. The system counted a treat as being removed only if there was a close range reading in front of the tray at the same time.

The false reading rate dropped considerably as seen below:

Logical sensor	W/O Fusion		Fusion	
	FP	FN	FP	FN
Face-Find	1.7%	27.5%	2.5%	0%
Food-Count	6.7%	76.7%	6.7%	1.7%

At this point it is helpful to step back and examine the sensing for the Hors d'Oeuvres, Anyone? entry in terms of the attributes listed in Sec. 6.3. Recall that the attributes for evaluating the suitability of an individual sensor were *field of view, range, accuracy, repeatability, resolution, responsiveness in target domain, power consumption, reliability,* and *size.* The field of view and range of the sensors was an issue, as seen by the differences in vision and thermal sensors for the face-finding behavior. The camera had a much better field of view than the thermal sensor, so it was used to focus the attention of the heat sensor. Repeatability was clearly a problem for laser with its high false positive/false negative rate. The sonars could not be used for estimating the location of a face because the resolution was too coarse. Each of the sensors had reasonable responsiveness from a hardware perspective, though the algorithms may not have been able to take advantage of them. Power consumption was not an issue because all sensors were on all the time due to the way the robots were built. Reliability and size of the hardware were not serious considerations since the hardware was already on the robots.

The algorithmic influences on the sensor design were *computational complexity* and *reliabilty.* Both were definitely a factor in the design of the perceptual schemas for the reactive behaviors. The robots had the hardware to support stereo range (two cameras with dedicated framegrabbers). This could have been used to find faces, but given the high computational complexity, even a Pentium class processor could not process the algorithm in real-time. Reliability was also an issue. The vision face finding algorithm was very unreliable, not because of the camera but because the algorithm was not well-suited for the environment and picked out extraneous blobs.

Finally, the sensing suite overall can be rated in terms of *simplicity, modularity,* and *redundancy.* The sensor suite for both Nomad robots can be considered simple and modular in that it consisted of several separate sensors, mostly commercially available, able to operate independently of each other. The sensor suite did exhibit a high degree of physical redundancy: one robot had dual sonar rings, and the sonars, laser, and camera pair could have been used for range, ignoring the placement of the shark teeth and the computational complexity. There was also a large amount of logical redundancy, which was exploited through the use of behavioral sensor fusion.

6.9   Summary

The success of a reactive system depends on the suitability of the robot's sensor suite. It is often more useful to think of sensing in terms of perceptual schemas or logical sensors needed to accomplish a task, rather than focus on the characteristics of a particular transducer or modality. Reactive perception may appear limited since it uses only behavior-specific representations and does not involve recognition. However, it supports a diversity of forms of perception, including behavioral sensor fusion. Advances in electronics have led to a plethora of range sensors and algorithms. Many of these are logically equivalent and can be used interchangeably; for example, with obstacle avoidance behaviors.

The design of a perceptual schema or a sensor suite requires a careful analysis. Each individual sensor should fit the task, power, and processing constraints. Likewise, the entire sensor suite should provide complete coverage of all perceptual processing required by the robot.

Almost all mobile robots have some form of proprioception, most likely shaft or wheel encoders used to estimate the distance traveled based on the number of times the motor has turned. Outdoor robots may carry GPS, and this trend is expected to increase as the cost of receivers goes down and inexpensive DGPS systems emerge.

Reactive navigation requires exteroception, whereby the robot observes the environment. Proprioception can guide a robot on a path, but exteroception can prevent it from hitting an unmodeled obstacle or falling off a cliff. The most common exteroceptive sensor on reactive robots is an ultrasonic transducer or sonar. An ultrasonic transducer is an active sensor which returns a single range reading based on the time-of-flight of an acoustic wave. Some of the difficulties associated with ultrasonics include erroneous readings due to specular reflection, crosstalk, and foreshortening. Other popular proximity sensors are IR and laser rangers.

Due to the low price and availability of consumer electronics, computer vision is becoming more common in robotic systems. Computer vision processing operates on images, regardless of the modality which generated it. Color coordinate systems tend to divide an image into 3 planes. The two most common color coordinate systems are RGB and HSV. HSV treats color in absolute terms, but RGB is favored by equipment manufacturers. A color space used in biomedical imaging, SCT, appears to be less sensitive to lighting conditions than RGB and RGB-derived HSV. Many reactive robots exploit color as an affordance. This can be done by thresholding an image and identifying regions of the appropriate color. A color affordance method which works well for objects with multiple colors is color histogramming. Stereo range finding is an important class of algorithms for navigation, though the computational complexity has prevented it being ported to many mobile robot applications. Laser range finders, particularly the inexpensive planar rangers, have grown in popularity over the past few years.

Despite the diversity of sensors and affordances inherent in the environment, reactive robotics is remarkable for its lack of sophistication in sensing. This may stem from the split between computer vision and robotics in the formative years of the field. Many roboticists still assume algorithms developed by computer vision specialists are too computationally expensive to work on commercially available on-board processors. This is no longer true, in part because of the increased computational power of general purpose chips. Readers are encouraged to explore the large body of literature on computer vision and free tools on the web.

6.10   Exercises

Exercise 6.1

Define sensor suite, active/passive sensors, dead reckoning, computer vision. †

Exercise 6.2

Compare and contrast the RGB and HSV color representations specifying the advantages and disadvantages of each type. †

Exercise 6.3

Ultrasonic sensors have many positive and negative attributes. Name and describe three positive and three negative attributes. †

Exercise 6.4

What is the difference between physical and logical redundancy? †

Exercise 6.5

Describe the three major problems of ultrasonic sensing, and define a hypothetical instance in which a robot would encounter each problem (such as a room with a large amount of glass surfaces). †

Exercise 6.6

Describe with examples the three attributes that should be considered for an entire sensing suite. †

Exercise 6.7

Consider a Lego Mindstorms robot. Classify the available sensors for it in terms of modalities.

Exercise 6.8

Describe the problems of specular reflection, cross talk, and foreshortening with an ultrasonic transducer. †

Exercise 6.9

List the metrics for rating individual sensors and a sensor suite, and apply these metrics to a particular application. †

Exercise 6.10

An alternative to a Denning ring is to mount one or more sonars on a mast and turn the mast. Turning gives the robot a 360° coverage. Which do you think would be better, a fixed ring or a panning mast? Would a panning mast reduce problems of foreshortening, cross-talk, and specular reflection.

Exercise 6.11

List and describe advantages and disadvantages of 3 different sensors, including one type of computer vision. †

Exercise 6.12

Describe all the different characteristics of sensors that must be evaluated when designing a sensor suite. In addition, give priorities for each to determine which you would consider to be the most and least important of these characteristics for a robot that was going to be designed for the 1994 AUVS Unmanned Ground Robotics Competition. †

Exercise 6.13

Pick a sensor suite that you think would do a good job if you were designing a robot for the 1995 UGV competition described in an earlier chapter. Explain what each sensor would do as well as describe the sensors and sensor suite in terms of the attributes listed in this chapter. †

Exercise 6.14

You are to design a sensor suite for a new robot for use by fire fighters. The robot is designed to seek out people in a smoke filled building. Keep in mind the following:

1. Visibility is often very limited due to smoke.

2. Heat can be both an attactive force (e.g. human) or repulsive (e.g. open flame).

3. Obstacles may have a wide variety of sound absorbtion (e.g. carpeting or furniture).

Describe the types of sensors that may be needed and how they will be used. Do not focus on how the robot moves around just on the sensors it will need to use. Extra credit: Comment on using simple voice recognition software and a microphone to seek out human voices (e.g., cries for help). †

Exercise 6.15

How are the concepts of logical sensors in robotics and polymorphism in object-oriented programming similar?

Exercise 6.16

Define *image function*. What is the image function for

a. the left-right images in a stereo pair?

b. the depth map?

Exercise 6.17

What are two disadvantages of light stripers?

Exercise 6.18

Consider an obstacle avoidance behavior which consists of a perceptual schema that provides a polar plot of range and motor schema which directs the robot to the most open sector. List all the logical sensors covered in this chapter that can be used interchangeably for the perceptual schema. Which of these are logically redundant? Physically redundant?

Exercise 6.19

Assume you had a mobile robot about 0.5 meters high and a planar laser range finder. What angle would you mount the laser at if the robot was intended to navigate

a. in a classroom?

b. in a hallway or reception area where the primary obstacle is people?

c. outdoors in unknown terrain?

State any assumptions your design is based on. Is there more information needed; if so, what?

Exercise 6.20   [*Programming*]

Write your own code to give you the threshold of a small interleaved image. †

Exercise 6.21   [*World Wide Web*]

Search for Kludge, another robot built by Ian Horswill. Describe Kludge's homemade whisker system and how well it works.

Exercise 6.22   [*Programming*]

Program a mobile robot to find and bump an orange tennis or soccer ball.

Exercise 6.23   [*Programming*]

Create a color histogram program. Construct the color histogram, *E*, for four different brightly colored objects, such as dolls of the South Park or the Simpsons cartoon
characters. Present the program with a different image, *I*, of one of the characters and
compute the histogram intersection with each of the four *E*. Does the highest match
correctly identify the character? Why or why not?

6.11   End Notes

For the roboticist's bookshelf.
Hobart Everett literally wrote the book, *Sensors for Mobile Robots*,[52] on robotic sensors, which provides both analytical details of sensors plus practical experience from
Everett's many years with the Navy work on robots. He has built a series of mobile
robots called ROBART (a pun on Everett's nickname, Bart); ROBART II has been in
continuous operation since 1982. Everett's laboratory has to be one of the most ideally
situated in the world. It is in San Diego, overlooks the Pacific Ocean, and is adjacent
to a frequently used volleyball court.

Hans Moravec.
If Joe Engelberger is known as the father of industrial robotics, Hans Moravec is best
known as the father of AI robotics. He has also become a well-known author, argu-
ing for the inevitability of machine intelligence in controversial books such as *Mind
Children*[94] and *Robot: mere machine to transcendent mind.*[96] His work with the Stanford Cart was a catalyzing event in attracting attention to robotics after the years of
slow progress following Shakey. Documentaries will occasionally run edited footage
of the Stanford Cart navigating outdoors, avoiding obstacles. Since the cart traveled in a stop-start fashion, with 15 minutes or so between updates, the location of
the shadows visibly change. Moravec's office mate, Rodney Brooks, helped with the
recording.

Undergraduates and sonars.
It is interesting to note that the first serious analysis of the Polaroid sonars was done
by an undergraduate at MIT, Michael Drumheller. Drumheller's paper, "Mobile Robot Localization Using Sonar," was eventually published in the *IEEE Transactions on
Pattern Analysis and Machine Intelligence* in 1987, and became a classic.

Ballard and Brown.
Dana Ballard and Chris Brown wrote the first textbook on computer vision, entitled
appropriately *Computer Vision*. Both have worked with robots, though Brown more
than Ballard. I met both of them at a workshop at a beach resort in Italy in early 1990.
I had just arrived from a harrowing bus ride from the airport and had to go past the
pool to my room in the hopes of recovering from jet lag before the meeting started in

the morning. As I walked past the pool, one of my friends said, "Oh, Chris Brown is over there!" I immediately turned to look for what I thought would be an older, dignified author wearing a suit and tie. Instead, I got soaked by a tall, youngish man impishly doing a cannonball into the pool. From that day on, I never assumed that textbook authors were dull and dignified.

The tallest roboticist.
Tom Henderson at the University of Utah was one of the founders of the concept of logical sensors. Henderson is also the tallest known roboticist, and played basketball in college for Louisiana State University.

Stereo with a single camera.
Ray Jarvis at Monash University in Austraila came up with a clever way of gathering rectified stereo images from a single camera. He used a prism to project two slightly different veiwpoints onto the lens of a camera, creating an image which had a different image on each side. The algorithm knew which pixels belong to each image, so there was no problem with processing.

USAR and Picking Up the Trash.
While picking up trash seems mundane, most people would agree that finding and rescuing survivors of an earthquake is not. The two tasks have much in common, as illustrated by the work of Jake Sprouse, and behaviors and schemas developed in one domain can be transferred to another. Sprouse was a member of the Colorado School of Mines' 1995 IJCAI competition team. The same vision program he wrote for finding "red" was used to find "international orange." Later, he extended the search strategies to incorporate aspects of how insects forage for food.[108]

Run over Barney.
The figures and materials on color histogramming used in this chapter were part of research work conducted by Dale Hawkins in persistence of belief. His use of a stuffed Barney doll started out from a class project: program a mobile robot to find a Barney doll and run over it. This is actually a straightforward reactive project. The Barney doll is a distinctive purple, making it easy for the vision system to find it. The project allowed the programmers to use the flat earth assumption, so trigonometry could be used to estimate the location to the doll based on the location in image coordinates. Hawkins' program was the clear winner, running completely over Barney. It also gave him vision code that he could reuse for his thesis.

Reactive soccer.
Color regions are often used to simplify tracking balls (and other robots) in robot soccer competitions such as RoboCup and MIROSOT. One amusing aspect is that many of these behaviors are purely reflexive; if the robot sees the ball, it responds, but if it loses the ball, it stops. Ann Brigante and Dale Hawkins programmed a No-

mad 200 to reflexively track a soccer ball to compare what would happen if the robot had some concept of object permanence. Because of the angle of the camera, the robot would lose sight of the ball when it was almost touching it. The behaviors that emerged worked, but always generated much laughter. The robot would see the ball and accelerate rapidly to its estimated location to "kick" it. When it got to the ball, it suddenly deccelerated but had enough momentum to bump the ball. The ball would slowly roll forward, back into the now-stationary robot's field of view. The robot would again jump forward, and the cycle would repeat endlessly.

Photographs and scanning.
Dale Hawkins, Mark Micire, Brian Minten, Mark Powell, and Jake Sprouse helped photograph robots, sensors, and demonstrations of perceptual behaviors.

7 The Hybrid Deliberative/Reactive Paradigm

Chapter objectives:

- Be able to describe the Hybrid Deliberative/Reactive paradigm in terms of i) sensing, acting, and planning and ii) sensing organization.

- Name and evaluate one representative Hybrid architecture in terms of: support for modularity, niche targetability, ease of portability to other domains, robustness.

- Given a list of responsibilities, be able to say whether it belongs in the deliberative layer or in the reactive layer.

- List the five basic components of a Hybrid architecture: sequencer agent, resource manager, cartographer, mission planner, performance monitoring and problem solving agent.

- Be able to describe the difference between managerial, state hierarchy, and model-oriented styles of Hybrid architectures.

- Be able to describe the use of state to define behaviors and deliberative responsibilities in state hierarchy styles of Hybrid architectures.

7.1 Overview

By the end of the 1980's, the trend in artificially intelligent robots was to design and program using the Reactive Paradigm. The Reactive Paradigm allowed robots to operate in real-time using inexpensive, commercially available processors (e.g., HC6811) with no memory. But the cost of reactivity, of course, was a system that eliminated planning or any functions which involved remembering or reasoning about the global state of the robot relative to its environment. This meant that a robot could not plan optimal trajectories (path planning), make maps, monitor its own performance, or even select the best behaviors to use to accomplish a task (general planning). Notice that not all of these functions involve planning per se; map making involves handling uncertainty, while performance monitoring (and the implied objective of what to do about degraded performance) involves problem solving and learning. In order to differentiate these more cognitively oriented functions from path planning, the term *deliberative* was coined.

DELIBERATIVE

The Reactive Paradigm also suffered somewhat because most people found that designing behaviors so that the desired overall behavior would emerge was an art, not a science. Techniques for sequencing or assembling behaviors to produce a system capable of achieving a series of sub-goals also relied heavily on the designer. Couldn't the robot be made to be smart enough to select the necessary behaviors for a particular task and generate how they should be sequenced over time?

Therefore, the new challenge for AI robotics at the beginning of the 1990's was how to put the planning, and deliberation, back into robots, but without disrupting the success of the reactive behavioral control. The consensus was that behavioral control was the "correct" way to do low level control, because of its pragmatic success, and its elegance as a computational theory for both biological and machine intelligence. As early as 1988, Ron Arkin was publishing work on how to add more cognitive functions to a behavioral system in the form of the *Autonomous Robot Architecture (AuRA)*. Many roboticists looked at adding layers of higher, more cognitive functions to their behavioral systems, emulating the evolution of intelligence. This chapter will cover five examples of architectures which illustrate this bottom-up, layering approach: *AuRA, Sensor Fusion Effects (SFX), 3T, Saphira,* and *TCA*. Other robot systems which do not strongly adhere to an architectural style, such as Rhino and Minerva, will be discussed in later chapters.

During the 1990's, members of the general AI community had become exposed to the principles of reactive robots. The concept of considering an intelligent system, or agent, as being situated in its environment, combined with the existence proof that detailed, Shakey-like world representations are not always necessary, led to a new style of planning. This change in planning was called *reactive planning*. Many researchers who had worked in traditional AI became involved in robotics. One type of reactive planner for robots, Jim Firby's *reactive-action packages (RAPs)*,[53] was integrated as a layer within the 3T architecture.[21] Architectures stemming from the planning community roots showed their traditional AI roots. They use a more top-down, hierar-

REACTIVE PLANNING

chical flavor with global world models, especially Saphira[77] and TCA.[131]

Regardless of the bottom-up or top-down inspiration for including non-behavioral intelligence, architectures which use reactive behaviors, but also incorporate planning, are now referred to as being part of the Hybrid Deliberative/Reactive Paradigm. At first, Hybrids were viewed as an artifact of research, without any real merit for robotic implementations. Some researchers went so far as to recommend that if a robot was being designed to operate in an unstructured environment, the designer should use the Reactive Paradigm. If the task was to be performed in a knowledge-rich environment, easy to model, then the Hierarchical Paradigm was preferable, because the software could be engineered specifically for the mission. Hybrids were believed to be the worst of both worlds, saddling the fast execution times of reactivity with the difficulties in developing hierarchical models.

The current thinking in the robotics community is that Hybrids are the best general architectural solution for several reasons. First, the use of asynchronous processing techniques (multi-tasking, threads, etc.) allow deliberative functions to execute independently of reactive behaviors. A planner can be slowly computing the next goal for a robot to navigate to, while the robot is reactively navigating toward its current goal with fast update rates. Second, good software modularity allows subsystems or objects in Hybrid architectures to be mixed and matched for specific applications. Applications which favor purely reactive behaviors can implement just the subset of the architecture for behaviors, while more cognitively challenging domains can use the entire architecture.

7.2 Attributes of the Hybrid Paradigm

The organization of a Hybrid Deliberative/Reactive system can be described as: **PLAN**, then **SENSE-ACT**. It is shown in Fig. 7.1. The **PLAN** box includes all deliberation and global world modeling, not just task or path planning. The robot would first plan how to accomplish a mission (using a global world model) or a task, then instantiate or turn on a set of behaviors (**SENSE-ACT**) to execute the plan (or a portion of the plan). The behaviors would execute until the plan was completed, then the planner would generate a new set of behaviors, and so on.

The idea of **PLAN**, then **SENSE-ACT** evolved from two assumptions of the Hybrid Paradigm. First, planning covers a long time horizon and requires global knowledge, so it should be decoupled from real-time execution

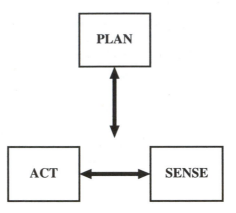

Figure 7.1   P,SA Organization of Hybrid Deliberative/Reactive Paradigm in terms of Primitives.

just on the software engineering principle of coherence (dissimilar functions should be placed in different objects). It is good for setting objectives and selecting methods, but not for making finely grained decisions. Another way DELIBERATION AND of stating this is that *deliberation works with symbols*, e.g., the goal is to pick up SYMBOLS a "Coca-Cola can," while reaction works with sensors and actuators, e.g., the percept is a "red blob" which exerts an attractive field. Second, planning and global modeling algorithms are computationally expensive, so they should be decoupled from real-time execution just from a standpoint of practicality because they would slow down the reaction rate.

The organization of sensing in the Hybrid architecture is more complex. Sensing is truly hybrid, as seen in Fig. 7.2. In the behaviors, sensing remains as it was for the Reactive Paradigm: local and behavior specific. But planning and deliberation requires global world models. Therefore, planning functions have access to a global world model. The model is constructed by processes independent of the behavior-specific sensing. However, both the perceptual schemas for the behaviors and the model making processes can share the same sensors. Furthermore, the model making processes can share the percepts created by the perceptual schemas for behaviors (eavesdrop) or it can have sensors which are dedicated to providing observations which are useful for world modeling but aren't used for any active behaviors.

The organization of the SENSE, PLAN, ACT primitives in the Hybrid Para-REACTOR digm is conceptually divided into a reactive (or *reactor*) portion and a deliber-DELIBERATOR ation (or *deliberator*) portion. Although many architectures will have discrete

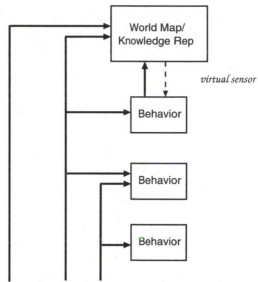

Figure 7.2 Sensing Organization in Hybrid Paradigm, showing that the global world model can have its own sensors, can "eavesdrop" on sensors or percepts used / created by behaviors, and can act as a virtual sensor for use by a behavior.

layers of functionalities within the reactor and deliberator, each architecture in the Hybrid Paradigm has obvious partitions between reactive and deliberative functions.

7.2.1   Characteristics and connotation of reactive behaviors in hybrids

The Hybrid Paradigm is an extension of the Reactive Paradigm, and from the above description, it would appear that the behavioral component is untouched. That is not entirely true. Behaviors in the Hybrid Paradigm have a slightly different connotation than in the Reactive Paradigm. In the Reactive Paradigm, "behavior" connotes purely reflexive behaviors. In the Hybrid Paradigm, the term "behavior" is usually more consistent with the ethological use and includes reflexive, innate, and learned behaviors. This can be SKILL VS. BEHAVIOR confusing, and at least one architecture uses the term *skill* instead of "behavior" to avoid confusion with purely reflexive behaviors. Also, Hybrid implementations tend to use assemblages of behaviors sequenced over time, rather than primitive behaviors. Because the Hybrid implementations are interested in more complex emergent behaviors, there is more diversity in methods for combining the output from concurrent behaviors.

7.2.2   Connotations of "global"

The term "global" is used almost synonymously with "deliberative" and "local" with "reactive." This can lead to significant confusion, because "global" isn't always truly global in Hybrids.

The deliberative portion of a Hybrid architecture contains modules and functions for things which are not easy to represent in reactive behaviors. Some of these functions clearly require a global world model; path planning and map making are probably the best examples. But other activities require global knowledge of a different sort. *Behavorial management* (planning which behaviors to use) requires knowing something about the current mission and the current (and projected) state of the environment. This is global knowledge in that it requires the module to know something outside of itself, as compared to a reactive behavior which can function without any knowledge of whether there are other behaviors actively executing. Likewise, *performance monitoring* to see if the robot is actually making progress to its goal, and problem solving is a global activity. Consider writing a program to diagnose whether the robot's not moving forward is a problem with the terrain (it's stuck in the mud) or a sensor (the shaft encoders don't report wheel turns correctly). In order to perform the diagnostics, the program has to know what the behaviors were trying to accomplish, if there are any other sensors or knowledge sources to corroborate any hypotheses, etc. Therefore, a deliberative function may not need a global world model, but may need to know about the internal workings of the robot on a global scale, if only to know what other modules or deliberative capabilities the program should interact with.

BEHAVORIAL
MANAGEMENT

PERFORMANCE
MONITORING

7.3   Architectural Aspects

The differences between various Hybrid Deliberative/Reactive architectures fall into three areas based on how they answer the following questions: *How does the architecture distinguish between reaction and deliberation? How does it organize responsibilities in the deliberative portion? How does the overall behavior emerge?* The difference between reaction and deliberation is a critical issue in building a successful, reusable object-oriented implementation. This determines what functionality goes in what modules, what modules have access to global knowledge (which leads to specifying public and friend classes in C++), and what that global knowledge (shared data structures) should be. Likewise, it is important to subdivide the deliberative portion into modules or objects. A good decomposition will ensure portability and reusability. While Hybrid architectures are most noteworthy for how they incorporate deliberation into mobile robotics, they also introduce some changes in the way reaction is organized. Many researchers found the two primary means of combining reactive behaviors—subsumption and potential field summation—to be limited. Since then at least three other mechanisms have been introduced: *voting* (in the DAMN architecture),[121] *fuzzy logic* (Saphira),[77] and *filtering* (SFX).[107]

The number of Hybrid architectures is rapidly increasing. This section attempts to introduce some conceptual organization on Hybrids in two ways. First, it offers a set of common components—essentially, things to look for in a Hybrid architecture. Second, it divides Hybrid into three broad categories: *managerial*, *state hierarchies*, and *model-oriented*.

7.3.1   Common components of hybrid architectures

While Hybrid architectures vary significantly in how they implement deliberative functionality, what they implement is fairly similar. Generally a Hybrid architecture has the following modules or objects:

SEQUENCER
- A *Sequencer* agent which generates the set of behaviors to use in order to accomplish a subtask, and determines any sequences and activation conditions. The sequence is usually represented as a dependency network or a finite state machine, but the sequencer should either generate this structure or be able to dynamically adapt it. Recall from Ch. 5 that assemblages of reactive behavior are manually constructed.

RESOURCE MANAGER
- A *Resource manager* which allocates resources to behaviors, including selecting from libraries of schemas. For example, a robot may have stereo vision, sonars, and IR sensors, all of which are capable of range detection. The behavioral manager would ascertain whether the IR sensors can detect at a sufficient range, the stereo vision can update fast enough to match the robot's desired velocity, and the sonars have enough power to produce reliable readings. In reactive architectures, the resources for a behavior were often hard-coded or hardwired, despite the ability of hu-

mans to use alternative sensors and effectors (e.g., opening a door with the other hand when the holding something in the preferred hand).

CARTOGRAPHER
- A *Cartographer* which is responsible for creating, storing, and maintaining map or spatial information, plus methods for accessing the data. The cartographer often contains a global world model and knowledge representation, even if it is not a map.

MISSION PLANNER
- A *Mission Planner* which interacts with the human, operationalizes the commands into robot terms, and constructs a mission plan. For example, the ideal robot assistant might be given a command: "Lassie, go get the sheriff." The mission planner would interpret that command to mean to first physically search for a person, identify him as a sheriff because of the uniform, attract his attention, and then lead him back to the current location. The mission planner might have access to information that sheriffs are most likely to be in their office, donut shops, or the last place they were seen. The plan might first be to navigate to the sheriff's office.

PERFORMANCE MONITORING AND PROBLEM SOLVING
- A *Performance Monitoring and Problem Solving* agent which allows the robot to notice if it is making progress or not. Notice that this requires the robot to exhibit some type of self-awareness.

7.3.2   Styles of hybrid architectures

MANAGERIAL STYLES
Architectural styles can be loosely divided into three categories. *Managerial styles* focus on subdividing the deliberative portion into layers based on the scope of control, or managerial responsibility, of each deliberative function. A Mission Planning module would be able to direct other, subordinate deliberative modules such as navigation, because Mission Planning (where to go) is more abstract than Path Planning (how to get there). *State hierarchies*

STATE HIERARCHIES
use the knowledge of the robot's state to distinguish between reactive and deliberative activities. Reactive behaviors are viewed as having no state, no self-awareness, and function only in the **Present**. Deliberative functions can be divided into those that require knowledge about the robot's **Past** state (where it is in a sequence of commands) and about the **Future** (mission and path planning). *Model-oriented styles* are more nebulous. They are characterized by behaviors that have access to portions of a world model, often to the point that they appear to have returned to the Hierarchical monolithic global world model.

MODEL-ORIENTED STYLES

7.4   Managerial Architectures

Managerial styles of Hybrid architectures are recognizable by their decomposition of responsibilities similar to business management. At the top are agents which do high level planning, then pass off the plan to subordinates, who refine the plan and gather resources, and pass those down to the lowest level workers, the reactive behaviors. Higher level agents can see the results of their subordinate lower level agents (essentially eavesdrop on them), and can give them directions. As with subsumption, a layer can only modify the layer below it. In Managerial styles, each layer attempts to carry out its directive, identify problems and correct them locally. Only when an agent cannot solve its own problem does it ask for help from a superior agent; the agent is said to *fail upwards* in this case.

FAIL UPWARDS

7.4.1   Autonomous Robot Architecture (AuRA)

AUTONOMOUS ROBOT
ARCHITECTURE
(AuRA)

Autonomous Robot Architecture (AuRA) is the oldest of the Hybrids. It was actually designed and implemented by Arkin at the same time Brooks was beginning to publish his work with subsumption. AuRA is based on schema theory, and consists of five subsystems, equivalent to object-oriented classes. Two of the subsystems comprise the deliberative portion: the Planner, and the Cartographer. The Planner is responsible for mission and task planning. It is subdivided into three components, equivalent to the Nested Hierarchical Controller[93] discussed in Ch. 2. The Cartographer encapsulates all the map making and reading functions needed for navigation. The Cartographer can also be given an *a priori* map. For example, a human operator might load in a map file for the Cartographer to use. The three components of the Planner would interact with the Cartographer through methods to obtain a path to follow, broken down into subsegments.

The Planner subsystem is divided into the Mission Planner, Navigator, and Pilot. The Mission Planner serves as the interface with the human, and the current implementation of AuRA has one of the most extensive and user friendly robot interfaces available. The Navigator works with the Cartographer to compute a path for the robot and break it into subtasks (go over the mountain to the water tower, follow the road along the ridge to the camp). The Pilot takes the first subtask (go over the mountain to the water tower) and gets relevant information (terrain, foliage types, what the water tower looks like) to generate behaviors. The Pilot portion of the Planning subsystem interacts with the Motor Schema Manager in the Motor subsystem, giv-

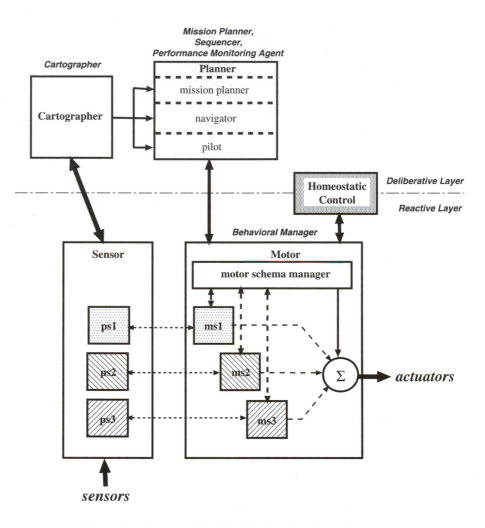

Figure 7.3   Layout of AuRA, showing the five subsystems.

ing it the list of behaviors it needs to accomplish the current subsegment. The Motor Schema Manager composes each behavior by examining the libraries of perceptual schemas in the Sensing subsystem and of motor schemas in the Motor subsystem. The motor schemas represent actions with potential fields, and the overall behavior emerges due to vector summation.

The Sensor and Motor subsystems make up the reactive portion of the architecture. These classes contain libraries of perceptual and motor schemas, which form the behavior schema. The schemas themselves can consist of assemblages of primitive schemas, coordinated by finite state machines. Schemas can share information, if necessary, through links established by the Motor Schema Manager. Behaviors are not restricted to being purely reflexive; behavior specific knowledge, representations, and memory is permitted within the schemas. The motor schemas, however, are restricted to potential fields.

The fifth subsystem, Homeostatic Control, falls into a gray area between deliberation and reaction. The purpose of Homeostatic control is to modify the relationship between behaviors by changing the gains as a function of the "health" of the robot or other constraints. As an example, consider a planetary rover operating on a rocky planet. The robot is tasked to physically remove rock samples from various locations around the planet and deliver them to a return vehicle. The return vehicle has a fixed launch date; it will blast off, returning to Earth on a set day and time no matter what. Now, the rover may be provided with default gains on its behaviors which produce a conservative behavior. It may stay two meters away from each obstacle, giving itself a wide margin of error. At the beginning of the mission, such a conservative overall behavior appears reasonable. Now consider what happens towards the time when the return vehicle is set to launch. If the robot is near the return vehicle, it should be willing to shave corners and reduce the margin by which it avoids obstacles in order to ensure delivery. The robot should be willing to perform the equivalent of sacrificing its own existence for the sake of the mission.

The issue becomes how to do homeostatic. Many aspects of AuRA are motivated by biology, and homeostatic control is no exception. Rather than put a module in the deliberative portion to explicitly reason about how to change the overall behavior of the robot, biology suggests that animals subconsciously modify their behaviors all the time in response to internal needs. For example, an animal who needs food becomes increasingly focused on finding food. Human behavior changes in response to insulin. Fortunately, changing the emergent behavior is straightforward in a potential fields representation of behaviors, since the output vector produced by each behavior can be scaled by a gain term. Returning to the case of the planetary rover rushing to make the last delivery, the gain on the move-to-goal behavior attracting the rover to the return vehicle should start going up, while the gain on the avoid-obstacle behavior should start going down as a function of time to launch.

The table below summarizes AuRA in terms of the common components and style of emergent behavior:

AuRA Summary	
Sequencer Agent	Navigator, Pilot
Resource Manager	Motor Schema Manager
Cartographer	Cartographer
Mission Planner	Mission Planner
Performance Monitoring Agent	Pilot, Navigator, Mission Planner
Emergent behavior	Vector summation, spreading activation of behaviors, homeostatic control

7.4.2   Sensor Fusion Effects (SFX)

Another managerial style of architecture is the Sensor Fusion Effects (SFX) architecture, which started out as an extension to AuRA by Murphy to incorporate pathways for sensing. The extension was to add modules to specify how sensing, including sensor fusion and handling sensor failures, are handled. Over time, SFX has reorganized both the reactive and deliberative components of AuRA although the two architectures remain philosophically identical. SFX is an example of how robustness can be built into an architecture. SFX has been used on eight robots for indoor office navigation, outdoor road following, and urban search and rescue.

Fig. 7.4 shows a neurophysiological model of sensing based on studies with sensing in cats. The model suggests that sensory processing is initially local to each sensor, and may have its own sensor-dependent receptive field. This is consistent with reactive robot behaviors, and at least with the motivation for sensor fission. Sensor processing then appears to branch, with duplicates going to the *superior colliculus* (a mid-brain structure responsible for motor behaviors) and the other to the *cerebral cortex* (responsible for more cognitive functions). The branching allows the same sensor stream to be used simultaneously in multiple ways. In SFX, the equivalent superior colliculus functions are implemented in the reactive layer, and cortical activities in the deliberative layer. Branching of perception is done through the use of whiteboards, common in numerous AI systems as global cognitive data structures.

The deliberative component is divided into modules or object classes, each of which is actually a software agent, a self-contained software program which specializes in some area of competence and can interact with other

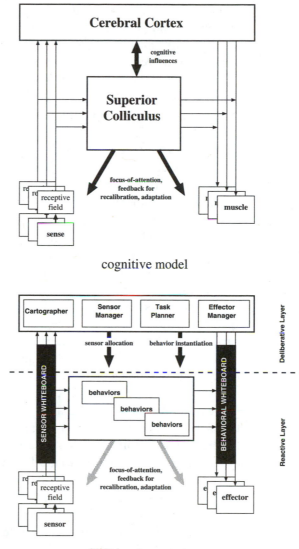

cognitive model

SFX implementation

Figure 7.4   The cognitive model used for the implementation of the Sensor Fusion Effects Architecture.

agents. The dominant agent is called the Mission Planner agent. This agent serves to interact with the human and specify the mission constraints to the other agents in the deliberative layer. The agents in the deliberative layer attempt to find (and maintain) a set of behaviors which can accomplish the mission while meeting the constraints. The software agents in each deliberative layer are peers; just as with behaviors, they operate independently of each other. But the nature of deliberation suggests that they have to negotiate with other peers to find a satisfactory set of behaviors to accomplish the current task. One way to think of this partitioning is that the Mission Planner acts as a president or CEO in a large company, giving directions, while the behaviors are the workers. The agents in the lower deliberative layer are middle-management, planning how to organize the workers' assignments, monitoring productivity, and adapting assignments if necessary.

Within the deliberative layer, the Task Manager, Sensing Manager, and Effector Manager serve as the resource managers. The resource manager functions are divided across managers because the types of knowledge and algorithms are different for managing sensors and actions. The managers use AI planning, scheduling, and problem solving techniques to determine the best allocation of effector and sensing resources given the set of motor and perceptual schemas for a behavior. They are not allowed to relax any constraints specified by the Mission Planner, so they essentially know what the robot is supposed to do, but only the Mission Planner knows why. The advantage of this middle-management layer is that it simplifies the AI techniques needed for behavioral management.

The Sensing Manager in SFX is particularly noteworthy because of its explicit commitment to performance monitoring and problem solving. It has two software agents for monitoring both the task performance and whether the habitat has changed (if so, a performance failure is likely to occur). If a behavior fails or a perceptual schema detects that sensor values are not consistent or reasonable, the Sensing Manager is alerted. It can then identify alternative perceptual schemas, or even behaviors, to replace the problematic behavior immediately. Imagine a mobile robot in a convoy of robots hauling food to refugees. If the robot had a glitch in a sensor, it shouldn't suddenly just stop and think about the problem. Instead, it should immediately switch to a back-up plan or even begin to smoothly slow down while it identifies a back-up plan. Otherwise, the whole convoy would stop, there might be wrecks, etc. Then working in a background mode, the Sensing Manager can attempt to diagnose the cause of the problem and correct it. In one demonstration, a robot using SFX resorted to shaking its camera to shake off a T-

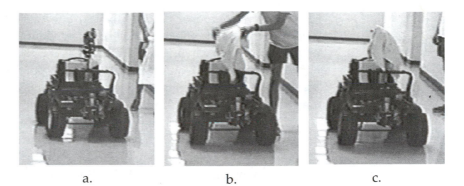

a.   b.   c.

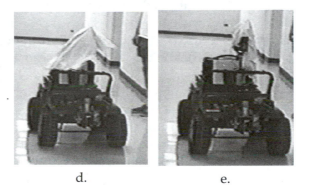

d.   e.

Figure 7.5   A robot using SFX to figure out that something is wrong with the camera. It cannot identify the problem, so it attempts to correct the problem by shaking.

Shirt covering the lens, as shown in Fig. 7.5.

The lower deliberative layer also contains a Cartographer agent and performance monitoring agents. The Cartographer is responsible for map making and path planning, while the performance agents attempt to observe the progress of the robot toward its goals and notice when the robot is unsuccessful, using work by Hughes.[71] An example is when a robot gets stuck in the mud on a dirt road. The follow-road behavior is executing correctly; it is seeing the road and giving actuator commands correctly. The shaft encoders show that the wheels are turning. So some other process with more self-awareness than a reactive behavior is needed to notice that the robot isn't moving. In this case, if the robot is moving, the vision should change over time, not remain the same.

The reactive component is also divided into two layers. In this case, the layers reflect *strategic* versus *tactical behaviors*, defined below. As noted earlier, just about every hybrid architecture has its own method of combining behaviors in the reactive portion. AuRA uses potential field combination, whereas SFX uses a filtering method. The SFX philosophy is similar to subsumption: there are some fundamental behaviors that should override other behaviors. The difference is that in SFX, it is the "lowest" tactical behaviors which do the subsuming, not the "higher" strategic ones.

The idea of a tactical behavior is best seen by example. Recall the case of obstacle avoidance with potential fields. The use of a repulsive field was simple, but could lead to a global minima, where the repulsion could cancel out any other motive fields such as move-to-goal. The NaTs[132] solution was to use the vector created by that other field as an input to the avoid-obstacle field. That vector would lead to a tangential field in addition to the repulsive field, resulting in an avoid-obstacle field which repulses the robot towards the direction it was heading in to begin with. In this case, the move-to-goal field was offering a strategic command; like a general, it was telling the troops to move ahead. But the avoid-obstacle field was like an infantry man; it was trying to go in the direction given by the general but not hit anything. The avoid-obstacle behavior filters the strategic direction (given by move-to-goal) with the immediate tactical situation (the presence of an obstacle).

Another example of a tactical behavior in SFX is speed-control. Speed-control in AuRA and many architectures is a by-product of the mechanism used for combining behaviors. The emergent speed in AuRA is the magnitude of the vector summed from all the active behaviors. In SFX, speed-control is considered a separate behavior. The safe velocity of a robot depends on many influences. If the robot cannot turn in place (in effect, turns like a car), it will need to be operating at a slow speed to make the turn without overshooting. Likewise, it may need to go slower as it goes up or down hills. These influences are derived from sensors, and the action is a template (the robot always slows down on hills), so speed control is a legitimate behavior. But the other behaviors should have some influence on the speed as well. So these other, strategic behaviors contribute a strategic speed to the speed-control behavior. If the strategic speed is less than the safe speed computed from tactical influences, then the output speed is the strategic speed. But if the tactical safe speed is lower, the output speed to the actuator is the tactical speed. Tactical behaviors serve as filters on strategic commands to

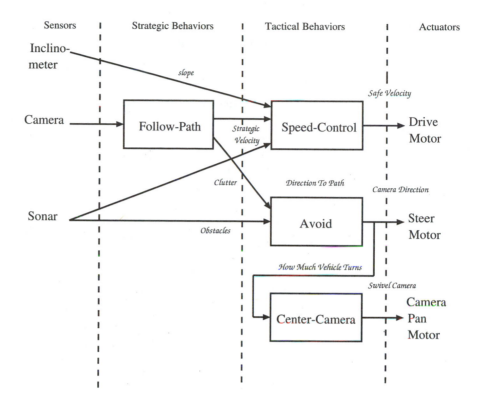

Sensors | Strategic Behaviors | Tactical Behaviors | Actuators

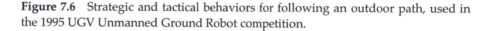

Figure 7.6 Strategic and tactical behaviors for following an outdoor path, used in the 1995 UGV Unmanned Ground Robot competition.

ensure that the robot acts in a safe manner in as close accordance with the strategic intent as possible. The interaction of strategic and tactical behaviors is still considered emergent behavior.

One outcome of the strategic-tactical partitioning was the discovery that every task to date could be done with one strategic behavior and several tactical behaviors. This means that the need to combine behaviors does not occur often, and so the combination mechanism is not particularly important. However, it should be emphasized that the strategic behaviors were often assemblages in the form of scripts. There were many strategic behaviors, but they were explicitly coordinated and controlled according to behavior-specific knowledge.

The table below summarizes SFX in terms of the common components and style of emergent behavior:

SFX Summary	
Sequencer Agent	Task Manager
Resource Manager	Sensing and Task Managers
Cartographer	Cartographer
Mission Planner	Mission Planner
Performance Monitoring Agent	Performance Monitor, Habitat Monitor
Emergent behavior	Strategic behaviors grouped into abstract behaviors or scripts, then filtered by tactical behaviors

7.5   State-Hierarchy Architectures

State-hierarchy styles of architectures organize activities by the scope of time knowledge. Since time is generally thought of as being **Present**, **Past**, and **Future**, state-hierarchy styles of architectures usually have 3 layers. Unfortunately, many other Hybrid architectures have 3 layers but with the layers meaning something totally different. Therefore, this book refers to them as state-hierarchies to emphasize the layering based on the state of knowledge. As with managerial styles, the organization is broken down into layers. Within each layer are peers of software agents or functions that accomplish the goals of that layer. As with managerial styles, a higher layer has access to the output of lower layers and can operate on the next lower layer.

7.5.1   3-Tiered (3T)

The 3T, or 3-Tiered, mobile robot architecture is the best example of a state-hierarchy system and is predominately used at NASA. The roots of 3T stem from continuing work at NASA, where aspects of Slack's NaT system,[132] Gat's subsumption-style ATLANTIS architecture,[57] and Firby's RAPs system[53] were merged at JPL under the initial direction of David Miller, and refined by Pete Bonasso and Dave Kortenkamp at NASA's Johnson Space Center. As the name suggests, 3T divides itself into 3 layers, one clearly reactive, one clearly deliberative, and one which serves as the interface between the two. Fig. 7.7 show the layers actually running on three different computers at NASA Johnson Space Center controlling the Extra-Vehicular Activity Helper-Retriever (EVAHR) robot simulator. 3T has been used primarily for planetary rovers, underwater vehicles, and robot assistants for astronauts.

Figure 7.7 Each of the 3T layers running on a separate computer, controlling the EVAHR robot. (Photograph courtesy of the National Aeronautics and Space Administration, Johnson Space Center.)

The top layer of 3T is Planner. It fulfills the duties of the mission planner and cartographer by setting goals and strategic plans. These goals are passed to the middle layer, called the Sequencer. The Sequencer uses a reactive planning technique called RAPs to select a set of primitive behaviors from a library and develops a task network specifying the sequence of execution for the behaviors for the particular subgoal. The Sequencer is responsible for the sequencer and performance monitoring functions of a generic Hybrid architecture. The Sequencer layer instantiates a set of behaviors (called *skills*) to carry out the plan. These behaviors form the bottom layer, called the Controller or Skill Manager. In order to avoid confusion with the connotations of purely reflexive behaviors left over from the Reactive Paradigm, 3T does not call its behaviors "behaviors." Its behaviors have the same broader scope as AuRA and SFX, permitting sensor fusion and assemblages of primitive behaviors. The preferred term is "skill" to distinguish its behaviors from the connotations of behaviors popularized by the subsumption architecture. A skill is often an assemblage of primitive skills; indeed, one of the interesting aspects of 3T is its foundation as a tool for learning assemblages.

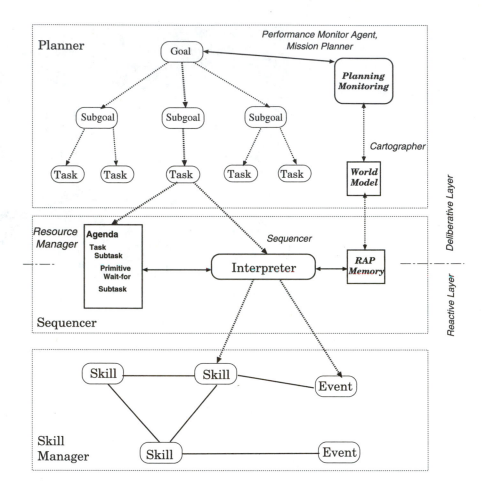

Figure 7.8 3T architecture.

A powerful attribute of the lower level is that the skills have associated *events*, which serve as checkpoints to verify explicitly that an action has had the correct effect. In some regards, events are equivalent to the innate releasing mechanisms; both let the world be its own best representation.

The three layers represent true deliberation, reactive planning, and reactive control. They also represent a philosophy organized by scope of state, rather than scope of responsibility. The Skill Manager layer is composed of skills that operate only in the **Present** (although with some allowances to permit the persistence of some behaviors when the stimulus temporarily disappears). The components in the Sequencer layer operate on state information reflecting memories about the **Past**, as well as the **Present**. Therefore, sequences of behaviors can be managed by remembering what the robot has already done and whether that was successful or not. This adds a great deal of robustness and supports performance monitoring. The Planner layer works with state information predicting the **Future**. It can also use information from the **Past** (what the robot has done or tried) and **Present** (what the robot is doing right now). In order to plan a mission, the planner needs to project what the environment will be and other factors.

UPDATE RATE.

In practice, 3T does not strictly organize its functions into layers by state (**Past, Present, Future**); instead it often uses *update rate*. Algorithms that update slowly are put in the Planner, while fast algorithms go in the Skill Manager layer. This appears to be a situation where the pragmatic considerations of computation influenced the design rules; in the early 1990's behaviors were very fast, reactive planning (especially RAPs and Universal Plans) were fast, and mission planning was very slow. However, many sensor algorithms involving computer vision were also slow, so they were placed in the Planner despite their low-level sensing function.

The table below summarizes 3T in terms of the common components and style of emergent behavior:

3T	
Sequencer Agent	Sequencer
Resource Manager	Sequencer (Agenda)
Cartographer	Planner
Mission Planner	Planner
Performance Monitoring Agent	Planner
Emergent behavior	Behaviors grouped into skills, skills grouped into task networks

7.6   Model-Oriented Architectures

Both the managerial and state-hierarchy styles of architectures evolved directly from the Reactive Paradigm. The designers sought to add more cognitive functionality to the Reactive Paradigm. As such, managerial and state-hierarchy styles are more bottom-up in flavor, emphasizing behaviors or skills as the basic building blocks. However, a new influx of researchers from the traditional AI community, particularly Stanford and SRI, has entered robotics and made a distinct contribution. Their architectures have a more top-down, symbolic flavor than managerial and state-hierarchies. One hallmark of these architectures is that they concentrate symbolic manipulation around a global world model. However, unlike most other Hybrid architectures, which create a global world model in parallel with behavior-specific sensing, this global world model also serves to supply perception to the behaviors (or behavior equivalents). In this case, the global world model serves as a virtual sensor.

The use of a single global world model for sensing appears to be a throwback to the Hierarchical Paradigm, and conceptually it is. However, there are four practical differences. First, the monolithic global world model is often less ambitious in scope and more cleverly organized than earlier systems. The world model is often only interested in labeling regions of the sensed world with symbols such as: hallway, door, my office, etc. Second, perceptual processing is often done with distributed processing, so that slow perceptual routines run asynchronously of faster routines, and the behaviors have access to the latest information. In effect, the "eavesdropping" on perception for behaviors is an equivalent form of distributed processing. Third, sensor errors and uncertainty can be filtered using sensor fusion over time. This can dramatically improve the performance of the robot. Fourth, increases in processor speeds and optimizing compilers have mitigated the processing bottleneck.

Two of the best known model-oriented architectures are the Saphira architecture developed by Kurt Konolige with numerous others at SRI, and the Task Control Architecture (TCA) by Reid Simmons which has been extended to do multi-task planning with the Prodigy system. The Saphira architecture comes with the ActivMedia Pioneer robots.

7.6.1 Saphira

SAPHIRA

The *Saphira* architecture, shown in Fig. 7.9, has been used at SRI on a variety of robots, including Shakey's direct descendents: Flakey and Erratic. The motivation for the architecture stems from the basic tenet that there are three keys to a mobile robot operating successfully in the open world: *coordination, coherence,* and *communication.*[77] A robot must coordinate its actuators and sensors (as has been seen through in the Reactive Paradigm), but it must also coordinate its goals over a period of time (which is not addressed by the Reactive Paradigm). Whereas the motivation for coordination is compatible with reactivity, coherence is an explicit break from the Reactive Paradigm.

COORDINATION,
COHERENCE,
COMMUNICATION

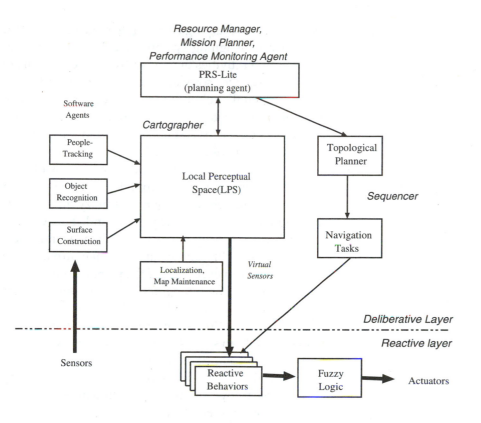

Figure 7.9 Simplifed view of Saphira architecture.

Coherence is essentially the ability of the robot to maintain global world worlds, which Konolige and Myers argue is essential for good behavioral performance and interacting with humans.[77] Finally, communication is important because robots have to interact with humans and, as will be seen in Ch. 8, other robots. This introduces the problem of having common frames of reference (anchors) for communicating.

PRS-LITE   The bulk of the architecture is concerned with planning, and uses a type of reactive planner called *PRS-lite* for Procedural Reasoning System-lite.[77] PRS-lite is capable of taking natural language voice commands from humans ("deliver this to John") and then operationalizing that into navigation tasks and perceptual recognition routines. Both planning and execution relies on the Local Perceptual Space, the central world model. Much processing is devoted to maintaining an accurate model of the world based on the robot's sensors and assigning symbolic labels to regions. Saphira also divides the deliberation activities among software agents. This provides a high degree of flexibility. Since software agents are independent, they don't even have to run on-board the robot they're controlling. In the 1996 AAAI Mobile Robot Competition,[78] robots running Saphira actually had some of their planning reside on a local workstation, transmitted through a radio link.[62] This will be covered in more detail in Ch. 8.

The reactive component of Saphira consists of behaviors. The behaviors extract *virtual sensor* inputs from the central world model, the Local Perceptual Space. The behavioral output is fuzzy rules, which are fused using fuzzy logic into a velocity and steer command. Fuzzy logic turns out to be a very natural way of fusing competing demands, and is less ad hoc than Boolean logic rules (e.g., "if x and y but not z, then turn left"). The behaviors are managed by the plan execution of the planned navigation tasks. The fuzzy logic mechanism for combining behaviors produces essentially the same results as a potential field methodology, as described by Konolige and Myers.[77] The Local Perceptual Space can improve the quality of the robot's overall behavior because it can smooth out sensor errors. Although this central processing introduces a computational penalty, the increases in processor power and clock speeds have made the computational costs acceptable.

VIRTUAL SENSOR

The table below summarizes Saphira in terms of the common components and style of emergent behavior:

Saphira	
Sequencer Agent	Topological planner, Navigation Tasks
Resource Manager	PRS-lite
Cartographer	LPS
Mission Planner	PRS-lite
Performance Monitoring Agent	PRS-lite
Emergent behavior	Behaviors fused with fuzzy logic

7.6.2 Task Control Architecture (TCA)

TASK CONTROL
ARCHITECTURE (TCA)

Reid Simmon's *Task Control Architecture (TCA)* has been used extensively by robots designed for NASA, including Ambler, Dante (Fig. 7.11), and service robots. It is also the intelligence inside Xavier (shown in Fig. 7.11, the Carnegie Mellon University robot which is accessible over the web). Xavier has has traveled autonomously over 210 kilometers in the hallways at CMU

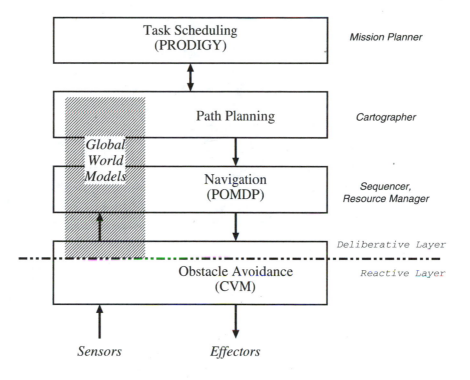

Figure 7.10   Layout of the Task Control Architecture.

in response to 30,000 requests by web users to navigate to a particular site.[130] TCA is more difficult to evaluate as a Hybrid architecture, in part because it has more of an operating system flavor than a general purpose architecture. Also, there are no behaviors per se. However, many of the low level tasks resemble behaviors, and TCA shares the hybrid philosophy of layering intelligence, and having lower modules fail upwards.

The basic layout of TCA for indoor navigation is presented in a somewhat different form than usual[131] in Fig. 7.10 to provide consistency with the terminology of this chapter. TCA uses dedicated sensing structures such as evidence grids (see Ch. 11) which can be thought of as a distributed global world model. Sensor information percolates up through the global models. The basic task flow is determined by the Task Scheduling Layer, which uses the Prodigy planner. (A layer is more along the lines of a software agent or a subsystem in other architectures.) This layer interacts with the user and determines the goals and order of execution. For example, if the robot is

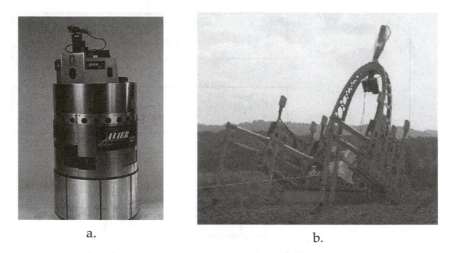

a.   b.

Figure 7.11   Two robots using TCA: a.) Xavier, a RWI robot at Carnegie Mellon University (photograph courtesy of Reid Simmons) and b.) Dante (photograph courtesy of NASA Ames Research Center).

given several jobs to drop, Prodigy can prioritize and optimize the schedule. Once the current task has been established, the Path Planning layer is engaged. Navigation is handled by a Partially Observable Markov Decision Process (POMDP, pronounced "pom D P") module which determines what the robot should be looking for, where it is, and where it has been. As with the relationship between strategic and tactical behaviors in SFX, the Obstacle Avoidance Layer takes the desired heading and adapts it to the obstacles CURVATURE-VELOCITY extracted from the evidence grid virtual sensor. The layer uses a *curvature-*
METHOD *velocity method* (CVM) to factor in not only obstacles but how to respond with a smooth trajectory for the robot's current velocity.

The table below summarizes TCA in terms of the common components and style of emergent behavior:

TCA	
Sequencer Agent	Navigation Layer
Resource Manager	Navigation Layer
Cartographer	Path-Planning Layer
Mission Planner	Task Scheduling Layer
Performance Monitoring Agent	Navigation, Path-Planning, Task-Scheduling
Emergent behavior	Filtering

7.7 Other Robots in the Hybrid Paradigm

One implicit criterion for evaluating the utility of a Paradigm and derivative architectures is its popularity. The Hybrid Paradigm describes many of the robots being developed in laboratories today. It is clearly popular. A large number of these robots fall into the Hybrid category by virtue of being "neither fish nor fowl," in this case being neither purely Reactive nor Hierarchical. Almost every robot has a set of functions that are equivalent to behaviors, though several have followed the lead of 3T in calling those functions by other names (e.g., "skills") to reduce the connotations of purely reflexive behaviors. Even architectures that started out as Hierarchical, namely Albus' Real-time Control Architecture[1] and Simmons' Task Control Architecture,[131] recast many of their functions into behavioral components.

One of the major influences on the mobile robot community has been the DARPA UGV Demo II and Demo III projects, which forwarded the state of the art in outdoor ground vehicle control and navigation. The tasks were well-suited for a hybrid approach: the idea was to give a HMMWV military jeep a map, a set of directions, and send it off. It would autonomously plan a route, drive along roads, then go off roads as needed. In a military reconnaissance mode, the HMMWV was expected to autonomously stay behind hills, avoid trees and rocks, and covertly position itself so that Reconnaissance, Surveillance, and Target Acquisition (RSTA, pronounced "rist-tah") sensors could peek over and find enemy locations. Demo II even had multiple HMMWVs traveling autonomously in formation.

The European Community ESPRIT agency has also significantly influenced mobile robotics, sponsoring research in automating highway vehicles via initiatives in the 1990's. The United States has shown some interest through several iterations of "intelligent vehicle highway systems" programs. The most notable of these automated vehicles were constructed by Dickmanns and Graefe in Germany[45] and the CMU Navlab led by Dean Pomerleau.[116]

A third influence on mobile robots has been NASA's push for autonomous planetary rovers, which culminated in the Mars Pathfinder mission with the Sojourner rover. Mapping a planet's surface is intrinsically a deliberative function, as is planning paths for optimal exploration. Unfortunately, from the Viking lander missions, Mars was known to be very rocky. The approaches quickly fell into camps. One, led by MIT, favored deploying many small, legged robots, such as Genghis, that would climb over small rocks and go around others. The "low-to-the-ground" viewpoint, which limits what a robot—and therefore, the scientists on Earth—can sense, would be overcome by the large number of robots. The other approach, characterized by Carnegie Mellon University's Ambler robot, proposed a single large robot with a higher viewpoint and stability. Ambler was built by "Red" Whitaker at the CMU Field Robotics Institute to be able to maintain a sensor platform at a level height by stepping over the majority of rocks, but at a tremendous penalty in size, weight, and power. In the end, planetary rover researchers have gravitated towards wheeled vehicles with some type of articulation to maintain stability, such as seen with Sandia National Laboratories' Rattler. An extension of the Ambler design philosophy was manifested in the Dante robots. These were built to rappel down steep canyons and volcanoes on Mars (and Earth). Dante was able to lower itself successfully most of the way into a volcano in Antarctica, but could not climb back out. It was dropped while being lifted out by a helicopter, twisting its frame.

7.8   Evaluation of Hybrid Architectures

In some regards, it is difficult to evaluate Hybrid architectures individually. Each architecture is still evolving and the deliberative component is being expanded practically daily. Returning to the four criteria set forth in the overview in Part I, it is interesting to evaluate the architectures as a whole.

In terms of support for modularity, each architecture is highly modular. Most are divided into layers, which are then subdivided into modules. As the software agent programming style for AI gains in popularity, probably more architectures will implement deliberative modules as independent specialists. AuRA and SFX clearly exhibit an organization which lends itself to object-oriented programming. The use of specialists also enhances the ease of portability.

Hybrids tend to have a high degree of niche targetability. The addition of the deliberative component allows Hybrids to be used for applications not appropriate for purely Reactive systems. However, the partitioning between reaction and deliberation allows the reactive portion to be used alone for purely reactive applications.

Another attractive aspect of Hybrid architectures is that they often explicitly attempt to ensure robustness. In the SFX and 3T architecture, modules within the various deliberative components attempt to monitor the performance of the reactive behaviors and either replace or adapt the configuration as needed.

An evaluation of Hybrid architectures would not be complete without asking the question, "so what's the difference between what Shakey could do (if it had had infinite computation power) and what a Hybrid can do?" Speed of execution aside, it is interesting to ponder whether the only fundamental difference is how Hierarchical and Hybrids achieve the same ends. Hybrids certainly explicitly reflect more of the principles of software engineering (modularity, coherence, design for reuse, etc.). The two paradigms also certainly reflect different attitudes toward world modeling. In the Hybrid Paradigm, global models are used only for symbolic functions. The frame problem either doesn't exist or is minor because 1) execution is reactive and therefore well-suited for unstructured environments, and 2) software agents can use agent-specific abstractions to exploit the structure of an environment in order to fulfill their particular role in deliberation. Global models are generally closed world, but the world is "closed" at the deliberative level. The robot can think in terms of a closed world, while it acts in an open world. Another major philosophical difference is the role of planning and execution. Under STRIPS, Shakey planned every move, down to the lowest level of granularity, and had problems confirming that an action had been accomplished. It should be noted that modern planners often produce only partial plans, then execute that part of the plan, note the results and plan the next step. It is not clear whether a SENSE, PLAN, ACT paradigm with a more suitable planner would produce a more intuitively appealing robot architecture. The final distinction between the Hierarchical and Hybrid Paradigms may be the influence of biology. The Hybrid Paradigm has its roots in ethology, and provides a framework for exploring cognitive science. The Hierarchical Paradigm is less clearly cognitively plausible, although both share the same cognitive motivation.

7.9 Interleaving Deliberation and Reactive Control

The primary contribution of a Hybrid architecture is to provide a template for merging deliberation and reaction. However, interleaving the two functions is often task dependent. In navigation, there is the issue of interleaving path planning and reactive execution of the path. Another issue is monitoring the progress of behaviors and terminating behaviors correctly.

One of the obvious task domains for a mobile robot is navigation, simply getting around in the world. Many robot architectures have well-developed modules for handling navigational tasks. In the early 1990's, navigation served as an excellent example of why deliberation and reaction were largely separate, and reinforced a "plan once, execute lots" mentality. However, advances in technology and new domains are causing researchers to rethink the strict separation.

By the early 1990's, many algorithms existed which if given a two or even three dimensional map could compute an optimal path for a robot to take through the world. These path planning algorithms exhibited several drawbacks. One was that they were all computationally expensive, taking between 5 and 15 minutes to execute. This prevented the robot from continuously generating the path. But as was seen with Shakey, if the robot tried to execute a pre-computed path, it would be vulnerable to unexpected changes in the world. That map would represent the best, currently available knowledge about the world: where obstacles were, unpassable terrain, etc. But a map is at best a representation of a closed world; it can't show what has changed since it was built, unless a robot goes there and senses it. So the robot can generate an optimal path, but it may discover an unmodeled obstacle blocking that path. If the robot was just using the precomputed path to navigate, it would have to stop, update the map with the newly discovered obstacle, then replan the optimal path, resulting in slow progress.

If the robot used reactive behaviors to navigate, there was no guarantee that it would make it to the goal any faster. Even if it headed off in the right direction, it might spend time getting into and out of box canyons. By letting the robot solely react to the world, it might make poor choices.

The common solution was to mix path planning and reaction by having a planning algorithm in the cartographer generate a complete optimal route for the robot to take, but then decompose that route into segments, usually straight lines. The end of each path segment is called a *waypoint*, because it is a point along the way to the final goal. Each waypoint can be a goal to reach, which can be accomplished by behaviors (move-to-goal(), avoid-obstacles()). When the robot reaches the first goal, the sequencer agent can give the behavioral manager the coordinates or landmarks for the next goal, and so on. Notice this allows computationally expensive path planning to occur only once, and then the behaviors take care of actually navigating.

WAYPOINT

As will be seen in Part II, this strategy has its own set of drawbacks. But for the most part it is a well-accepted means of partitioning deliberation and reaction in navigation. However, with the advent of the Intel Pentium and Sparc microprocessors, the computational demands of path planning algorithms have been mitigated. Algorithms which ran on the order of once every 10 minutes can now execute once every second. As a result, the mismatches in planning and reaction times are no longer a compelling reason to enforce a strict separation of deliberation and reaction. However, the software engineering reason for the partition remains: things which operate on symbols and global information should be in the deliberator; things which operate directly on sensors and actuators should be in the reactor.

The above example of Navigation illustrates a top-down interleaving of deliberation and reaction. The deliberative layer(s) decompose the mission into finer and finer steps until it arrives at a set of behaviors capable of accomplishing the first subgoal. Another example of interleaving deliberation and reaction is the role of the deliberative layer(s) in supplying the reactor with expectations and virtual sensors. And it is important to note that deliberation can be triggered bottom-up as well.

It is not always the case that the deliberator generates the set of behaviors, turns them on, and lets them execute until they either complete the subtask or fail. In the case of sensing, it might be desirable for the deliberator to make some of the global models being constructed available to the behaviors. For example, consider a robot vehicle following a road. Now suppose that it is looking for the large tree, since it is supposed to turn right at the intersection after the tree. In order to maintain the correct sequence of behaviors, the deliberator has a global world model where trees are noted. The reactive behaviors of following a road and avoid an obstacle do not need the explicit representation of a tree. But what if the tree casts a shadow which might confuse the follow-path behavior and cause it to give the robot incorrect steering commands? In this case, it would be useful if the information about the presence of a tree could be absorbed by the behavior. One way to do this is to permit methods on the world model to act as virtual sensors or perceptual schema. Then the follow-road behavior could use the virtual sensor, which tells the behavior when the road boundaries extracted by the vision sensor are probably distorted, to ignore affected regions in the image that would normally be observed by the vision sensor. This is an example of how the SELECTIVE ATTENTION deliberative layer can aid with *selective attention*, or filtering of perception for a context.

But the reactor may wish to trigger deliberation under many circumstances. Most of these cases involve failure or exception handling. Suppose that a sensor breaks and the perceptual schema cannot produce a percept. The schema cannot diagnose itself. Therefore, its failure would cause a deliberative function, such as the Sensing Manager in SFX, to be triggered. If the Sensing Manager cannot find a replacement perceptual schema or equivalent behavior, then it can no longer meet the constraints imposed by the Mission

Planner. In the SFX system, the Sensing Manager would trigger the Mission Planner. The Mission Planner presumably has the intelligence to relax constraints on the mission, or in practice to alert the human supervisor. This is an example of "failing upwards," where a lower level module fails and a higher level, or smarter, module has to take over.

COGNIZANT FAILURE   Failing upwards is also known as a *cognizant failure*, meaning that the failure takes some amount of awareness of the context to resolve, not that the cognition itself has failed. Erann Gat motivated the need for cognizant failures through the "Wesson Oil" problem.[57] In old Wesson Oil TV advertisements, a mother would be cooking chicken in oil when she would have to stop to rush her son to the emergency room for treatment of a broken arm. Ideally the mother would not only turn off the stove but remove the chicken from the oil. In the commercial, the mother neglects to remove the chicken. Since she is using Wesson Oil, the chicken isn't ruined when they return. The point of the Wesson Oil problem for robotics is what happens when a set of reactive behaviors are turned off in the middle of a sequence? In many cases, it may not be just a simple act of de-instantiating the behaviors and activating new ones. There may be behaviors in the sequence that have to execute or disaster will occur (turn off the stove) as well behaviors which must run or lead to merely undesirable side effects (chicken sits in oil if it is not removed). All of this means that the sequencer must know why a failure or need to change behaviors has occurred and what the intent of the current sequence is. Deliberation is definitely not trivial!

7.10   Summary

The Hybrid Deliberative-Reactive Paradigm can be thought of as **PLAN**, then **SENSE-ACT (P,S-A)**. The **SENSE-ACT** portion is always done with reactive behaviors, while **PLAN** includes a broader range of intelligent activities than just path or mission planning. Planning can be interleaved with execution; then for the most part, the robot plans a set of behaviors which will execute for a long time. Sensing is also hybrid; the reactive portion uses local, behavior-specific representations while the deliberative portion uses global world models.

Architectures in the Hybrid paradigm usually encapsulate functionality into modules. The basic modules are the *mission planner, sequencer agent, behavioral manager, cartographer,* and *performance monitor*. Hybrid architectures always have portions which are recognizably deliberative and reactive. The rule of thumb is that functions which operate on symbolic information go in the deliberative layer, or deliberator, while functions which transform sensor data into actuator commands go in the reactive layer, or reactor. The reactive component is organized by behaviors, but the definition of behavior is wider than the purely reflexive behaviors in the Reactive Paradigm. Behaviors may be called skills or by other names to eliminate confusion with reflexive behaviors. Hybrid architectures also exhibit a wide variety of mechanisms for combining behaviors, including subsumption, potential field combination, filtering, voting, and fuzzy logic. The reactive portion tends to make more use of assemblages of behaviors than in the Reactive Paradigm.

The deliberative component is often subdivided into layers. The layering may reflect scope in managerial responsibilities or in time horizon. Layers often consist of modules implemented as software agents. These agents may have agent-specific world models or share a single global world model. The world model can also serve as a virtual sensor for use by behaviors.

Managerial styles of architectures favor a bottom-up organization, concentrating on layering planning on top of behaviors and behavior management. Deliberation is based on whether symbols are being manipulated. The overall behavior emerges as a function of the behavioral layer. State-hierarchies divide deliberation and reaction by the state, or scope of knowledge, available to the modules or agents operating at that layer. The three states are Past, Present, Future. Responsibilities are organized into planning and sequencing components. The overall emergent behavior is more due to the sequencing of behaviors, or skills, rather than concurrency. Model-based styles favor a top-down organization, focusing on the creation and maintenance of a global world model. The world model then serves as a virtual sensor to the behaviors and as a data structure for planning. Often the software agents within the deliberative layer in all three architectural styles exhibit self monitoring and problem solving abilities, and fail upwards if the mission cannot be accomplished. As such, they distribute planning and problem-solving.

7.11 Exercises

Exercise 7.1

Describe the Hybrid paradigm in terms of:

a. sensing, acting, and planning, and

b. sensing organization.

Exercise 7.2

Decide whether each of the following is deliberative or behavioral: path planning, resource allocation, map making, avoiding obstacles, navigation.

Exercise 7.3

Name and evaluate the following architectures in terms of support for modularity, niche targetability, ease of portability to other domains, robustness.

a. AuRA

b. SFX

c. 3T

d. Saphira

e. TCA

Exercise 7.4

Why do behavioral management and performance monitoring require global knowledge?

Exercise 7.5

How does the Hybrid Paradigm address the frame problem and the open world?

Exercise 7.6

List the five basic components of a Hybrid architecture.

Exercise 7.7

Describe the difference between managerial, state hierarchy, and model-oriented styles of Hybrid architectures and give one example of each.

Exercise 7.8

Describe the use of state (**Past, Present, Future**) to define behaviors and deliberative responsibilities in a state-hierarchy architecture.

Exercise 7.9   [*Advanced Reading*]

Search for technical papers on *Cog*, Rodney Brooks' controversial humanoid robot project. What paradigm best describes the architecture and why?

Exercise 7.10   [*Advanced Reading*]

Look up technical reports on Shakey. Compare Shakey with the Hybrid architectures. Now consider the possible impact of the radical increases in processing power since the 1960's. Do you agree or disagree with the statement that Shakey would be as capable as any Hybrid if it were built today? Justify your answer. (This question was posed by Tom Garvey of SRI.)

Exercise 7.11 *[Advanced Reading]*

Read more about the Saphira architecture in "The Saphira Architecture for Autonomous Mobile Robots" by Kurt Konolige and Karen Myers in *Artificial Intelligence and Mobile Robots*.[77] They describe the system built for a demonstration for the TV special, *Scientific American Frontiers*. Summarize the behaviors and agents used. How would the same tasks be accomplished using AuRA, SFX, 3T, or TCA?

7.12 End Notes

For the roboticist's bookshelf.

Behavior-Based Robotics by Ron Arkin[10] is the most complete work on AI robotics. It has a comprehensive list of influential robot architectures, and explores in detail many of the issues only lightly touched upon in this book. Well worth reading and using as a reference.

About Saphira and Pioneer robots.

So why did RWI/ActivMedia choose the Saphira architecture for their Pioneer line? Because the Pioneer robot is based on a robot designed by a class taught at Stanford by Kurt Konolige, one of the architects of Saphira.

Foam-henge and the importance of architectures.

One criticism that applies to many of the Hybrid architectures is that they have moved away from subsumption or vector summation to more open-ended methods such as voting, rule-based arbitration, fuzzy logic, etc. There are definitely cases where there is a single best action to take. For example, consider what happened at a 1995 demonstration of the UGV Demo II program. The demonstration took place at the Martin Marietta (now Lockheed Martin) facility near Denver, Colorado. The Martin team was responsible for integrating various research contracts into a form usable by the HMMWV and for hosting demos. To help with the demo, they had several very large foam boulders created for the demo by a California special effects company. That way, the team could arrange the boulders in challenging positions to test the Demo II vehicles (versus trying to move real boulders). The boulders eventually became nicknamed "Foam-henge" as a play on Stonehenge.

The demonstration involving Foam-henge started with the audience standing at the rise of a canyon. Foam-henge was placed in the middle of the predicted path for an autonomous HMMWV. This was intended to be a test of its ability to detect and respond to unmodeled obstacles. The audience watched as a HMMWV navigating slowly, but autonomously, out of the canyon. The vehicle approached Foam-henge, then stopped, clearly detecting the boulder nearest it. Still stopped, the front wheels of the robot turned hard to the right. The wheels then turned hard to the left. Just as quickly, the wheels returned to the straight position, and the HMMWV accelerated straight into the boulder! In this case, the behavior arbiter (a precursor of DAMN)[121] had apparently viewed the choices between avoiding to the right and left as equal and thereby cancelling each other out.

About "Red" Whitaker.
William Whitaker used to have red hair, hence the nickname. Whitaker has had an impressive career focusing on building the hardware for industrial applications of mobile robots, including the robots used to clean up Chernobyl (through the company RedZone Robotics) and Three-Mile Island. Typically, the robots are teleoperated or contain software developed by other CMU scientists such as Reid Simmons and Tony Stentz.

Dante and the media.
The Dante project received heavy media coverage, and percolated into the entertainment industry. A small, Dante-like robot appears in the movie, *Dante's Peak*, as part of the team of vulcanologists led by Pierce Brosnan. The robot is continually breaking in the movie, which is unfortunately an all-too-accurate reflection of the current state of robotics. In the "Firewalker" episode of the TV series *The X-Files*, a robot looking like an Odetics "spider" robot is down in a volcano and broadcasts disturbing images implying that the vulcanologists have been attacked by a mysterious life form. The culprit turned out to be a scientist who had quit taking his medication.

EVAHR.
The EVAHR project was cancelled in the mid 1990's. It was envisioned as a jet-pack with arms to help astronauts construct the space station. The heuristic is that less than 20% of the research conducted by NASA will actually be integrated into a flight package.

8 *Multi-agents*

Chapter Objectives:

- Define the types of *control regimes, cooperation strategies,* and *goals* in multi-agents.

- Given a description of an intended task, a collection of robots, and the permitted interactions between robots, design a multi-agent system and describe the system in terms of heterogeneity, control, cooperation, and goals.

- Compute the *social entropy* of a team.

- Be able to program a set of homogeneous reactive robots to accomplish a foraging task.

- Describe use of social rules and internal motivation for emergent societal behavior.

8.1 Overview

This chapter explores artificial intelligence methods for coordinating and controlling collections of mobile robots working on completing a task. Collections of two or more mobile robots working together are often referred to SOCIETIES as teams or *societies* of multiple mobile robots, or more concisely *multi-agents*. MULTI-AGENTS Multi-agent teams are desirable for many reasons. In the case of planetary explorers or removing land mines, more robots should be able to cover more area. Like ants and other insects, many cheap robots working together could replace a single expensive robot, making multi-agents more cost effective. SWARM ROBOTS Indeed, the term *swarm robots* is becoming popular to refer to large numbers of robots working on a single task. Another motivation of multiple robots is redundancy: if one robot fails or is destroyed, the other robots can continue and complete the job, though perhaps not as quickly or as efficiently. Rodney Brooks at MIT first proposed to NASA that teams of hundreds of inexpensive ant-like reactive robots be sent to Mars in a technical report entitled "Fast, Cheap and Out of Control"[30] in part because having many robots meant that several robots could be destroyed in transit or during landing without a real impact on the overall mission.

Multi-agent teams are becoming quite popular in robot competitions, especially two international robot soccer competitions: RoboCup and MIROSOT. In these competitions, teams of real or simulated robots play soccer against other teams. The soccer task explicitly requires multiple robots that must cooperate with each other, yet react as individuals.

Readers with a strong background in artificial intelligence may notice similarities between teams of mobile robots and teams of software agents ("webots" which search the web and "knowbots" which do data mining). Those similarities are not accidental; software and physical agents fall into a research area in Artificial Intelligence often referred to as *Distributed Artificial Intelligence (DAI)*. Most of the issues in organizing teams of robots apply to software agents as well. Arkin,[10] Bond and Gasser,[119] Brooks,[26] and Oliveira et al.[113] all cite the problems with teams of multiple agents, condensed here as:

DISTRIBUTED
ARTIFICIAL
INTELLIGENCE (DAI)

- *Designing teams is hard.* How does a designer recognize the characteristics of a problem that make it suitable for multi-agents? How does the designer (or the agents themselves) divide up the task? Are there any tools to predict and verify the social behavior?

- *There is a "too many cooks spoil the broth" effect.* Having more robots working on a task or in a team increases the possibility that individual robots with unintentionally *interfere* with each other, lowering the overall productivity.

INTERFERENCE

- *It is hard for a team to recognize when it, or members, are unproductive.* One solution to the "too many cooks spoil the broth" problem is to try engineering the team so that interference cannot happen. But this may not be possible for every type of team or the vagaries of the open world may undermine that engineering. To defend itself, the team should be capable of monitoring itself to make sure it is productive. This in turn returns to the issue of communication.

- *It is not clear when communication is needed between agents, and what to say.* Many animals operate in flocks, maintaining formation without explicit communication (e.g., songs in birds, signals like a deer raising its tail to display white, speaking). Formation control is often done simply by perceiving the proximity to or actions of other agents; for example, schooling fish try to remain equally close to fish on either side. But robots and modern telecommunications technology make it possible for all agents in a team to literally know whatever is in the mind of the other robots, though at a computational and hardware cost. How can this unparalleled ability be exploited? What happens if the telecommunications link goes bad? Cell phones aren't 100% reliable, even though there is tremendous consumer pressure on cell phones, so it is safe to assume that robot communications will be less reliable. Is there a language for multi-agents that can abstract the important information and minimize explicit communication?

- *The "right" level of individuality and autonomy is usually not obvious in a problem domain.* Agents with a high degree of individual autonomy may create more interference with the group goals, even to the point of seeming "autistic."[113] But agents with more autonomy may be better able to deal with the open world.

The first question in the above list essentially asks *what are the architectures for multi-agents?* The answer to that question at this time is unclear. Individual members of multi-agent teams are usually programmed with behaviors, following either the Reactive (Ch. 4) or Hybrid Deliberative/Reactive (Ch. 7) paradigms. Recall that under the Reactive Paradigm, the multiple behaviors acting concurrently in a robot led to an *emergent behavior*. For example, a robot might respond to a set of obstacles in a way not explicitly programmed in. Likewise in multi-agents, the concurrent but independent actions of each robot leads to an *emergent social behavior*. The group behavior can be different from the individual behavior, emulating "group dynamics" or possibly "mob psychology." As will be seen in this chapter, fairly complex team actions such as flocking or forming a line to go through a door emerge naturally from reactive robots with little or no communication between each other. But as with emergent behavior in individual robots, emergent social behavior is often hard to predict. Complete architectures for designing teams of robots are still under development; Lynne Parker's ALLIANCE architecture[114] is possibly the most comprehensive system to date. The whole field of multi-agents is so new that there is no consensus on what are the important dimensions,

EMERGENT SOCIAL
BEHAVIOR

or characteristics, in describing a team. For the purposes of this chapter, *heterogeneity, control, cooperation,* and *goals* will be used as the dimensions.[117]

8.2   Heterogeneity

HETEROGENEITY

HETEROGENEOUS
TEAMS
HOMOGENEOUS TEAMS

Heterogeneity refers to the degree of similarity between individual robots that are within a collection. Collections of robots are characterized as being either heterogeneous or homogeneous. *Heterogeneous teams* have at least two members with different hardware or software capabilities, while in *homogeneous teams* the members are all identical. To make matter more confusing, members can be homogeneous for one portion of a task by running identical behaviors, then become heterogeneous if the team members change the behavioral mix or tasks.

8.2.1   Homogeneous teams and swarms

Most multi-agent teams are homogeneous swarms. Each robot is identical, which simplifies both the manufacturing cost and the programming. The biological model for these teams are often ants or other insects which have large numbers of identical members. As such, swarms favor a purely reactive approach, where each robot operates under the Reactive Paradigm. Insect swarms have been modeled and mimicked since the 1980's. The proceedings of the annual conference on the Simulation of Adaptive Behavior (also called "From Animals to Animats") is an excellent starting point.

An example of a successful team of homogeneous robots is Ganymede, Io, and Callisto fielded by Georgia Tech. These three robots won first place in the "Pick Up the Trash" event of the 1994 AAAI Mobile Robot Competition,[129] also discussed in Ch. 5. Recall that the objective of that event was to pick up the most trash (coca-cola cans) and deposit it in a refuse area. The majority of the entries used a single agent, concentrating on model-based vision for recognizing trash, cans, and bins and on complex grippers.

The three identical robots entered by Georgia Tech were simple, both physically and computationally, and are described in detail in a 1995 *AI Magazine* article.[19] The robots are shown in Fig. 8.1, and were constructed from an Intel 386 PC motherboard mounted on a radio-controlled toy tracked vehicle. The robots had a miniature wide-angle video camera and framegrabber. The flapper-style grippers had an IR to indicate when something was in the gripper. The robots also had a bump sensor in front for collisions. The robots were painted fluorescent green.

Each robot was programmed with a sequence of simple reactive behaviors (renamed here for clarity), following the reactive layer of Arkin's AuRA architecture described in Ch. 4:

wander-for-goal This behavior was instantiated for two goals: trash and trashcan. The motor schema was a random potential field, the perceptual schema was color blob detection, where trash="red" and trashcan="blue."

move-to-goal This behavior also had two different goals: trash and trashcan. The motor schema was an attractive potential field, and the perceptual schema for the trash and trashcan were the same as in the wander-for-goal.

avoid-obstacle This behavior used the bump switch as the perceptual schema, and a repulsive field as the motor schema.

avoid-other-robots The three robots did not communicate with each other, instead using only the repulsive field created by avoid-other-robots to reduce interference. The motor schema was a repulsive potential field (linear dropoff), while the perceptual schema detected "green."

grab-trash The robot would move toward the trash until the perceptual schema reported that the IR beam on the gripper was broken; the motor schema would close the gripper and back up the robot.

drop-trash When the robot reached the trashcan with trash in its gripper, the motor schema would open the gripper and back up the robot, and turn 90 degrees.

8.2.2   Heterogeneous teams

A new trend in multi-agents is *heterogeneous teams*. A common heterogeneous team arrangement is to have one team member with more expensive computer processing. That robot serves as the team leader and can direct the other, less intelligent robots, or it can be used for special situations. The danger is that the specialist robot will fail or be destroyed, preventing the team mission from being accomplished.

One interesting combination of vehicle types is autonomous air and ground vehicles. Researchers as the University of Southern California under the direction of George Bekey have been working on the coordination of teams of ground robots searching an area based on feedback from an autonomous

Figure 8.1   Georgia Tech's winning robot team for the 1994 AAAI Mobile Robot Competition, Pick Up the Trash event. (Photograph courtesy of Tucker Balch and AAAI.)

miniature helicopter. This combination permits the team to send a human observer a comprehensive view of a particular site, such as a hostage situation.

A special case of a cooperative, heterogeneous team of robots has been dubbed *marsupial robots*. The motivation for marsupial robots stemmed from concerns about deploying micro-rovers for applications such as Urban Search and Rescue. Micro-rovers often have limited battery power, which they can't afford to spend just traveling to a site. Likewise, micro-rovers may not be able carry much on-board processing power and need to have another, more computationally powerful workstation do proxy (remote) processing. A marsupial team consists of a large robot which carries one or more smaller robots to the task site, much like a kangaroo mother carries a joey in her pouch. Like a joey, the daughter robot is better protected in the pouch and can conserve energy or be recharged during transport. The mother can protect a delicate mechanism or sensor from collisions while it navigates through an irregular void. The mother can also carry a payload of batteries to recharge (feed) the daughter. It can serve as a proxy workstation, moving to maintain communications. The mother is likely to be a larger robot, while the daughter might be a micro-rover with sensors very close to the ground. The mother will have a better viewpoint and sensors, so in some circumstances it can communicate advice to the smaller daughter to help it cope with a "mouse's eye" view of the world. A teleoperator can also control

a.

b.

Figure 8.2   Two views of a marsupial robot team at University of South Florida. a.) Silver Bullet is the "mother" connected by an umbilical tether to a tracked chemical inspection robot Bujold, the "daughter." b.) Bujold exits from the rear of the jeep. (Photographs by Tom Wagner.)

the daughter more easily in some situations by looking through the mother's camera.

At this time, there appear to be only two physically realized implementations of autonomous marsupials: the University of South Florida teams, one of which is shown in Fig. 8.2, and the robots at the US Department of Energy's Idaho National Energy and Engineering Laboratory (INEEL).[3] The USF team is the only one where a mother robot carries a micro-rover inside the structure to protect it. The Mars Pathfinder mission is similar to a marsupial robot in that a micro-rover was transported to a mission site and the transport vehicle served as a support mechanism. However, our definition of marsupial assumes the mother is a fully mobile agent and can recover and retask the micro-rover.

8.2.3   Social entropy

SOCIAL ENTROPY

The above examples show how different heterogeneous teams can be. One rough measure of the degree of heterogeneity is the *social entropy* metric created by Tucker Balch.[16] (Entropy is a measure of disorder in a system, especially in the sense of the Third Law of Thermodynamics. It was also adapted by Shannon for use in information theory to quantify the amount or quality of information in a system.) The point of social entropy is to assign a numerical value for rating diversity (or disorder) in a team. The number should be 0 if all team members are the same (homogeneous). The number should have the maximum value if all the team members are different. The number of team members which are different should make the overall number higher.

To compute social entropy, consider a marsupial team $\mathcal{R}$ with a mother robot and three identical (hardware and software) micro-rovers. The formula for the social entropy, $Het(\mathcal{R})$, is:

$$(8.1)\quad Het(\mathcal{R}) \quad = \quad -\sum_{i=1}^{c} p_i \log_2(p_i)$$

CASTES There are two types of robots in the team, called *castes* or c: the mother and the daughters. Therefore $c = 2$. The term p_i is the decimal percent of robots belonging to caste c_i. If $i = 1$ for the mother, and $i = 2$ for the daughters:

$$(8.2)\quad p_1 \quad = \quad \frac{1}{4} = 0.25$$
$$p_2 \quad = \quad \frac{3}{4} = 0.75$$

Substituting into Eqn. 8.1 (and remembering that $\log_2 n = \frac{\log_{10} n}{\log_{10} 2}$), the social entropy is:

$$(8.3)\quad Het(\mathcal{R}) \quad = \quad -\sum_{i=1}^{c} p_i \log_2(p_i)$$
$$= \quad -(0.25 \log_2 0.25 + 0.75 \log_2 0.75)$$
$$= \quad -((-0.50) + (-0.31))$$
$$= \quad 0.81$$

Now consider a case where the daughters are not identical. Suppose that one of the three micro-rovers has a different sensor suite and behaviors from the other two. In that case $c = 3$, where $p_1 = \frac{1}{4}$, $p_2 = \frac{2}{4}$, and $p_3 = \frac{1}{4}$. Substituting into Eqn. 8.1 yields 1.5. Since $1.5 > 0.81$, the marsupial team with the different daughter is more diverse that the marsupial team with all identical daughters.

8.3   Control

CENTRALIZED CONTROL
DISTRIBUTED CONTROL

Control of multi-agents can fall in a spectrum bounded by *centralized control* and *distributed control* regimes. In centralized control, the robots communicate with a central computer. The central computer distributes assignments, goals, etc., to the remote robots. The robots are essentially semi-autonomous, with the centralized computer playing the role of a teleoperator in a teleoperated system. In distributed control, each robot makes its own decisions and acts independently. Of course, there is a range of regimes between fully centralized and fully distributed; the robots can interact with a central controller to receive new goals, then operate for the duration of the mission in a distributed manner.

Examples of full and partial centralized control can be found by comparing the RoboCup and MIROSOT robot soccer competitions. In those soccer competition events, teams of robots are controlled remotely by a central computer. In the small sized league of RoboCup and MIROSOT, teams of three, very small self-contained robots (7.5cm x 7.5cm x 7.5cm) play on a 130cm x 90cm arena with an orange golf ball serving as the miniature soccer ball. Each robot had a unique pattern of bright colors to make it visible from the overhead cameras, and the overhead camera is connected to a central processor. The robots communicate with the central processor over a radio link. In MIROSOT, the central processor commands each robot by supplying the direction to move. In RoboCup, the central processor can give either explicit directions or just locations of other robots and the ball, letting the robot's on-board behaviors generate the (one hopes) correct response. Fig. 8.3 shows a view of the small-sized league from the 1998 RoboCup World Cup.

MIROSOT robots are more drone-like than their RoboCup counterparts, since they are not required to carry any on-board sensing. They represent the extreme of centralized control, where everything must go through a single computer, much like the battle-droids in the *Star Wars* movie, *The Phantom Menace*. RoboCup robots are required to have some type of on-board

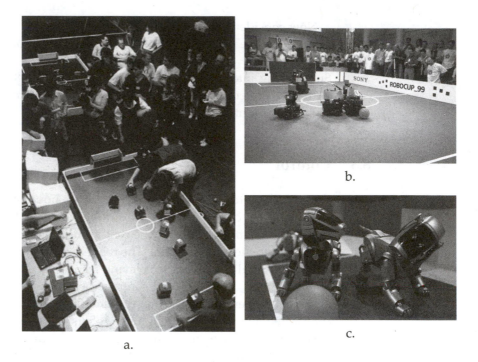

a.

b.

c.

Figure 8.3   RoboCup soccer competition: a.) Overhead view of the RoboCup playing field and teams for the small-sized league (overhead camera is not shown), b.) Mid-sized league, and c.) Legged league using Sony Aibo robots. (Photographs ©The RoboCup Federation 1999. All rights reserved.)

sensing for reflexive obstacle avoidance. In the RoboCup case, the robots must have a set of basic tactical behaviors (see Ch. 7), but may either receive strategic commands from the central computer or have on-board strategic behaviors. This type of control is conceptually equivalent to the Hybrid Reactive-Deliberative Paradigm, where the reactive layer physically resides on the robot and the deliberative layer resides on the central workstation.

Distributed control is more natural for soccer playing than centralized control, because each player reacts independently to the situation. An example of distributed control in robot soccer playing is the mid-sized league in RoboCup. Notice that in robot soccer the robots are inherently heterogeneous. Although they may be physically the same, each robot is programmed with a different role, most especially Goalie, Striker, and Defender.

Likewise, there are significant advantages to planning and learning strategies, two deliberative functions. Manuela Veloso and Peter Stone have used RoboCup as a test domain for research in deliberation.

8.4 Cooperation

COOPERATION
ACTIVE COOPERATION

Cooperation refers to how the robots interact with each other in pursuing a goal. Robots can show *active cooperation* by acknowledging one another and working together. Note that this does not necessarily mean the robots communicate with each other. For example, in robot soccer, one robot can pass the ball to another robot as part of an offensive play. The cooperation does not require communication—if a robot has the ball, can't see goal and can see team mate, then it passes to team mate, but this does require being aware of the teammates.

NON-ACTIVE
COOPERATION

More often robots are programmed to exhibit *non-active cooperation*, whereby they individually pursue a goal without acknowledging other robots but cooperation emerges. The choice of cooperation schemes is often influenced by the sensory capabilities of the robots. Active cooperation requires that robot be able to distinguish its peer robots from other aspects of the environment. In the case of the Georgia Tech entry, each robot was covered in fluorescent green poster paper easily segmented as a color region. If the robots had not been green, they would have been treated as obstacles to be avoided. Non-active cooperation has attracted much interest in the robotics community because it requires very little sensing or behaviors.

PHYSICAL
COOPERATION

RECONFIGURABLE
ROBOTS

COOPERATIVE
MOBILITY

It is easy to think of cooperation in terms of robots working together on a task. Another aspect of cooperation is *physical cooperation*, where the robots physically aid each other or interact in similar ways. Marsupial robots are certainly a type of physical cooperation, especially during deployment and docking. An even more exciting type of cooperation occurs between *reconfigurable robots*. One of the first such systems was proposed by Toshio Fukuda, called CEBOT for "celluar robot system."[31] These are small identical robots that hook up to form a useful robot. Another aspect of reconfigurable robots is *cooperative mobility*, where one robot might come over and help another robot in trouble. Shigeo Hirose simulated robots which could link up with each other to gain more stability or traction in rough terrain.[67]

8.5   Goals

The final dimension for characterizing a collection of multi-agents is how the robot works on a goal. If all the robots in the collection work on attaining the same explicit goal, then they are said to share a single goal, versus having individual goals.

An example of robots working a single goal is the winning team for the Office Navigation event in the 1996 AAAI Mobile Robot Competition.[78] The office navigation event had a robot that was supposed to search a series of rooms, find an empty conference room, and then go to a list of rooms where people were and tell them that a meeting was going to begin in the empty conference room. The event was originally conceptualized as a single agent task, but the SRI entry under the direction of Kurt Konolige consisted of three robots.[62] Each of the three robots ran the Saphira architecture (see Ch. 7) and were coordinated by a central workstation. While the robots were responsible for autonomous navigation, their goals were set by the central strategy agent. Even though they were navigating through different parts of the office maze, the robots were working on a single goal and the software agents on the central workstation were explicitly coordinating the actions of the robots. The robots were able to find an empty room and inform the attendees in 4 minutes and 30 seconds. The next best time was close to 10 minutes.

An example of purely reactive robots working on individual goals is a problem originally posed by Ron Arkin:[9] a group of robotic space "ants" foraging for mineral rich asteroids or Near Earth Objects (NEOs). If each robot in the group forages for its own asteroid, then they have individual goals. (Notice that a behavior that permits them to notice other robots and be repulsed will help disperse the robots.) If the robots are programmed so that they will all go to one specific asteroid, then they share a common goal.

Emergent cooperation is not the same thing as having a single goal. For example, suppose the robotic space ants are programmed to go to the nearest *non-moving* asteroid and bring it back to base. Each robot might have a set of behaviors: find-stationary-asteroid, move-to-asteroid, push-asteroid-to-home, and avoid-robots. The find-stationary-asteroid could be done with a random potential field (in 3 dimensions, of course). An attractive "asteroid-tropic" potential field could be used for the move-to-asteroid behavior. Likewise an attractive field could be used for the push-asteroid-to-home behavior, where the robot tries to stay behind the asteroid as it moves to home rather than avoid the asteroid. Avoid-robot could be done with a repulsive field. These behaviors give the robots individual goals, since there is no awareness of the goals of the other team members.

Now consider what happens when a robot ant encounters an asteroid it can't move. The robot stays there pushing. Eventually another robot will come along because the asteroid is not moving. As it is attracted to the "dark side" of the asteroid, it will come into range of the first robot. What happens? The avoid-robot behavior should be instantiated, causing the first robot to move over a bit. The second robot will also feel a repulsive force and slow down. As the first robot moves out of the way, the angle of repulsion changes, forcing the second robot to move sideways as well, as it continues to move to the asteroid. Together, the interaction between the two robots should cause them to naturally balance themselves behind the asteroid and push together. The point is that the robots were not explicitly directed to all work on the same NEO; they were each directed to find their own NEO, but circumstances led them to the same one.

8.6 Emergent Social Behavior

The examples of heterogeneity, cooperation, control, and goals give some hint of how an overall social behavior emerges from the actions of autonomous robots. The robot teams often are the result of extensive design efforts, where the teams aren't too large to interfere with each other, and are optimally sized for the particular task, etc. Many researchers are exploring the issues of what happens when the designer doesn't have a choice about the size of the robot population. How do social behaviors emerge in those cases? And how can social rules or conventions be established to make the team self-regulating and productive? This section summarizes two approaches: creating social rules for the robots to follow, and allowing internal motivation to cause the robots to adapt their behavior to problems.

8.6.1 Societal rules

Maja Mataric has focused her research on how group dynamics might emerge in herds of multiple agents operating under fully distributed control. She explored the impact of density and the impact of societal rules on overall team performance.[90] Each IS Robotics R2 robot was programmed with behaviors using the Subsumption architecture. She set up a scenario where up to 20 identical robots (now known as "The Nerd Herd") were given the same location as a goal. The goal, however, was on the other side of a partition with a narrow door, permitting only one robot to pass through the partition at a

Figure 8.4   The Nerd Herd. (Photograph courtesy of USC Interaction Laboratory.)

time. The robots were placed randomly on the same side of the partition and started moving at the same time.

IGNORANT
COEXISTENCE In the first set of demonstrations, the robots functioned with *ignorant coexistence*. The robots coexisted in a team, but did not have any knowledge of each other. A robot treated another robot as an obstacle. Each robot had the equivalent of a move-to-goal and an avoid-obstacle behavior. Since robots were treated as obstacles, once the robots gathered at the opening, they spent most of their time avoiding each other. The team as a whole made slow progress through the door to the goal location. Worse yet, the larger the number of robots fielded, the larger the traffic jam, and the longer to get all the team members through.

INFORMED
COEXISTENCE In the second demonstration, *informed coexistence*, the robots were allowed to recognize each other and given a simple social rule governing inter-robot interactions. In addition to move-to-goal and avoid-obstacle, a third behavior was created for avoiding robots. If a robot detected another robot, it would stop and wait for time p. If the blocking robot was still in the way after p, the robot would turn left and then resume moving to the goal. The result of the new behavior was to reduce the traffic jams, and the group got through the door in about the same time as a single agent going back and forth through the opening 20 times.

INTELLIGENT
COEXISTENCE The real surprise came in the third demonstration, *intelligent coexistence*.

Figure 8.5 Robots cooperatively tracking an object under the ALLIANCE architecture. (Photograph courtesy of Oak Ridge National Laboratories.)

The social behavior for avoiding robots was replaced with another heuristic: the robots were repulsed from other robots, but as it moves away, it tries to move in the same direction as a majority of other robots. (Each robot broadcast its heading over a radio transmitter to compensate for the inability to recognize each other by vision or sonar, so that isn't considered communication.) As a result, the robots exhibited a flocking behavior and went through the door in single file! The need to go in the same direction created a tendency to form a line, while repulsion caused the robots to essentially create spaces for robots to merge into line. Together the two effects created a strong need to go through the door single file, even though there was no such explicit direction. Not only were traffic jams reduced, but the overall task was accomplished faster.

8.6.2 Motivation

In Mataric's work, the robots reduced interference through simple social rules with no communication, but the members of the team could not actively help out failed colleagues or change tasks dynamically. Lynne Parker has attempted to address the larger issues of robustness and fault tolerance with the ALLIANCE architecture,[114] an outgrowth of the Subsumption architecture. The central idea is that members in the team can either observe or "hear" the progress of others in teams, as well as their own progress. If they get frustrated with their own progress, they should stop what they're doing and move on to something else. Likewise, if a robot is free and another robot has been unable to accomplish a task, it should try to complete the unfinished task. This is particularly useful for tasks where there is a logical sequence of behaviors, where all of a particular task (like dusting) needs to be done for an area before the robots begin working on another task (e.g., sweeping). These MOTIVATION changes in behaviors are regulated by a simple mechanism: *motivation*. The motivation of a robot to do a task is regulated by two internal motivations, ROBOT IMPATIENCE *robot impatience* and *robot acquiescence*. The more frustrated a robot with gets ROBOT ACQUIESCENCE with another robot's performance on t_i, the higher the impatience associated with that task t_i. Likewise, the more frustrated a robot gets with its own performance for a task, the higher the acquiescence. If the frustration threshold is exceeded, then the robot either takes over the unfinished task or abandons its current task and changes behavior.

Fig. 8.6 shows the time trace for an example of motivation for two space ants foraging for asteroids. (This example isn't really a sequential series of tasks in the manner used by ALLIANCE, but this conveys the elegance of motivation.) In this case, the reactive space ants have to either broadcast what they're doing or be able to perceive the other's progress. This makes it a bit different than the "no communication" approach. At time 0, both robots start by looking for asteroids. (We assume there is no frustration for the find task.) Both see asteroid A1, but Robot 1 is the first there. Robot 1 has now taken responsibility for Task 1 (T1), pushing A1 to home. Even though A1 is still stationary at time 3, Robot 2 does not join in as it would in the no-communication method. Instead, it begins to accrue impatience about T1. Once Robot 1 begins to push A1, it starts accruing frustration in the form of acquiescence. As with the no-communication example, a single robot cannot push the asteroid.

While Robot 1 is trying to push asteroid A1, Robot 2 sees and moves to asteroid A2. All the while its impatience over T1 is growing. At time 7, Robot 2 is trying unsuccessfully to push asteroid A2 (task T2) and its acquiescence counter is increasing. Also at time 7, Robot 2's patience with Robot 1 and task T1 has been exceeded. It pushes T1 onto its stack of things to do when it completes its curent task. Meanwhile, at time 9, Robot 1 gives up on T1. Although it is frustrated with Robot 2, it assumes that T2 is still under control and so begins to forage again. Finally, at time 10, the frustration over T2 reaches the limit and Robot 1 is free to help Robot 2.

time	Robot 1	Robot 2
0	find-stationary-asteroid	find-stationary-asteroid
1	sees A1	sees A1
2	move-to-asteroid(A1)	move-to-asteroid(A1)
3	arrives at A1	resumes find-stationary-asteroid
4	push-asteroid-to-home(A1) T1-acquiescence++	find-stationary-asteroid T1-impatience++
5	push-asteroid-to-home(A1) T1-acquiescence++	sees A2 T1-impatience++
6	push-asteroid-to-home(A1) T1-acquiescence++	move-to-asteroid(A2) T1-impatience++
7	push-asteroid-to-home(A1) T1-acquiescence++ T2-impatience++	push-asteroid-to-home(A2) T1-impatience>limit put T1 on stack T2-acquiescence++
8	push-asteroid-to-home(A1) T1-acquiescence++ T2-impatience++	push-asteroid-to-home(A2) A1-impatience++ T2-acquiescence++
9	T1-acquiescence>limit gives up on T1 find-stationary-asteroid T2-impatience++	push-asteroid-to-home(A2) T2-acquiescence++
10	T2-impatience>limit now attempts T2 move-to-asteroid(A2)	T2-acquiescence++
11	push-asteroid-to-home(A2) T2-acquiescence = 0	push-asteroid-to-home(A2) T2-acquiescence = 0
12	arrives at HOME	arrives at HOME

Figure 8.6   Example of how the internal motivation in ALLIANCE might be extended to work with two space ants.

8.7   Summary

In summary, many tasks favor the use of many cheap robots rather than a single expensive one. These collections of multiple robots are often referred to as multi-agents. Individual robots in a multi-agent team are generally programmed with behaviors, most often as purely reactive systems, but occasionally with a hybrid architecture. As with an overall behavior emerging on a single reactive agent, societies of reactive agents often exhibit an emergent societal behavior.

Multi-agent societies can be characterized according to where they fall on at least four dimensions (since multi-agent theory is relatively new, even for robotics, new dimensions may surface over time). Heterogeneity refers to whether the member robots are identical in software and hardware. Cooperation may be either active or non-active, while control may fall in the spectrum from fully distributed to fully centralized. A robot society may have a single, explicitly shared goal or each robot may have its own goal. When communication between agents is appropriate is a pervasive, open question.

From a practical side, the emphasis in multi-agents has been on how favorable group dynamics emerge from teams of homogeneous, purely reactive robots while operating under distributed control. Problems in emergent societal behaviors such as interference and the need to adapt to the open world can often been addressed by specifying social rules and internal motivation. However, more interest is emerging in robots that have either heterogeneous software or hardware capabilities, such as marsupial and reconfigurable robots. The diversity of a heterogeneous team can be captured somewhat by the social entropy metric.

8.8   Exercises

Exercise 8.1

Give three reasons why multi-agents are desirable. Describe the general attributes of applications which are well-suited for multi-agents, and give one example.

Exercise 8.2

Define the following:

a. heterogeneity

b. control

c. cooperation

d. goals

Exercise 8.3

Consider the example of space ants. What would happen if the first robot communicated with the other robots to recruit them to help move the asteroid? Would the behaviors or the goal structure necessarily change? Why or why not?

Exercise 8.4

Draw a FSA or write a script to coordinate the sequencing of the Pick Up the Trash behaviors for Io, Ganymede, and Callisto.

Exercise 8.5

Describe three approaches to societal behavior: social rules, internal motivation, and leadership.

Exercise 8.6

Were the behaviors for the Nerd Herd purely reactive? Why or why not?

Exercise 8.7   [*Programming*)]

Implement the space ant example with 3-5 robots capable of phototaxis and dead reckoning.

a. Multi-agent foraging. Start with only a phototropic and avoid-robot behavior, where a robot is an obstacle that isn't a light. The program will start with an empty world consisting of a light (you may need to make a "bigger light" by placing lights next to each other). Between 2 and 5 phototropic robots will be placed at different random starting locations in the world. Each will wander through the world, avoiding obstacles, until it comes to a light. Then it will move directly to the light (attractive field). If more than one robot is attracted to the same light, they should center themselves evenly around the light. Compare this with the program in Ch. 5 which had a single robot forage for lights. Which gets more lights faster?

b. Cooperating to bring the food home. Now add the push-to-home behavior where the robot wants to be on a straight line behind the light to home. What happens now?

Exercise 8.8   [*World Wide Web*]

Visit the RoboCup web site at www.robocup.org. Which team has performed the best over the past 3 years? Describe the multi-agent organization in terms of control and cooperation.

Exercise 8.9   [*Advanced Reading*]

Read Ed Durfee's humorous invited paper on DAI, "What Your Computer Really Needs to Know, You Learned in Kindergarten" (proceedings of the *Tenth National Conference on Artificial Intelligence*, 1992). For each of his ten issues ("Share Everything," "Play Fair," etc.), describe how this applies to robots. For each issue give an example of how it applies to a robot team described in this chapter.

Exercise 8.10   [*Advanced Reading*]

Read and summarize "Behavior-Based Formation Control for Multirobot Teams," by Tucker Balch and Ron Arkin in *IEEE Transactions on Robotics and Automation*, vol. 14, no 6., 1998.

Exercise 8.11   [*Science Fiction*]

Watch the movie "Silent Running" about a team of three mobile robots (Huey, Dewey, and Louie) working on a space station. Classify their teamwork in terms of heterogeneity, control, cooperation and goals.

8.9   End Notes

For further reading.
Chapter 9, "Social Behavior," of *Behavior-Based Robotics* by Ron Arkin has a detailed and comprehensive presentation of the ethology, philosophical considerations, and different robot architectures for multi-agents. It is well worth reading.

Swarms and flocks.
The references to swarm robots are too numerous to cite here; many papers explore details of insect behavior and coordination strategies as well as provide simulations. Jean-Louis Deneubourg has produced many interesting articles synthesizing insights form insect colonies into a form useful for programming mobile robots. As noted in *Behavior-Based Robotics*, Craig Reynolds' work in computer graphic simulation of flocks of in "Flocks, herds, and schools: A distributed behavior model," in *Computer Graphics*, 1987, showed how flocks emerge from simple, individual interactions.

"Fast, Cheap and Out of Control: The Movie."
The term "Fast, Cheap and Out of Control" later became the title of a 1997 award-winning documentary by Errol Morris on four men, including Rodney Brooks. The movie title implied that Morris saw human kind shifting from highly individualistic relations with the world developed over time (as seen by the lion tamer and topiary gardener) to decentralized, reactive mobs. Although the movie is not about robotics per se, it features interviews with Brooks and contains stunning shots of some of Brooks' robots walking over broken glass, shining like diamonds in the bright lights. Maja Mataric, one of Brooks' students at the time of the filming, can be seen in one of the shots wearing shorts.

Languages for multi-agents.
Researchers are beginning to work on languages for multi-agent coordination, including Holly Yanco and Lynn Stein at MIT.

Robot soccer.
There is some dispute over which competition was the first robot soccer competition: MIROSOT or RoboCup. RoboCup was originally proposed by Minoru Asada, a noted Japanese researcher in visually guided mobile robots, in 1995 for the 1997 IJ-CAI, giving researchers two years to prepare. Hiroaki Kitano has been responsible for much of the organization of the competition and funding from the Sony Corporation (among others). MIROSOT was started by Jong-Kwan Kim in Korea in 1996, a year after RoboCup was announced but a year before the first official RoboCup game.

Robot name trivia.
More robots are being named after women these days. The robots in Lynne Parker's laboratory at Oak Ridge National Laboratory are named after women pioneers in

computer science. Rogue at Carnegie Mellon University was named after the woman mutant from the *X-Men* comics (to complement the robot Xavier, named after the wheeled super hero). The robots in my lab at the University of South Florida are named after women science fiction authors. (Except one robot which was named after the Coors beer, Silver Bullet, while I was out of town.)

More robot name trivia.
The Nerd Herd consists of IS Robotics R2 robots which look like toasters. Brightly colored toasters, but toasters nonetheless. The 20 robots are named for things that come out of toasters, for example, Bagel.

PART II

Navigation

Contents:

Overview

The first three chapters in this part focus on navigation, a critical ability for a robot that claims to be mobile. Navigation remains one of the most challenging functions to perform, in part because it involves practically everything about AI robotics: sensing, acting, planning, architectures, hardware, computational efficiencies, and problem solving. Reactive robots have provided behaviors for moving about the world without collisions, but navigation is more purposeful and requires deliberation. In particular, a robot needs to be able to plan how to get a particular location. Two different categories of techniques have emerged: *topological navigation* and *metric navigation*, also known as *qualitative navigation* and *quantitative navigation*, respectively. Another important class of problems is how to make maps, which introduces the issue of how the robot can accurately localize itself as it moves, despite the problems seen with proprioceptive sensors in Ch. 6. The final chapter provides an overview of robots and AI techniques on the horizon.

TOPOLOGICAL
NAVIGATION
METRIC NAVIGATION
QUALITATIVE
NAVIGATION
QUANTITATIVE
NAVIGATION

The Four Questions

Part I presented the material in a historical sequence, following the steps in development of the three AI robotic paradigms. Navigation is more of a collection of specific algorithms than a linear progression; therefore the material is organized by functionality. The functions of navigation can be expressed by four questions presented below.

Where am I going? This is usually determined by a human or a mission planner. A planetary rover may be directed to move to a far away crater and look for a specific rock in the caldera. Roboticists generally do not include this as part of navigation, assuming that the robot has been directed to a particular goal.

What's the best way there? This is the problem of path planning, and is the area of navigation which has received the most attention. Path planning methods fall into two categories: qualitative and quantitative (or metric). Qualitative path planning methods will be covered in Ch. 9, while metric methods will be presented in Ch. 10.

Where have I been? Map making is an overlooked aspect of navigation. As a robot explores new environments, it may be part of its mission to map the environment. But even if the robot is operating in the same environment (e.g., delivering mail in an office building), it may improve its performance by noting changes. A new wall may be erected, furniture rearranged, paintings moved or replaced. Or, as discovered by Xavier, one of the indoor robots at the Robotics Institute at Carnegie Mellon University, certain hallways and foyers are too crowded at specific times of the day (end of class, lunchtime) and should be avoided.

Where am I? In order to follow a path or build a map, the robot has to know where it is; this is referred to as localization. However, as has already been seen in Ch. 6, a robot is very poor at dead reckoning. Imagine what happens to map making when a robot goes around the perimeter of a room but cannot record its footsteps. Localization can be relative to a local environment (e.g., the robot is in the center of the room), in topological coordinates (e.g., in Room 311), or in absolute coordinates (e.g., latitude, longitude, altitude). Both map making and localization are covered in Ch. 11.

The Rhino and Minerva Tour Guide Robots (shown in Fig. II) provide an excellent example of how these four questions arise naturally in applications.[139] Rhino and Minerva were designed by researchers from CMU and the University of Bonn to perform all the functions of a tour guide in a museum, including leading groups of people to exhibits upon request and answering questions. Rhino hosted tours of the Deutsches Museum in Bonn, Germany, while Minerva was used in the Smithsonian's National Museum of History in Washington, DC.

The tour guide robots had to know where they were at any given time (localization) in order to answer questions about an exhibit or give directions to another exhibit. Minerva also could create a custom tour of requested exhibits, requiring it to know how to get to each of the exhibits (path planning). The tour path had to be reasonably efficient, otherwise the robot might have the group pass a targeted exhibit repeatedly before stopping at it. This also means that the robot had to remember where it had been. Rhino operated using a map of the museum, while Minerva created her own. An important aspect of the map was that it included the time needed to navigate between exhibits, not just the distance. This time of information allows a planner to factor in areas to avoid at certain times of day. For example,

a.

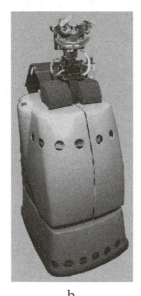

b.

Figure II.1 Two Tour Guide Robots: a) Rhino in the Deutsches Museum in Bonn (in the center), and b) a close up of the more emotive Minerva. (Photographs courtesy of Sebastian Thrun and Wolfram Burgard.)

Xavier at CMU has learned to avoid cutting through a particular foyer when classes are changing, since the density of people moving about slows down its progress.

Criteria for Evaluating Path Planners

Although it should be clear by the end of Part II that navigation is more than path planning, path planning is the most obvious aspect of navigation from a programmer's standpoint. A designer has a wide variety of techniques to choose from, spanning close to 30 years of research. As with everything else robotic, the choice of technique depends on the ecological niche the robot will operate in. The criteria for evaluating the suitability of a path planner includes:

1. *Complexity.* Is the algorithm too computationally or space intensive to execute or reside within the limitations of the robot?

2. *Sufficiently represents the terrain.* Many researchers work in indoor environments, which are flat. Outdoor robots may be operating in rough terrain with steep inclines or undesirable areas, such as slippery sand or mud. If the path planning algorithm is built to generate paths from a binary representation (a region is either navigable or not), then it may lead the robot into trouble if it is applied to a more diverse environment.

3. *Sufficiently represents the physical limitations of the robot platform.* Robots have physical limitations. The most profound limitation which impacts path planning is whether a robot is holonomic or not. Recall that holonomic robots can turn in place. Since they can spin on a dime, the path planning algorithm doesn't have to consider the steering radius of the robot. Likewise, robots may not be round. Robots made for research purposes such as Nomad 200's, Khepera, and RWI B-series are often round so that when they turn in place, they won't bump into anything. A robot which is not round introduces more complexity. In order to turn in a narrow hall, it may have to "watch its back" to make sure it doesn't bump anything.

4. *Compatible with the reactive layer.* Path planners are deliberative by definition. But in a Hybrid style of architecture, the reactive layer will be responsible for carrying out the path. A technique which simplifies this transformation is desirable.

5. *Supports corrections to the map and re-planning.* Path planning requires an a priori map, which may turn out to be seriously wrong. Therefore, a robot may start out with one map, discover it is incorrect, and need to update the map and re-plan. Clearly techniques which permit the existing plan to be repaired rather than be scrapped and computed from scratch are desirable.

The Impact of Sensor Uncertainty

Since navigation is a fundamental capability of a mobile robot, researchers have been investigating navigational techniques since the 1960's. But as was seen in Part I, it was only since the early 1990's that robots became affordable, and had on-board sensing and reasonable computational power. As a result, most researchers in navigation were forced to develop techniques using simulators and assumptions about how real robots would physically work.

Two of the most pervasive assumptions of these researchers turned out to be unfortunate in retrospect. First, it was generally assumed that the robot could localize itself accurately at each update. This assumption was based in part on another assumption: that sensors would give an accurate representation of the world. As was seen just with sonars in Ch. 6, this is often not true. Sensors are always noisy and have vulnerabilities.

Therefore, a robot has to operate in the presence of uncertainty. In the Reactive Paradigm, the way in which the sensors were coupled with the actuators accepted this uncertainty. If the sonar or IR returned an incorrect range reading, the robot may appear to start to avoid an imaginary obstacle. However, the process of moving often eliminated the source of the noisy data, and soon the robot was back to doing the right thing. Uncertainty becomes more serious when dealing with map making and localization; therefore a new wave of techniques has been developed to smooth over sensor noise and ascertain the correct state of the world. These methods are mathematical in nature and are covered in Ch. 11.

Navigation and the Robotic Paradigms

The questions posed call to mind deliberation. Planning, just from the name alone, is deliberative. Map making and localization imply memory and labeling specific locations (room, hall, river, canyon); these are symbolic representations and so also fit the notion of deliberation from the Hybrid Paradigm. Most of the techniques presented in Part II will go into the deliberative component of Hybrid architectures.

One important observation is that the four questions of navigation largely ignore an implicit fifth question: *how am I going to get there?* Based on Part I, the obvious answer is "by using reactive behaviors." But navigation is deliberative, and the issue of integrating deliberation and reaction for navigation in a Hybrid architecture is still largely open. Work addressing this issue of interleaving planning and execution is presented in Ch. 9.

Spatial Memory

The answer to *what's the best way there?* depends on the representation of the world that the robot is using. The world representation will be called SPATIAL MEMORY the robot's *spatial memory*.[63] Spatial memory is the heart of the cartographer object class (or its equivalent) in a Hybrid architecture, as described in Ch. 7.

Spatial memory should provide methods and data structures for processing and storing output from current sensory inputs. For example, suppose a robot is directed to "go down the hall to the third red door on the right." Even for the coordination and control of reactive behaviors, the robot needs to operationalize concepts such as "hall," "red," "door" into features to look for with a perceptual schema. It also needs to remember how many red doors it has gone past (and not count the same door twice!). It would also be advantageous if the robot sensed a barrier or dead-end and updated its map of the world.

Spatial memory should also be organized to support methods which can extract the relevant expectations about a navigational task. Suppose a robot is directed this time to to "go down the hall to the third door on the right." It could consult its spatial memory and notice that odd numbered doors are red, and even numbered are yellow. By looking for "red" and "yellow" in addition to other perceptual features of a door, the robot can more reliably identify doors, either by focus of attention (the robot only runs door detection on red and yellow areas, not every image) or by sensor fusion (more sources of data means a more certain percept).

Spatial memory supports four basic functions:

ATTENTION   1. *Attention.* What features, landmarks to look for next?

REASONING   2. *Reasoning.* Can that surface support my weight?

PATH PLANNING   3. *Path planning.* What is the best way through this space?

4. *Information collection.* What does this place look like? Have I ever seen it before? What has changed since the last time I was here?

Spatial memory takes two forms: *route*, or *qualitative*, and *layout*, or *metric*, representations. Route representations express space in terms of the connections between landmarks. An example of a route representation is when a person gives directions propositionally (as a list): "go out of the parking lot, and turn left onto Fowler Drive. Look for the museum on the right, and turn left at next traffic light." Notice that is perspective dependent; landmarks that are easy for a human to see may not be visible to a small robot operating close to the floor. Route representations also tend to supply orientation cues: "out of the parking lot" (versus being contained in it), "turn left," "on the right." These orientation cues are egocentric, in that they assume the agent is following the directions at each step.

Layout representations are the opposite of route representations. When a person gives directions by drawing a map, the map is a layout representation. Layout representations are often called metric representations because most maps have some approximate scale to estimate distances to travel. The major differences between layout and route representations are the viewpoint and utility. A layout representation is essentially a bird's-eye view of the world. It is not dependent of the perspective of the agent; the agent is assumed to be able to translate the layout into features to be sensed. The layout is orientation and position independent. Layout representations can be used to generate a route representation, but this doesn't necessarily work the other way. (Consider how easy it is to read a map and give verbal directions to a driver, versus drawing an accurate map of a road you've only been on once.) Most maps contain extra information, such as cross streets. An agent can use this information to generate alternative routes if the desired route is blocked.

While spatial memory is clearly an important key to robust navigation, it does involve memory, representation, and planning. The successes of the Reactive Paradigm suggest that for robots "less is more." Therefore, it merits considering how much spatial memory an agent needs to navigate. This is a gray area. The amount of representation needed depends on many factors. How accurately and efficiently does the robot have to navigate? Is time critical, or can it take a slightly sub-optimal route? Navigational tasks which require optimality tend to require more dense and complex world representations. What are the characteristics of the environment? Are there landmarks to provide orientation cues? Are distances known accurately? What are the sources of information about that environment that specify terrains, surface properties, obstacles, etc.? What are the properties of the available sensors in that environment?

End Notes

Invasion of the robot tour guides. . .
The success of Rhino and Minerva, coupled with the interesting technical challenges posed by navigating through buildings crowded with people, has prompted other groups to create robot tour guides. A group also at the CS department at CMU developed SAGE, a tour guide for the Carnegie Museum in Pittsburgh, under the direction of Illah Nourbakhsh.

9 *Topological Path Planning*

Chapter Objectives:

- Define the difference between a *natural* and *artificial landmark* and give one example of each.

- Given a description of an indoor office environment and a set of behaviors, build a relational graph representation labeling the *distinctive places* and *local control strategies* using gateways.

- Describe in one or two sentences: *gateway, image signature, visual homing, viewframe, orientation region.*

- Given a figure showing landmarks, create a topological map showing landmarks, landmark pair boundaries, and orientation regions.

9.1 Overview

TOPOLOGICAL
NAVIGATION

Topological, route, or *qualitative navigation* is often viewed as being more simple and natural for a behavior-based robot. Certainly people frequently give other people routes as directives; therefore it seems natural to expect a robot to be able to parse commands such as "go down the hall, turn to the left at the dead end, and enter the second room on the right." Even without a map of where everything is, there is enough information for navigation as long as the robot knows what a "hall," "dead-end," and "room" is.

Route representations fall into one of two approaches:

1. **Relational.** Relational techniques are the most popular, and can be thought of as giving the robot an abbreviated, "connect the dots" graph-style of spatial memory.

2. **Associative.** Relational techniques tend to focus on the graph-like representation of spatial memory. Associative techniques focus on coupling sensing with localization in a manner which parallels the tight coupling of sensing to acting found in reflexive behaviors.

Because relational techniques use an explicit representation, they can support path planning. Associative techniques are better for retracing known paths.

9.2   Landmarks and Gateways

LANDMARK   Topological navigation depends on the presence of landmarks. A *landmark* is one or more perceptually distinctive features of interest on an object or locale of interest. Note that a landmark is not necessarily a single, self-contained object like "red door." A landmark can be a grouping of objects; for example, "McDonald's" means a tall sign, bright building of a certain shape, and a parking lot with a lot of activity. Another outdoor landmark might be a "stand of aspen trees."

Landmarks are used in most aspects of navigation. If a robot finds a landmark in the world and that landmark appears on a map, then the robot is localized with respect to the map. If the robot plans a path consisting of segments, landmarks are needed so the robot can tell when it has completed a segment and another should begin. If a robot finds new landmarks, they can be added to its spatial memory, creating or extending a map.

GATEWAYS   Dave Kortenkamp popularized a particularly interesting special case of landmarks: *gateways*.[79] A gateway is an opportunity for a robot to change its overall direction of navigation. For example, an intersection of two hallways is a gateway; the robot can choose to go straight or turn left or right. Because gateways are navigational opportunities, recognizing gateways is critical for localization, path planning, and map making.

ARTIFICIAL LANDMARKS
NATURAL LANDMARKS   Landmarks may be either *artificial* or *natural*. The terms "artificial" and "natural" should not be confused with "man-made" and "organic." An artificial landmark is a set of features added to an existing object or locale in order to either support recognition of the landmark or some other perceptual activity. An interstate highway exit sign is an example of an artificial landmark. It is put there with the purpose of being easy to see (retro-reflective) and the white-on-green font is sized for optimal visibility (perceptual activity is reading the sign). A natural landmark is a configuration of exisiting features selected for recognition which were not expressly designed for the

perceptual activity. If someone gives directions to their house, "take the second right after the McDonald's," the McDonald's is being used as an orientation cue for navigation to their house. Clearly, the McDonald's was not built with the purpose of being a navigational cue to a private home. The fact that it was used for another purpose means it is a natural landmark.

CRITERIA FOR
LANDMARKS
Regardless of whether a landmark is artificial or natural, it must satisfy three criteria:

1. *Be readily recognizable.* If the robot can't find the landmark, it isn't useful.

2. *Support the task dependent activity.* If the task dependent activity is simply an orientation cue ("take the second right after the McDonald's"), then being recognized is enough. Suppose a landmark is intended to provide position estimation to guide docking the space shuttle to a space station. In that case, the landmark should make it easy to extract the relative distance to contact.

3. *Be perceivable from many different viewpoints.* If the landmark is widely visible, the robot may never find it.

Fig. 9.1 shows artificial landmarks constructed for use in the 1992 AAAI Mobile Robot Competition.[42] Each robot was supposed to follow a route between any sequence of waypoints in an arena. The teams were allowed to mark the waypoints with artificial landmarks. Each waypoint is readily recognizable by the checkerboard pattern. The task dependent activity of going to the correct waypoint is facilitated by the cylindrical barcodes which are unique for each station. Notice that the use of a cylinder guaranteed that landmarks would be perceivable from any viewpoint in the arena.

A good landmark has many other desirable characteristics. It should be passive in order to be available despite a power failure. It should be perceivable over the entire range where the robot might need to see it. It should have distinctive features, and, if possible, unique features. Distinctive features are those which are locally unique; they appear only as part of the landmark from every viewpoint of the robot in that region of the world (e.g., there is only one McDonald's on Busch Boulevard). If the feature occurs only once in the entire region of operations (e.g., there is only one McDonald's in Tampa), then the feature would be considered globally unique. In addition to being perceivable for recognition purposes, it must be perceivable for the task. If the robot needs to position itself to within 0.5 meters of the landmark, then the landmark must be designed to achieve that accuracy.

Figure 9.1 Artificial landmarks used in the 1992 AAAI Mobile Robot Competition. (Photograph courtesy of AAAI.)

9.3   Relational Methods

Relational methods represent the world as a graph or network of nodes and edges. Nodes represent gateways, landmarks, or goals. Edges represent a navigable path between two nodes, in effect that two nodes have a spatial relationship. Additional information may be attached to edges, such as direction (N,S,E,W), approximate distance, terrain type, or the behaviors needed to navigate that path. Paths can be computed between two points using standard graph algorithms, such as Dijkstra's single source shortest path algorithm. (See any algorithm textbook for details.)

One of the earliest investigations of relational graphs for navigation was by Smith and Cheeseman.[133] They represented the world as a relational graph, where the edges represented the direction and distance between nodes. They

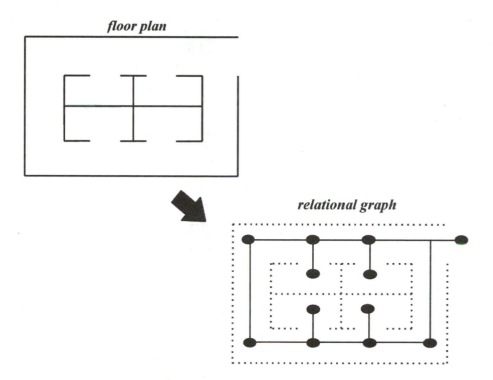

Figure 9.2 Representation of a floor plan as a relational graph.

simulated what would happen if a robot used dead-reckoning to navigate. As would be expected from the section on proprioception in Ch. 6, they found that the error would continually increase and soon the robot would be unable to reach any of the nodes.

9.3.1 Distinctive places

DISTINCTIVE PLACE

Kuipers and Byun tied relational graphs to sensing in their seminal work with distinctive places.[81] A *distinctive place* is a landmark that the robot could detect from a nearby region called a neighborhood. Their work was motivated by research in cognitive science indicating that spatial representation in the animal kingdom forms a multi-level hierarchy. (More recent studies suggest this hierarchy isn't as clearly partitioned as previously thought.) The lowest level, or most primitive way of representing space, was by identifying landmarks (doors, hallways) and the procedural knowledge to travel

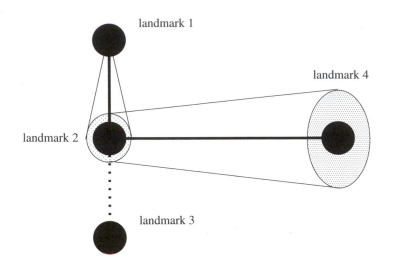

Figure 9.3   Propagation of error in a relational graph.

between them (follow-hall, move-thru-door). The next layer up was topological. It represented the landmarks and procedural knowledge in a relational graph, which supported planning and reasoning. The uppermost level was metric, where the agent had learned the distances and orientation between the landmarks and could place them in a fixed coordinate system. Higher layers represented increasing intelligence.

Kuipers and Byun's representation is of particular interest. Each node represents a distinctive place. Once in the neighborhood, the robot can position itself in a known spot relative to the landmark using sensor readings. One example of a distinctive place was a corner. (Kuipers and Byun worked in simulation; this did not turn out to be realistic with sonars.) The idea was that the robot could repeatably move around in the neighborhood the corner until, for example, 1 meter from each wall. Then the robot would be localized on the map.

LOCAL CONTROL
STRATEGY

HILL-CLIMBING
ALGORITHM

An arc or edge in the relational graph was called a *local control strategy*, or *lcs*. The local control strategy is the procedure for getting from the current node to the next node. When the robot senses the landmark it is filling in values for a set of features. The robot uses a *hill-climbing algorithm*. The hill-climbing algorithm directs the robot around in the neighborhood until a measurement function (e.g., how far away the walls are) indicates when the robot is at a position where the feature values are maximized (e.g., both

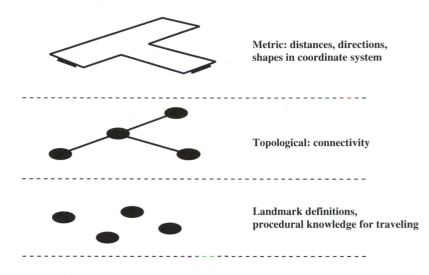

Metric: distances, directions,
shapes in coordinate system

Topological: connectivity

Landmark definitions,
procedural knowledge for traveling

Figure 9.4   Multi-level spatial hierarchy, after Byun and Kuipers.[81]

are 1 meter away). The point where the feature values are maximized is the distinctive place. The hill-climbing algorithm is a very simple approach. The idea is that for most hills, if you always choose the next step which is the highest (you can't look ahead), then you will get to the top quickly. Hence, the robot always moves in the direction which appears to cause the most postive change in the measurement function.

Although developed independently of each other, reactive behaviors map nicely onto distinctive places and local control strategies, as shown in Fig. 9.6. Consider a robot navigating down a wide hall to a dead-end. The local control strategy is a behavior, such as `follow-hall`, which operates in conjunction with a releaser, `look-for-corner`. The releaser is an exteroceptive cue. When it is triggered, the robot is in the neighborhood of the distinctive place, and the released behavior, `hillclimb-to-corner(distance=1)`, directs the robot to 1 meter from each wall.

9.3.2   Advantages and disadvantages

The distinctive place concept eliminates any navigational errors at each node. The robot may drift off-course because the hall is wide, but as soon as it reaches the neighborhood, it self-corrects and localizes itself. Kuipers and Byun were able to show in simulation how a robot with dead reckoning er-

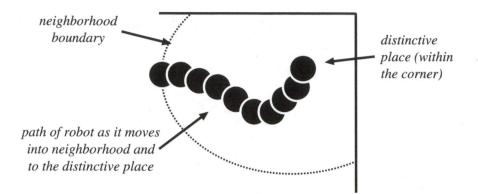

Figure 9.5 A robot reacting to a corner and moving to a distinctive place within the neighborhood.

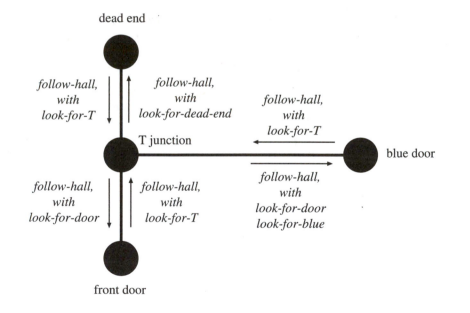

Figure 9.6 Behaviors serving as local control strategies, and releasers as means of signalling the entrance to a neighborhood.

rors could use multiple trips between nodes to build up a reasonable metric map, since most of the errors would average out. Another attractive aspect of the distinctive place approach is that it supports discovery of new landmarks as the robot explores an unknown environment. As long as the robot found something distinctive that it could reliably localize itself to, it could be put on a topological map. Then as it repeatedly moved to it, the robot could construct a metric map.

Returning to the discussion of landmarks, it should be noticed that a landmark must be unique to a node pair. There can't be any corners in the real world that are not on the graph between the nodes or else the robot will localize itself incorrectly.

The distinctive place approach as originally formulated encountered some problems when behavior-based roboticists began to apply it to real robots. One of the most challenging problems was perception. Good distinctive places are hard to come by; configurations that seemed useful to humans, like corners, proved difficult to reliably sense and localize against. Features that were easy to sense often were too numerous in the world, and so were not locally unique. Another challenge was learning the local control strategy. As the robot explored an unknown environment, it was easy to imagine that it could find distinctive places. But how did it learn the appropriate local control strategy? In an indoor environment, the robot might resort to always using wall following, even though other behaviors would be better suited. How would it ever try something different? Another open issue is the problem of indistinguishable locations. The issue of indistinguishable locations has also been tackled to some degree by work with probablistic methods, which will be covered in Ch. 11.

9.4 Associative Methods

ASSOCIATIVE METHODS

Associative methods for topological navigation essentially create a behavior which converts sensor observations into the direction to go to reach a particular landmark. The underlying assumption is that a location or landmark of interest for navigation usually has two attributes:

PERCEPTUAL STABILITY

1. *perceptual stability*: that views of the location that are close together should look similar

PERCEPTUAL DISTINGUISHABILITY

2. *perceptual distinguishability*: that views far away should look different.

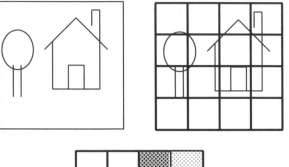

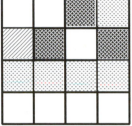

Figure 9.7   Derivation of an image signature. Clockwise from the upper left: a raw image, the image partitioned into 16 sections, and the image with the sections values shown as crosshatching.

These principles are implicit in the idea of a neighborhood around a distinctive place. If the robot is in the neighborhood, the views of the landmark look similar. The main difference is that associative methods use very coarse computer vision.

9.4.1   Visual homing

Work done by Nelson,[111] and later by Engelson,[50] relied on an image signature. An image signature is created by partitioning an image into sections. Fig. 9.7 shows an image partitioned into 16 sections. Next, each section is examined and a measurement is made of some attribute in the section. Some possible measurements are the edge density (the number of pixels with edges divided by the number of pixels in the section), dominant edge orientation (the angle the majority of the edges are pointing), average intensity, and so on. The image signature reduces the image to n measurements. One way to think of this is that it changes the resolution of the image into 16 pixels.

Notice that the image signature in the figure forms a pattern. If the robot

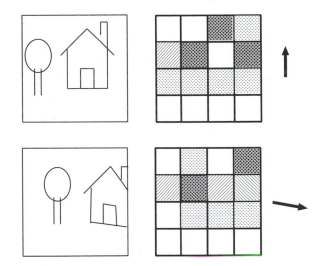

Figure 9.8   Image measurements and the appropriate response from two different views.

is in the neighborhood of the location, then the image measurements should be approximately the same pattern as the image signature, only the pattern may be offset due to the not-quite-at-the-right-place viewpoint.

If the robot can identify the image signature, or portion of it, in the current image, it will then know whether to turn left or right to localize itself relative to the location. The use of image signatures to direct a robot to a specific location is called visual homing. The inspiration for visual homing came from Nelson's research into how bees navigate. It is easy to speculate that baby bees are learning the image signatures of their hive as they execute the zoom in/out behavior described in Ch. 3. In that case, the compound eyes serve as de facto partitions of what to humans would be a single image.

9.4.2   QualNav

AUTONOMOUS LAND
VEHICLE (ALV)

Levitt and Lawton took the ideas of neighborhoods and visual homing to an extreme for outdoor navigation over large distances as part of the Defense Advance Research Projects Agency (DARPA) *Autonomous Land Vehicle (ALV)* project in the late 1980's.[85] At that time, topological navigation using relational graphs appeared promising for indoor environments, but seemed to resist application to outdoor terrains. Part of the challenge was the notion of

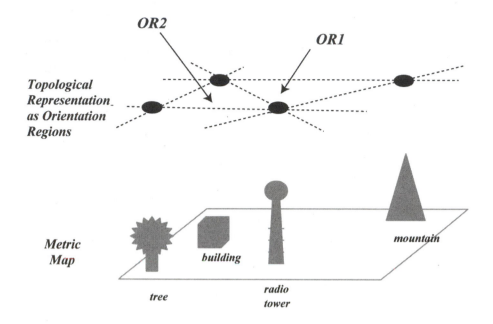

Figure 9.9   Division of an outdoor area into orientation regions, after Levitt and Lawton.[85]

localization. With that challenge went the associated question of what could the robot use as a landmark. The land vehicle might be expected to travel for 50 miles deliberately avoiding obvious landmarks such as houses, road intersections, and radio towers. The idea was to have a robot vehicle capable of stealthily scouting an area and seeing if enemy forces were nearby. The robot vehicle has to provide some indication of where it found the enemy forces as well as return to base.

Inside of trying to localize the vehicle to a particular landmark, the idea behind *QualNav*[85] (an acronym for "qualitative navigation") was to localize the vehicle to a particular *orientation region*, or a patch of the world. The orientation region is defined by *landmark pair boundaries*. A landmark pair boundary is an imaginary line drawn between two landmarks. As seen in the figure below, drawing lines between all the candidate landmark pairs will partition the world into orientation regions, although the orientation regions may be very oddly shaped.

An orientation region is conceptually similar to a neighborhood. Within an orientation region, all the landmarks appear in the same relationship. If

QualNav
ORIENTATION REGION
LANDMARK PAIR
BOUNDARIES

the vehicle is in OR1, the landmarks are found in the same order if the robot always turns in the same direction (either always clockwise or always counter-clockwise): building-mountain-tower. If the vehicle is in OR2, the landmarks will be tree-building-intersection.

An interesting attribute of orientation regions and landmark pair boundaries is that the vehicle can directly perceive when it has entered a new orientation region. For example, as the robot moves from OR1 to OR2, the building-tower landmark pair boundary is in front of it, then is on both sides of the vehicle, and is finally behind it. The transition is a perceptual event, and does not require knowledge about the distance of the landmarks, just that the relationship of the landmarks to the robot has just changed.

The use of orientation regions allows the robot to create an outdoor topological map as it explores the world, or to localize itself (coarsely) to a metric map. The robot does not have to be able to estimate the range to any of the landmarks.

How the robot navigates inside an orientation region has the flavor of visual homing. The robot may need to retrace its path as precisely as possible through an orientation region. (A military robot might need to return without being seen.) Without knowing the range to the landmarks bounding the orientation region, the robot is helpless. But if it has to remember the angles to each landmark every n minutes, it can move to follow the angles. A set of angles remembered at a point along the path is called a viewframe.

One amusing aspect of the viewframe approach is that it assumed the robot had cameras literally in the back of its head. Unfortunately the ALV vehicle did not; all the sensors faced forward. Daryl Lawton tells the story of trying to convince the union driver of the vehicle to stop every 10 feet and do a 360° turn so he could record the viewframes. After much pleading, the driver finally honored the request, though it wasn't clear if he ever understood why the crazy scientist wanted a high-tech truck capable of autonomous navigation to go in circles every 10 feet!

Associative methods are interesting because of the tight coupling of sensing to homing. The image signature and viewframe concepts do not require the robot to recognize explicitly what a landmark is, only that it is perceptually stable and distinguishable for the region of interest. Unfortunately associative methods require massive storage and are brittle in the presence of a dynamic world where landmarks may be suddenly occluded or change. Of course, this is more problematic for indoor environments than outdoor ones.

Figure 9.10   A student testing an unidentified entry in the competition arena at the 1994 AAAI Mobile Robot Competition "Office Delivery" event. (Photograph courtesy of AAAI.)

9.5   Case Study of Topological Navigation with a Hybrid Architecture

This section presents a case study of topological navigation using the SFX architecture in the 1994 AAAI Mobile Robot Competition by a team of undergraduates from the Colorado School of Mines. The 1994 competition had an office navigation event.[129] Each robot was placed in a random room, then had to navigate out of the room and to another room within 15 minutes. Entrants were given a topological map, but weren't allowed to measure the layout of the rooms and halls. This case study reviews how the topological map was entered, the activities of the Cartographer, how scripts (discussed in Ch. 5) were used to simplify behavioral management, and the lessons learned.

9.5.1   Path planning

The topological map was entered as an ASCII file in Backus-Naur Form. A sample map is shown in Fig. 9.11. The input map consists of three node types: room (R), hall (H), and foyer (F). The world is assumed to be orthogonal. Since edges between nodes can be in only four directions, it is convenient to refer to them as north (N), south (S), east (E), and west (W), where N is set arbitrarily in the map. The robot is given its starting node but as an extra challenge, the robot is not given the direction it is initially facing relative to the map. The topological map is structurally correct, but does not necessarily represent if a corridor or door is blocked. Such blockages may occur or be moved at any time. An additional assumption is that the outside of each door is marked with a landmark such as a room number or room name.

The Cartographer in SFX is responsible for constructing the route. It takes as input a gateway type of topological map and a start node and goal node, and produces a list of nodes representing the best path between the start and goal. The cartographer operates in two steps: preprocessing of the map to support path planning, and path planning. The preprocessing step begins by building a database of the nodes in the input map, reclassifying the corridor nodes which represent a hall to door connection as Hd.

Once the start and goal nodes are known, the Cartographer eliminates extraneous gateways. A Hd node may be connected to a room which is not visitable, that is, it is neither the goal room, the start room, or a room with more than one door. If that occurs, then both the R and Hd node entries are eliminated from the database. A sample input graphical topological representation for a metric map is shown in Fig. 9.11. If R3 was selected as the start node and R7 the goal, the refined graphical representation is as shown in Fig. 9.11. Note that Hd3-R1 and Hd4-R6 were eliminated because they were not associated with the start or goal rooms and could not be used as a shortcut since they had only one entrance. Gateway nodes such as H10 remain in the path because they may be useful if a blocked path occurs. For example, if the robot is going down the hallway from H11 to H8 and the path is blocked, the robot will need to return to a known location in order to reorient itself and replan. However, if the H10 is eliminated, then the robot must return to the very beginning of the corridor, because it does not know where it is with respect to H10. To solve this dilemma of traveling the same part of the corridor possibly three times, the cartographer maintains nodes which represent possible alternative strategies. Different types of gates, tasks, and robot capabilities will lead to different preprocessing strategies.

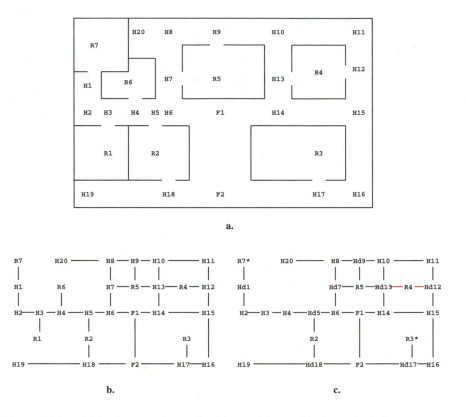

a.

b.   **c.**

Figure 9.11   a.) Metric map of an office layout, b.) graphical topological representation, and c.) refined graph for traveling from R3 to R7.

An optimal path is computed using Dijkstra's single source shortest path algorithm. The algorithm generates the shortest path by considering the costs between each pair of connected nodes; the costs are expressed as the length or weight of an edge in the graph. Since the topological representation is not metric, connections between the nodes reflect *preferences* in constructing routes. These preferences are expressed as edge weights. In this implementation, navigating through foyers was considerably more computationally expensive and unreliable; therefore the edge weighting for any path subsegment originating from a foyer was set at 3. The edge weight for going from a room to another room was set at 2 to discourage the robot from finding solutions which were "impolite" (e.g., cutting through people's offices). All other connections were set to 1.

The Task Manager in SFX uses the path computed by the cartographer to select the appropriate *abstract navigation behavior* (Ch. 5) for traveling between a particular pair of nodes. It maintains a pointer to the current node and the next intended node from the path. The current and next node type determine TRANSITION TABLE   the appropriate behavior according to the *transition table* shown below:

From	To			
	H	F	R	H
H	Navigate-hall	Navigate-hall	Undefined	Navigate-hall
F	Navigate-hall	Navigate-foyer	Navigate-door	Navigate-hall
R	Undefined	Navigate-door	Navigate-door	Navigate-door
Hd	Navigate-hall	Navigate-hall	Navigate-door	Navigate-hall

The transition table shows that not all combinations of nodes are permitted; by definition, the robot cannot move from a hall node H to a room node R without going through a Hd node. Also, the table is not necessarily symmetrical. In the case of rooms, navigate-door must be employed to either enter or exit, but the case of moving to a foyer will use different strategies depending on whether the robot is traversing a hall or a foyer. The ANB itself uses the information in the database entries for the nodes as parameters for instantiating the script to the current waypoint pair.

One novel aspect of this implementation is how the Task Manager handles a blocked path; it does not reverse the currently instantiated abstract navigation behavior (ANB). If the obstacle avoidance behavior posts to the whiteboard structure that a BLOCKED condition has occurred, the Task Manager terminates the currently active abstract navigation behavior. Because the robot is between nodes, the Task Manager directs the robot to return to the current node. But it triggers a simple move-to-goal behavior, which allows the robot to reorient itself more quickly than reinstantiating the abstract navigation behavior with new parameters.

Once the robot has returned to approximately the last known location, the Task Manager requests a new path from the Cartographer. The Cartographer removes the connection between the current and intended nodes, then recomputes a new path with the current node as the start. Once the new path is completed, the Task Manager resumes control.

Fig. 9.12 demonstrates the robot moving through the map handed out at the actual AAAI Mobile Robot Competition. The start node is R7 and the goal is R2. The cartographer computes the path as R7-H1-H2-H5-R2, eliminating H3 and H4 because they are not relevant for this task.

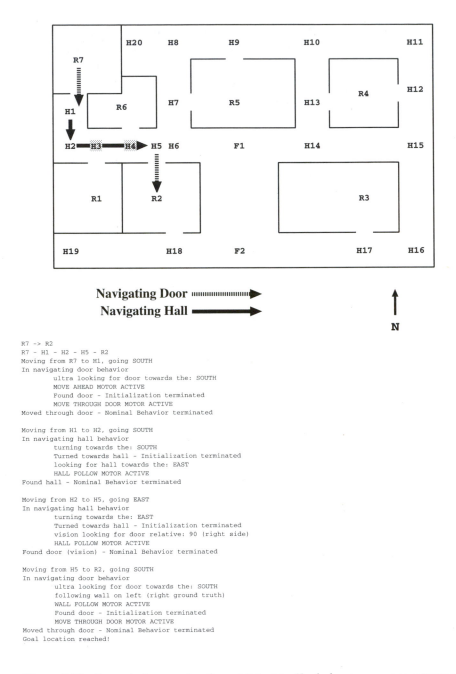

```
R7 -> R2
R7 - H1 - H2 - H5 - R2
Moving from R7 to H1, going SOUTH
In navigating door behavior
        ultra looking for door towards the: SOUTH
        MOVE AHEAD MOTOR ACTIVE
        Found door - Initialization terminated
        MOVE THROUGH DOOR MOTOR ACTIVE
Moved through door - Nominal Behavior terminated

Moving from H1 to H2, going SOUTH
In navigating hall behavior
        turning towards the: SOUTH
        Turned towards hall - Initialization terminated
        looking for hall towards the: EAST
        HALL FOLLOW MOTOR ACTIVE
Found hall - Nominal Behavior terminated

Moving from H2 to H5, going EAST
In navigating hall behavior
        turning towards the: EAST
        Turned towards hall - Initialization terminated
        vision looking for door relative: 90 (right side)
        HALL FOLLOW MOTOR ACTIVE
Found door (vision) - Nominal Behavior terminated

Moving from H5 to R2, going SOUTH
In navigating door behavior
        ultra looking for door towards the: SOUTH
        following wall on left (right ground truth)
        WALL FOLLOW MOTOR ACTIVE
        Found door - Initialization terminated
        MOVE THROUGH DOOR MOTOR ACTIVE
Moved through door - Nominal Behavior terminated
Goal location reached!
```

Figure 9.12 Scenario for moving from R7 to R2. Shaded gateways are extraneous and discarded by the planner.

As shown by the output, the Cartographer computes the path shown in the first line. The second line shows that the current navigational task is to move from R7 to H1. The Task Manager selects navigate-door and it begins by looking for the door since the user did not specify where it was. By examining the database, the door is known to be to the south. Therefore, the behavior initiates the move-ahead behavior in the south direction. When the door is found, the initialization phase of the abstract behavior is over and the nominal activity of moving through the door is triggered. Once the robot is through the door, the nominal behavior is terminated, terminating the entire abstract behavior as well.

The next navigational task is to move from H1 to H2, again in the direction south. The task manger selects navigate-hall. The task of moving from H2 to H5 is interesting because it shows that the termination condition for hall following is different than for H1 to H2. Since H5 is a gateway to a room of interest, a different perceptual process is used to visually identify the room. Once the door has been identified visually, the robot is considered at H5. The H5-R2 connection instantiates navigate-door. However, in this case, the ultrasonics has not yet identified the door opening and so the initialization phase consists of wall following until the door opening is recognized. Then the nominal behavior is activated and the robot moves into the room, successfully completing the task.

The second simulation shown in Fig. 9.13 uses the sample topological map provided prior to the competition. The intended path was R1-H1-F1-H8--H0-R0, but H8-H0 was blocked. As shown in the figure, the robot detects that the path is blocked and uses move to goal to return to H8. The Cartographer updates the topological map and computes a new route and the robot resumes execution, in this case H8-F1-H5-H6-H7-H0-R0. The output of the script below shows the robot confirming the nodes H5 and H6 even though the plan did not have them enter the associated rooms. These nodes were kept in the path because if another blocked hall was encountered, the robot would then be able to return to either R5 or R6 and attempt to use a route through the door between.

9.5.2 Navigation scripts

The path planning and execution components are clearly deliberative. The Cartographer is maintaining a map in the form of a graph and is monitoring progress. The transition table takes the role of a high level sequencer. Scripts

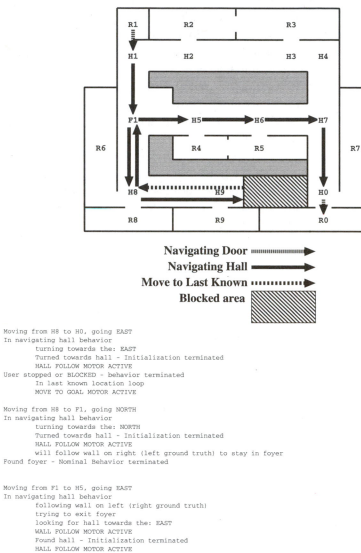

Figure 9.13   Scenario for moving from R1 to R0 with blocked path.

are used to specify and carry out the implied details of the plan in a modular and reusable way.

The implementation consisted of three scripts for navigating doors, halls, and foyers. The pseudocode for `navigate-door` is shown below in C^{++} style and takes advantage of the indexing properties of the switch statement:

```
switch(door)
case door-not-found:
      //initialization phase
      //follow wall until find door
      if wall is found
            wallfollow to door
      else
            move-ahead to find a wall
case door-found:
      //nominal activity phase
      move-thru-door(door-location)
```

The nominal behavior, `move-thru-door`, is self-terminating, so there is no separate termination condition. The perception of the door is the key determinant in what the robot does.

The `navigate-hall` is used for traveling between corridors, foyers and corridors, and from corridors to corridor/door nodes. It has two different starting conditions. One condition is that the robot is in a foyer and detects a hall. Since the hall may be somewhat ahead and the `hallfollow` behavior assumes the robot is in the hall, the script has the robot employ `wallfollow` to find the hall, then begin following the hall. The task manager uses the directional information stored in the database to determine which wall of the foyer to follow. In the other condition the robot is already in a hall. Since the robot is not guaranteed to be facing the centerline of the hall (ANBs have no knowledge of what was done prior to their instantiation except via global variables), the sub-script turns it to line itself up with the desired hall.

```
switch(hall)
case not-facing-hall:
      //initialization phase
      if starting in a FOYER
```

```
                    if hall-not-found
                        wallfollow until find the hall
                    else
                        if not facing hall
                            turn to face hall
              else starting in a HALL
                    if not facing hall
                        turn to face hall
        case facing-hall:
            //nominal activity phase
            hallfollow until next gateway
```

The `navigate-hall` ANB terminates when the next expected gateway (the next node in the path) is found. There are three behaviors which look for gateways. `hallwatch` looks for the ultrasonic signature of a hall in the expected direction; `foyerwatch` similarly looks for foyers, and the robot uses vision through the `confirm-door` behavior to detect the landmark associated with the room. These behaviors run concurrently with the nominal behaviors.

The `navigate-foyer` ANB is used to move the robot between two foyers. It assumes that two foyers' nodes connected are a connvenient representation of a single large foyer with entries from different directions (i.e., multiple gateways into the foyer). The script moves the robot n feet into the first foyer in the direction of the second foyer. This gets the robot away from potentially confusing ultrasonic signatures. Then the task manager determines which side of the foyer to wall-follow until the next expected gateway is detected. There is no case statement in the pseudocode since the sequence of activities is fixed.

```
            //step 1
            move-to-goal(n, dir) in direction of next foyer
            //step 2
            wallfollow until next gateway is detected
```

9.5.3   Lessons learned

The CSM team did not place at the AAAI competition; the robot suffered a series of hardware failures, causing both the power supply and the sonars to fail. The robot was eventually fixed and the software worked fine. The tests before and after the competition offered several practical lessons.

First, it is critical to build the abstract navigation behaviors out of robust primitives. The biggest problem with the implementation has not been with the scripts per se, but rather with the quality of the primitive behaviors. If the robot cannot reliably detect an open doorway while it is following a wall around a room, it will never exit no matter what the script says. Second, contention for sensing resources is an emerging issue for robotic control schemes. The video camera on the robot did not have a pan mechanism; essentially, Clementine's directional control is the camera effector. In one instantiation of the `navigate-hall` behavior between a H node and a Hd node, the nominal behavior of `hallfollow` frequently pointed Clementine and her camera away from the anticipated location of the door, interfering with the `confirm-door` perceptual behavior used to terminate `navigate-hall`. Even at slow speeds, Clementine frequently missed the door. One alternative is to let the two active behaviors take turns with control of the robot. This leads to a move, stop, sense scenario which slowed the robot's progress and still allowed the robot to roll past the door.

Note that the representation and path planning algorithm support the addition of metric information. The metric distance between every visited could be stored in the database. The distance could be attached to the reference index in the node class, much the same as the nodes connected to the N, E, S, W are stored. One problem with simply attaching the metric distance is deciding what distance value to use. If `wallfollow` takes the robot around the perimeter of a foyer in order to exit, the distance traveled will not reflect the straight line distance between nodes. Nor is the measure bidirectional; going N-S through the foyer could be significantly longer than S-N if the foyer is asymmetric and the robot follows different walls each time. On the other hand, if the width of a foyer were known, the robot might possibly be able to use dead reckoning to move directly across it to the desired exit. The impact of obstacles lengthening the distance traveled can also be a problem, especially if the obstacles are people moving down a hall. A short hall can take a long time to navigate if it is cluttered during one visit, but a short time during another. Another difficulty with adding metric distances is how to use it effectively. Metric distances may not be known for all pairs of nodes, making it difficult to apply Dijkstra's algorithm. Likewise, distance may be only one factor in selecting a route; our current implementation prefers going through halls versus taking short cuts between rooms. Utility theory can be used to quantitify the impact of these competing concerns.

9.6   Summary

Landmarks simplify the *where am I?* problem by providing orientation cues. Gateways are a special case of landmarks which reflect a potential for the robot to change directions (turn down a different road or hall, enter a room, etc.). There are two categories of qualitative navigation methods: *relational* and *associative*. Relational methods relate *distinctive places* (nodes) to each other by the *local control strategies (lcs)*, or behaviors, needed to travel between them (edges), forming a graph. The robot can use the graph to plan a path using techniques such as the single source shortest path algorithm. It executes the path by employing the behavior associated with that edge it is traversing. When it sees the landmark of the location, it is in the neighborhood, and then can use another behavior, such as hill-climbing, to localize itself relative to the landmark. Associative methods directly couple perception with acting. An image can be compared to a image signature or a viewframe to generate the next movement for the robot to take. Relational methods are commonly used for topological navigation.

9.7   Exercises

Exercise 9.1

List the four questions associated with navigation.

Exercise 9.2

List and describe the criteria for evaluating a path planner.

Exercise 9.3

Describe the difference between route and metric representations of space.

Exercise 9.4

Define the difference between natural and artificial landmarks and give one example of each.

Exercise 9.5

Define a gateway. What gateways would be in a museum? What sensors would be needed to reliably detect them?

Exercise 9.6

Build a relational graph representation labeling the distinctive places and local control strategies using gateways for a floor of a building on campus.

Exercise 9.7

Describe each in one or two sentences: gateway, image signature, visual homing, viewframe, orientation region.

Exercise 9.8

Create a topological map showing landmarks, landmark pair boundaries, and orientation regions for an area of campus.

Exercise 9.9

Consider the spatial hierarchy of Kuipers and Byun. Do these three levels fit naturally within a Hybrid architecture? How would they be implemented in a state-hierarchy style? A model-oriented style?

Exercise 9.10

Did Minerva use topological navigation? What did it use for landmarks?

Exercise 9.11   [*World Wide Web*]

Visit the Minerva site as http://www.cs.cmu.edu/~Minerva. Write a one-page paper summarizing the project.

Exercise 9.12   [*Advanced Reading*]

Read the scientific papers at the Minerva web site. Describe:

a. The path planner used and evaluate it using the criteria presented in this overview.

b. Discuss the impact of sensor uncertainty on Minerva's navigation and how it was addressed.

c. List which of the four functions of spatial memory were used.

Exercise 9.13   [*Advanced Reading*]

Read the article about the two winners of the 1992 AAAI Mobile Robot Competition in Congdon et al.[38] Describe each team's use of landmarks and topological navigation strategy.

Exercise 9.14   [*Programming*]

Look up the following algorithms and describe how they work. Can they be used interchangeably?

a. Dijkstra's single source shortest path

b. hill-climbing

Exercise 9.15   [*Programming*]

Design a visual landmark and implement a hill-climbing algorithm to localize the robot relative to the landmark.

Exercise 9.16   [*Programming*]

Design 4 unique landmarks.

   a. Program the robot to visit each landmark in any order specified by a user.

   b. Place the landmarks at different locations. Implement Dijkstra's single source shortest path algorithm to compute the shortest path between two points specified by a user.

   c. Implement a *minimal spanning tree* algorithm to allow the robot to visit all way-points efficiently.

9.8   End notes

Of batteries and topological navigation.
The CSM entry did not place due to massive hardware failures with the power supply on Clementine. At one point, the team was using the car battery from the school van parked outside the Seattle Convention Center. We'd drive up, park, I'd take the battery out in the open, and walk into the convention center, and we'd return it to the van to drive to their housing in the wee hours of the morning. No security guard or policeman ever said a word. See the Summer 1995 issue of *AI Magazine* for an article on the winners.

Topological navigation examples.
The figures and printouts of the topological navigation system used by the CSM team were prepared by Paul Wiebe.

10 *Metric Path Planning*

Chapter objectives:

- Define *Cspace, path relaxation, digitization bias, subgoal obsession, termination condition.*

- Explain the difference between graph and wavefront planners.

- Represent an indoor environment with a *generalized Voronoi graph*, a *regular grid*, or a *quadtree*, and create a graph suitable for path planning.

- Apply the A* search algorithm to a graph to find the optimal path between two locations.

- Apply wavefront propagation to a regular grid.

- Explain the differences between continuous and event-driven replanning.

10.1 Objectives and Overview

QUANTITATIVE NAVIGATION

Metric path planning, or *quantitative navigation*, is the opposite of topological navigation. As with topological methods, the objective is to determine a path to a specified goal. The major philosophical difference is that metric methods generally favor techniques which produce an optimal, according to some measure of best, while qualitative methods seem content to produce a route with identifiable landmarks or gateways. Another difference is that WAYPOINTS metric paths are usually decompose the path into subgoals consisting of *way-points*. These waypoints are most often a fixed location or coordinate (x,y). These locations may have a mathematical meaning, but as will be seen with meadow maps, they may not have a sensible correspondence to objects or landmarks in the world. Topological navigation focused on subgoals which are gateways or locations where the robot could change its primary heading.

The terms "optimal" and "best" have serious ramifications for robotics. In order to say a path is optimal, there is an implied comparison. As will be seen, some metric methods are able to produce an optimal path because they consider all possible paths between points. This can be computationally expensive. Fortunately, some algorithms (especially one named "A*" for reasons that will be discussed later) are more clever about rejecting non-optimal paths sooner than others.

Surprisingly, an optimal path may not appear optimal to the human eye; for example, a mathematically optimal path of a world divided into tiles or grids may be very jagged and irregular rather than straight. The ability to produce and compare all possible paths also assumes that the planning has access to a pre-exisiting (or *a priori*) map of the world. Equally as important, it assumes that the map is accurate and up to date. As such, metric methods are compatible with deliberation, while qualitative methods work well with more reactive systems. As a deliberative function, metric methods tend to be plagued by the same sorts of difficulties that were seen in Hierarchical systems: challenges in world representation, handling dynamic changes and surprises, and computation complexity.

COMPONENTS OF
METRIC PATH
PLANNERS

Metric path planners have two components: the *representation* (data structure) and the *algorithm*. Path planners first partition the world into a structure amenable for path planning. They use a variety of techniques to represent the world; no one technique is dominant, although regular grids appear to be popular. The intent of any representation is to represent only the salient features, or the relevant configuration of navigationally relevant objects in the space of interest; hence the term configuration space. Path planning algorithms generally work on almost any configuration space representation, although as with any algorithm, some methods work better on certain data structures. The algorithms fall into two broad categories: those which treat path planning as a graph search problem, and those which treat path planning as a graphics coloring problem. Regardless of what algorithm is used, there is always the issue in a Hybrid architecture of when to use it. This is sometimes called the issue of interleaving reaction and planning.

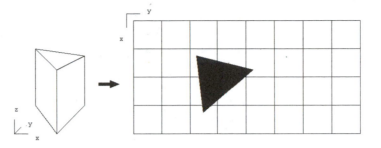

Figure 10.1   Reduction of a 6DOF world space to a 2DOF configuration space.

10.2   Configuration Space

CONFIGURATION SPACE

The physical space robots and obstacles exist in can be thought of as the world space. The *configuration space,* or *Cspace* for short, is a data structure which allows the robot to specify the position (location and orientation) of any objects and the robot.

DEGREES OF FREEDOM

A good Cspace representation reduces the number of dimensions that a planner has to contend with. Consider that it takes six dimensions (also called *degrees of freedom* or DOF) to represent precisely where an object is. A person may specify the location of the object as a (x, y, z) coordinate in some frame of reference. But an object is three-dimensional; it has a front and back, top and bottom. Three more degrees are needed to represent where the front of the chair is facing, whether it is tilted or not, or even upside down. Those are the Euler (pronounced "Oiler") angles, ϕ, θ, γ, also known as pitch, yaw, and roll.

Six degrees of freedom is more than is needed for a mobile ground robot in most cases for planning a path. The z (height) coordinate can be eliminated if every object the robot sits on the floor. However, the z coordinate will be of interest if the robot is an aerial or underwater vehicle. Likewise, the Euler angles may be unnecessary. Who cares which way the robot is facing if all the robot wants to do is to plan a path around it? But the pitch of a planetary rover or slope of an upcoming hill may be critical to a mission over rocky terrain.

Fig. 10.1 shows a transformation of an object into Cspace. In general, metric path planning algorithms for mobile robots have assumed only two DOF, including for the robot. For path planning purposes, the robot can be modeled as round so that the orientation doesn't matter. This implicitly assumes

HOLONOMIC   the robot is *holonomic*, or can turn in place. Many research robots are sufficiently close to holonomic to meet this assumption. However, robots made
from radio-controlled cars or golf carts are most certainly not holonomic.
Much work is being done in non-holonomic path planning, where the pose
of the robot must be considered (i.e., can it actually turn that sharply without
colliding?), but there no one algorithm appears to be used in practice. This
chapter will restrict itself to holonomic methods.

10.3   Cspace Representations

The number of different Cspace representations is too large to include more
than a coarse sampling here. The most representative ones are Voronoi diagrams, regular grids, quadtrees (and their 3D extension, octrees), vertex
graphs, and hybrid free space/vertex graphs. The representations offer different ways of partitioning free space. Any open space not occupied by an
object (a wall, a chair, an un-navigable hill) is free space, where the robot is
free to move without hitting anything modeled. Each partition can be labeled with additional information: "the terrain is rocky," "this is off-limits
from 9am to 5am," etc.

10.3.1   Meadow maps

Many early path planning algorithms developed for mobile robots assumed
that the robot would have a highly accurate map of the world in advance.
This map could be digitized in some manner, and then the robot could apply
various algorithms to convert the map to a suitable Cspace representation.
An example of a Cspace representation that might be used with an *a priori*
MEADOW MAP   map is the *meadow map* or hybrid vertex-graph free-space model.
Meadow maps transform free space into convex polygons. Convex polygons have an important property: if the robot starts on the perimeter and
goes in a straight line to any other point on the perimeter, it will not go out of
the polygon. The polygon represents a safe region for the robot to traverse.
The path planning problem becomes a matter of picking the best series of
polygons to transit through. Meadow maps are not that common in robotics,
but serve to illustrate the principles of effecting a configuration space and
then planning a path over it.
The programming steps are straightforward. First, the planner begins with
a metric layout of the world space. Most planners will increase the size of
every object by the size of the robot as shown in Fig. 10.2; this allows the

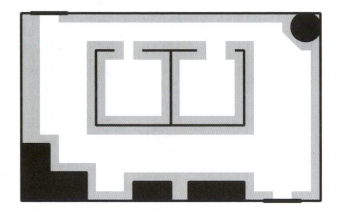

Figure 10.2 A *a priori* map, with object boundaries "grown" to the width of the robot (shown in gray).

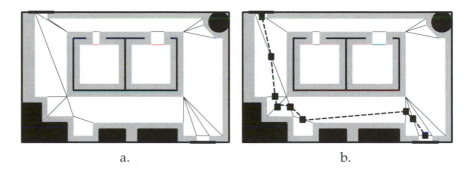

a.   b.

Figure 10.3 Meadow maps: a.) partitioning of free space into convex polygons, and b.) generating a graph using the midpoints.

planner to treat the robot as if it were a point, not a 2D object. Notice how from the very first step, path planners assume holonomic vehicles.

The next step in the algorithm is to construct convex polygons by considering the line segments between pairs of some interesting feature. In the case of indoor maps, these are usually corners, doorways, boundaries of objects, etc. The algorithm can then determine which combination of line segments partitions the free space into convex polygons.

The meadow map is now technically complete, but it is not in a format that supports path planning. Each convex polygon represents a safe passage for the robot. But there is still some work to be done. Some of the line segments

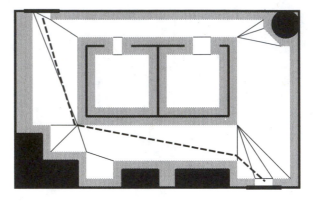

Figure 10.4   String tightening as a relaxation of an initial path.

forming the perimeter aren't connected to another a polygon (i.e., they are part of a wall), so they should be off limits to the planning algorithm. Also, as can be seen by the above figure, some of the line segments are quite long. It would make a difference to the overall path length where the robot cuts across the polygon. It is hard for the planner to discretize a continuous line segment. So the issue becomes how to specify candidate points on the polygon. One solution is to find the middle of each line segment which borders another polygon. Note that each of these midpoints becomes a node, and if edges are drawn between them, an undirected graph emerges. A path planning algorithm would determine the best path to take.

One disadvantage of a meadow map, indeed of any Cspace representation, is evident on inspection of Fig. 10.3: any path which is chosen will be somewhat jagged. Each of the inflection points is essentially a waypoint. One outcome of the partitioning process is that the free space is divided up in a way that makes sense geometrically, but not necessarily for a robot to actually travel. Why go halfway down the hall, then angle off? This may be mathematically optimal on paper, but in practice, it seems downright silly. Chuck Thorpe at CMU devised a solution to paths generated from any kind of discretization of free space.[138] Imagine that the path is a string. Now imagine pulling on both ends to tighten the string (the technical name for this is PATH RELAXATION *path relaxation*) This would remove most of the kinks from the path without violating the safe zone property of convex polygons.

Meadow maps have three problems which limit their usefulness. One problem is that the technique to generate the polygons is computationally

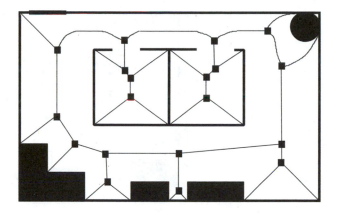

Figure 10.5 Graph from a generalized Voronoi graph (GVG). (Graph courtesy of Howie Choset.)

complex. But more importantly, it uses artifacts of the map to determine the polygon boundaries, rather than things which can be sensed. Unless the robot has accurate localization, how does it know it is halfway down a long, featureless hall and should turn 30°? The third major disadvantage is that it is unclear how to update or repair the diagrams as the robot discovers discrepancies between the *a priori* map and the real world.

10.3.2 Generalized Voronoi graphs

GENERALIZED
VORONOI GRAPHS

Generalized Voronoi Graphs, or *GVGs*, are a popular mechanism for representing Cspace and generating a graph. Unlike a meadow map, a GVG can be constructed as the robot enters a new environment, thereby creating a topological map as shown by Howie Choset at CMU.[36]

VORONOI EDGE

The basic idea of a GVG is to generate a line, called a *Voronoi edge*, equidistant from all points. As seen in Fig. 10.5, this line goes down the middle of hallways and openings. The point where many Voronoi edges meet is known as a *Voronoi vertex*. Notice the vertices often have a physical correspondence to configurations that can be sensed in the environment. This makes it much easier for a robot to follow a path generated from a GVG, since there is an implicit local control strategy of staying equidistant from all obstacles.

If the robot follows the Voronoi edge, it will not collide with any modeled obstacles, because it is staying "in the middle." This obviates the need to grow the obstacle boundaries. Edges serve as freeways or major thorough-

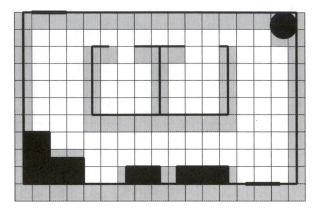

Figure 10.6   Regular grid.

fares. It should also be noted that the curved edges in a GVG do not matter to graph theory or graph algorithms. It is only the length, not the physical reality, of the edges that make any difference.

10.3.3   Regular grids

Another method of partitioning the world space is a regular grid. The regular grid method superimposes a 2D Cartesian grid on the world space, as shown in Fig. 10.6. If there is any object in the area contained by a grid element, that element is marked occupied. Hence, regular grids are often referred to as occupancy grids. Occupancy grids will be detailed in Ch. 11.

Regular grids are straightforward to apply. The center of each element in the grid can become a node, leading to a highly connected graph. Grids are either considered *4-connected* or *8-connected*, depending on whether they permit an arc to be drawn diagonally between nodes or not.

4-CONNECTED
NEIGHBORS
8-CONNECTED
NEIGHBORS
DIGITIZATION BIAS

Unfortunately, regular grids are not without problems. First, they introduce *digitization bias*, which means that if an object falls into even the smallest portion of a grid element, the whole element is marked occupied. This leads to wasted space and leads to very jagged objects. To reduce the wasted space, regular grids for an indoor room are often finely grained, on the order of 4- to 6-inches square. This fine granularity means a high storage cost, and a high number of nodes for a path planning algorithm to consider.

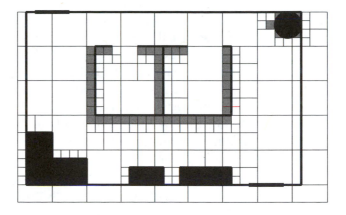

Figure 10.7 Quadtree Cspace representation.

10.3.4 Quadtrees

QUADTREES A variant on regular grids that attempts to avoid wasted space is *quadtrees*. Quadtrees are a recursive grid. The representation starts out with grid elements representing a large area, perhaps 64-inches square (8 by 8 inches). If an object falls into part of the grid, but not all of it, the Cspace algorithm divides the element into four (hence the name "quad") smaller grids, each 16-inches square. If the object doesn't fill a particular sub-element, the algorithm does another recursive division of that element into four more sub-elements, represented a 4-inches square region. A three dimensional quadtree is called an octree.

10.4 Graph Based Planners

INITIAL NODE
GOAL NODE
As seen in the previous section, most Cspace representations can be converted to graphs. This means that the path between the *initial node* and the *goal node* can be computed using graph search algorithms. Graph search algorithms appear in networks and routing problems, so they form a class of algorithms well understood by computer science. However, many of those algorithms require the program to visit each node on the graph to determine the shortest path between the initial and goal nodes. Visiting every node may be computationally tractable for a sparsely connected graph such as derived from a Voronoi diagram, but rapidly becomes computationally expensive for a highly connected graph such as from a regular grid. Therefore, there has

been a great deal of interest in path planners which do a "branch and bound" style of search; that is, ones which prune off paths which aren't optimal. Of course, the trick is knowing when to prune!

The A* search algorithm is the classic method for computing optimal paths for holonomic robots. It is derived from the A search method. In order to explain how A* works, A search will be first presented with an example, then A*. Both assume a metric map, where the location of each node is known in absolute coordinates, and the graph edges represent whether it is possible to traverse between those nodes.

The A search algorithm produces an optimal path by starting at the initial node and then working through the graph to the goal node. It generates the optimal path incrementally; each update, it considers the nodes that could be added to the path and picks the best one. It picks the "right" node to add to the path every time it expands the path (the "right node" is more formally known as the plausible move). The heart of the method is the formula (or evaluation function) for measuring the plausibility of a node:

$$f(n) = g(n) + h(n)$$

where:

- $f(n)$ measures how good the move to node n is

- $g(n)$ measures the cost of getting to node n from the initial node. Since A expands from the initial node outward, this is just the distance of the path generated so far plus the distance of the edge to node n

- $h(n)$ is the cheapest cost of getting from n to goal

Consider how the formula is used in the example below. Assume that a Cspace representation yielded the graph in Fig. 10.8.

The A search algorithm begins at node A, and creates a decision tree-like structure to determine which are the possible nodes it can consider adding to its path. There are only two nodes to choose from: B and C.

In order to determine which node is the right node to add, the A search algorithm evaluates the plausibility of B and C by looking at the edges. The plausibility of B as the next move is:

$$f(B) = g(B) + h(B) = 1 + 2.24 = 3.24$$

where $g(B)$ is the cost of going from A to B, and $h(B)$ is the cost to get from B to the goal E.

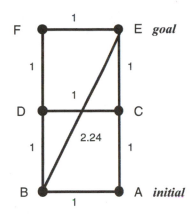

Figure 10.8   Graph for A search algorithm.

The plausibility of C is:

$$f(C) = g(C) + h(C) = 1 + 1 = 2.0$$

where $g(C)$ is the cost of going from A to C, and $h(C)$ is the cost of getting from C to E. Since $f(C) > f(B)$, the path should go from A to C.

But this assumes that $h(n)$ was known at every node. This meant that the algorithm had to recurse in order to find the correct value of $h(n)$. This leads to visiting all the nodes.

A search is guaranteed to produce the optimal path because it compares all possible paths to each other. A* search takes an interesting approach to reducing the amount of paths that have to be generated and compared: it compares the possible paths to the best possible path, even if there isn't a path in the real world that goes that way. The algorithm estimates h rather than checks to see if there is actually a path segment that can get to the goal in that distance. The estimate can then be used to determine which nodes are the most promising, and which paths have no chance of reaching the goal better than other candidates and should be pruned from the search.

Under A* the evaluation function becomes:

$$f^*(n) = g^*(n) + h^*(n)$$

where the $*$ means that the functions are estimates of the values that would

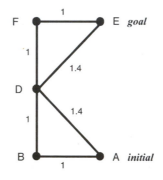

Figure 10.9   An A* example.

have been plugged into the A search evaluation. In path planning, $g^*(n)$ is the same as $g(n)$: the cost of getting from the initial node to n, which is known through the incremental build of the path. $h^*(n)$ is the real difference. So what is a way to estimate the cost of going from n to the goal? Furthermore, how can we be sure that the estimate will be accurate enough that we don't end up choosing a path which isn't truly optimal? This can be done by making sure that $h^*(n)$ will never be smaller than $h(n)$. The restriction that $h^*(n) \leq h(n)$ is called the *admissibility condition*. Since $h^*(n)$ is an estimate, it is also called a *heuristic function*, since it uses a rule of thumb to decide which is the best node to consider.

ADMISSIBILITY
CONDITION
HEURISTIC FUNCTION

Fortunately, there is a natural heuristic function for estimating the cost from n to the goal: the Euclidean (straight line) distance. Recall that the locations of each node are known independently of the edges. Therefore, it is straightforward to compute the straight line distance between two nodes. The straight line distance is always the shortest path between two points, barring curvature of the earth, etc. Since the real path can never be shorter than that, the admissibility condition is satisfied.

To see how A* uses this to actually eliminate visiting nodes, consider the example in Fig. 10.9. As with A search, the first step in A* is to consider the choices from the initial node.

The choices are B and D, which can be thought of as a search tree (see Fig. 10.10a) or as a subset of the original graph (see Fig 10.10b). Regardless

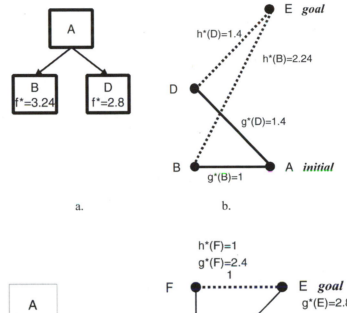

a.   b.

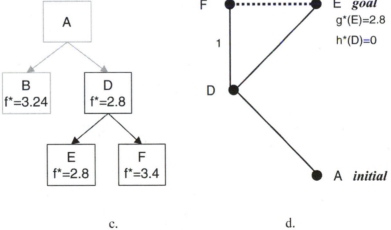

c.   d.

Figure 10.10   a.) What A* "sees" as it considers a path A-?-E, and b.) the original graph. c.) What A* "sees" from considering a path A-D-?-E, and d.) the associated graph.

of how it is visualized, each node is evaluated to determine which is the most plausible move. The above figure shows what the algorithm "sees" at this point in the execution. The choices evaluate to:

$$f^*(B) \quad = \quad g^*(B) + h^*(B) = 1 + 2.24 = 3.24$$
$$f^*(D) \quad = \quad g^*(D) + h^*(D) = 1.4 + 1.4 = 2.8$$

A path going from $A - D-? - E$ has the potential to be shorter than a path going from $A - B-? - E$. So, D is the most plausible node. Notice that A* can't eliminate a path through B because the algorithm can't "see" a path that actually goes from D to E and determine if it is indeed as short as possible.

At step 2, A* recurses (repeats the evaluation) from D, since D is the most plausible, as shown in Fig. 10.10.

The two options from D are E and F, which are evaluated next:

$$f^*(E) \quad = \quad g^*(E) + h^*(E) = 2.8 + 0 = 2.8$$
$$f^*(F) \quad = \quad g^*(F) + h^*(F) = 2.4 + 1.0 = 3.4$$

Now the algorithm sees that E is the best choice among the leaves of the search tree, including the branch through B. (If B was the best, then the algorithm would have changed branches.) It is better than F and B. When it goes to expand E, it notices that E is the goal, so the algorithm is complete. The optimal path is $A - D - E$, and we didn't have to explicitly consider $A - B - F - E$. There are other ways to improve the procedure described so far. $f^*(F)$ didn't need to be computed if the algorithm looks at its choices and sees that one of them is the goal. Any other choice has to be longer because edges aren't allowed to be negative, so $D - F - E$ has to be longer than $D - E$.

Another important insight is that any path between A and E has to go through D, so the B branch of the search tree could have been pruned. Of course, in the above example the algorithm never had an opportunity to notice this because B was never expanded. It's easy to imagine in a larger graph that there might be a case where after several expansions through D, the leaf at B in the search tree came up the most plausible. Then the algorithm would have expanded A and seen the choices were D. Since D already occurred in another branch, with a cheaper $g^*(D)$, the B branch could be safely pruned.

This is particularly useful when A* is applied to a graph created from a regular grid, where the resulting graph is highly connected.

One very attractive feature of the A* path planner is that it can be used with any Cspace representation that can be transformed into a graph. The major impact that Cspace has on the A* planner is how many computations it takes to find the path.

A limitation of A* is that it is very hard to use for path planning where there are factors other than distance to consider in generating the path. For example, the straight line distance may be over rocky terrain or sand that poses a risk to the robot. Likewise, the robot may wish to avoid going over hills in order to conserve energy, but at the same time might wish to go down hills whenever possible for the same reason. In order to factor in the impact of terrain on the path costs, the heuristic function $h^*(n)$ has to be changed. But recall that the new heuristic function must continue to satisfy the admissibility condition: $h^* \leq h$. If the new h^* just takes the worst case energy cost or safety cost, it will be admissible, but not particularly useful in pruning paths. Also, gaining energy going downhill is essentially having an edge in the graph with a negative weight, which A* can't handle. (Negative weights pose an interesting problem in that the robot can get into a loop of rolling down a hill repeatedly because it's an energy-efficient solution rather than actually making forward progress! Bellman-Ford types of algorithms deal with this situation.)

10.5   Wavefront Based Planners

Wavefront propagation styles of planners are well suited for grid types of representations. The basic principle is that a wavefront considers the Cspace to be a conductive material with heat radiating out from the initial node to the goal node. Eventually the heat will spread and reach the goal, if there is a way, as shown in the sequence in Fig. 10.11. Another analogy for wavefront planners is region coloring in graphics, where the color spreads out to neighboring pixels. An interesting aspect of wavefront propagation is that the optimal path from all grid elements to the goal can be computed as a side effect. The result is a map which looks like a potential field. One of the many wavefront types of path planners is the Trulla algorithm developed by Ken Hughes.[106] It exploits the similarities with a potential field to let the path itself represent what the robot should do as if the path were a sensor observation.

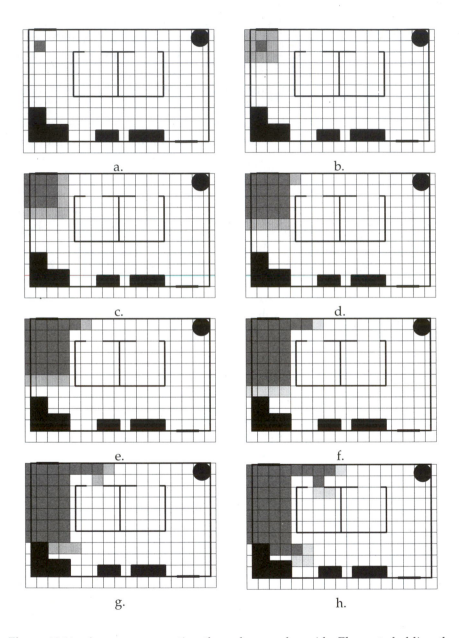

Figure 10.11 A wave propagating through a regular grid. Elements holding the current front are shown in gray, older elements are shown in dark gray.

An attractive feature of wavefront propagation is how it treats terrain types. A modeled obstacle can have a conductivity of 0.0 (no heat can be propagated through that grid element), while an open area has infinite conductivity. But undesirable terrains, which are traversable, but not desirable to go across, can be given a low value of conductivity. This means that heat will travel slower through undesirable regions. But it may turn out that this is the best path, even with the loss through the undesirable regions. A wavefront naturally handles the tradeoffs between a longer path through desirable terrain versus taking shortcuts through less desirable terrain.

The examples in Fig. 10.12 use the Trulla planner. Undesirable terrain is shown on the Trulla display in gray, obstacles in black and open areas in white. The intensity of gray reflects the degree of undesirability of the terrain. In Fig. 10.12a, the robot Clementine can move over an extension cord but would prefer not to, as shown by the gray region. The path planner accordingly routes her around the cord. In Fig. 10.12 this isn't possible due to the placement of obstacles. Therefore, she has to cut through.

10.6   Interleaving Path Planning and Reactive Execution

Most path planning algorithms are employed in a strictly plan once, then reactively execute style. Almost all techniques break a path into segments; even a wavefront planner actually produces a goal location (waypoint) for each directional vector. This is well suited for a Hybrid architecture with a Cartographer handing off path segments, or an entire path, for a Sequencer. The Sequencer can then employ a series of move-to-goal behaviors, deactivating and re-instantiating the behavior as a new subgoal is met. Unfortunately there are two problems with reactive execution of a metric path as described above: *subgoal obsession* and the lack of *opportunistic replanning*.

SUBGOAL OBSESSION
OPPORTUNISTIC
REPLANNING

Subgoal obsession is when the robot spends too much time and energy trying to reach the exact subgoal position, or more precisely, when the termination conditions are set with an unrealistic tolerance. The problem with termination conditions for subgoals is best defined by an example. Suppose the next waypoint is at location (35, 50). If the robot has shaft encoders or GPS, this should be straightforward to do in theory. In practice, it is very hard for a robot, even a holonomic robot, to reach any location exactly because it is hard to give the robot precise movement. The robot may reach (34.5, 50). The behavior sees the goal is now 0.5 meters ahead, and move again to attempt to reach (35, 50). On that move, it may overshoot and end up at (35.5, 50.5).

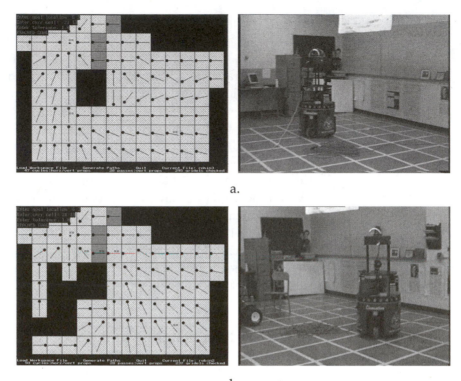

a.

b.

Figure 10.12   a.) Trulla output and photo of Clementine navigating around cord. b.) Trulla output and photo of Clementine navigating over the cord.

Now it has to turn and move again. A resulting see-sawing set of motions emerges that can go on for minutes. This wastes time and energy, as well as makes the robot appear to be unintelligent. The problem is exacerbated by non-holonomic vehicles which may have to back up in order to turn to reach a particular location. Backing up almost always introduces more errors in navigation.

To handle subgoal obsession, many roboticists program into their move-to-goal behaviors a tolerance on the terminating condition for reaching a goal. A common heuristic for holonomic robots is to place a tolerance of +/- the width of the robot. So if a cylindrical, holonomic robot with a diameter of 1 meter is given a goal of (35, 50), it will stop when $34.5 < y < 35.5$ and 49.5

$< y < 50.5$. There is no common heuristic for non-holonomic robots, because the maneuverability of each platform is different. A more vexing aspect of subgoal obsession is when the goal is blocked and the robot can't reach the terminating condition. For example, consider a subgoal at the opposite end of a hall from a robot, but the hall is blocked and there is no way around. Because the robot is executing reactively, it doesn't necessarily realize that it isn't making progress. One solution is for the Sequencer to estimate a maximum allowable time for the robot to reach the goal. This can be implemented either as a parameter on the behavior (terminate with an error code after n seconds), or as an internal state releaser. The advantage of the latter solution is that the code can become part of a monitor, leading to some form of self-awareness.

Related to subgoal obsession is the fact that reactive execution of plans often lacks opportunistic improvements. Suppose that the robot is heading for Subgoal 2, when an unmodeled obstacle diverts the robot from its intended path. Now suppose that from its new position, the robot can perceive Subgoal 3. In a classic implementation, the robot would not be looking for Subgoal 3, so it would continue to move to Subgoal 2 even though it would be more optimal to head straight for Subgoal 3.

The need to opportunistically replan also arises when an *a priori* map turns out to be incorrect. What happens when the robot discovers it is being sent through a patch of muddy ground? Trying to reactively navigate around the mud patch seems unintelligent because choosing left or right may have serious consequences. Instead the robot should return control to the Cartographer, which will update its map and replan. The issue becomes how does a robot know it has deviated too far from its intended path and needs to replan?

D* ALGORITHM

Two different types of planners address the problems of subgoal obsession and replanning: the *D* algorithm* developed by Tony Stentz[136] which is a variant of the A* replanning algorithm, and an extension to the Trulla algorithm. Both planners begin with an *a priori* map and compute the optimal path from every location to the goal. D* does it by executing an A* search from each possible location to the goal in advance; this converts A* from being a single-source shortest path algorithm into an all-paths algorithm. This is computationally expensive and time-consuming, but that isn't a problem since the paths are computed when the robot starts the mission and is sitting still. Since Trulla is a wavefront type of planner, it generates the optimal path between all pairs of points in Cspace as a side effect of computing the path from the starting location to the goal.

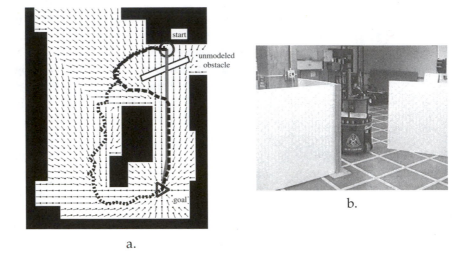

Figure 10.13 Layout showing unmodeled obstacle. a.) Gray line shows expected path, long dashed line the actual path with Trulla, and short dashed line shows purely reactive path. b.) *Clementine* opportunistically turning.

Computing the optimal path from every location to the goal actually helps with reactive execution of the path. It means that if the robot can localize itself on the *a priori* map, it can read the optimal subgoal for move-to-goal on each update. If the robot has to swing wide to avoid an unmodeled obstacle in Fig. 10.13, the robot automatically becomes redirected to the optimal path without having to replan. Note how the metric path becomes a virtual sensor, guiding the move-to-goal behavior replacing the direct sensor data. This is a rich mechanism for the deliberative and reactive components of Hybrid architectures to interact.

This approach eliminates subgoal obsession, since the robot can change "optimal" paths reactively and opportunistically move to a closer waypoint. As with most things in life, too much of a good thing is bad. At some point though, the sheer number of unmodeled obstacles might force the robot to get trapped or wander about, changing subgoals but making no real progress. The D* solution to this problem is to continuously update the map and dynamically repair the A* paths affected by the changes in the map. D* represents one extreme on the replanning scale: *continuous replanning*.

CONTINUOUS
REPLANNING

Continuous replanning has two disadvantages. First, it may be too computationally expensive to be practical for a robot with an embedded processor and memory limitations, such as a planetary rover. Second, continuous re-planning is highly dependent on the sensing quality. If the robot senses an unmodeled obstacle at time T1, it computes a new path and makes a large course correction. If it no longer senses that obstacle at time T2 because the first reading was a phantom from sensor noise, it will recompute another large course correction. The result can be a robot which has a very jerky motion and actually takes longer to reach the goal.

EVENT-DRIVEN
REPLANNING

In the cases of path planning with embedded processors and noisy sensors, it would be desirable to have some sort of *event-driven* scheme, where an event noticeable by the reactive system would trigger replanning. Trulla uses the dot-product of the intended path vector and the actual path vector. When the actual path deviates by 90° or more, the dot product of the path vector and the actual vector the robot is following becomes 0 or negative. Therefore the dot product acts as an affordance for triggering replanning: the robot doesn't have to know why it is drifting off-course, only that it has drifted noticeably off-course.

This is very good for situations that would interfere with making progress on the originally computed path, in effect, situations where the real world is less amenable to reaching the intended goal. But it doesn't handle the situation where the real world is actually friendlier. In Fig. 10.14, an obstacle thought to be there really isn't. The robot could achieve a significant savings in navigation by opportunistically going through the gap.

Such opportunism requires the robot to notice that the world is really more favorable than originally modeled. A continuous replanner such as D* has a distinct advantage, since it will automatically notice the change in the world and respond appropriately, whereas Trulla will not notice the favor-able change because it won't lead to a path deviation. It is an open research question whether there are affordances for noticing favorable changes in the world that allow the robot to opportunistically optimize it path.

10.7 Summary

Metric path planning converts the world space to a configuration space, or *Cspace*, representation that facilitates path planning. Cspace representations such as generalized Voronoi diagrams exploit interesting geometric prop-erties of the environment. These representations can then be converted to graphs, suitable for an A* search. Since Voronoi diagrams tend to produce sparser graphs, they work particularly well with A*. Regular grids work

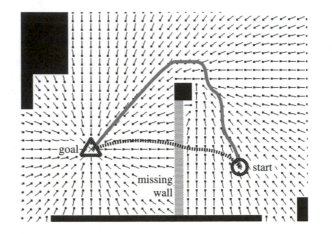

Figure 10.14 Opportunity to improve path. The gray line is the actual path, while the dashed line represents a more desirable path.

well with wavefront planners, which treat path planning as an expanding heat wave from the initial location.

Metric path planning tends to be expensive, both in computation and in storage. However, they can be interleaved with the reactive component of a Hybrid architecture, where the Cartographer gives the Sequencer a set of waypoints. Two problems in interleaving metric path planning with reactive execution are subgoal obsession and when to replan. Optimal path planning techniques for *a priori* fixed maps are well understood, but it is less clear how to update or repair the path(s) without starting over if the robot encounters a significant deviation from the *a priori* map. One solution is to continuously replan if resources permit and sensor reliability is high; another is event-driven replanning which uses affordances to detect when to replan.

Cspace representations and algorithms often do not consider how to represent and reason about terrain types, and special cases such as the robot actually conserving or generating energy going downhill are usually ignored. A possibly even more serious omission is that popular path planners are applicable for only holonomic vehicles.

10.8   Exercises

Exercise 10.1
Represent your indoor environment as a GVG, regular grid, and quadtree.

Exercise 10.2

Represent your indoor environment as a regular grid with a 10cm scale. Write down the rule you use to decide how to mark a grid element empty or occupied when there is a small portion overlapping it.

Exercise 10.3

Define *path relaxation*.

Exercise 10.4

Consider a regular grid of size 20 by 20. How many edges will a graph have if the neighbors are

a. 4-connected?

b. 8-connected?

Exercise 10.5

Convert a meadow map into a graph using:

a. the midpoints of the open boundaries, and

b. the midpoints plus the 2 endpoints.

Draw a path from A to B on both graphs. Describe the differences.

Exercise 10.6

Apply the A* search algorithm by hand to a small graph to find the optimal path between two locations.

Exercise 10.7

What is a heuristic function?

Exercise 10.8

Apply wavefront propagation to a regular grid.

Exercise 10.9

Subgoal obsession has been described as a problem for metric planners. Can hybrid systems which use topological planning exhibit subgoal obsession?

Exercise 10.10

Trulla uses a dot product of 0 or less to trigger replanning, which corresponds to 90° from the desired path. What are the advantages or disadvantages of 90°? What would happen if Trulla used 45° or 135°?

Exercise 10.11

Describe the difference between *continuous* and *event-driven replanning*. Which would be more appropriate for a planetary rover? Justify your answer.

Exercise 10.12   [*Programming*]

Obtain a copy of the Trulla simulator suitable for running under Windows. Model at least three different scenarios and see what the path generated is.

Exercise 10.13   [*Programming*]

Program an A* path planner. Compare the results to the results for the Dijkstra's single source shortest path program from Ch. 9.

10.9   End Notes

For a roboticist's bookshelf.
Robot Motion Planning by Jean-Claude Latombe of Stanford University is the best-known book dealing with configuration space. [82]

Voronoi diagrams.
Voronoi diagrams may be the oldest Cspace representation. *Computational Geometry: Theory and Applications* [44] reports that the principles were first uncovered in 1850, although it wasn't until 1908 that Voronoi wrote about them, thereby getting his name on the diagram.

On heuristic functions for path planning.
Kevin Gifford and George Morgenthaler have explored some possible formulations of a heuristic function for path planning over different terrain types. Gifford also developed an algorithm which can consider the energy savings or capture associated with going downhill. [60]

Trulla.
The Trulla algorithm was developed by Ken Hughes for integration on a VLSI chip. Through grants from the CRA Distributed Mentoring for Women program, Eva Noll and Aliza Marzilli implemented it in software. The algorithm was found to work fast enough for continuous updating even on an Intel 486 processor. Dave Hershberger helped write the display routines used in this book.

11 *Localization and Map Making*

Chapter Objectives:

- Describe the difference between *iconic* and *feature-based* localization.

- Be able to update an occupancy grid using either Bayesian, Dempster-Shafer, or HIMM methods.

- Describe the two types of formal exploration strategies.

11.1 Overview

The two remaining questions of navigation are: *where am I?* and *where have I been?* The answers to these questions are generally referred to as *localization* and *map-making*, respectively. Both are closely related, because a robot cannot create an accurate map if it does not know where it is. Fig. 11.1 shows a hallway in black in a building. The hallway makes a complete circuit around the center of the building. The gray shows the hallway as sensed by a mobile robot. The mobile robot senses, updates the map with the portions of the hallway that have come into view, then moves, updates, and so on. In this case, it uses shaft encoders to determine where it has moved to and how to update the map.

As can been seen from the figure, as well as discussions in Ch. 6, shaft encoders are notoriously inaccurate. Worse yet, the inaccuracies are highly dependent on surfaces. For example, the robot's wheel will slip differently on carpet than on a polished floor. Developing an error model to estimate the slippage is often unrealistically difficult. The shaft encoder problem might appear to be eliminated by new hardware technology, especially GPS and MEMS (micro electrical-mechanical systems) inertial guidance systems (INS).

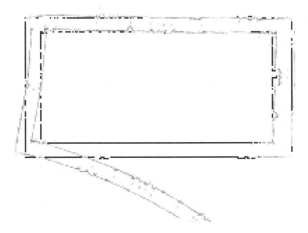

Figure 11.1   A map of a circuit of a hallway created from sonars by a Nomad 200 showing the drift in localization. The ground truth is in black.

URBAN CANYONS

However, GPS only works reliably outdoors. The signal is often unobtainable indoors, in tunnels, or in cities with large buildings (sometimes referred to as *urban canyons*). MEMS inertial navigation devices are small, but suffer from significant inaccuracies and have not been packaged in a way to be easily used with robots.

Researchers have attempted to solve the localization problem in a number of ways. The first approach was to simply ignore localization errors. While this had the advantage of being simple, it eliminated the use of global path planning methods. This was part of the motivation and appeal of purely reactive systems, which had a "go until you get there" philosophy. Another approach was to use topological maps, which have some symbolic information for localization at certain points such as gateways, but don't require continuous localization. Unfortunately, for reasons discussed in Ch. 9, it is hard to have unique gateways. The move to topological mapping gave rise to a whole subfield of reasoning about indistinguishable locations.

More sophisticated systems either identified natural landmarks which had noticeable geometric properties or added artificial landmarks. One robot proposed for a Canadian mining company intended to navigate through relatively featureless mine shafts by dropping beacons at different intersections, much like Hansel and Gretel dropping cookie crumbs for a path. (This inspired much humorous discussion of the merits of the biological equivalent of robot droppings and robots imitating animals that "mark" their territory in the wild.) Other techniques attempted to match the raw sensor data to an *a priori* map using interpretation trees or similar structures. One of the many problems with these techniques is that the sensor data rarely comes in a form amenable to matching against a map. Consider attempting to match noisy sonar data to the layout of a room. In the end, the basic approach used by most systems is to move a little, build up a small map, match the new map to the last map, and merge it in, then merge the small map with the overall map. The use of small, local maps for localization brings the process back full circle to the need for good map-making methods.

Localization algorithms fall into two broad categories: *iconic* and *feature-based*. Iconic algorithms appear to be the more popular in practice, in part because they usually use an occupancy grid. Occupancy grids are a mechanism for fusing sensor data into a world model or map. Fusion is done either following an algorithm provided by a formal theory of evidence, either Bayesian or Dempster-Shafer, or by a popular quasi-evidential method known as HIMM. Since occupancy grids fuse sensor data, the resulting map does not contain as much sensor noise. Many Hybrid architectures also use the occupancy grid as a *virtual sensor* for obstacle avoidance.

The chapter first covers occupancy grids, which are also known as certainty and evidence grids. Since sonars are a popular range sensor for mapping and obstacle avoidance, the chapter next covers sonar sensor models and the three methods for using sensor models to update a grid: Bayesian, Dempster-Shafer, and HIMM. The Bayesian and Dempster-Shafer methods can be used with any sensor, not just range from sonar. The comparison of the three methods discusses practical considerations such as performance and ease in tuning the method for a new environment. Iconic localization is described next. It is useful for metric map building and generally uses an occupancy grid-like structure. Feature-based localization, which is better suited for topological map building, is discussed next. Feature-based methods have become popular with the advent of partially ordered Markov decision process (POMDP) methods to simplify reasoning about them; POMDPs are outside the scope of this book but the basic localization strategy is presented. The chapter ends with a brief description of frontier and Voronoi methods of using the data in an occupancy grid to direct exploration of an unknown environment.

11.2   Sonar Sensor Model

All methods of updating uncertainty require a sensor model. Models of sensor uncertainty can be generated in a number of ways. *Empirical methods* for generating a sensor model focus on testing the sensor and collecting data as to the correctness of the result. The frequency of a correct reading leads to a belief in an observation; the set of beliefs from all possible observations form the model. *Analytical methods* generate the sensor model directly from an understanding of the physical properties of the device. *Subjective methods* rely on a designer's experience, which are often an unconscious expression of empirical testing.

One robotic sensor which has been heavily studied is the Polaroid ultrasonic transducer, or sonar. This chapter will use Polaroid sonars as an example; however, the principles of scoring and fusing belief apply to any sensor. Most roboticists have converged on a model of sonar uncertainty which looks like Fig. 11.2, originally presented in Ch. 6.

SONAR MODAL PARAMETERS

The *basic model of a single sonar beam* has a field of view specified by β, the half angle representing the width of the cone, and R, the maximum range it can detect. This field of view can be projected onto a regular grid. The grid will be called an *occupancy grid*, because each element l (for eLement) in the grid will hold a value representing whether the location in space is occupied or empty. As shown in Fig. 11.2, the field of view can be divided into three regions:

OCCUPANCY GRID ELEMENT L

Region I: where the affected elements are probably occupied (drawn as a "hill"),

Region II: where the affected elements are probably empty (drawn as a "valley"), and

Region III: where the condition of the affected elements is unknown (drawn as a flat surface).

Given a range reading, Region II is more likely to be really empty than Region I is to be really occupied. Regardless of empty or occupied, the readings are more likely to be correct along the acoustic axis than towards the edges. Recall that this is in part because an obstacle which was only along one edge would be likely to reflect the beam specularly or generate other range errors.

While the sensor model in Fig 11.2 reflects a general consensus, there is much disagreement over how to convert the model into a numerical value

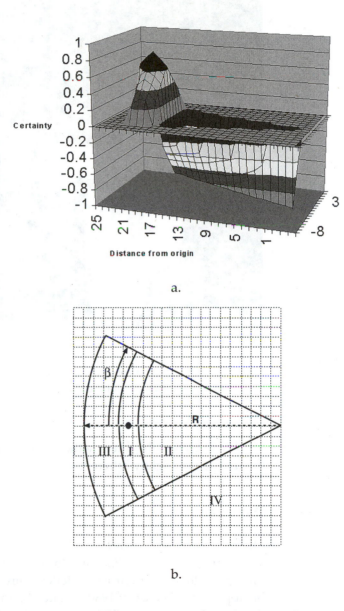

a.

b.

Figure 11.2   A sensor model for a sonar: a.) three dimensional representation and b.) two dimensional representation projected onto an occupancy grid.

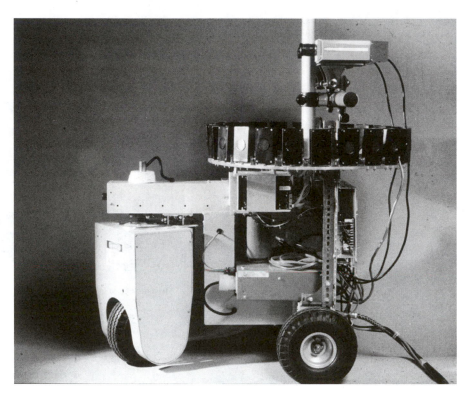

Figure 11.3   Neptune, a robot using occupancy grids during the early 1980's. (Photograph courtesy of Hans Moravec.)

for belief. Each of the three methods covered in the following sections does the translation slightly differently.

11.3   Bayesian

The most popular evidential method for fusing evidence is to translate sensor readings into *probabilities* and to combine probabilities using *Bayes' rule*. Elfes and Moravec at Carnegie Mellon University pioneered the probabilistic approach in the early 1980's. Later Moravec turned to a form of Bayes' Rule which uses probabilities expressed as *likelihoods* and *odds*.[95] This has some computational advantages and also side-steps some of the problems with priors. The likelihood/odds formulation is equivalent to the traditional approach presented here. In a Bayesian approach, the sensor model generates conditional probabilities of the form $P(s|H)$. These are then converted to $P(H|s)$ using Bayes' rule. Two probabilities, either from two different sensors sensing at the same time or from two different times, can be fused using Bayes' rule.

11.3.1 Conditional probabilities

PROBABILITY
FUNCTION

To review, a *probability function* scores evidence on a scale of 0 to 1 as to whether a particular event **H** (**H** stands for "hypothesis") has occurred given an experiment. In the case of updating an occupancy grid with sonar readings, the experiment is sending the acoustic wave out and measuring the time of flight, and the outcome is the range reading reporting whether the region being sensed is Occupied or Empty.

Sonars can observe only one event: whether an element $grid[i][j]$ is Occupied or Empty. This can be written $\mathbf{H} = \{H, \neg H\}$ or $\mathbf{H} = \{Occupied, Empty\}$.

The probability that H has really occurred is represented by $P(H)$:

$$0 \leq P(H) \leq 1$$

An important property of probabilities is that the probability that H didn't happen, $P(\neg H)$, is known if $P(H)$ is known. This is expressed by:

$$1 - P(H) = P(\neg H)$$

As a result, if $P(H)$ is known, $P(\neg H)$ can be easily computed.

UNCONDITIONAL
PROBABILITIES

Probabilities of the form $P(H)$ or $P(\neg H)$ are called *unconditional probabilities*. An example of an unconditional probability is a robot programmed to explore an area on Mars where 75% of the area is covered with rocks (obstacles). The robot knows in advance (or *a priori*) that the next region it scans has $P(H = Occupied) = 0.75$.

Unconditional probabilities are not particularly interesting because they only provide *a priori* information. That information does not take into account any sensor readings, S. It is more useful to a robot to have a function that computes the probability that a region $grid[i][j]$ is either Occupied or Empty given a particular sensor reading s. Probabilities of this type are called *conditional probabilities*. $P(H|s)$ is the probability that H has really occurred given a particular sensor reading s (the "$|$" denotes "given"). Unconditional probabilities also have the property that $P(H|s) + P(\neg H|s) = 1.0$.

CONDITIONAL
PROBABILITIES

In an occupancy grid, $P(Occupied|s)$ and $P(Empty|s)$ are computed for each element, $grid[i][j]$, that is covered by a sensor scan. At each grid element, the tuple of the two probabilities for that region is stored. A tuple can be implemented as a C struct

```
typedef struct {
    double   occupied;
    double   empty;
} P;


P occupancy_grid[ROWS][COLUMNS];
```

Probabilities provide a representation for expressing the certainty about a region $grid[i][j]$. There still needs to be a function which transfers a particular sonar reading into the probability for each grid element in a way that captures Fig. 11.2. One set of functions which quantify this model into probabilities is given below.

For every grid element falling into **Region I**:

$$
\begin{aligned}
P(Occupied) &= \frac{(\frac{R-r}{R}) + (\frac{\beta-\alpha}{\beta})}{2} \times Max_{occupied} \\
P(Empty) &= 1.0 - P(Occupied)
\end{aligned}
$$

(11.1)

where r and α are the distance and angle to the grid element, respectively. The $\frac{\beta-\alpha}{\beta}$ term in Eqn. 11.1 captures the idea that the closer the grid element is to the acoustic axis, the higher the belief. Likewise, the nearer the grid element is to the origin of the sonar beam, the higher the belief (the $\frac{R-r}{R}$ term). The $Max_{occupied}$ term expresses the assumption that a reading of occupied is never fully believable. A $Max_{occupied} = 0.98$ means that a grid element can never have a probability of being occupied greater than 0.98.

It is important to note that Region I in Fig. 11.2 has a finite thickness. Due to the resolution of the sonar, a range reading of 0.87 meters might actually be between 0.82 and 0.92 meters, or 0.87±0.05 meters. The ±0.05 is often called TOLERANCE a *tolerance*. It has the impact of making Region I wider, thereby covering more grid elements.

Each grid element in **Region II** should be updated using these equations:

$$
\begin{aligned}
P(Occupied) &= 1.0 - P(Empty) \\
P(Empty) &= \frac{(\frac{R-r}{R}) + (\frac{\beta-\alpha}{\beta})}{2}
\end{aligned}
$$

(11.2)

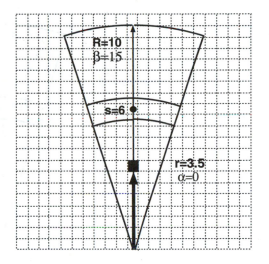

Figure 11.4 Example 1: Updating an element in Region II (sonar reading of 6).

Note that unlike an element in Region I, an element in Region II can have a probability of being empty of 1.0.

To see how these formulas would be applied, consider the example in Fig. 11.4. The sonar has returned a range reading of 6.0 feet with a tolerance of ± 0.5 feet. The $Max_{occupied}$ value is 0.98. The robot is shown on a grid, and all elements are measured relative to it. The element of interest $grid[i][j]$ is shown in black, and is at a distance $r = 3.5$ feet and an angle of $\alpha = 0°$ from the robot. In a computer program, r and α would be computed from the distance and arctangent between the element of interest and the element representing the origin of the sonar, but for the sake of focus, these examples will give r and α.

The first step is to determine which region covers the element. Since $3.5 < (6.0 - 0.5)$, the element is in Region II. Therefore, the correct formulas to apply are those in Eqn. 11.2:

$$
\begin{aligned}
P(Empty) &= \frac{(\frac{R-r}{R})+(\frac{\beta-\alpha}{\beta})}{2} &= \frac{(\frac{10-3.5}{10})+(\frac{15-0}{15})}{2} &= 0.83 \\
P(Occupied) &= 1.0 - P(Empty) &= 1 - 0.83 &= 0.17
\end{aligned}
$$

The example in Fig. 11.5 shows an element in Region I. The probability for the element in black is computed the same way, only using the equations for that region.

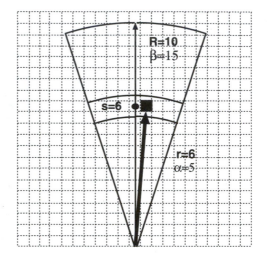

Figure 11.5   Example 2: Updating a element in Region I (sonar reading at 6).

$$P(Occupied) = \frac{(\frac{R-r}{R})+(\frac{\beta-\alpha}{\beta})}{2} \times Max_{occupied} = \frac{(\frac{10-6}{10})+(\frac{15-5}{15})}{2} \times 0.98 = 0.52$$
$$P(Empty) = 1.0 - P(Occupied) = 1 - 0.52 = 0.48$$

11.3.2   Conditional probabilities for $P(H|s)$

The sensor model represents $P(s|H)$: the probability that the sensor would return the value being considered given it was really occupied. Unfortunately, the probability of interest is $P(H|s)$: the probability that the area at $grid[i][j]$ is really occupied given a particular sensor reading. The laws of probability don't permit us to use the two conditionals interchangeably. However, Bayes' rule does specify the relationship between them:

(11.3) $$P(H|s) = \frac{P(s|H)P(H)}{P(s|H)P(H) + P(s|\neg H)P(\neg H)}$$

Substituting in *Occupied* for H, Eqn. 11.3 becomes:

(11.4) $$P(Occupied|s) = \frac{P(s|Occupied)\boxed{P(Occupied)}}{P(s|Occupied)\boxed{P(Occupied)} + P(s|Empty)\boxed{P(Empty)}}$$

$P(s|Occupied)$ and $P(s|Empty)$ are known from the sensor model. The other terms, $P(Occupied)$ and $P(Empty)$, are the unconditional probabilities, or *prior probabilities* sometimes called *priors*. The priors are shown in

Eqn. 11.4 in boxes. If these are known, then it is straightforward to convert the probabilities from the sonar model to the form needed for the occupancy grid.

In some cases, such as for a planetary rover, there may be some knowledge that produces the prior probabilities. In most cases, that knowledge isn't available. In those cases, it is assumed that $P(Occupied) = P(Empty) = 0.5$. Using that assumption, the probabilities generated for the example in Fig. 11.5 can be transformed as follows.

For $grid[i][j]$:

$$
\begin{aligned}
P(s = 6|Occupied) &= 0.62 \\
P(s = 6|Empty) &= 0.38 \\
P(Occupied) &= 0.5 \\
P(Empty) &= 0.5
\end{aligned}
$$

Substituting into Eqn. 11.4 yields:

$$
\begin{aligned}
P(Occupied|s = 6) &= \frac{(0.62)(0.5)}{(0.62)(0.5) + (0.38)(0.5)} = 0.62 \\
P(Empty|s = 6) &= \frac{(0.38)(0.5)}{(0.38)(0.5) + (0.62)(0.5)} = 0.38
\end{aligned}
$$

The use of 0.5 for the priors made $P(Occupied|s)$ numerically equivalent to $P(s|Occupied)$, but in general $P(H|s) \neq P(s|H)$.

11.3.3 Updating with Bayes' rule

Now that there is a method for computing conditional probabilities of the correct form, the question becomes how to fuse it with other readings. The first update is simple. Each element in the occupancy grid is initialized with the *a priori* probability of being occupied or empty. Recall that this is generally implemented as a data structure consisting of two fields. If the *a priori* probabilities are not known, it is assumed $P(H) = P(\neg H) = 0.5$. The first observation affecting $grid[i][j]$ can use Bayes' rule to compute a new probability and replace the prior $P(H) = 0.5$ with the new value.

But what about the second observation? Or an observation made from another sonar at the same time? It turns out that in both cases, Bayes' rule can be used iteratively where the probability at time t_{n-1} becomes the prior and is combined with the current observation (t_n).

To see this, consider the following derivation. For n multiple observations, $s_1, s_2, \ldots s_n$, Bayes' rule becomes:

$$(11.5) \quad P(H|s_1, s_2, \ldots s_n) = \frac{P(s_1, s_2, \ldots s_n|H)P(H)}{P(s_1, s_2, \ldots s_n|H)P(H) + P(s_1, s_2, \ldots s_n|\neg H)P(\neg H)}$$

This introduces the problem of generating $P(s_1, s_2, \ldots s_n|H)$. Ideally, this requires a sonar model of getting occupied and empty values for all $grid[i][j]$ with n combinations of sensor readings. Fortunately, if the reading from s_1 can be considered the result of a different experiment than s_2 and the others, $P(s_1, s_2, \ldots s_n|H)$ simplifies to $P(s_1|H)P(s_2|H) \ldots P(s_n|H)$. Now, the program only has to remember all previous $n-1$ readings. Since there is no way of predicting how many times a particular grid element will be sensed, this creates quite a programming problem. The occupancy grid goes from being a two dimensional array with a single two field structure to being a two dimensional array with each element a potentially very long linked list. Plus, whereas Eqn. 11.3 involved 3 multiplications, updating now takes $3(n-1)$ multiplications. The computational overhead begins to be considerable since an element in a hallway may have over 100 observations.

Fortunately, by clever use of $P(H|s)P(s) = P(s|H)P(H)$, a recursive version of Bayes' rule can be derived:

$$(11.6) \quad P(H|s_n) = \frac{P(s_n|H)P(H|s_{n-1})}{P(s_n|H)P(H|s_{n-1}) + P(s_n|\neg H)P(\neg H|s_{n-1})}$$

So at each time a new observation is made, Eqn. 11.6 can be employed and the result stored at $grid[i][j]$. The rule is commutative, so it doesn't matter in what order two or more simultaneous readings are processed.

11.4   Dempster-Shafer Theory

An alternative theory of evidence is *Dempster-Shafer theory* which produces results similar to Bayesian probabilities. It is a much newer theory, originating in the work of A.P. Dempster, a mathematician at Harvard, during the 1960's with extensions by Glen Shafer in 1987.[126] Whereas Bayes' rule relies on evidence being represented by probability functions, Dempster-Shafer theory represents evidence as a *possibilistic* belief function. Possibilistic means that the function represents *partial evidence*. For example, a reading may provide direct evidence for an event **H**, but, due to occlusions, it may not be perceiving the entire object. Therefore, there is a possibility that the evidence could be higher than was reported. The possibilistic belief functions, also called Shafer belief functions, are combined used Dempster's rule of combination. The rule of combination is very different from Bayes' rule, although they provide similar results. Unlike Bayes' rule, Dempster's rule has a term which indicates when multiple observations disagree. This *conflict metric* can be used by the robot to detect when its occupancy grid may be subject to errors.

11.4.1 Shafer belief functions

Belief is represented by Shafer belief functions in Dempster-Shafer theory. The belief functions serve the same purpose as probabilities in Bayesian evidential reasoning, although they are quite different in flavor. Instead of measuring the probability of a proposition, belief functions measure the *belief mass, m*. Each sensor contributes a belief mass of 1.0, but can distribute that mass to any combination of propositions. This can be illustrated by a direct comparison with probabilities.

A probability function quantifies the evidence for a set of outcomes, **H** = $\{H, \neg H\}$. A belief function calls the set of propositions the *frame of discernment*, signifying what can be discerned (or observed) by an observer or sensor. The frame of discernment is either abbreviated by *FOD* or represented by capital theta, Θ. The frame of discernment for an occupancy grid is:

$$\Theta = \{Occupied, Empty\}$$

Unlike in probability theory, **H** = Θ does not have to be composed of mutually exclusive propositions. A belief function can represent that the sensor had an ambiguous reading, that it literally doesn't know what is out there. The sensor can distribute some of its quanta of belief mass to the proposition that the area is occupied, but it can also mark a portion of its belief mass to being unable to tell if the area is occupied or empty.

The number of all possible subsets that the belief mass can be distributed to by a belief function is 2^{Θ} or 2 raised to the power of the number of elements in the set Θ. For the case of an occupancy grid, the possible subsets are: $\{Occupied\}$, $\{Empty\}$, $\{Occupied, Empty\}$, and the empty set $\emptyset$. Belief that an area is $\{Occupied, Empty\}$ means that it is either Occupied or Empty. This is the same set as Θ, and represents the "don't know" ambiguity (if any) associated with a sensor observation. The term *dontknow* will be used instead

of Θ to reduce confusion when belief mass is assigned to the proposition
{*Occupied, Empty*}.

A belief function *Bel* must satisfy the following three conditions:

1. $Bel(\emptyset) = 0$. This prohibits any belief to be assigned to the empty set $\emptyset$ or
   "nothing." A sensor may return a totally ambiguous reading, but it did
   make an observation. The practical ramification for occupancy grids is
   that there are only 3 elements for belief: *Occupied*, *Empty*, and Θ.

2. $Bel(\Theta) = 1$. This specifies the quantum of belief to be 1. Just as with
   Bayesian probabilities where $P(H) + P(\neg H) = 1.0$, Condition 2 means
   that $Bel(H) + Bel(\neg H) + Bel(\Theta) = 1.0$.

3. For every positive integer n and every collection $A_1, \ldots, A_n$ of subsets of
   Θ,

$$Bel(A_1 \ldots A_n) \geq \sum_{I \subset \{1,\ldots,n\}; I \neq \emptyset} (-1)^{|I|+1} Bel(\bigcap_{i \in I} A_i)$$

This says that more than one belief function contributing evidence over
Θ can be summed, and that the resulting belief in a proposition can be
higher after the summation.

To summarize, a belief function representing the belief that an area $grid[i][j]$
is expressed as a tuple with three members (unlike the two in probabilities),
occupied, empty, dontknow. The belief function can be written as:

$Bel = m(Occupied), m(Empty), m(dontknow)$

An occupancy grid using belief functions would have a data structure similar to the `typedef struct P` used in a Bayesian grid. One possible implementation is:

```
typedef struct {
  double  occupied;
  double  empty;
  double  dontknow;
} BEL;

BEL occupancy_grid[ROWS][COLUMNS];
```

An interesting property of belief functions is that the total belief mass can be assigned to *dontknow*, or $m(dontknow) = 1.0$. This means the observer is completely uncertain, and the belief function is humorously called VACUOUS BELIEF the *vacuous belief function*. The vacuous belief function is equivalent to the FUNCTION $P(H) = P(\neg H) = 0.5$ assignment in Bayesian probabilities. It is also used to initialize the occupancy grid if there is no *a priori* belief.

11.4.2 Belief function for sonar

Returning the sonar model in Sec. 11.2, the Shafer belief function for a sonar reading can be expressed as:

For **Region I:**

$$
\begin{aligned}
m(Occupied) &= \frac{\left(\frac{R-r}{R}\right) + \left(\frac{\beta-\alpha}{\beta}\right)}{2} \times Max_{occupied} \\
m(Empty) &= 0.0 \\
m(dontknow) &= 1.00 - m(Occupied)
\end{aligned}
$$
(11.7)

For **Region II:**

$$
\begin{aligned}
m(Occupied) &= 0.0 \\
m(Empty) &= \frac{\left(\frac{R-r}{R}\right) + \left(\frac{\beta-\alpha}{\beta}\right)}{2} \\
m(dontknow) &= 1.00 - m(Empty)
\end{aligned}
$$
(11.8)

The main conceptual difference between the probability and the Shafer belief function is that any uncertainty in the reading counts as belief mass for "don't know."

Returning to the examples in Figs. 11.4 and 11.5, the computations are largely the same. For Example 1:

$$
\begin{aligned}
m(Occupied) &= 0.0 \\
m(Empty) &= \frac{\left(\frac{R-r}{R}\right)+\left(\frac{\beta-\alpha}{\beta}\right)}{2} = \frac{\left(\frac{10-3.5}{10}\right)+\left(\frac{15-0}{15}\right)}{2} = 0.83 \\
m(dontknow) &= 1.0 - m(Empty) = 1 - 0.83 = 0.17
\end{aligned}
$$

Resulting in:

$$Bel = m(Occupied) = 0.0, m(Empty) = 0.83, m(dontknow) = 0.17$$

For Example 2:

$$m(Occupied) = \frac{\left(\frac{R-r}{R}\right) + \left(\frac{\beta-\alpha}{\beta}\right)}{2} \times Max_{occupied}$$

$$= \frac{\left(\frac{10-6}{10}\right) + \left(\frac{15-5}{15}\right)}{2} \times 0.98 = 0.52$$

$$m(Empty) = 0.0$$

$$m(dontknow) = 1.0 - m(Occupied)$$

$$= 1 - 0.52 = 0.48$$

Resulting in:

$$Bel = m(Occupied) = 0.52, m(Empty) = 0.0, m(dontknow) = 0.48$$

The belief function produced by the sonar model is now ready to be combined with any other observations. It is the equivalent of $P(H|s)$. Recall that the sonar model generated the probability of $P(s|H)$ and Bayes' rule had to be applied with an assumption of $P(H) = P(\neg H)$ to convert it $P(H|s)$.

11.4.3 Dempster's rule of combination

In theory there are many possible ways to combine belief functions. The most popular is the original rule, called *Dempster's rule of combination* or the *orthogonal sum*. Dempster's rule treats combining two belief functions, Bel_1 and Bel_2, as if they represented a physical intersection. Dempster's rule is very similar to Bayes' rule in that it can be applied to any two belief functions as long as they are independent. This means that the rule can be applied to observations about l from overlapping sonars or readings made at two different times.

Dempster's rule of combination is notationally dense, so a graphical example will be given first, followed by the formal mathematical expression.

Consider the case where two observations about $grid[i][j]$ need to be combined. Both observations believe that $grid[i][j]$ is in Region I. Suppose the two belief functions are:

$$Bel_1 = m(Occupied) = 0.4, m(Empty) = 0.0, m(dontknow) = 0.6$$
$$Bel_2 = m(Occupied) = 0.6, m(Empty) = 0.0, m(dontknow) = 0.4$$

Fig. 11.6a shows that the two belief functions can be represented as a numberline of length 1.0 corresponding to the one quanta of belief mass. The

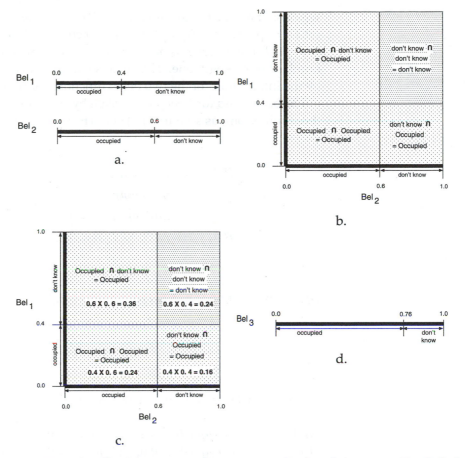

Figure 11.6   Graphical description of Dempster's rule of combination. a.) Two belief functions as numberlines, b.) transformed into axes of a unit square, c.) associated belief mass, and d.) resultant belief function.

numberline can be divided up into the mass associated with each focal element; note that since the masses all add up to 1.0, the order of the elements on the line does not matter.

In Dempster's rule, the two numberlines form orthogonal axes, forming a square of unit area 1.0. The interior of the square can be divided into subregions representing the belief in the focal element produced by the set intersection from the two axes.

The set intersections are shown in Fig. 11.6b. Note that there are four subregions: three for *Occupied* and one for *dontknow*. Since *dontknow* is the set $\Theta = \{Occupied, Empty\}$, the intersection of *dontknow* and *Occupied* is *Occupied*. The subregions of a square of unit 1.0 area can be projected onto a numberline of length one. This means that the "area" of belief mass created by the intersections of the two belief functions forms a third belief function!

The belief mass for *Occupied* is taken by summing the areas of each of the three subregions, as seen in Fig. 11.6c. Therefore, the orthogonal sum is:

$$
\begin{aligned}
Bel_1 &= m(Occupied) = 0.4, \\
       & \quad m(Empty) = 0.0 \\
       & \quad m(dontknow) = 0.6 \\
Bel_2 &= m(Occupied) = 0.6, \\
       & \quad m(Empty) = 0.0, \\
       & \quad m(dontknow) = 0.4 \\
Bel_3 = Bel_1 \oplus Bel_2 &= m(Occupied) = 0.76, \\
       & \quad m(Empty) = 0.0, \\
       & \quad m(dontknow) = 0.24
\end{aligned}
$$

Now consider the case where the two readings are contradictory:

$$
\begin{aligned}
Bel_1 &= m(Occupied) = 0.4, m(Empty) = 0.0, m(dontknow) = 0.6 \\
Bel_2 &= m(Occupied) = 0.0, m(Empty) = 0.6, m(dontknow) = 0.4
\end{aligned}
$$

As shown in Fig. 11.7, there is now a region where the intersection of Occupied and Empty occurs. Since these are mutually exclusive propositions, the resulting set intersection is the empty set $\emptyset$. The emergence of a subregion associated with $\emptyset$ is a problem. Recall from the definition of a Shafer belief function that no belief mass can be assigned to $\emptyset$. But if the area of 0.24 associated with $\emptyset$ is simply left out, the resulting combined belief function will not equal 1.0.

Dempster's rule solves this problem by *normalizing* the belief function; the area for $\emptyset$ is distributed equally to each of the non-empty areas. Each area gets a little bigger and they now all sum to 1.0. The normalization can be carried out by noticing that the belief mass for a particular proposition C is really the sum of all k areas with set C divided by the total area of valid

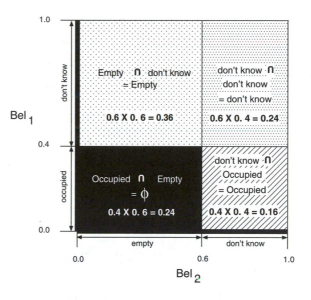

Figure 11.7   Example of the need for normalization.

belief. For the previous example the total area of valid belief was 1.0, so the belief for a set was computed as:

$$m(C) = \frac{\sum_k (m(C_k)}{1.0}$$

If a portion of that area belongs to $\emptyset$ (or there are p areas for $\emptyset$), then the total area is $1.0 - m(\emptyset)$:

$$m(C) = \frac{\sum_k (m(C_k)}{1 - \sum_p m(\emptyset_p)}$$

Normalizing leads to:

$$
\begin{aligned}
m(Occupied) &= \frac{0.16}{1-0.24} &= 0.21 \\
m(Empty) &= \frac{0.36}{1-0.24} &= 0.47 \\
m(dontknow) &= \frac{0.24}{1-0.24} &= 0.32
\end{aligned}
$$

This idea of summing up the areas for a particular proposition and normalizing can be captured with a mathematical formula known as *Dempster's rule.* It specifies the combined probability mass assigned to each C_k, where C is the set of all subsets produced by $A \cap B$. The rule is:

$$(11.9) \quad m(C_k) = \frac{\sum_{A_i \cap B_j = C_k; C_k \neq \emptyset} m(A_i) m(B_j)}{1 - \sum_{A_i \cap B_j = \emptyset} m(A_i) m(B_j)}$$

where the focal elements of Bel_1 and Bel_2 are:

$$Bel_1 = A = \{A_1, \dots, A_i\}$$
$$Bel_2 = B = \{B_1, \dots, B_j\}$$

The computation is repeated k times, once for every distinct subset that emerged from the orthogonal sum, and results in

$$Bel_3 = m(C_1), m(C_2), \dots m(C_k)$$

For the case of any occupancy grid, there are only three possible focal elements (*Occupied*, *Empty*, and *dontknow*). Dempster's rule reduces to:

$$m(Occupied) = \frac{\sum_{A_i \cap B_j = Occupied} m(A_i) m(B_j)}{1 - \sum_{A_i \cap B_j = \emptyset} m(A_i) m(B_j)}$$

$$m(Empty) = \frac{\sum_{A_i \cap B_j = Empty} m(A_i) m(B_j)}{1 - \sum_{A_i \cap B_j = \emptyset} m(A_i) m(B_j)}$$

$$m(don'tknow) = \frac{\sum_{A_i \cap B_j = dontknow} m(A_i) m(B_j)}{1 - \sum_{A_i \cap B_j = \emptyset} m(A_i) m(B_j)}$$

11.4.4   Weight of conflict metric

Normalizing contradictory evidence may produce a justifiable measure of evidence, but a robot needs to be aware of such discordances. Instead, the renormalization term can be viewed as a measure of the conflict between the pair of belief functions. The larger the area assigned to $\emptyset$, the more disagreement between the two beliefs about the FOD. Shafer defines such a measure in the *weight of conflict* metric, Con:[126]

$$(11.10) \quad Con(Bel_1, Bel_2) = \log(\frac{1}{1 - \kappa}); \; where \; \kappa = \sum_{A_i \cap B_j = \emptyset} m_1(A_i) m_2(B_j)$$

Con takes a value between 0 and ∞; as $\kappa \to 0.0$, $Con \to 0.0$, and as $\kappa \to 1.0$, $Con \to \infty$. It is additive, which means that the conflict from a summation of more than two belief functions can be measured. Recent work by Murphy[102] has begun to use *Con* to indicate when more sensing is necessary to disambiguate readings. *Con* can be stored as a fourth field in the BEL structure, but most Dempster-Shafer implementations of occupancy grids do not.

11.5   HIMM

The *Histogrammic in Motion Mapping (HIMM)* algorithm developed by Borenstein and Koren[23] at the University of Michigan provides a different approach to scoring whether a particular element in an occupancy grid is occupied or empty. The motivation for HIMM stemmed from a need to improve obstacle avoidance. In order to safely run their Cybermotion robot, CARMEL, at its top speed of 0.8 meters/sec, they needed to update an occupancy grid on the order of 160ms. The processor was a 20MHz 80386, fast for 1992, but still quite slow. The Bayesian model at that time was well accepted but the sheer number of computations involved in updating prevented the algorithm from a satisfactory fast execution. HIMM was developed as a quasi-evidential technique where it scores certainty in a highly specialized way suitable for sonars.

The University of Michigan's robotics team entered CARMEL in the 1992 AAAI Mobile Robot Competition, shown in Fig. 11.5. CARMEL resoundingly won first place that year in the task of navigating between a series of waypoints marked by landmarks on posts. By using HIMM in conjunction with the *vector field histogram (VFH)* obstacle avoidance algorithm, CARMEL was able to navigate at velocities an order of magnitude higher than the other entries, and avoided obstacles of all sizes more reliably. After that, HIMM and occupancy grids became standard on many platforms.

11.5.1   HIMM sonar model and updating rule

HIMM uses a simple sonar model shown in Fig. 11.9. The model has two striking features in contrast to the sonar model in Fig. 11.2. First, only elements along the acoustic axis are updated. This eliminates up to 90% of the grid elements that are updated by Bayesian and Dempster-Shafer methods, thereby significantly reducing the order complexity. It is important to note that the sonar reading is the same for Bayesian, Dempster-Shafer, and HIMM; HIMM interprets the information from the sonar reading differently and over fewer elements than the other methods. Second, the uncertainty score is expressed as an integer from 0 to 15, which means each element

Figure 11.8   CARMEL at the 1992 AAAI Mobile Robot Competition. (Photograph courtesy of David Kortenkamp and AAAI.)

can be represented by a byte, rather than a structure containing at least two floating point numbers.

The sonar model also shows the updating rule. In HIMM, the l are incremented with I each time the acoustic axis of a sonar reading passes over it. If an l is empty, the increment I is -1. Occupied l is incremented with $I = +3$. This implies that HIMM believes a region is occupied more than it believes the intervening regions are empty; this is the opposite of evidential methods. The update rule also is computationally efficient; it reduces scoring to addition and subtraction of integers, which takes far fewer CPU clock cycles to execute than multiplication and division of floating point numbers. The

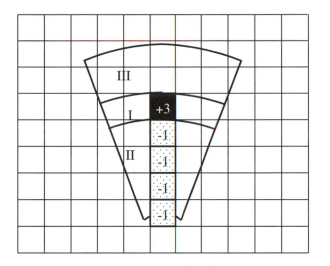

Figure 11.9 HIMM sonar model.

basic formula is given below:

$$grid[i][j] = grid[i][j] + I \qquad \text{where } 0 \leq grid[i][j] \leq 15$$

(11.11)
$$I = \begin{cases} I^+ & \text{if occupied} \\ I^- & \text{if empty} \end{cases}$$

While it should be clear that HIMM executes much more quickly than true evidential methods, it may not be clear why it would produce more reliable occupancy grids for navigation. Updating along the acoustic axis leads to a small sample size, as shown in Fig. 11.10. This means a wall (shown in gray dots) would be appear on the grid as a series of one or more small, isolated "posts." There is a danger that the robot might think it could move between the posts when in fact there was a wall there. If the robot moves, the gaps get filled in with subsequent readings. HIMM works best when the robot is moving at a high velocity. If the velocity and grid update rates are well matched, the gaps in the wall will be minimized as seen in Fig. 11.10a. Otherwise, some gaps will appear and take longer to be filled in, as shown in Fig. 11.10b. HIMM actually suffers in performance when the robot moves slowly because it sees too little of the world.

Fig. 11.11 shows the application of Eqn. 11.11 to an occupancy grid for a series of 8 observations for a single sonar. In the example, the HIMM sonar model is shown as a rectangle with darker outlines. For simplicity, the range

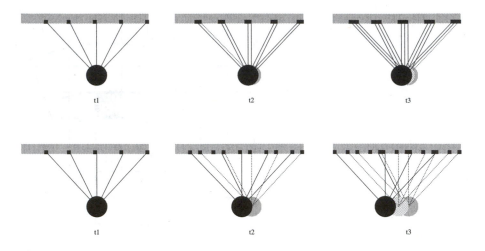

Figure 11.10   HIMM updating example for a wall a.) when velocity and update rates are well matched, and b.) when update rate is slower than velocity, leading to holes.

returned by the sonar is always 3 grid elements long: therefore 1 element will be scored as occupied and 2 elements will scored as empty. Also, the robot's motions are such that the sonar is always facing "up" and aligned with the grid. The grid is initialized to 0, indicating that the robot assumes that the world is empty.

11.5.2   Growth rate operator

A disadvantage of HIMM is that the scattered sampling means that a particular element $grid[i][j]$ may get only one or two updates. This has two ramifications. First, it means the values in the grid tend to be low; an element that is occupied and only has two updates has a score of 6, which is less than half of the maximum score of 15 for occupancy. Second, small obstacles such as poles or chairs which present a small profile to the sonar versus a wall never receive a high score. One way to handle this is to change the scoring increments. If this is done, the updating process tends to produce maps with many phantom obstacles.

Another approach is to consider nearby grid elements. A heuristic is that the more neighbors an element has which are occupied, the more likely there is something really there and its score should be increased. Note that this is handled in evidential methods by having a sonar model with a large β.

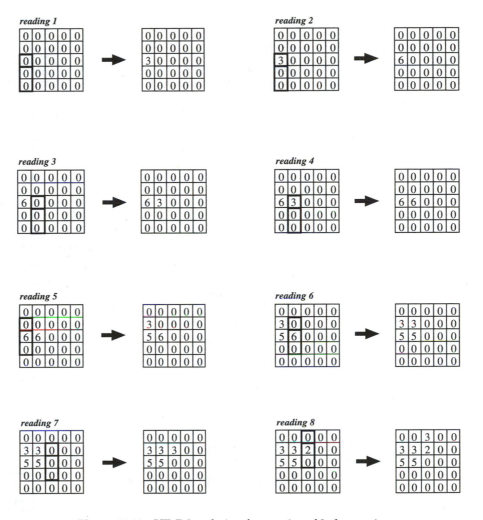

Figure 11.11 HIMM updating for a series of 8 observations.

HIMM instead uses a companion mechanism called a *Growth Rate Operator* or *GRO* to capture this heuristic.

Figure 11.12 shows the GRO and how it works. When an element $grid[i][j]$ is updated with an occupied reading, GRO is applied as an extra step. The GRO uses a *mask*, W, to define "neighbors." Masks are a common data structure in robotics and computer vision used to define an area of interest on an array, grid, or image. The mask is literally a small array overlaid on the oc-

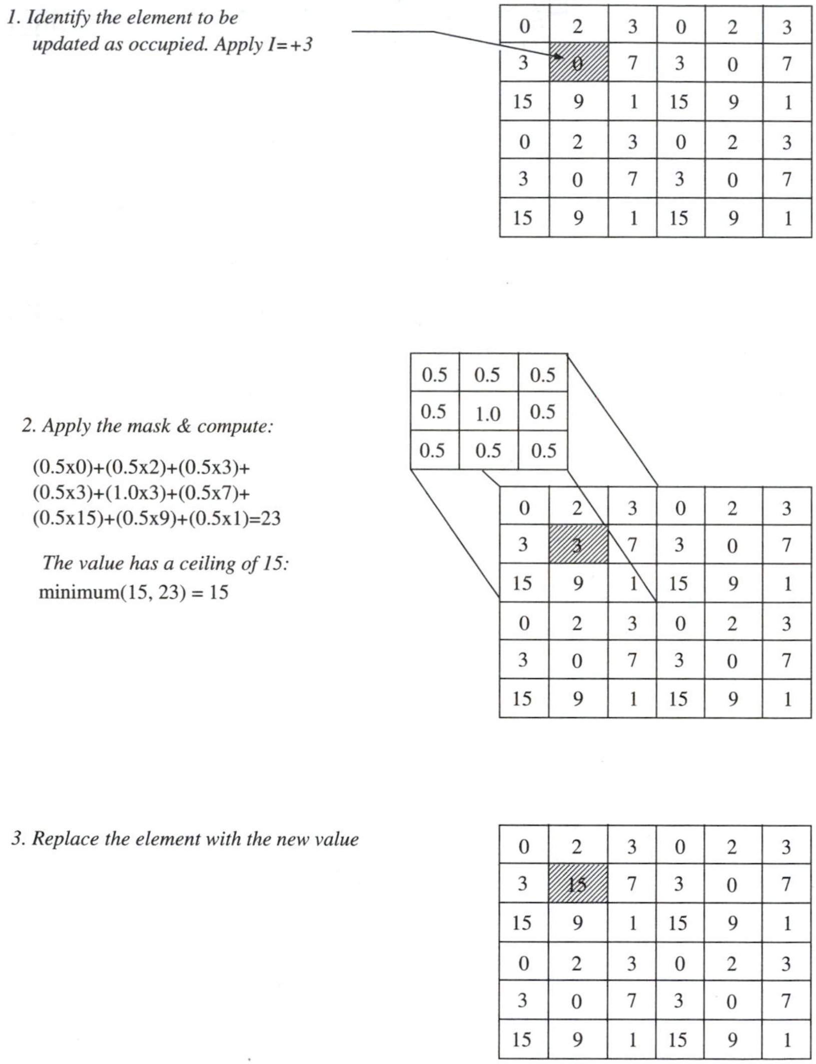

1. Identify the element to be updated as occupied. Apply I=+3

0	2	3	0	2	3
3	0	7	3	0	7
15	9	1	15	9	1
0	2	3	0	2	3
3	0	7	3	0	7
15	9	1	15	9	1

2. Apply the mask & compute:

(0.5x0)+(0.5x2)+(0.5x3)+
(0.5x3)+(1.0x3)+(0.5x7)+
(0.5x15)+(0.5x9)+(0.5x1)=23

The value has a ceiling of 15:
minimum(15, 23) = 15

0.5	0.5	0.5
0.5	1.0	0.5
0.5	0.5	0.5

0	2	3	0	2	3
3	3	7	3	0	7
15	9	1	15	9	1
0	2	3	0	2	3
3	0	7	3	0	7
15	9	1	15	9	1

3. Replace the element with the new value

0	2	3	0	2	3
3	15	7	3	0	7
15	9	1	15	9	1
0	2	3	0	2	3
3	0	7	3	0	7
15	9	1	15	9	1

Figure 11.12   The GRO mechanism. Only the effects of incrementing an occupied element are shown.

cupancy grid. The center of the mask fits directly over $grid[i][j]$. In this case, the mask is a 3x3 mask; it has 3 columns and 3 rows. A 3x3 mask represents that $grid[i][j]$ has 8 neighbors that should be considered. Masks of larger sizes can be applied using the same method; larger sizes will grow the score of clusters of occupied regions much quicker since it considers the influence of more neighbors.

While the more occupied neighbors $grid[i][j]$ has should increase the score, the increase should also be affected by neighbor's score. For example, the fact that l has an occupied neighbor should increase the score, but if the score of the neighbor is low, $grid[i][j]$'s score shouldn't increase very much. Therefore each element of the mask contains a weighting factor. In Fig. 11.12, the mask W has a center with 1.0 and the surrounding elements are 0.5. When $grid[i][j]$ is updated as occupied, the update now has essentially two steps:

$$grid[i][j] = grid[i][j] + I$$

This is the standard HIMM updating, but now it only produces a temporary value for $grid[i][j]$ that will be used in the next step. The second step is to apply the weighting specified by the mask, W.

$$grid[i][j] = \sum_{p,q=-1\ldots1} grid[i][j] \times W[i+p][j+q]$$

Note that the mask W is given indices from $-1\ldots1$. This is telling the program to start with the element 1 row "up" and 1 column "to the left" of the grid element. This expands to:

$$
\begin{aligned}
grid[i][j] \quad = \quad & (grid[i-1][j-1] * 0.5) + (grid[i-1][j] * 0.5) + \\
& (grid[i-1][j+1] * 0.5) + (grid[i][j-1] * 0.5) + \\
& (grid[i-1][j] * 1.0) + (grid[i][j+1] * 0.5) + \\
& (grid[i+1][j-1] * 0.5) + (grid[i+1][j] * 0.5) + \\
& (grid[i+1][j+1] * 0.5)
\end{aligned}
$$

Fig. 11.13 shows the difference in the final occupancy grid if GRO is used instead of the basic HIMM in Fig. 11.11. The resulting occupancy grid now shows that there is definitely an obstacle present. In 8 readings, GRO was able to reflect the presence of an obstacle that the basic HIMM updating rule could have only approached with 40 readings.

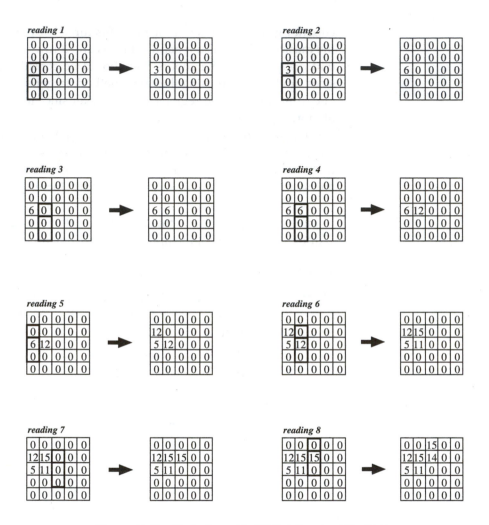

Figure 11.13   Updating with GRO, following Fig. 11.11.

The advantage of GRO is that it is very sensitive to potential obstacles. But that leads to its disadvantage: obstacles tend to be bigger and persist longer than is appropriate. Obstacles tend to be bigger because sonar errors and errors in localization make the readings around a small object much larger. Since the noisy readings are near the true readings, GRO scores them very high, adding to the perceived size of the object. As long as the robot is not trying to navigate in cluttered, narrow areas, this is not a significant problem.

11.6   Comparison of Methods

Occupancy grid methods have their unique advantages and disadvantages. Bayesian and Dempster-Shafer theory are formal theories, and other readings from other sensor modalities, such as range from stereo or a laser, can be easily fused as long as there is a sensor model. HIMM is limited to sonars but it has significant computational advantages. As seen in Fig. 11.14, all three produce similar occupancy grids, with a slight advantage going to Bayesian and Dempster-Shafer grids. In practice, Bayesian and Dempster-Shafer have fewer parameters to tune, making them more straightforward to adapt to new environments.

11.6.1   Example computations

The similarities and differences between the three methods is best seen by an example. The following example covers how to initialize the occupancy grid, compute the score at a grid element for a sensor reading, update the grid, and repeat for three different observations.

Step 1: Initialize the Occupancy Grid.
Consider a robot beginning to map a new area. The occupancy grid shown in Fig. 11.15 covers an area of 12 units by 10 units. The grid is an array of size 24 x 21, with 2 grid elements per unit of distance. The grid starts in an initial unsensed state. In a Bayesian approach, each element in the grid would be a structure P with two fields: $P(Occupied)$ and $P(Empty)$. The value of each field depends on the unconditional probability that the area represented by the grid is occupied or empty. Unless there is some prior knowledge, the assumption is that an element has equal chances of being occupied or empty. This translates to $P(Occupied) = P(Empty) = 0.5$. Every element in the grid would start with (0.5, 0.5). In a Dempster-Shafer implementation, each element in the grid would be a structure Bel with three fields: $m(Occupied), m(Empty)$ and $m(dontknow)$. Since the grid represents areas that have not been sensed, the entire belief mass m is initialized as $m(dontknow) = 1.0$. Every element in the grid would start with (0.0, 0.0, 1.0). Every element in a HIMM occupancy grid would be a single 8-bit integer, and would be initialized to 0.

Consider how three different sonar updates create a certainty value for a particular grid element, $grid[3][10]$, shown in Fig. 11.15. At time t_1, the sonar

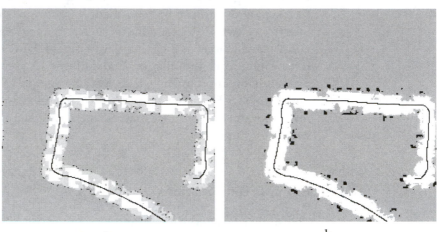

a.   b.

c.

Figure 11.14   Comparison of occupancy grids generated from the same set of readings in a favorable hallway by a.) Bayesian, b.) Dempster-Shafer, and c.) HIMM. The Bayesian and Dempster-Shafer maps show the path of the robot, while the HIMM map does not. The HIMM map is slightly offset due to show spurious readings.

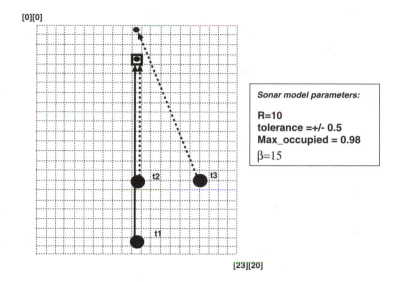

Figure 11.15   Example occupancy grid size 24 x 21 elements, showing the robot's position and range reading for three updates. (Only the acoustic axis is shown.)

reading returns 9.0. The robot is at $grid[21][10]$, so $grid[3][10]$ is 9 units away from the robot ($r = 9$) with an α of $0°$.

The first step in updating a particular grid element is to see if the sonar reading affects that grid element. For Bayesian and Dempster-Shafer uncertainty models, the grid element must satisfy two conditions:

- $|\alpha| \leq |\beta|$, the grid element is within the angular field of view of the sonar model, and

- $r \leq s + tolerance$, the grid element is within the upper bound of the range reading.

Based on those tests, $grid[3][10]$ is affected by the reading at t_1. Since HIMM considers only grid elements on the acoustic axis, the key tests are:

- $\alpha = 0$, the grid element is on the acoustic axis of the sonar model, and

- $r \leq s + tolerance$, the grid element is within the upper bound of the range reading.

$grid[3][10]$ passes these tests, so it is also affected by the sonar model in HIMM.

Step 2: Compute the uncertainty of the observation.
The second step is to compute the uncertainty score of an observation, remembering that a grid element will only have a score if it is covered by the
sonar reading. This computation can be done in a series of sub-steps. The
process begins by determining whether $grid[3][10]$ falls in Region I or Region II, since this specifies which equations or increment to use. Region I,
Occupied, extends for $s \pm tolerance$. The test for falling in Region I is the
same for all three methods: if r satisfies $s - tolerance \leq r \leq s + tolerance$,
then it is in Region I. In this case, $s = 9$, $tolerance = 0.5$, and $r = 9$, and the
substitution results in $9 - 0 \leq 9 \leq 9 + 0.5$ being true. Therefore $grid[3][10]$ is
in Region I.

At this point, the three methods diverge in computing the "score" from
the reading at t_1. The next step in Bayesian methods is to compute the prob-
ability, $P(s|Occupied)$, that the sensor s will correctly report that $grid[3][10]$
is *Occupied* if there is really something at $s = 9$. This is done using Eqn. 11.1:

$$
\begin{aligned}
P(s|Occupied) &= \frac{\left(\frac{R-r}{R}\right) + \left(\frac{\beta-\alpha}{\beta}\right)}{2} \times Max_{occupied} \\
&= \frac{\left(\frac{10-9}{10}\right) + \left(\frac{15-0}{15}\right)}{2} \times 0.98 = 0.54 \\
P(s|Empty) &= 1.0 - P(s|Occupied) \\
&= 1.0 - 0.54 = 0.46
\end{aligned}
$$

Dempster-Shafer theory uses Eqn. 11.8, which produces essentially the
same score for the sensor reading as with the Bayesian method:

$$
\begin{aligned}
m(Occupied) &= \frac{\left(\frac{R-r}{R}\right) + \left(\frac{\beta-\alpha}{\beta}\right)}{2} \times Max_{occupied} \\
&= \frac{\left(\frac{10-9}{10}\right) + \left(\frac{15-0}{15}\right)}{2} \times 0.98 = 0.54 \\
m(Empty) &= 0.0 \\
m(dontknow) &= 1.00 - m(Occupied) \\
&= 1.0 - 0.54 = 0.46
\end{aligned}
$$

The HIMM score is the I term in Eqn. 11.11. Since $grid[3][10]$ is in Region 1
of the HIMM sonar model, $I = I^+ = +3$.

Step 3: Update the current score with the past score and update the occupancy grid.

The third step in the updating process is to combine the score for the grid element from the current reading with the previous score stored there.

The Bayesian method uses the recursive form of Bayes' rule, Eqn. 11.6:

$$(11.12) \quad P(H|s_n) = \frac{P(s_n|H)P(H|s_{n-1})}{P(s_n|H)P(H|s_{n-1}) + P(s_n|\neg H)P(\neg H|s_{n-1})}$$

where s_{n-1} terms are from the reading stored at $grid[3][10]$ and the s_n terms are the current reading. Substituting *Occupied* for H and *Empty* for $\neg H$, $P(s_n|H)$ becomes:

$$P(s_{t_1}|O) = 0.54$$
$$P(s_{t_1}|E) = 0.46$$
$$P(s_{t_0}|O) = 0.50$$
$$P(s_{t_0}|E) = 0.50$$

This yields:

$$
\begin{aligned}
P(O|s_{t_1}) &= \frac{P(s_{t_1}|O)P(O|s_{t_0})}{P(s_{t_1}|O)P(O|s_{t_0}) + P(s_{t_1}|E)P(E|s_{t_0})} \\
&= \frac{(0.54)(0.50)}{(0.54)(0.50) + (0.46)(0.50)} \\
&= 0.54 \\
P(E|s_{t_1}) &= 1 - P(O|s_{t_1}) = 0.46
\end{aligned}
$$

The Dempster-Shafer updating takes the belief function stored at $grid[3][10]$ at time t_0 and combines it with the current belief function. This can be written recursively as:

$$(11.13) \quad Bel'_{t_n} = Bel_{t_n} \oplus Bel'_{t_{n-1}}$$

The $'$ means that the value is the one after any combination, so $Bel'_{t_{n-1}}$ is the value currently stored at $grid[i][j]$ and Bel'_{t_n} is the value that will be stored at $grid[i][j]$ after the update. The method uses Dempster's rule of combination given in Eqn. 11.9 and reprinted below:

$$(11.14) \quad m(C_k) = \frac{\sum_{A_i \cap B_j = C_k; C_k \neq \emptyset} m(A_i)m(B_j)}{1 - \sum_{A_i \cap B_j = \emptyset} m(A_i)m(B_j)}$$

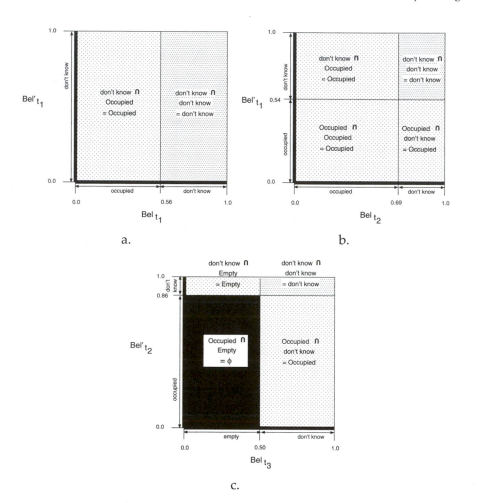

Figure 11.16   Applying Dempster's rule after three updates for the example.

The first step in applying Dempster's rule is determine the focal elements C_k in the combined belief Bel that result from the set intersection of the focal elements A_i from t_{n-1} and B_j from t_n. Although this can be done analytically, it is easier to sketch the unit square out, as shown in Fig. 11.16a.

The total belief has only two focal elements, $Occupied$ and $dontknow$. There is no belief mass for $\emptyset$. The computation of the belief mass is:

$$m(Occupied) \quad = \quad \frac{(1.0)(0.54)}{1.0 - 0.0} = 0.54$$

$$m(dontknow) \quad = \quad \frac{(1.0)(0.46)}{1.0 - 0.0} = 0.46$$

Therefore, the updated belief at $grid[3][10]$ is:

(11.15) $m(Occupied) = 0.54, m(Empty) = 0.0, m(dontknow) = 0.46$

The HIMM updating is governed by Eqn. 11.11, below. Since $grid[3][10]$ is in the HIMM occupied region, the increment term I is $I^+ = 3$.

$$
\begin{aligned}
grid[3][10] \quad &= \quad grid[3][10] + I^+ \\
&= \quad 0 + 3 = 3
\end{aligned}
$$

Step 4: Repeat Steps 2 and 3 for each new reading.
At t_2, the robot has translated forward. The sonar reading is 6.0. The grid element is now 6.0 units away with an $\alpha = 0°$. $grid[3][10]$ still falls in Region I for all three updating methods. The application of Eqn. 11.1 produces a probability of $P(s|Occupied) = 0.69, P(s|Empty) = 0.31$, a belief function of $m(Occupied) = 0.69, m(Empty) = 0.0, m(dontknow) = 0.31$, and a HIMM increment of +3.

Updating the grid produces an increase in the occupancy score, as would be expected, given two direct sonar observations of an object. The Bayesian updating is:

$$
\begin{aligned}
P(O|s_{t_2}) \quad &= \quad \frac{P(s_{t_2}|O)P(O|s_{t_1})}{P(s_{t_2}|O)P(O|s_{t_1}) + P(s_{t_2}|E)P(E|s_{t_1})} \\
&= \quad \frac{(0.69)(0.54)}{(0.69)(0.54) + (0.31)(0.46)} \\
&= \quad 0.72 \\
P(E|s_{t_2}) \quad &= \quad 1 - P(O|s_{t_2}) = 0.28
\end{aligned}
$$

The Dempster-Shafer updating generates a higher occupancy score, which can also be seen from Fig. 11.16b. The final score is:

$$
\begin{aligned}
m(Occupied) \quad &= \quad \frac{(0.54)(0.69) + (0.46)(0.69) + (0.54)(0.31)}{1.0 - 0.0} \\
&= \quad 0.86 \\
m(dontknow) \quad &= \quad \frac{(0.46)(0.31)}{1.0 - 0.0} = 0.14 \\
m(Empty) \quad &= \quad 0.0
\end{aligned}
$$

The HIMM updating scheme is simple where:

$$grid[3][10] \ = \ grid[3][10] + 3$$
$$= \ 3 + 3 = 6$$

At t_3, the sonar returns a value of 8.5 units. The robot has moved to the side and rotated; it is now 6.7 units from the grid element with an α of $5°$. In this case $grid[3][10]$ is in Region II for the Bayesian and Dempster-Shafer sonar models, and is not affected by the HIMM model at all.

The probability score for the Bayesian model is computed using Eqn. 11.2 instead of Eqn. 11.1:

$$P(s|Empty) \ = \ \frac{(\frac{R-r}{R}) + (\frac{\beta - \alpha}{\beta})}{2}$$
$$= \ \frac{(\frac{10-6.7}{10}) + (\frac{15-5}{15})}{2} = 0.50$$
$$P(s|Occupied) \ = \ 1.0 - P(s|Empty) = 1.0 - 0.50 = 0.50$$

The result happens to be an almost even probability that $grid[3][10]$ is occupied. This probability is then substituted into Bayes rule (Eqn. 11.6) with the previously stored probability:

$$P(O|s_{t_3}) \ = \ \frac{P(s_{t_3}|O)P(O|s_{t_0})}{P(s_{t_3}|O)P(O|s_{t_0}) + P(s_{t_1}|E)P(E|s_{t_0})}$$
$$= \ \frac{(0.50)(0.72)}{(0.50)(0.72) + (0.50)(0.28)}$$
$$= \ 0.72$$
$$P(E|s_{t_3}) \ = \ 1 - P(O|s_{t_3}) = 0.28$$

The Dempster-Shafer belief function is computed using Eqn. 11.9, yielding $m(Occupied) = 0.0, m(Empty) = 0.50), m(dontknow) = 0.50)$. The difference between the probability and belief function is that the $\neg Empty$ score was assigned to $P(s|Occupied)$ in the Bayesian method and to $m(dontknow)$ in the Dempster-Shafer. The combination is shown in Fig. 11.16c, and produces:

$$m(Occupied) \ = \ \frac{(0.86)(0.5)}{1.0 - (0.86)(0.5)} = 0.76$$

$$m(dontknow) = \frac{(0.14)(0.5)}{1.0 - (0.86)(0.5)} = 0.12$$

$$m(Empty) = \frac{(0.14)(0.5)}{1.0 - (0.86)(0.5)} = 0.12$$

Since $grid[3][10]$ is not affected by the HIMM sonar model for the reading at t_3, there is no update.

The above computations can be summarized as follows. The score for $grid[3][10]$ at each observation is:

sonar certainty:	Bayesian		Dempster-Shafer			HIMM
	$P(s\|O)$	$P(s\|E)$	$m(O)$	$m(E)$	m(*dontknow*)	
t_1	0.54	0.46	0.56	0.00	0.46	+3
t_2	0.69	0.31	0.69	0.00	0.31	+3
t_3	0.50	0.50	0.00	0.50	0.50	n/a

Notice the differences in the Bayesian and Dempster-Shafer scores. The numbers are the same, but where those numbers go is quite different. At t_2, both methods score the occupancy of the grid element as 0.69. But the Bayesian scores the emptiness as 0.31, while Dempster-Shafer doesn't commit to the area being empty; rather it can't tell if it is empty or occupied. At t_3, there is no HIMM score because $grid[3][10]$ is not covered by the HIMM sonar model's field of view.

The updated value of $grid[3][10]$ after each observation, that is, the combination of the current score with the previous score, is:

after update:	Bayesian		Dempster-Shafer			HIMM
	$P(O\|s)$	$P(E\|s)$	$m(O)$	$m(E)$	m(*dontknow*)	
t_1	0.54	0.46	0.54	0.00	0.46	3
t_2	0.72	0.28	0.86	0.00	0.14	6
t_3	0.72	0.28	0.76	0.12	0.12	6

Notice that the end results of the Bayesian and Dempster-Shafer fusion methods are very similar, though the intermediate values are different. In the HIMM, the value of $grid[3][10]$ after t_3 is 6 because nothing is done to it after t_2; it is neither incremented nor decremented.

11.6.2   Performance

Fig. 11.14 shows the three methods used to generate occupancy grids for data collected from the same hallway. Performance scores are easy to compute. The ground truth is expressed as a "perfect" occupancy grid, manually constructed with occupied points receiving 1.0 or 15 values and empty grid elements 0. The performance can be computed as the sum of the differences on a grid element by grid element basis:

$$(11.16) \qquad score = \sum_{i,j} |truth[i][j] - grid[i][j]|$$

Low scores mean there was less difference between the perfect map and the sensed map.

Bayesian and Dempster-Shafer theory produce essentially the same results. This is not surprising since they both use the same model of uncertainty for sonars. The major difference between Bayesian and Dempster-Shafer is the weight of conflict metric.

HIMM tends to be less accurate than Bayesian or Dempster-Shafer theory, as would be expected from a method that only updates along the acoustic axis. But HIMM has almost an order of magnitude fewer elements to update on average after each reading, making it much faster to execute.

Two solutions are available to improve Bayesian and Dempster-Shafer performance. The first is to convert all floating point numbers to integers. The area of coverage can be dynamically adapted as a function of the robot speed. When the robot is going fast, it can't afford to spend much time updating the occupancy grid. At that point, it becomes reasonable to update only along the acoustic axis. Errors due to the obstacle not being on the axis will be smoothed out as the robot quickly moves to a new position and receives updates. In this case, the β term in the sensor model changes as a function of speed. Murphy, Gomes, and Hershberger did a comparison of Dempster-Shafer and HIMM with variable β; their results showed that the adaptive approach produced better grids than a fixed β or HIMM. [103]

11.6.3   Errors due to observations from stationary robot

All three methods produce incorrect results if the robot is stationary and repeatedly returns the same range reading. HIMM is particularly vulnerable to errors due to incorrect readings reinforcing extreme values on the grid. Due to updating on the acoustic axis, only a very small part of the world is updated after each observation. As a result, the robot sees a wall as a set of isolated poles. If the wall is far enough away, the gaps between "poles" can be quite large, causing the robot to attempt to head through them and then have to avoid as subsequent updates prove the previous map wrong. If the robot is experiencing incorrect or missing readings from specular reflection or crosstalk, obstacles might be missed or appear at the wrong distance. If the robot is stationary, HIMM will generate high belief in an incorrect map. Bayesian and Dempster-Shafer theory also suffer from the same defect. Since they usually cover a larger area, the problem with gaps in walls is usually avoided. But problems with phantom readings still cause incorrect maps.

The plots of the rate of accrual of belief show that multiple identical readings will cause the robot to quickly believe that its occupancy grid is correct. Once $P(H|S)$ or $m(H)$ reach 1.0, there is no revision downward. HIMM can revise belief because it subtracts strictly based on the current reading. But HIMM must have a new, contradictory reading to cause this to happen.

The reason Bayesian and Dempster-Shafer methods degenerate when the robot is stationary and receives multiple, identical readings is because the assumption that the observations are independent has been violated. If the robot is at the same location sensing the same object, the value of reading $S_{t_{n+1}}$ is likely to be the same as S_{t_n}. Since the robot hasn't moved, the observations cannot be considered to be taken from two different experiments or by two different observers. This serves as a cautionary note about making simplifying assumptions: it is important to understand when those assumptions lead to counterproductive results.

11.6.4   Tuning

Fig. 11.14 shows the performance of the three updating methods for a hallway with significant specular reflection. All three methods show the hallway as being wider than it really is. This would be a serious problem for navigation and obstacle avoidance. The sensor noise was not eliminated by the use of an occupancy grid. In many cases, a large amount of sensor noise can be eliminated by tuning the model and updating algorithms.

Therefore an important criterion for an algorithm is how easily it can be tuned for a particular environment. For example, in environments which provoke a high degree of specular reflection in sonars, a $\beta < 8°$ is often used to reduce the registration of noise in the occupancy grid. Why put false readings into the grid over a large area that will take several contradictory readings to eliminate? It can often take one or more days to tune a set of sonars which were producing near perfect occupancy grids in a laboratory for a new building.

3 WAYS TO TUNE   Occupancy grids can be tuned for a task environment in at least three ways. One way is to leave all the algorithms the same but concentrate on adjusting the physical equipment. For example, the time of flight of sound

depends on the density of air, so if a robot is going from sea level to high mountains, an adjustment factor can be added to the raw readings. Another approach is to change the threshold on what the robot considers a "really occupied" region. Lowering the threshold makes the interpretation of the occupancy map more conservative; more occupied regions that may be phantoms are treated as if they were real. This typically doesn't work well in cluttered or narrow environments because the robot can get blocked in by false readings. Increasing the threshold can make the robot less sensitive to small occupied regions which may not get many readings. Finally, a common solution is to slow the robot's velocity down; however, this exacerbates sensor noise in HIMM/GRO updating mechanisms and to a lesser degree in Bayesian and Dempster-Shafer.

TUNING BAYESIAN MODEL

Other possibilities for tuning the performance include changing the sonar model and the update rules. In practice, only two aspects of the Bayesian sonar model are tuned: the field of view and the prior probability that an area is occupied. In difficult environments, the range R accepted as valid is often shortened. A robot might treat a range reading greater than 4 feet as being empty even though the sonar range is theoretically covers 25 feet or more. The rationale is that the likelihood that long readings are accurate is small and the robot is more interested in obstacles nearby. Of course, this can limit the robot's maximum safe velocity since it may be able to cover a distance faster than it can determine reliably that there is anything in it. Likewise, the β for the field of view is often adjusted. In Sec. 11.3, the prior probability was assumed to be $P(H) = P(\neg H) = 0.5$. However, this isn't necessarily true. In some cases, the area to be covered is actually more likely to be occupied. Consider a robot operating in a narrow hallway. Compare the hallway to the area that can be covered by the robots sonars. Most of the field of view is likely to be occupied, which may argue for a $P(H) \geq P(\neg H)$. Moravec's ongoing work in sonar-based occupancy grids has shown improvement based on using more accurate priors. However, this requires the robot or designer to gather data in advance of the robot being able to use the data. There is work in adaptive learning of the parameters.

TUNING DS MODEL

Dempster-Shafer theoretic methods have less to tune. Priors are not required as with Bayesian; Dempster-Shafer assigns all unsensed space a belief of $m(dontknow) = 1.0$. If there is prior information, the appropriate expectations can be placed into the grid. However, this is rarely if ever done. Tuning with Dempster-Shafer consists primarily of changing the field of view parameters, β and R.

TUNING HIMM

HIMM/GRO have many more parameters that can be tuned, which can often be a disadvantage in the field as tweaking more than one can have conflicting side effects. The basic increments, I^+ and I^- are often changed. Less frequently, the size of the mask W and the individual weights $W_{p,q}$ are changed.

11.7 Localization

Fig. 11.1 shows a metric map built up from sensor data using shaft encoders to localize. As can be seen, the shaft encoders are so inaccurate that the hallways never connect.

ICONIC
FEATURE-BASED
LOCALIZATION

Localization can either use raw sensor data directly (*iconic*) or use features extracted from the sensor data (*feature-based*). For example, iconic localization would match current sensor readings to data fused with the previous sensor measurements in the occupancy grid. Feature-based localization might first extract a corner from the sonar data or occupancy grid, then on the next data acquisition, the robot would extract the corner and compute the true change in position. Feature-based localization is conceptually similar to the idea of *distinctive places* in topological navigation, in the sense that there are features in the environment that can be seen from several viewpoints.

Current metric map-making methods rely heavily on iconic localization, and many methods use some form of continuous localization and mapping. Essentially the robot moves a short distance and matches what it sees to what it has built up in its map. Map matching is made more complex by the uncertainties in the occupancy grid itself: what the robot thought it was seeing at time t_{n-1} may have been wrong and the observations at t_n are better. These methods can be extremely accurate, though are often computationally expensive.

There is rising interest in feature-based methods for topological map-making because gateways are of interest for maps and can be readily perceived. The primary issue in topological map-making is the possibility that the robot mistakes one gateway for another, for example, interprets an intersection with a hallway as a door.

Shaffer et al. compared iconic and feature-based methods.[127] They concluded that iconic methods were more accurate for localization than feature-based methods with fewer data points. Also, they noted that iconic methods impose fewer restrictions on the environment (such as having to know the types of features that will be available). However, feature-based algorithms were often faster because there was less data to match during the localization

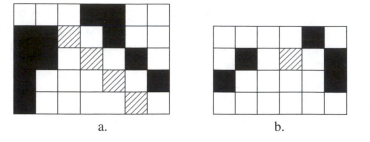

Figure 11.17 Example of a.) a global map constructed from previous readings and b.) a new local observation that must be fit to the global map. Shaded elements in a. represent possible matches to the shaded element in b.

process. This ignored the cost of feature extraction, however. Feature-based algorithms were also better able to handle poor initial location estimates. So if the robot was placed in an office building and told it was facing North when it was facing South, it would be able to correct that error after it encountered one or more gateways.

An important point to remember about localization is that no technique handles a dynamic environment. If there are people moving about, each local update will be different and it may be next to impossible for the robot to match the past and current observations. If the robot is localizing itself to an *a priori* map, it cannot tolerate a large number of discrepancies between the map and the current state of the real world. For example, furniture shown in one place on the map but which is actually in another is hard to handle. Likewise, a hallway in a hospital which is usually clear but suddenly cluttered with gurneys and equipment presents a challenge.

11.7.1 Continuous localization and mapping

In order to eliminate the problems with shaft encoders or other *proprioceptive* techniques, current localization methods use *exteroception*. Exteroceptive methods involve the robot matching its current perception of the world with its past observations. Usually the past observations are the map itself. Once the true position of the robot is known with respect to the map, the current
REGISTRATION   perception is then added to the map in a process often called *registration*.

As seen in Fig. 11.17, matching the current observation to past observations is not as simple as it sounds. The robot has moved from *a* to *b* according to its shaft encoders. It has created a map in the form of an occupancy grid, shown in Fig. 11.17a. However, the robot can have significant (and different amounts of) errors in each of its three degrees of freedom, (x, y, θ). As a result, based on the current, or local, observation, the robot could actually be in any one of the shaded elements. Actually, if the robot was facing a different orientation, the number of possible matches of the local observation to the global map increases. The shaft encoders provide a set of possible locations, not a single location, and orientations; each possible (x, y, θ) will be called a

POSE   *pose*.

In theory, the "local" occupancy grid built from current range readings should help determine which location is correct. If the robot has not moved very far, then a large portion of the grid should match what is already in the global map. As can be seen in Fig. 11.17, the current sensor readings have at least three possible fits with the global occupancy grid, or map. The possibilities get higher if the uncertainty in the local and global grids are considered. Unfortunately, there is no guarantee the the current perception is correct; it could be wrong, so matching it to the map would be unreliable.

Localization methods, therefore, attempt to balance competing interests. On one hand, more frequent localization is good. The less the robot has moved, the smaller the set of possible poses to be considered. Likewise, the less the robot has moved, the more likely there is to be an intersection of current perception with past perceptions. But if the robot localizes itself every time it gets a sensor reading, the more likely it is that the current observation will have noise and that the method will produce the wrong match. So there are tradeoffs between 1) localizing after every sensor update and 2) localizing after n sensor updates which have been fused. Usually the choice of n is done by trial and error to determine which value works well and can execute on the particular hardware (processor, available memory). Notice that the issues in balancing these issues are similar to those of balancing continuous versus event-driven replanning discussed in Ch. 10.

LOCAL OCCUPANCY   The general approach to balancing these interests is shown in Fig. 11.18. In
GRID   order to filter sensor noise, the robot constructs a *local occupancy grid* from the
GLOBAL OCCUPANCY   past n readings. After n readings, the local grid is matched to the *global occu-*
GRID   *pancy grid* or map. Matching is done k times, one for every possible (x, y, θ) pose generated from the shaft encoder data. In order to generate k, the robot has to consider the translation of the robot (which $grid[i][j]$ the robot is actually occupying) and the rotation of the robot (what direction θ it is facing). In theory, the possible number of poses, k, is actually infinite. Consider just the θ error for a "move ahead 1 meter" command, which might be between -5°

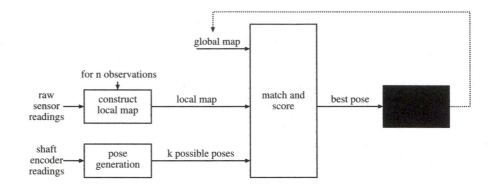

Figure 11.18   Flowchart showing the continuous localization and mapping process. Mapping phase is shown shaded.

and +10°, because the robot has a tendency to drift to the right and because it initially might not be pointed straight. This is a range of real values, so the possible values to consider are infinite! In order to make this tractable the *pose generation function* has to convert this continuous range into discrete units, much as an occupancy grid represents area with elements of a finite width and height. The function might only consider θ errors in increments of 5°. In that case, the possible poses will consider only $\theta = -5, 0, 5, 10$. Of course, the pose generation function has to discretize the errors in the x and y degrees of freedom too. A pose generation function may return on the order of 128 different poses to consider. In order to cut down on the computations while the robot is navigating, a pose generation function might use a lookup table which stores possible poses for a particular motion computed in advance.

POSE GENERATION FUNCTION

The localization algorithm must match the local occupancy grids to the global occupancy. To do this, it essentially overlays the center of the local grid at the k pose onto the global grid. This marks a set of grid elements which overlap in both grids. The algorithm scores how well the values in the local grid match the values in the overlapping global occupancy grid. Since the local and global grids will have uncertainty values, the matching function must somehow account for this. There are a variety of possible measures; Eqn. 11.16 can be adapted as an example of a simple one:

$$score = \sum_{k=i,j}^{K} |global[i][j] - local[i][j]|$$

Once the score for all matches has been computed, the algorithm chooses the pose with the best score. This (x, y, θ) is declared the correct current position of the robot on the global grid and is used to update the robot's odometry. The process then repeats.

A good example is the continuous localization component of the ARIEL system[125] developed under the direction of Alan Schultz at the US Naval Research Laboratory. ARIEL runs on Nomad 200 bases that have both sonar and a structured light rangefinder for range detection, but can be used with any type of sensor that returns range data that is fused into the occupancy grids according to an appropriate sensor model.

The localization process is illustrated in Fig. 11.19c. The local occupancy grid is called the Short-Term Perception Map, and it covers the area that the robot can ideally sense; it is only about as large as the sensor coverage. Fig. 11.19a shows an example of a short-term perception map generated by the sonars in a large room. The grid is constructed by fusing range data with a variant of the Bayesian combination method.

A second, global occupancy grid, the Long-Term Perception Map, represents the robot's larger environment. It covers an area such as an entire room, and is illustrated in Fig. 11.19b. In terms of updating, it serves as an *a priori* map.

The robot's odometry obtained from shaft encoders drifts with motion, so the continuous localization process adapts the frequency of relocalization with the distance traveled. More frequent localization reduces the amount of motion between each attempt, which in turn reduces the odometric drift, and fewer poses are needed to adequately cover the uncertainty in position, which in turn decreases the computational effort.

As the robot moves, sensor data is obtained and fed into the Short-Term Map. Every two feet (which corresponds to about 800 individual sensor readings), the matching function estimates the possible choices k, and for each pose compares the match between the mature Short-Term Map and the Long-Term Map. The pose with the best fit is chosen, and the robot's odometry is updated.

Fig. 11.20 shows the results of using the ARIEL continuous localization and mapping process to map a previously unknown environment (a 70-foot-long hallway). ARIEL was able to reduce the errors in the final map (both the dimensions of the hall and how well the maps lined up) by 75% compared to maps generated by just shaft encoder localization.

But what if the environment is dynamic? After the Long-Term Map is obtained, if a hallway is obstructed or a door is closed, the robot needs to

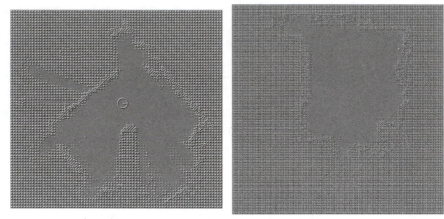

a.   b.

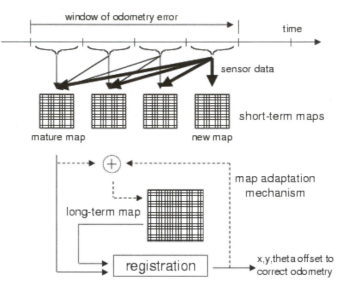

c.

Figure 11.19   Continuous localization in ARIEL: a.) short-term perception map. Height of pixels indicates the certainty, b.) long-term perception map, and c.) registration of short-term perception map with long-term map. (Figures courtesy of the Navy Center for Applied Research in Artificial Intelligence, Naval Research Laboratory.)

be able to notice the change so that it can react accordingly. To allow this, ARIEL has a map adaptation mechanism (the dashed lines in Fig. 11.19c).

After each localization, the Short-Term Map is integrated into the Long-Term Map at the determined pose using Bayes' rule. Changes in the environment sensed by the robot and put into the Short-Term Perception Map therefore make their way into the Long-Term Map, where they can be used for improved localization (e.g. when a box shows up in a previously feature-less hallway) and planning (e.g. planning a path to a goal via another route). In this way, the robot maintains its ability to stay localized despite changes in the environment while adding the ability to react to those changes.

Although continuous localization can be computationally intensive, the fusion of sensor data over each element in the Short-Term Map would be done for obstacle avoidance anyway. The added cost of the registration is periodic and can be performed in parallel on a separate processor to reduce its impact. The map adaptation mechanism has a small cost, as it reuses the fused data in the Short-Term Map, rather than resensing and fusing the individual sensor data into the Long-Term Map. Overall, the NRL algorithm is able to localize at about a 1Hz rate on a Pentium II class processor.

11.7.2   Feature-based localization

Feature-based localization has two flavors. One flavor is similar to continuous localization and mapping: the robot extracts a feature such as a wall, opening, or corner, then tries to find the feature in the next sensor update. The feature acts as a local, natural landmark. As noted earlier in Ch. 9, the use of natural landmarks can be challenging for navigation in general, especially since a "good" set of features to extract may not be known in advance. Trying to find and use natural landmarks for accurate localization is at least doubly hard.

The second flavor is really an extension of topological navigation. The robot localizes itself relative to topological features such as gateways. It may not know how long a hallway is, but it knows what the end of the hallway looks like and important information (e.g., the hallway terminates in a t-junction and has 3 doors on the left and 3 on the right). Once the robot has constructed a topological map, it can locate itself.

An interesting question that has been considered by many researchers is what happens when a robot is given a topological map (such as in Fig. 11.21), told it was at Position A, and was really at Position B? How would the robot ever notice it was misinformed, rather than assume its sensors were re-

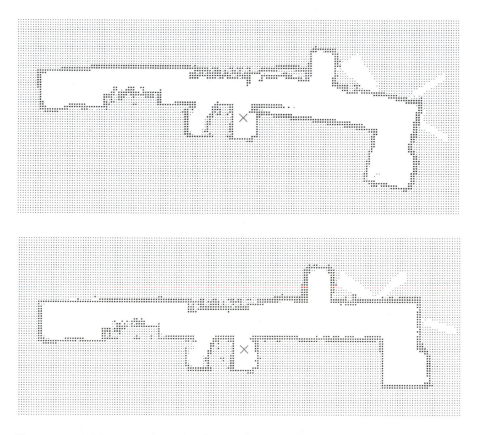

Figure 11.20   Mapping of a 70-foot hall without continuous localization (upper) and with (lower). (Figure courtesy of the Navy Center for Applied Research in Artificial Intelligence, Naval Research Laboratory.)

porting erroneous readings? And, how many moves would it take to find a unique path that would permit the robot to localize itself? These questions were explored by the AAAI Mobile Robot Competitions from 1993 through 1996.

Sensor uncertainty plays a large role in localization, even in a topological map. Nourbakhsh, Power, and Birchfield, who won the AAAI competition in 1994,[112] collected large amounts of data with their robot's sonar range finders. They wrote algorithms to detect walls, closed doors, open doors, and hallways. Even with their best algorithms, the sonar noise was such that a hallway had about a 10% chance of being classified as an open door, while

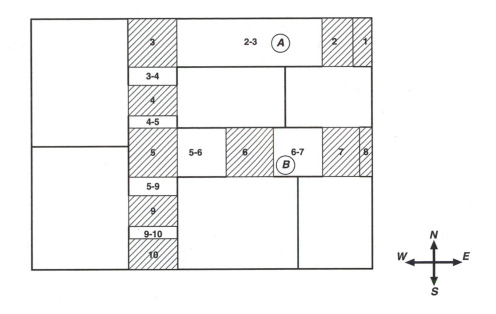

Figure 11.21 State-sets of a topological layout of an office building.

a wall had a 30% chance of being seen as a closed door. To factor in this sensor uncertainty, most roboticists use techniques based on a probabilistic method known as Partially Observable Markov Decision Processes (POMDP, pronounced "pom D P"). POMDPs are beyond the scope of this book, but the basic idea is illustrated by the quasi-evidential *state-set progression* methodology developed by Illah Nourbakhsh.[112]

Returning to Fig. 11.21, it can be seen that there are 10 gateways. The gateways are labeled with a single number and represent a state where the robot can localize itself relative to the map. (The numbering is arbitrary.) Notice that the hallways are not gateways. The robot knows that it is in a hallway, but unless it uses continuous localization and mapping, it does not know where it is in the hallway (e.g., how close it is to the next gateway). Since hallways can be considered as the state of the robot which is between gateways, the hallway are labeled with two numbers, *gateway − gateway*, representing the pair of gateways the robot is between.

If the robot "wakes up" and senses it is in a hallway facing east, it knows it is in one of the following states: {{2-3},{5-6},{6-7}}. So it is currently in one of three possible states. As it moves and detects a gateway, the new information should reduce the possible states. For example, it the robot starts moving east, it will encounter different gateways based on where it really is. The possible *progression* of the states from the initial set of states is:

- $\{2-3\} \rightarrow \{3\}$, where $\{3\}$ is a $wall_{right}$, $hall_{left}$, $wall_{front}$

- $\{5-6\} \rightarrow \{5\}$, where $\{5\}$ is a $hall_{right}$, $hall_{left}$, $wall_{front}$

- $\{6-7\} \rightarrow \{6\}$, where $\{6\}$ is a $wall_{right}$, $door_{left}$, $hall_{front}$

Therefore if the robot encounters a $door_{left}$, the set of possible states representing its location on the topological map reduces to $\{6\}$.

The above method works very well for indoor environments with orthogonal intersections. The challenge becomes how to handle sensor noise; there is a large possibility the robot will misclassify the door as a hallway. This would lead to a belief that the robot was more likely to be at $\{3\}$ rather than at $\{6\}$. The basic solution is to keep track of the probabilities of where the robot is at and then after many moves, the probability that the robot was at $\{6\}$ eventually becomes 1.0.

11.8   Exploration

Exploration attempts to answer the question of *where haven't I been?* versus *where am I?* A central concern in exploration is how to cover an unknown area efficiently. One way is to do this with a random search; the robot literally wanders around randomly (using a random potential field). After some (often very large) period of time, statistics indicate it should have covered the entire area. Another reactive method is to permit a short-term persistence of proprioception (odometry). Then the robot is repulsed by areas that have been recently visited. This can be implemented as a repulsive field, generated by every visited cell in a coarse occupancy grid or for every previous heading. This "avoid past" behavior[17] when combined with the random potential field drives the robot towards new areas.

Another behavioral approach is to exploit evidential information in the occupancy grid. As the robot explores a new area, many cells on the grid will be unknown, either $P(Occupied) = P(Empty)$ in a Bayesian system or $m(dontknow) = 1$ in a Dempster-Shafer implementation. The robot takes the centroid of the unknown area and uses that as a goal for a move-to-goal. As it moves to the goal (in conjunction with avoid-obstacle), new sensor readings will update the occupancy grid, reducing the amount and location of unknown areas, and creating a new goal. Hughes and Murphy[105] showed that this move-to-unknown-area behavior was suitable for indoor exploration and even localization. While the above behavior-oriented approaches are simple and easy to implement, they often are inefficient, especially when presented with two or more unexplored areas. Suppose a robot has encountered a hallway intersection; how does it choose which area to explore?

Two basic styles of exploration methods have emerged which rank unexplored areas and make rational choices: *frontier-based* and *generalized Voronoi graph* methods. Both work well for indoor environments; it is less clear how these work over large open spaces. Both use behaviors for navigation, but are different in how they set the navigational goals. This section provides a highly simplified overview of each method.

11.8.1 Frontier-based exploration

Frontier-based exploration was pioneered by Brian Yamauchi.[125] The approach assumes the robot is using a Bayesian occupancy grid (a Dempster-Shafer grid can be used as well). As shown in Fig. 11.22, when a robot enters a new area, there is a boundary between each area that has been sensed and is open and the area that has not been sensed. (The boundary between occupied areas and unknown areas are not interesting because the robot cannot go through the occupied area to sense what is behind it.) There are two such

FRONTIER boundaries in Fig. 11.22; each of these lines form a *frontier* that should be explored.

The choice of which frontier to be explored first can be made in a variety of ways. A simple strategy is to explore the nearest frontier first. Another is to explore the biggest frontier first. Since the world is unknown, the robot has no way of knowing if upon reaching a big frontier it will discover a wall just a meter away. This means that the robot might move across a room, briefly explore one area, then return back to almost at its starting point, explore that area, and then go to another place, and so on. In practice, this doesn't happen that often with indoor environments.

The size of the frontier can be measured by the number of edge cells. Every cell in the occupancy grid that the boundary runs through is considered an edge. If an edge "touches" an edge in one of its eight surrounding neighbors, the edges are connected and form the line. In order to eliminate the effects of

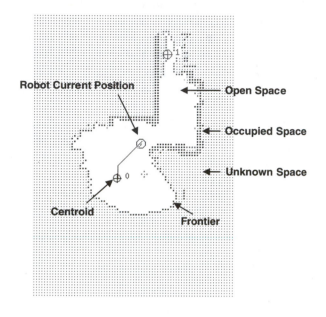

Figure 11.22 Example of a robot exploring an area using frontier-based method. (Figure courtesy of the Navy Center for Applied Research in Artificial Intelligence, Naval Research Laboratory.)

sensor noise there is usually a threshold of the minimum of number of cells in a line before it can be treated as a frontier.

Once the robot has chosen a frontier to investigate, it must decide precisely where to head. A good goal that will get the robot to the frontier is the centroid, (x_c, y_c), of the edges in the frontier line. x and y is the location of the centroid, either in map coordinates or the i,j indices in the grid. The centroid for a two dimensional object is the center, or the "average" (x, y) location. The computation for the centroid in pseudocode is:

```
x_c = y_c = count = 0
for every cell on the frontier line with a location of (x, y)
   x_c = x_c + x
   y_c = y_c + y
   count++
```

```
x_c = x_c/count
y_c = y_c/count
```

Once the centroid has been established, the robot can navigate either using reactive move-to-goal and avoid-obstacle behaviors, plan a path and reactively execute the path, or continuously replan and execute the path. Regardless, once the robot is at the frontier, the map is updated and new frontiers may be discovered. These frontiers are then evaluated, a new one is chosen, and the rest are stored.

11.8.2   Generalized Voronoi graph methods

Another method of deciding how to explore a space is to have the robot build a reduced generalized Voronoi graph (GVG) as it moves through the world. This method has been used extensively by Howie Choset.[35;34]

To review Ch. 10, as the robot moves, it attempts to maintain a path that places it equidistant from all objects it senses. Essentially, the robot tries to move ahead but stay in the "middle" or at a tangent to surrounding objects. This path is a GVG edge, the same as would be generated by decomposing the space into a Voronoi graph. Generating and following the path is straightforward to do with a behavior.

When the robot comes to a dead end or a gateway, there are multiple GVG edges that the robot could follow. As shown in Fig. 11.23, dead ends produce two GVG edges. But in this case, the robot can perceive that both of these edges end at objects, so there is no reason to follow them. The robot can then backtrack along the path it had been on, either to the start or to another branch. If the robot encounters branches in the GVG edges, it can choose one at random to follow.

Fig. 11.23 shows how the robot would explore the an area. For convenience, the figure shows the entire GVG that would be drawn *after* the robot had fully explored the area. The robot would begin by sensing the walls on each side (without any recognition that it was in a hall). The sensed area is shown in light gray. It would attempt to center itself between the walls while moving perpendicular to the line of intersection. Eventually it reaches an intersection. This creates two edges, neither of which appears to terminate at an object. It arbitrarily chooses the left edge and saves the right. It does this repeatedly, as seen in Fig. 11.23b. It continues up the hall until it comes to the dead end. The robot then backtracks using the same edge behavior (stay in the middle). It continues to favor exploring to the left until it comes to a dead end in the lower left, then backtracks as shown in Fig. 11.24a. The robot continues to explore and backtrack until the entire area is covered, as shown in Fig. 11.24b.

11.9   Summary

Map-making converts a local, or robot-centered, set of sensor observations into a global map, independent of robot position. One of the most common data structures used to represent metric maps is the *occupancy grid*. An occupancy grid is a two dimensional array regular grid which represents a fixed area in an absolute coordinate system. Grids have a high resolution, on the order of 5-10 cm per grid element.

Greater accuracy is obtained in occupancy grids by fusing together multiple uncertain sensor readings. Sensor fusion requires a *sensor model* for translating a sensor reading into a representation of uncertainty, and an *update rule* for combining the uncertainty for a pair of observations. Bayesian methods use a *probabilistic* sensor model, representing uncertainty as probabilities and updating with Bayes' rule. Dempster-Shafer methods use a *possibilistic* sensor model with Shafer belief functions combined by Dempster's rule. HIMM uses an *ad hoc* sensor model and update rule. HIMM is less accurate and harder to tune, but requires significantly less computation than traditional implementations of Bayesian or Dempster-Shafer methods. Because of the improvement due to sensor fusion, occupancy grids are often used for obstacle avoidance, serving as a virtual sensor for reactive behaviors.

Producing a global map based in a fixed coordinate system requires localization. In general, the more often the robot is able to localize itself, the more accurate the map. However, localization is often computationally expensive so it may not be run at the same update rate as reactive behaviors. Raw sensor data, especially odometry, is imperfect and confounds the localization and map-making process. Most techniques concurrently map and localize.

The two categories of localization methods are *iconic* and *feature-based*. Of the two, iconic methods are better suited for metric map-making and occupancy grids. They fit raw observations into the map directly. An example is creating a local short-term occupancy grid from sonar readings, then after three moves, matching that grid to the long-term occupancy grid.

Feature-based methods perform less well for metric map-making, but work satisfactorily for topological map-making. Feature-based methods match current observations to the map by matching features rather than raw sen-

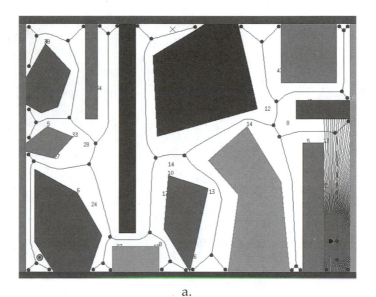

a.

b.

Figure 11.23   Example of a robot exploring an indoor area using a GVG method. a.)
The robot starts in the lower right corner and b.) explores the center. The black lines
indicate the ideal GVG, the white lines indicate the portion of the GVG that the robot
has traveled. (Figures courtesy of Howie Choset.)

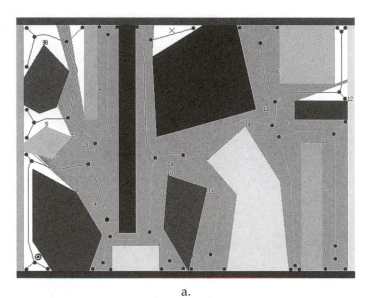

a.

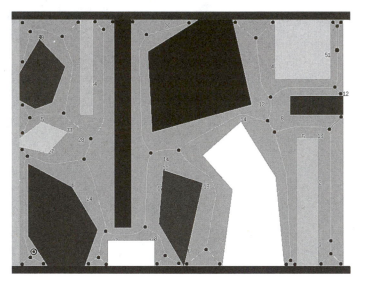

b.

Figure 11.24 Example of a robot exploring an indoor area using a GVG method, continued. a.) reaches a dead end and backtracks, and b.) completely covers the area, though it hasn't traveled all edges. (Figures courtesy of Howie Choset.)

sor readings. The features can be either local features such as a corner, or more topologically significant, such as a landmark or gateway. The choice of features gives rise to two problems: the certainty with which a feature can be detected (how likely is the robot to miss a hallway on its left) and reasoning about indistinguishable locations (one hallway intersection looks like another). Topological localization can be done by matching the gateways encountered with the expected gateways given on a topological map. All existing map-making methods tend to break in the presence of changing environments.

Formal exploration strategies for mapping new areas fall into two categories of techniques: *frontier-based* and *GVG*. Frontier-based methods look as the perimeter of the of sensed region on an occupancy grid and then rank areas to explore. Voronoi methods represent the explored world as a Voronoi diagram and use geometric properties to ensure that open areas are opportunistically explored as the robot moves.

11.10   Exercises

Exercise 11.1

An important property of an occupancy grid is that it supports *sensor fusion*. Define sensor fusion in one or two sentences and give two examples.

Exercise 11.2

What is the difference between an occupancy grid, a certainty grid, and an evidence grid?

Exercise 11.3

What is the difference between iconic and feature-based localization?

Exercise 11.4

List the desirable attributes of a landmark. Discuss why or why not each of the following might make a good landmark for feature-based localization:

a. Corner

b. Intersection of hallways

c. Open doorway

Exercise 11.5

Name three applications where metric map-making might be useful.

Exercise 11.6

Why is localization important in map-making?

Exercise 11.7

Suppose a localization algorithm had an order complexity of $O(m \times n)$, where m is the number of columns and n is the number of rows in the occupancy grid. Therefore if the algorithm operated over a 10×10 grid, approximately 100 operations would be executed for localization. What would be the number of operations if the grid were:

a. 100×100?

b. 1000×1000?

c. 5000×2000?

Exercise 11.8

Repeat the previous problem where the order complexity is $O((m \times n)^2)$.

Exercise 11.9

Consider a robot beginning to map a new area (the occupancy grid is at an initial unsensed state), and how three different sonar updates create a certainty value for a particular grid element. The sonar model is: range is 12, it's $\beta = 15°$, the $Max_{occupancy} = 0.98$, and the tolerance is $pm1.0$. At time $t1$, the sonar reading returns 10.0. The grid element of interest is 9.5 units away from the robot with an α of 0.0. At $t2$, the robot has translated sideways. The sonar reading is 11.0. The grid element is now 9.5 units away with an $\alpha = 14.0$. At $t3$, the sonar returns a value of 8.5 units. The robot has moved to the side and rotated; it is now 9.0 units from the grid element with an α of 5°.

a. What is the initial value of every element in the occupancy grid for

- i) Bayesian
- ii) Dempster-Shafer
- iii) HIMM

b. Fill in the probabilities for the *grid element for each sensor reading*:

sonar	Bayesian		Dempster-Shafer			HIMM
certainty:	$P(s\|O)$	$P(s\|E)$	$m(O)$	$m(E)$	m(*dontknow*)	
t1						
t2						
t3						

c. Fill in the values for the *grid element after every update*:

after	Bayesian		Dempster-Shafer			HIMM
update:	$P(O\|s)$	$P(E\|s)$	$m(O)$	$m(E)$	m(*dontknow*)	
t1						
t2						
t3						

Exercise 11.10

Construct a series of readings that using the HIMM update rule would produce the same final grid as produced by GRO in Fig. 11.13.

Exercise 11.11

Consider how the robot moves from one frontier to another in frontier-based exploration. What are the advantages and disadvantages of explicitly planning a path between frontier centroids versus using a purely reactive move-to-goal and avoid set of behaviors?

Exercise 11.12

Compare frontier-based exploration with GVG exploration. Is one better suited for certain environments than the other?

Exercise 11.13

Consider how both exploration strategies (frontier and GVG) often have to choose between possible areas to explore and then save the choices not taken for further exploration. Which data structure do you think would be better to store the choices, a stack or a priority queue? Why?

Exercise 11.14   [*Programming*]

Write a program that displays a sonar model on a 26 by 17 grid. The origin of the sonar should be at (26,8), with a $\beta = 15°$. Assume a sensor reading of $s = 10$ with a tolerance of 2 units.

a. Create a simple ASCII display. Each element should be labeled with the number of its corresponding region: 1, 2, or 3. For elements outside of the field of view, the label is 4.

b. Create a simple Bayesian display. Each element should be labeled with the correct $P(s|Occupied)$ value .

c. Create a simple Dempster-Shafer display. Each element should be labeled with the correct $m(Occupied)$ value (Dempster-Shafer).

d. Save the data from parts b. and c. and put in a spreadsheet or plotting program. Display as a 3D plot.

Exercise 11.15   [*Programming*]

Write a program for a robot which moves to the centroid of an unknown area. Test it for a variety of room configurations, and describe where it stops in each case.

Exercise 11.16   [*Advanced Reading*]

Read "Dervish: An Office-Navigating Robot," by Illah Nourbakhsh, and "Xavier: A Robot Navigation Architecture Based on Partially Observable Markov Decision Process Models," by Sven Koenig and Reid Simmons in *Artificial Intelligence and Mobile Robots: Case Studies of Succesful Robot System*, ed. Kortenkamp, Bonasso, Murphy, 1998. Describe how these approaches would work for the example in Fig. 11.21. Comment on the similarities and differences.

11.11   End Notes

Robot name trivia.
CARMEL stands for Computer Aided Robotics for Maintenance, Emergency, and Life Support. Many of Moravec's robots are named for (distant) planets: Neptune, Uranus, Pluto.

Uncertainty and mapping.
The figures of hallways were generated by Brian Sjoberg and Jeff Hyams at the University of South Florida and Bill Adams at the Naval Research Laboratory. Alan Schultz and Bill Adams also provided the description of ARIEL.

12 *On the Horizon*

Chapter Objectives:

- Define: *polymorphism, adjustable autonomy.*

- Be familiar with trends in AI robotics, both in research and in society.

12.1 Overview

At this point in time, AI robotics remains largely a research or specialized scientific endeavor. There has been some move to commercialize the progress made by the Reactive Paradigm, as seen by the popularity of Lego Mindstorms and Sony Aibo, but overall the field is nascent, waiting for what software gurus call the "killer app." This chapter attempts to identify new trends on the horizon.

Ch. 1 offered a timeline of the historical forks in the development of robotics. This is repeated in Fig. 12.1 for convenience. In retrospect, the most unfortunate fork was not the split between industrial and AI robots in the 1960's, but rather the split between vision and robotics communities. As can be seen from Ch. 4, the success of a robot is based largely on its perceptual capabilities. Vision is a powerful modality, and was overlooked by researchers due to high hardware prices and high computational demands.

Now there are signs of the two communities reuniting. Many computer vision groups are now working with mobile robots. Early forays by the vision community into robotics could be characterized as being "disembodied" or separating vision from the rest of the robot. Robots were a way of getting a series of images over time, rather than an opportunity to explore how to organize vision such that a robot could use it in real-time. One of the first computer vision scientists to take a more principled approach to merging

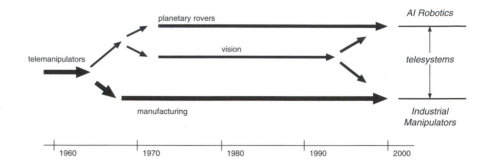

Figure 12.1   A timeline showing forks in development of robots.

vision and robotics was Avi Kak at Purdue University. His Cybermotion robot was one of the first to navigate in hallways using vision; in this case, a technique known as a Hough (pronounced "huff") transform.[80] In the early 1990's, with slow hardware, the robot could go 8 to 9 meters per second. The computer vision community went through the equivalent of a Reactive movement, moving to approaches now called *animate vision*, *purposive vision*, and *active vision*.

Another positive influence to reunite robotics and vision has been the various DARPA and ESPIRIT projects in mobility. Both agencies have provided funding for large-scale projects, such as fully autonomous off-road and highway vehicles. The size of the projects require hundreds of researchers from many universities to collaborate, providing the opportunity to cross-fertilize the fields.

A more cost-effective motivation to have roboticists work with vision, and vice versa, has been the various robot competitions. The prestigious AAAI Mobile Robot Competitions have changed the events and the rules each year to reward researchers who use computer vision in creative ways, instead of relying on the standard sonars. A newer event, RoboCup, mandates vision. There is no other way to play soccer than to see the ball and the players in real-time. The competitions have already spawned at least one commercial product: the Cognachrome fast vision board developed by Newton Labs. The ground and aerial robot competitions sponsored by the Association for Unmanned Vehicle Systems also promote the integration of computer vision with robotics, but winning those competitions still largely depends on hardware, not software algorithms.

The central theme of the first part of this book has been the paradigms of robotics. The Reactive and Hybrid Paradigms have been in dominance for a decade. It is reasonable to expect that a new paradigm is on the horizon. If so, that paradigm shift might be the addition of a fourth robot primitive, *learning*. Right now, robots have emergent behavior from manually coded schemas and deliberative functions. Certainly, learning exists in biological systems. The lack of a computational theory of learning and of bridge-builders such as Arbib, Brooks, and Arkin is possibly delaying this next step.

This is not to say that exciting work has not been going on in robot learning. Connell and Mahadevan published an influential book, *Robot Learning*, in 1993, and researchers such as Patty Maes have demonstrated multi-legged insect robots waking up and learning to walk within minutes. Leslie Kaebling has recently been recognized by AAAI for her work with robot learning. The field of robotic learning is growing rapidly and it is too large to cover in this book, but techniques such as *neural networks* and *genetic algorithms* are making increasing contributions and roboticists should keep an eye on developments in those communities.

The past suggests that the future will involve vision and paradigms. What trends can be gleaned from the current state of robotics? One assessment is that mobile robots are now truly mobile; they have demonstrated that they can reliably navigate. Given the ability to navigate, what would further shape the field? The rest of this chapter explores the potential impact of four "usual suspects": *hardware advances*, *software trends*, *emerging applications*, and *changing societal expectations*.

In terms of hardware, mobile robot design has been largely static for the past four or five years, centered about three main types or "species." There are the round, mostly holonomic research robots such as those made by Nomadic, RWI, Cybermotion, and Denning. Another robot species is that of the somewhat fragile insectoids. An in-between size of robot, somewhere on the order of a large radio-controller car powered with a laptop, has also emerged, most notably the Pioneers and B-12. New developments have led to *polymorphic* or *shape-shifting* robots, in addition to continued progress in reconfigurable platforms. Aerial and underwater platforms are also becoming more mainstream.

Software advances, particularly in *agency*, are also likely to have a profound influence on mobile robotics. As noted in Ch. 1, the Reactive movement contributed significantly to the rise of software agents, especially webots and know-bots. Now the rapid assimilation and commercial development of these concepts, combined with the "thin client" and "appliance" movement, suggest that these intellectual children will return home and teach their parents new tricks. Another software trend is the push for software toolkits and better development environments for robots. Georgia Tech's Mission Lab software package is one example of a toolkit that enables rapid assemblage of behaviors. [92]

For whatever reason, robots are being considered for a broader set of applications than ever before. In the 1960's, robots were targeted for hazardous operations, including nuclear processing and space exploration. In the 1970's and 1980's, robots became identified with manufacturing. The 1990's have seen a shift from manufacturing to entertainment, medical, personal care, and humanitarian efforts.

A subtle, but noticeable, change has been societal expectations of robots. Throughout the 1960's, 1970's, and 1980's, robots were envisioned as solitary creatures, working on dirty, dull, and dangerous tasks. This view changed a bit in the research community with the appearance of robot societies. Regardless of whether it was one smart robot or a colony of stupid robots, the human was nowhere to be found. Or the human was present, but actively supporting the robot. Now there is an expectation that robots will be interacting with humans. The end of the century has already seen robot pets and robot tour guides. Work is being done in medical robots and in personal care for the elderly and disabled.

12.2   Shape-Shifting and Legged Platforms

POLYMORPHISM
SHAPE-SHIFTING

One of the biggest changes in platforms is the recent move towards *polymorphism* (from "multiple" and "change"), literally *shape-shifting* robots. Snake-like robots constitute an important class of shape-shifters. These robots have a high number of joints and are difficult to control, but have the potential advantage of being able to conform to twists and turns in narrow passages. Fig. 12.2 shows a snake at CMU exploring a search and rescue site.

Traditional tracked vehicle designs are being reworked to provide polymorphism. Perhaps the best known is the IS Robotics' Urban robot shown in Fig. 12.3. The Urban has a set of front flippers. It can use the flippers to help navigate over rough terrain, raise the sensor platform for a better view, and to right itself should it fall over. Another polymorphic tracked vehicle is the Inuktun VGTV shown in Fig. 12.4.

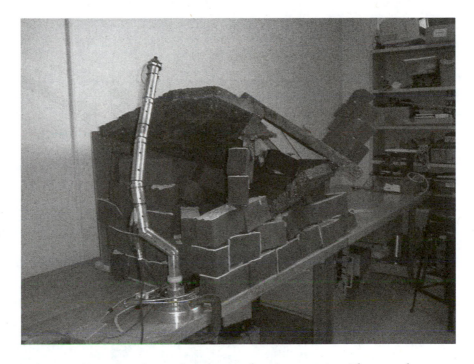

Figure 12.2   A snake robot exploring a search and rescue site. (Photograph courtesy of Howie Choset.)

Shape-shifting almost certainly necessitates an ecological approach to programming. For example, adaptation with a current shape regime is a gradual refinement of shape or posture, as in a robot lowering itself to fit into an increasingly smaller tunnel. This type of deformation is a direct response to the environment; it doesn't matter what type of material is making the tunnel smaller, the robot must get smaller to squeeze in. This suggests that the most elegant software approach will be to use a reactive behavior. For example, cockroaches and rats both exhibit a thigmotropic behavior: they prefer to be touching something. Cockroaches, in particular, like to be squeezed on all sides. In order to accomplish this, roaches and rats use feedback from cilia and hair distributed throughout their bodies to determine proximity. Once again, it is clear that the task, sensors, platforms, and intelligence must co-evolve to create a truly useful robot.

LEGGED LOCOMOTION   Another major hardware advance is *legged locomotion*. Legs have certain advantages for moving through rugged terrain and for power consumption.

Figure 12.3   IS Robotics' Urban vehicle, with flippers raising the robot body. (Photographs courtesy of IS Robotics.)

a.

b.

c.

Figure 12.4 An Inuktun VGTV in a.) full upright position, b.) half upright, and c.) flat.

Early work in the 1980's by Ken Waldron with the Ohio State Hexapod was disappointing from an AI standpoint. The traditional control theory methods for operating the hexapod were unable to provide real-time control with the processors of the time. In the end, the robot had to be teleoperated. Marc Raibert had a major impact on legged locomotion in the mid-1980's. He created a series of one-, two-, and four-legged robots for his PhD thesis, based in part on studies of gaits in animals.[118] One outcome of these studies was the understanding that one- and two-legged control were simply degenerate cases of multi-legged control; therefore the same simple gait control programs could be applied to all legged platforms. Although the control was biologically motivated, the hopping mechanisms were built like pogo-sticks. The field is concentrating now on maintaining balance, getting up (and sitting down), and dynamically adapting the gaits to terrain using more sophisticated legs.

12.3   Applications and Expectations

In his 1950 book, *The Human Use of Human Beings: Cybernetics and Society*, Norbert Wiener argued that robots could free people from being used inappropriately; for example, working in hazardous situations, allowing them to be "used" as human beings. Many of the applications being pursued by AI robotics researchers are fulfilling that potential. In addition to the traditional applications of nuclear and hazardous waste management, robots are now DEMINING being developed for humanitarian purposes. One area is *demining*, where land mines endangering civilians are safely removed and disposed of. An-URBAN SEARCH AND other effort is focusing on *urban search and rescue*. The Oklahoma City bomb-RESCUE ing in the US, and earthquakes in Japan, Mexico, Taiwan, and Turkey have offered painful lessons. Though no robots were available for those rescue efforts, it has become clear that robots could enter places dogs and humans cannot, and reduce the risk to workers as they search through area of dubious structural integrity.

Robots can be used for more commonplace tasks. Several companies have struggled to field reliable janitorial robots. This introduces a new challenge: robots' close proximity with humans. Robot pets are certainly intended to be with humans. The Sony Aibo dog (Fig. 12.5) is perhaps the best known of the robot pets to enter the commercial market. Humans interact with other agents in an emotional way. For example, people communicate in non-verbal ways such as facial expressions. Many researchers are now working on physically expressive interfaces, where the robot literally has a face and changes expresses with moods. Kismet, shown in Fig. 12.6 is one example. Minerva, the tour guide robot discussed in the Overview of Part II, used a similar robot face. Data collected during her stay at the Smithsonian indicated that the audience preferred the expressive face.[139]

Robots are also being examined for health care. One target audience is the elderly. Robots could be used to help pick up and retrieve objects, notice when a person has fallen or is trouble, and even to keep an invalid company. Much of the robotic technology developed for autonomous vehicles can be adapted for use by the disabled. Fig. 12.7 shows a semi-autonomous wheelchair developed by Holly Yanco at MIT and demonstrated at AAAI in 1996. The wheelchair uses sonars to simplify the task of going through doorways and areas of clutter. A wheelchair-bound person might not have the fine motor control needed to efficiently negotiate those situations; therefore the same behaviors for autonomy can reduce the need for a person to be intimately a part of the control loop. Although the robotic wheelchair can go

Figure 12.5 The Sony Aibo robot pet. (Photograph courtesy of the Sony Corporation, Aibo©The Sony Corporation.)

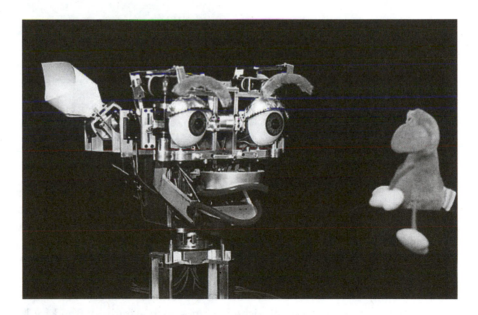

Figure 12.6 Kismet. (Photograph courtesy of the MIT Artificial Intelligence Laboratory.)

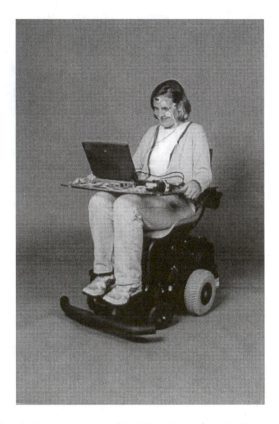

Figure 12.7   Wheelesley, a robotic wheelchair being guided by a person using the Boston University EagleEyes system.   (Photograph courtesy of Holly Yanco and AAAI.)

through a door or navigate through an obstacle course by itself, the human can take control over as much of the wheelchair as desired. This is often ADJUSTABLE AUTONOMY referred to as *adjustable autonomy*. The human is allowed to dynamically adjust the level of autonomy of the robotic agent. Note that this is confluence of ideas from the teleoperation community from Ch. 1 with the autonomy community.

As society shifts to expecting robots to work with and around humans, the ecological niche becomes increasingly defined by human workspaces. Everything the robot interacts with is designed for human ergonomics and unlikely to be reengineered. At one time, the prevailing line of thought was to deliberately avoid designing humanoid robots. Due to hardware and control limitations, there was no way a robot could mimic even a portion of human physiology. Now the pendulum is swinging towards humanoid robots, fueled in part by the need for robots to act in human spaces and by advances such as with legged locomotion.

Humanoid robots have been pursued by many research groups, especially Japanese. Human-like functionality seems to favor an implementation under the Hybrid Paradigm. The Honda humanoid robot, shown in Fig. 12.8a, is possibly the most successful to date, and certainly the most convincing. Most observers report a feeling that there is a person inside a space suit, just crouched a bit lower than usual. A quick look to the leg joints and feet make it clear that it is not an costumed person. The motivation for the robot stemmed from the company setting a long-term research challenge. The two keywords which described Honda's future market was "intelligent" and "mobility." The most advanced form of intelligent mobility is an autonomous mobile robot. The hardest form of a mobile robot is humanoid. Ergo, the research goal became a humanoid robot.

Rodney Brooks has also been working on a humanoid robot, *Cog*, since the mid-1990's. Cog is currently without legs, and much of the effort has been directed at vision and learning. Cog is shown in Fig. 12.8b.

NASA Johnson Space Center has moved from the EVAHR concept discussed in Ch. 7 to the more humanoid *robonaut* shown in Fig. 12.8. Robonaut is a human-sized robot complete with a stereo vision head, a torso, two arms and two five-fingered hands.

12.4   Summary

The field of AI robotics has created a large class of robots with basic physical and navigational competencies. At the same time, society has begun to move towards the incorporation of robots into everyday life, from entertainment to health care. Whereas robots were initially developed for dirty, dull, and dangerous applications, they are now being considered for personal assistants. Regardless of application, robots will require more intelligence, not less.

12.5   Exercises

Exercise 12.1

Define *polymorphism*. List the challenges for sensing and intelligent control for a polymorphic platform.

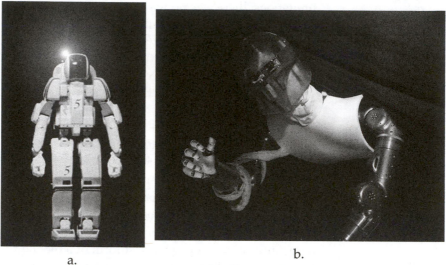

a.   b.

c.

Figure 12.8   Humanoid robots: a.) the Honda humanoid robot (photograph courtesy of Honda Corporation), b.) Robonaut, an anthropomorphic robot under development at NASA's Johnson Space Center (photograph courtesy of NASA), and c.) Cog playing with two MIT students. (Photograph courtesy of the MIT Artificial Intelligence Laboratory.)

Exercise 12.2

Consider designing a robot platform for urban search and rescue. What are the advantages and disadvantages of polymorphism? What are the advantages and disadvantages of a humanoid platform?

Exercise 12.3

Define *adjustable autonomy*. What teleoperation scheme does it most closely resemble? Is there a real difference between it and teleoperation?

Exercise 12.4

Propose a robot or robot society for the humanitarian applications below. Specify the Paradigm and architecture you would use. Justify your answer.

a. Demining.

b. Urban search and rescue.

Exercise 12.5   [*Advanced Reading*]

Look up and define *neural networks*. How are they being used for robotics? What makes them different from other approaches? Who are the researchers using neural networks?

Exercise 12.6   [*Advanced Reading*]

Look up and define *genetic algorithms*. How are they being used for robotics? What makes them different from other approaches? Who are the researchers using genetic algorithms?

Exercise 12.7   [*World Wide Web*]

Do a web search and report on the types of robot pets currently available or proposed. What is the motivation for each pet? What are the difficult issues being addressed?

Exercise 12.8   [*World Wide Web*]

Search the web for more information about the Honda humanoid robot, Cog, and Robonaut. Compare and contrast the motivation and objectives of each.

12.6   End Notes

Robots that run. And topple and fall . . .
Marc Raibert's thesis was published as *Legged Robots that Balance* in 1986. A video of his thesis work was also published. The video contained a blooper reel, showing memorable events such as when the one-legged hopper jumped *on* an obstacle instead of over it. The blooper reel did not detract from the scientific contributions;

instead it actually added confidence that Raibert's remarkable results were not the results of over-engineering the demonstrations.

The one-legged hopper appears for a few seconds in the movie "Rising Sun." Sean Connery and Wesley Snipes walk past it as they enter a high-tech research center. It has been reported that it took several days to get the hopper hopping long enough, coordinated with the actors, for the film.

Robonaut.
Bob Savely provided the photo of Robonaut.

The controversy over Cog.
Cog has a very ambitious set of goals, announced in a talk.[29] The goals looked a bit like science fiction author Robert Heinlein's "Future History," a timeline of all the books and stories that Heinlein intended to write. Although Heinlein had not written the stories yet, the timeline itself was published by John Campbell. Heinlein made good, writing almost every book and story on the timeline by the end of his 40+ year career. Progress with Cog has been relatively slow, despite frequent coverage by science magazines, leading many in the community to criticize the project as premature. Marvin Minsky, co-founder of the MIT AI Laboratory (which Brooks now directs), has repeatedly declared that "Cog is not a research project, it's a press release." As with all other aspects of AI robotics, time will tell.

Bibliography

[1] Albus, J., and Proctor, F.G., "A Reference Model Architecture for Intelligent Hybrid Control Systems," proceedings of the *International Federation of Automatic Control*, San Francisco, CA, June 30–July 5, 1996.

[2] Allocca, J. A., and Stuart, A., *Transducers: Theory and Application*, Prentice-Hall, 1984.

[3] Anderson, M.O., McKay, M.D., Richardson, B.S., "Multirobot Automated Indoor Floor Characterization Team," proceedings of the *1996 IEEE International Conference on Robotics and Automation*, Minneapolis, MN, April, 1996, pp. 1750–1753.

[4] Anderson, T.L., and Donath, M., "Animal Behavior as a Paradigm for Developing Robot Autonomy," *Robotics and Autonomous Systems*, vol. 6, 1990, pp. 145–186.

[5] Arbib, M., "Perceptual Structures and Distributed Motor Control," *Handbook of Physiology—The Nervous System II*, ed. Brooks, pp. 1449–1465, 1981.

[6] Arbib, M., "Schema Theory," *The Handbook of Brain Theory and Neural Networks*, Michael A. Arbib, ed., MIT Press, pp. 830–834.

[7] Arbib, M., and Liaw, J.-S., "Sensorimotor transformations in the worlds of frogs and toads," *Computational Theories of Interaction and Agency*, Philip Agre and Stanley J. Rosenschein, ed., MIT Press, 1996, pp. 53–80.

[8] Arkin, R.C., "Towards Cosmopolitan Robots: Intelligent Navigation in Extended Man-Made Environments," COINS Technical Report 87-80, *Computer and Information Science*, University of Massachusetts at Amherst, 1987.

[9] Arkin, R., personal communication, 1988.

[10] Arkin, R., *Behavior-Based Robotics*, MIT Press, 1998.

[11] Arkin, R., and MacKenzie, D., "Temporal Coordination of Perceptual Algorithms for Mobile Robot Navigation," *IEEE Transactions on Robotics and Automation*, vol. 10, no. 3, June, 1994, pp. 276–286.

[12] Arkin, R.C. and Murphy, R.R., "Autonomous Navigation in a Manufacturing Environment," *IEEE Transactions on Robotics and Automation*, vol. 6, no. 4, August, 1990, pp. 445–454.

[13] Arkin, R. C., Riseman, E. M., and Hansen, A., "AuRA: An Architecture for Vision-Based Robot Navigation," proceedings of the *DARPA Image Understanding Workshop*, Los Angeles, CA, February, 1987, pp. 417–413.

[14] *Artificial Intelligence and Mobile Robots*, D. Kortenkamp, P. Bonasso, R. Murphy, editors, MIT Press, 1998.

[15] Asimov, I., *I, Robot*, Bantam Books, 1994 (reprint).

[16] Balch, T., "Social Entropy: a New Metric for Learning Multi-Robot Teams," proc. *10th International FLAIRS Conference*, 1997.

[17] Balch, T.R. and Arkin R.C., "Avoiding the Past: A Simple but Effective Strategy for Reactive Navigation," *IEEE International Conference on Robotics and Automation*, 1993.

[18] Balch, T., and Arkin, R.C., "Behavior-Based Formation Control for Multirobot Teams," *IEEE Transactions on Robotics and Automation*, vol. 14, no. 6, 1999, pp. 926–939.

[19] Balch, T., Boone, G., Collins, T., Forbes, H., MacKenzie, D., and Santamaria, J., "Io, Ganymede, and Callisto: A Multiagent Robot Trash-Collecting Team," *AI Magazine*, vol. 16, no. 2, 1995, pp. 39–51.

[20] Barlow, J.B., "General Principles: The Senses Considered as Physical Instruments," *The Senses*, ed. Barlow, J.B., and Mollon, J.B., Cambridge University Press, 1982, pp. 1–34.

[21] Bonasso, R.P., Firby, J., Gat, E., Kortenkamp, D., Miller, D., and Slack, M., "A Proven Three-tiered Architecture for Programming Autonomous Robots," *Journal of Experimental and Theoretical Artificial Intelligence*, vol. 9, no. 2, 1997.

[22] Borenstein, J., and Koren, Y., "The Vector Field Histogram- Fast Obstacle Avoidance for Mobile Robots," *IEEE Transactions on Robotics and Automation*, vol.7, no.3, June, 1991, pp. 278–288.

[23] Borenstein, J., and Koren, Y., "Histogramic In-Motion Mapping for Mobile Robot Obstacle Avoidance," *IEEE Transactions on Robotics and Automation*, vol.7, no.4, August, 1991, pp. 535–539.

[24] Bower, T.G.R., "The Evolution of Sensory Systems," *Perception: Essays in Honor of James J. Gibson*, ed. by R.B. MacLeod and H.L. Pick, Jr., Cornell University Press, Ithaca, NY, 1974, pp. 141–153.

[25] Braitenberg, V., *Vehicles: Experiments in Synthetic Psychology*, MIT Press, 1984.

[26] Brooks, R., "Challenges for Complete Creature Architectures," proceedings of *First Intenational Conference on Simulation of Adaptive Behavior*, pp. 434–443.

[27] Brooks, R.A., "A Robust Layered Control System for a Mobile Robot," IEEE *Journal of Robotics and Automation (now IEEE Transactions on Robotics and Automation)*, vol. 1, no. 1, 1986, pp. 1–10.

[28] Brooks, R., *Cambrian Intelligence: The Early History of the New AI*, MIT Press, 1999.

[29] Brooks, R., Breazeal, C., Irie, R., Kemp, C., Marjanovic, M., Scassellati, B., Williamson, M., "Alternative Essences on Intelligence," proceedings *AAAI-98*, 1998, pp. 961–968.

[30] Brooks, R., and Flynn, A., "Fast, Cheap and Out of Control," AI Memo 1182, MIT AI Laboratory, December, 1989.

[31] Cai, A.; Fukuda, T.; Arai, F., "Information sharing among multiple robots for cooperation in cellular robotic system," proceedings *1997 IEEE/RSJ International Conference on Intelligent Robot and Systems*, vol. 3, pp. 1768–74.

[32] Cattaneo, M., Cavalchini, A.G., Rogonoi, G.L., "Design and construction of a robotic milking system," Sixth International Conference on Computers in Agriculture, Cancun, Mexico, June 1996, pp. 155–60.

[33] Cervantes-Perez, F., "Visuomotor Coordination in Frogs and Toads," *The Handbook of Brain Theory and Neural Networks*, Michael A. Arbib, ed., MIT Press, pp. 1036–1042.

[34] Choset, H. and Burdick, J., "Sensor Based Motion Planning: Incremental Construction of the Hierarchical Generalized Voronoi Graph," To appear in *International Journal of Robotics Research*, 2000.

[35] Choset, H. and Burdick, J., "Sensor Based Motion Planning: The Hierarchical Generalized Voronoi Graph," to appear in *International Journal of Robotics Research*, 2000.

[36] Choset, H. and Burdick, J., "Sensor Based Motion Planning: The Hierarchical Generalized Voronoi Graph," to appear in the *International Journal of Robotics Research.*

[37] *Concise International Encyclopedia of Robotics: Applications and Automation*, Richard C. Dorf, editor-in-chief, John Wiley and Sons, Inc., NY, 1990.

[38] Congdon, C., Huber, M., Kortenkamp, D., Konolige, K., Myers, K., Saffiotti, A., and Ruspini, E., "Carmel vs. Flakey: A Comparison of Two Winners," *AI Magazine*, vol. 14, no. 1, Spring 1993, pp. 49–57.

[39] Connell, J., *Minimalist Mobile Robotics: A Colony Architecture for an Artificial Creature*, Academic Press, 1990.

[40] Connolly, C.I., and Grupen, R.A., "The applications of harmonic functions to robotics," *Journal of Robotic Systems*, vol. 10, October 1993, pp. 931–946.

[41] Dean, T., Allen, J., and Aloimonis, Y., *Artificial Intelligence: Theory and Practice*, Benjamin/Cummings Publishing, 1995.

[42] Dean, T., Bonasso, R.P., "1992 AAAI Robot Exhibition and Competition," *AI Magazine*, vol. 14, no. 1, Spring 1993, pp. 35–48.

[43] Dean, T., and Wellman, M., *Planning and Control*, Morgan Kaufmann Publishers, San Mateo, CA, 1991.

[44] deBerg, M., vanKreveld, M., Overmars, M., Schwarzkoph, O., *Computational Geometry: Theory and Applications*, Springer-Verlag, 1999.

[45] Dickmanns, E.D. and Graefe, V., "Dynamic Monocular Machine Vision," *Int. J. Machine Vision and Applications*, vol. 1, 1988, pp. 223–240.

[46] daaper. Draper, B., Collins, J., Brolio, A. Hanson and E. Riseman. "The Schema System," *International Journal of Computer Vision*, vol. 2, 1989, pp. 209–250.

[47] Drumheller, M., "Mobile Robot Localization Using Sonar", *IEEE Transactions on Pattern Analysis and Machine Intelligence*, vol. 9, no . 2, Mar 1987, pp. 325–332.

[48] Duchon, A.P., and Warren, W.H., "Robot Navigation form a Gibsonian Viewpoint," *1994 IEEE International conference on Systems, Man, and Cybernetics*, vol. 3, pp. 2272–7.

[49] Edwards, G.R., Burnard, R.H., Bewley, W.L., and Bullock, B.L., "The Ground Vehicle Manager's Associate," *Tech Report AIAA-94-1249-CP*, 1994, pp. 520–526.

[50] Engelson, S. P., and McDermott, D. V., "Passive Robot Map Building with Exploration Scripts," *Technical Report: YALEU/DCS/TR-898*, Yale University, Dept. of Computer Science, March, 1992.

[51] Erickson, J., "Supervised Space Robots are Needed in Space Exploration," *Conference on Intelligent Robotics in Field, Factory, Service, and Space, NASA Conference Publication 3251*, vol. 2, 1994, pp. 705–716.

[52] Everett, H.R., *Sensors for Mobile Robots: Theory and Application*, A. K. Peters, Ltd, Wellesley, MA, 1995.

[53] Firby, R.J., Kahn, R.E., Prokopwicz, P.N., and Swain, M.J., "An Architecture for Vision and Action," proceedings of *1995 International Joint Conference on Artificial Intelligence*, Morgan Kaufmann Pub., San Mateo, CA, vol. 1, 1995, pp. 72–79.

[54] Firby, R.J.,Prokopwicz, P.N., Swain, M.J.,Kahn, R.E., and Franklin, D., "Programming CHIP for the IJCAI-95 Robot Competition," *AI Magazine*, Spring 1996, pp. 71–81.

[55] Fowler, M., Scot, K., Booch, G., *UML Distilled*, 2nd ed., Addison-Wesley, 1999.

[56] Gardner, H., *The Mind's New Science*, Basic Books, Inc., New York, 1987.

[57] Gat, E., "Reliable Goal-directed Reactive Control for Real-World Autonomous Mobile Robots," Ph.D. dissertation, Dept. of Computer Science, Virginia Polytechnic Institute and State University, 1991.

[58] Gat, E., "Three-layer Architectures," *Artificial Intelligence and Mobile Robots*, D. Kortenkamp, R. Bonasson, R. Murphy, editors, MIT Press, 1998.

[59] Gibson, J.J., *The Ecological Approach to Visual Perception*, Houghton Mifflin, Boston MA, 1979.

[60] Gifford, K.K., and Morgenthaler, G.W., "Optimal Path Coverage Strategies for Planetary Rover Vehicles," *46th International Astronautical Federation Congress*, Oslo, Norway, October, 1995.

[61] Graefe, V. and Kuhnert, K.-D., "Toward a Vision-Based Robot with a Driver's License," *Proceedings, IEEE International Workshop on Intelligent Robots and Systems*, (IROS'88), Tokyo, 1988, pp. 627–632.

[62] Guzzoni, D., Cheyer, A., Julia, L., and Konolige, K., "Many Robots Make Short Work: Report of the SRI International Mobile Robot Team," *AI Magazine*, Spring, vol. 18, no. 1, 1997, pp. 55–64.

[63] Haber, R.N., and Haber, L., "Why mobile robots need a spatial memory," SPIE *Sensor Fusion III*, vol. 1383, 1990, pp. 411–424.

[64] *The Handbook of Artificial Intelligence*, A. Barr and E. Feigenbaum, editors, William Kaufmann, Inc., 1981.

[65] Henderson, T., and Shilcrat, E., "Logical Sensor Systems," *Journal of Robotics Systems*, vol. 1, no.2, 1984, pp. 169–193.

[66] Hinkle, D., Kortenkamp, D, Miller, D., "The 1995 Robot Competition and Exhibition," *AI Magazine*, vol. 17, no. 1, Spring 1996, pp. 31–45.

[67] Hirose, S., untitled talk at the Planetary Rover Technology and Systems Workshop, *1996 IEEE International Conference on Robotics and Automation*, April, 1996.

[68] Honderd, G, Jongkind, W, Klomp, C., Dessing, J., and Paliwoda, R., "Strategy and control of an autonomous cow-milking robot system," *Robotics and Autonomous Systems*, vol. 7, no. 2–3, pp. 165–79.

[69] Horn, B.K.P., *Robot Vision*, MIT Press, 1986.

[70] Horswill, I., "Polly: A Vision-Based Artificial Agent," proceedings *AAAI-93*, July 1993, pp. 824–829.

[71] Hughes, K., "Managing sensor performance uncertainty in a multi-sensor robotic system," Ph. D. thesis, Computer Science and Engineering, University of South Florida, 1994.

[72] Hughes, K, and Murphy, R., "Ultrasonic robot localization using Dempster-Shafer theory," *SPIE Stochastic Methods in Signal Processing, Image Processing, and Computer Vision*, 1992.

[73] *Humanitarian Demining: Developmental Technologies 1998*, CECOM NVESD, DoD Humanitarian Demining R&D Program, Fort Belvoir, VA 22060-5606.

[74] Hyams, J., Powell, M., Murphy, R.R., "Position Estimation and Cooperative Navigation of Micro-rovers Using Color Segmentation," to appear *Autonomous Robots*, special issue on CIRA'99.

[75] Iberall, T. and Lyons, D., "Towards Perceptual Robotics," proceedings of *1984 IEEE International Conference on Systems, Man and Cybernetics*, Halifax, NS, Canada, Oct. 10–12, 1984, pp. 147–157.

[76] Jones, J., Flynn, A., Seiger, B., *Mobile Robots: Inspiration to Implementation*, second ed., A.K. Peters, 1998.

[77] Konolige, K., and Myers, K., "The Saphira Architecture for Autonomous Mobile Robots," *Artificial Intelligence and Mobile Robots*, D. Kortenkamp, R. Bonasson, R. Murphy, editors, MIT Press, 1998.

[78] Kortenkamp, D, Nourbakhsh, I., and Hinkle, D., "The 1996 AAAI Mobile Robot Competition and Exhibition," *AI Magazine*, Spring, vol. 18, no. 1, 1997, pp. 55–64.

[79] Kortenkamp, D., and Weymouth, T., "Topological Mapping for Mobile Robots using a Combination of Sonar and Vision Sensing," proceedings *AAAI-94*, 1994, pp. 974–984.

[80] Kosaka, A. and Kak, A.C., "Fast Vision-Guided Mobile Robot Navigation using Model-Based Reasoning and Prediction of Uncertainties," proceedings *Computer Vision, Graphics, and Image Processing – Image Understanding*, November 1992, pp. 271–329.

[81] Kuipers, B, and Byun, Y.T., "A Robot Exploration and Mapping Strategy Based on a Semantic Hierarchy of Spatial Representations," *Robotics and Autonomous Systems*, vol. 8, 1991, pp. 47–63.

[82] Latombe, J.C., *Robot Motion Planning*, Kluwer Academic, 1990.

[83] Lee, D., "The Functions of Vision," *Modes of Perceiving and Processing Information*, ed. by H.L. Pick, Jr. and E. Saltzman, John Wiley and Sons, NY, 1978, pp. 159–170.

[84] LeGrand, R., and Luo, R.C., "LOLA: Object Manipulation in an Unstructured Environment," *AI Magazine*, vol. 17, no. 1, 1996, pp. 63–70.

[85] Levitt, T.S., and Lawton, D.T., "Qualitative Navigation for Mobile Robots," *AI Journal*, vol. 44, no. 3, Aug 1990, pp. 305–360.

[86] Lewis, H.R., Papadimitriou, C.H., *Elements of the Theory of Computation*, Prentice-Hall, Inc., Englewood Cliffs, New Jersey, 1981.

[87] Lim, W., and Eilbert, J., "Plan-Behavior Interaction in Autonomous Navigation," *SPIE Mobile Robots V*, Boston, MA, Nov. 8-9, 1990, pp. 464–475.

[88] Marr, D., *Vision: A Computational Investigation into the Human Representation and Processing of Visual Information*, W.H. Freeman and Co., 1982.

[89] Mataric, M., "Behavior-Based Control: Main Properties and Implications," proceedings of *Workshop on Intelligent Control Systems, IEEE International Conference on Robotics and Automation*, Nice, France, 1992.

[90] Mataric, M.,"Minimizing Complexity in Controlling a Mobile Robot Population," proceedings, *1992 IEEE International Conference on robotics and Automation*, Nice, France, May, 1992, pp. 830–835.

[91] Matthies, L., and Elfes, A., "Probabilistic Estimation Mechanisms and Tesselated Representations for Sensor Fusion," *SPIE Sensor Fusion: Spatial Reasoning and Scene Interpretation*, vol. 1003, 1988, pp. 1–11.

[92] McKenzie, D.C.; Arkin, R.C.; Cameron, J.M., "Multiagent mission specification and execution," *Autonomous Robots*, vol.4, no.1, 1997, p. 29–52.

[93] Meystel, A., "Knowledge Based Nested Hierarchical Control," in *Advances in Automation and Robotics*, vol. 2, Ed. G. Saridis, JAI Press, Greenwich, CT, 1990, pp. 63–152.

[94] Moravec, H., *Mind Children*, Harvard University Press, 1988.

[95] Moravec, H.P., "Sensor Fusion in Certainty Grids for Mobile Robots," *AI Magazine*, vol. 9, no. 2, Summer, 1988, pp. 61–74.

[96] Moravec, H., *Robot: Mere Machine to Transcendent Mind*, Oxford Press, 1998.

[97] Murphy, R.R., "A Strategy for the Fine Positioning of a Mobile Robot using Texture," proceedings of *SPIE Mobile Robots IV*, Philadephia, PA, Nov. 5-10, 1989, pp. 267–279.

[98] Murphy, R. R., "An Artificial Intelligence Approach to the 1994 AUVS Unmanned Ground Vehicle Competition," *1995 IEEE International Conference on Systems, Man and Cybernetics*, Oct. 1995, Vancouver, BC., pp. 1723–1728.

[99] Murphy, R.R., "Biological and Cognitive Foundations of Intelligent Sensor Fusion," *IEEE Transactions on Systems, Man, and Cybernetics*, vol. 26, No. 1, Jan, 1996, pp. 42–51.

[100] Murphy, R.R, "Use of Scripts for Coordinating Perception and Action," *IROS-96*, Nov. 1996, Osaka, Japan, pp. 156–161.

[101] Murphy, R., "1997 International Ground Robotics Vehicle Competition," Robotics Competition Corner, *Robotics and Autonomous Systems*, Elsevier, vol. 20, 1997.

[102] Murphy, R., "Dempster-Shafer Theory for Sensor Fusion in Autonomous Mobile Robots," *IEEE Transactions on Robotics and Automation*, vol. 14, no. 2, April, 1998.

[103] Murphy, R.R., Gomes, K., and Hershberger, D., "Ultrasonic Data Fusion as a Function of Robot Velocity," *1996 SPIE Sensor Fusion and Distributed Robotic Agents*, Nov. 1996, Boston, MA., pp. 114–126.

[104] Murphy, R. R., Hawkins, D.K., and Schoppers, M.J., "Reactive Combination of Belief Over Time Using Direct Perception," *IJCAI-97*, Nagoya, Japan, Aug. 1997, pp. 1353–1358.

[105] Murphy, R.R., and Hughes, K., "Ultrasonic Robot Localization using Dempster-Shafer Theory," *SPIE Stochastic Methods in Signal Processing, Image Processing, and Computer Vision*, invited session on Applications for Vision and Robotics, San Diego, CA, July 19-24, 1992.

[106] Murphy, R., Hughes, K., Noll, E., and Marzilli, A., "Integrating Explicit Path Planning with Reactive Control for Mobile Robots using Trulla," *Robotics and Autonomous Systems*, no. 27, 1999, pp. 225–245.

[107] Murphy, R., and Mali, A., "Lessons Learned in Integrating Sensing into Autonomous Mobile Robot Architectures," *Journal of Experimental and Theoretical Artificial Intelligence special issue on Software Architectures for Hardware Agents,* vol. 9, no. 2, 1997, pp. 191–209.

[108] Murphy, R., and Sprouse, J., "Strategies for Searching an Area with Semi-Autonomous Mobile Robots," *2nd Conference on Robotics for Challenging Environments,* June 1-6, 1996, Albuquerque, NM. pp. 15–21.

[109] Neisser, U., *Cognition and Reality,* W.H. Freeman, 1976.

[110] Neisser, U., "Direct Perception and Recognition as Distinct Perceptual Systems," address presented to the Cognitive Science Society, August, 1991.

[111] Nelson, R.C., "Visual homing using an associative memory," *Biological Cybernetics,* vol. 65, no. 4, 1991, pp. 281–291.

[112] Nourbakhsh, I., Powers, R., Birchfield, S., "DERVISH: an office-navigating robot," *AI Magazine,* vol. 16, no. 2, pp. 53–60.

[113] Oliveira, E., Fischer, K., and Stephankova, O., "Multi-agent systems: which research for which applications," *Robotics and Autonomous Systems,* vol. 27, 1999, pp. 91–106.

[114] Parker, L.E., "ALLIANCE: An Architecture for Fault Tolerant Multirobot Cooperation," *IEEE Transactions on Robotics and Automation,* vol. 14, no. 2, pp. 2200–240.

[115] Penrose, Roger, *The Emperor's New Mind: Concerning Computers, Minds, and the Laws of Physics,* Oxford University Press, Oxford, 1989.

[116] Pomerleau, D., and Jochem, T., "Rapidly Adapting Machine Vision for Automated Vehicle Steering," *IEEE Expert,* Apr., 1996.

[117] Premvuti, S., and Yuta, S., "Considerations on the cooperation of muliple autonomous mobile robots," proceedings of *IEEE International Workshop on Intelligent Robots and Systems (IROS),* 1990.

[118] Raibert, M., *Legged Robots that Balance,* MIT Press, 1986.

[119] *Readings in Distributed Artificial Intelligence,* A. Bond and L. Gasser, editors, Morgan Kaufmann, 1988.

[120] Rich, E., and Knight, K., *Artificial Intelligence,* McGraw Hill Text, 1991.

[121] Rosenblatt, J.K, and Thorpe, C.E., "Combining Multiple Goals in a Behavior-Based Architecture," proceedings *1995 IEEE/RSJ International Conference on Intelligent Robots and Systems,* Pittsburgh, PA, Aug. 5-9, 1995, pp. 136–141.

[122] Schach, S, *Classical and Object-Oriented Software Engineering,* 3rd edition, Richard D. Irwin publishers, 1996.

[123] Schank, R. C., and Riesbeck, C. K., *Inside Computer Understanding: Five Programs Plus Miniatures,* Lawrence Erlbaum Associates, Hillsdale, NJ, 1981.

[124] Schöne, H., *Spatial Orientation: The Spatial Control of Behavior in Animals and Man*, translated by C. Strausfeld, Princeton University Press, NJ, 1984.

[125] Schultz, A., Adams, W., and Yamauchi, B., "Integrating Exploration, Localization, Navigation and Planning With a Common Representation," *Autonomous Robots*, vol. 6 no. 3, May 1999, pp. 293–308.

[126] Shafer, G., *A Mathematical Theory of Evidence*, Princeton University Press, 1976.

[127] Shaffer, G., Gonzalez, J., Stentz, A., "Comparison of two range-based pose estimators for a mobile robot," *SPIE Mobile Robots VI*, Boston, MA, USA; Nov. 1992, pp. 661–7.

[128] Sheridan, T., "Space Teleoperation Through Time Delay: Review and Prognosis," *IEEE Transactions on Robotics and Automation*, vol. 9, no. 5, Oct. 1993, pp. 592–605.

[129] Simmons, R., *AI Magazine*, Summer, vol. 16, no. 2, 1995, pp. 19–30.

[130] Simmons, R., Fernandez, J., Goodwin, R., Koenig, S., O'Sullivan, J., "Xavier: An Autonomous Mobile Robot on the Web," *Robotics and Automation Society Magazine*, June, 1999.

[131] Simmons, R., Goodwin, R., Haigh, K., Koenig, S., and O'Sullivan, J., "A Layered Architecture for Office Delivery Robots," proceedings *Autonomous Agents 97*, 1997, pp. 245–252.

[132] Slack, M., "Navigation templates: mediating qualitative guidance and quantitative control in mobile robots," *IEEE Transactions on Systems, Man and Cybernetics*, vol. 23, no. 2, 1993, p. 452–66.

[133] Smith, R., and Cheeseman, P., "On the Representation of and Estimation of Spatial Uncertainty," *International Journal of Robotics Research*, vol. 5, 1986, pp. 56–68.

[134] "Sojourner's 'Smarts' Reflect Latest in Automation," JPL Press Release, Aug. 8, 1997.

[135] Stark, L., and Bowyer, K., *Generic Object Recognition Using Form and Function*, World Scientific, 1996.

[136] Stentz, A., "The Focussed D* Algorithm for Real-Time Replanning," proceedings *1995 International Joint Conference on Artificial Intelligence,*Montreal, CA, Aug. 1995, pp. 1652–1659.

[137] Swain, M., and Ballard, D., "Color indexing," *International Journal of Computer Vision*, vol. 7, 1991, pp. 11–32.

[138] Thorpe, C.E., "Path Relaxation: Path Planning for a Mobile Robot," *1984 International Conference on AI (AAAI-84)*, 1984, pp. 318–321.

[139] Thrun,S., Bennewitz, M., Burgard, M., Dellaert, F., Fox, D., Haehnel, C., Rosenberg, C., Roy, N., Schulte, J., and Schulz, D., "MINERVA: A second generation mobile tour-guide robot," proceedings *1999 IEEE International Conference on Robotics and Automation*, vol. 3, pp. 1999–2005.

[140] Umbaugh, Scott E. C. *Computer Vision and Image Processing*, Englewood Cliffs, NJ:Prentice-Hall, 1998.

[141] Uttal, W. R., "Teleoperators," *Scientific American*, December 1989, pp. 124–129.

[142] Wampler, C., "Teleoperators, Supervisory Control," *Concise International Encyclopedia of Robotics: Applications and Automation*, R. C. Dorf, editor-in-chief, John Wiley and Sons, Inc., 1990, p. 997.

[143] Winston, P.H., *Artificial Intelligence*, Addison-Wesley, 1992.

Index